SUGAR BOWL CLASSIC | A HISTORY

BY MARTY MULÉ | mainstream media international ©2008

ACKNOWLEDGEMENTS:

This project stands on the shoulders of many Sugar Bowlers, players and coaches too numerous to list. We acknowledge their help.

Special thanks goes to the late Mary Frances Digby and Pie Dufour, who helped fill in the events of the early years, Peter Finney, and editors Ed Cassiere, Ted Lewis and Brian Ambridge for their keen eyes and insights.

– MJM

PHOTOGRAPHY CREDITS:

A heartfelt thanks to the following for their outstanding photographic contributions that helped make this book an work of art all on its own.

Allsport	Tim Alexander	Charles Kantrow	Wally Porter
Associated Press	Brian Bahr	Heinz Kluetmeier	Charlie Riedel
Collegiate Images	John Biever	Barry Lawrence	Robert Rogers
Getty Images	Darren Carroll	Andy Lyons	Stephen Savioa
Sports Illustrated	Andrew Cohoon	Richard Mackson	Steven Senne
Sports Imagery	Jim Dietz	Dave Martin	Jamie Squire
Sugar Bowl Archives	Bill Frakes	Peter Read Miller	Matthew Stockman
Times-Picayune	Chris Graythen	Ronald Modra	Damian Strohmeyer
NFL	Michael Hebert	Patrick Murphy-Racey	George Tiedemann

THE PUBLISHER:

CLEARWATER: 712 Grand Central Street • Clearwater, FL 33756 • Phone: 727-462-0300
TAMPA: 201 North Franklin Street Ste. 3415 • Tampa, FL 33602 • Phone: 813-549-6470
ATLANTA: 70 Mansell Court East Ste. 105 • Roswell, GA 30076 • Phone: 678-366-1211

Visit **www.gommi.com** for more information.

EXECUTIVES **Chuck Warner** CEO **Jonathan Wilson** President **David Jacobstein** COO
Mark Prince VP of Business Development & Publishing **ART** **Stacy Kovatch** Creative Director **Robyn Weber** Art Director
Jesse Swaney Senior Graphic Artist **Josh Gullinese** Graphic Artist

COPYRIGHT:

THE CONTENTS

STILL STANDING	4
NEW ORLEANS: THE CRADLE OF CHAMPIONS	6
2008 BCS CHAMPIONSHIP - LSU VS. OHIO STATE	8
HOW IT CAME TO BE	16
1935 - TULANE VS. TEMPLE	22
1936 - TCU VS. LSU	26
1937 - SANTA CLARA VS. LSU	30
1938 - SANTA CLARA VS. LSU	34
1939 - TCU VS. CARNEGIE TECH	38
1940 - TEXAS A&M VS. TULANE	42
1941 - BOSTON COLLEGE VS. TENNESSEE	46
1942 - FORDHAM VS. MISSOURI	50
1943 - TENNESSEE VS. TULSA	54
1944 - GEORGIA TECH VS. TULSA	58
1945 - DUKE VS. ALABAMA	62
1946 - OKLAHOMA A&M VS. ST. MARY'S	66
1947 - GEORGIA VS. UNC	70
1948 - TEXAS VS. ALABAMA	74
1949 - OKLAHOMA VS. UNC	78
1950 - OKLAHOMA VS. LSU	82
1951 - KENTUCKY VS. OKLAHOMA	86
1952 - MARYLAND VS. TENNESSEE	90
1953 - GEORGIA TECH VS. MISSISSIPPI	94
1954 - GEORGIA TECH VS. WEST VIRGINIA	98
1955 - NAVY VS. MISSISSIPPI	102
1956 - GEORGIA TECH VS. PITTSBURGH	106
1957 - BAYLOR VS. TENNESSEE	110
1958 - MISSISSIPPI VS. TEXAS	114
1959 - LSU VS. CLEMSON	118
1960 - MISSISSIPPI VS. LSU	122
1961 - MISSISSIPPI VS. RICE	126
1962 - ALABAMA VS. ARKANSAS	130
1963 - MISSISSIPPI VS. ARKANSAS	134
1964 - ALABAMA VS. MISSISSIPPI	138
1965 - LSU VS. SYRACUSE	142
1966 - MISSOURI VS. FLORIDA	146
1967 - ALABAMA VS. NEBRASKA	150
1968 - LSU VS. WYOMING	154
1969 - ARKANSAS VS. GEORGIA	158
1970 - MISSISSIPPI VS. ARKANSAS	162
1971 - TENNESSEE VS. AIR FORCE	166
1972 - OKLAHOMA VS. AUBURN	170
1972 - OKLAHOMA VS. PENN STATE	174
1973 - NOTRE DAME VS. ALABAMA	178
1974 - NEBRASKA VS. FLORIDA	182
1975 - ALABAMA VS. PENN STATE	186
1977 - PITTSBURGH VS. GEORGIA	192
1978 - ALABAMA VS. OHIO STATE	196
1979 - ALABAMA VS. PENN STATE	200
1980 - ALABAMA VS. ARKANSAS	204
1981 - GEORGIA VS. NOTRE DAME	208
1982 - PITTSBURGH VS. GEORGIA	214
1983 - PENN STATE VS. GEORGIA	220
1984 - AUBURN VS. MICHIGAN	224
1985 - NEBRASKA VS. LSU	228
1986 - TENNESSEE VS. MIAMI	232
1987 - NEBRASKA VS. LSU	238
1988 - AUBURN VS. SYRACUSE	244
1989 - FLORIDA STATE VS. AUBURN	250
1990 - MIAMI VS. ALABAMA	256
1991 - TENNESSEE VS. VIRGINIA	264
1992 - NOTRE DAME VS. FLORIDA	272
1993 - ALABAMA VS. MIAMI	280
1994 - FLORIDA VS. WEST VIRGINIA	288
1995 - FLORIDA STATE VS. FLORIDA	296
1995 - VIRGINIA TECH VS. TEXAS	304
1997 - FLORIDA VS. FLORIDA STATE	312
1998 - FLORIDA STATE VS. OHIO STATE	320
1999 - OHIO STATE VS. TEXAS A&M	328
2000 - FLORIDA STATE VS. VIRGINIA TECH	336
2001 - MIAMI VS. FLORIDA	344
2002 - LSU VS. ILLINOIS	352
2003 - GEORGIA VS. FLORIDA STATE	360
2004 - LSU VS. OKLAHOMA	368
2005 - AUBURN VS. VIRGINIA TECH	376
2006 - WEST VIRIGINIA VS. GEORGIA	384
2007 - NOTRE DAME VS. LSU	392
2008 - HAWAII VS. GEORGIA	400
THEY WERE THE PATHFINDERS	408

STILL STANDING

The Sugar Bowl fits many descriptions. It is a shining show-case of college football; it is a generous benefactor to chari-ties, and a far-reaching sponsor of amateur competition in other sports on the collegiate and prep levels; it is a tourist magnet in what has become a tourist-oriented town.

As much as anything, though, the Sugar Bowl is a miracle.

Still standing, still functioning, still a major destination point for high-achieving college football programs, is a feat noth-ing short of wondrous after the destruction and horror of the worst natural disaster in American history.

Hurricane Katrina transformed a picturesque place once mu-sically described as a "Land of Dreamy Scenes" into a night-marish waterworld. Eighty percent of New Orleans was submerged for weeks; and even that mighty structure that had become the modern symbol of the old town, the Super-dome, home of the Sugar Bowl, was a casualty, its roof par-tially stripped by the rampaging winds, its insides open to torrential rains.

Katrina's devastation was so complete, more than 1.2 million people across the Gulf region had to be evacuated to other parts of the country. So did the Sugar Bowl, which four months after the cataclysmic event, staged its 72nd game, but in Atlanta, 500 miles to the east of the French Quarter.

The still largely broken and traumatized city of New Orleans is yet to return to its former self.

But the Sugar Bowl hasn't missed a beat, playing three games since, counting the one in Atlanta, and putting on the 2008 BCS national championship extravaganza.

To anyone who actually saw the wide-spread carnage left in Katrina's wake the Sugar Bowl's perseverance and continuity would have to be categorized as nothing short of miraculous.

The Sugar's sister major bowls, the older, upper tier games formed in the early days of the 20th Century – the Rose, Or-ange and Cotton – have all endured hardships. The Rose, sim-ilar to the Sugar, once also had to be moved. The 1942 Rose

Bowl game was switched from Pasadena to Durham, N.C. because in the early days of World War II, as a precaution against enemy attack, the military wished to avoid large crowds on the West Coast. The game between Oregon State and Duke was played at the home of the Blue Devils.

But the analogy ends there. The Rose Bowl stadium was never torn apart, fans were not suddenly dispersed far from their homes and perhaps unable to attend even if they wanted. There was never a fear for the very future of the Rose Bowl.

The Rose was born in the infancy of the 20th Century, and the Sugar, the Orange and the Cotton came along in the unlikeliest of times – in the middle of the Great Depression. They all somehow came through that, as well as other dangerous moments like World War II and the terrorist attacks of September 11, 2001. They've all survived, and flourished.

No other postseason game, though, has gone through what the Sugar went through with Katrina, which could easily have killed the game. The Doomsday Storm was a life-altering event, for people, businesses, and sports. Life in the Crescent City in every way has been reconfigured. The Sugar

Bowl, really, against the odds, however, never failed to answer the bell.

If Fred Digby, the guiding spirit of the Sugar Bowl, didn't get the game off the ground in 1935, he could have done it in 1936, or 1937, or whenever. If Paul Hoolahan, the current executive director, hadn't kept the game alive in 2006, the Sugar Bowl might well have expired, along with so much else in post-Katrina New Orleans.

It was nothing less than inspirational when the Sugar Bowl returned to New Orleans, and the Superdome, with an eye-catching pairing of, appropriately, America's favorite college team, Notre Dame, and Louisiana's beloved LSU Tigers.

That Sugar Bowl, as much as anything, turned into a powerful symbol of the city, state and bowl game collectively rising from a watery canvas like a heavyweight champion recovering from an unlucky punch – a vivid demonstration that the Sugar Bowl had weathered the storm.

It was a miracle.

NEW ORLEANS: THE

"We're No. 1!"

That historic football battle-cry has been shrieked more times with meaning in New Orleans than anywhere else – thanks obviously to the Sugar Bowl.

The second BCS national championship game – using the new "stand alone" concept, meaning it has no official connection to any other game, like the Sugar Bowl – was played in New Orleans. But, obviously, without the Sugar Bowl's historical importance, the title game would have been held elsewhere. Over the course of eight decades, with all the different polls and all the varying methods of determining national champions – featuring those from the early days that were named at the end of the regular season, those picked after the bowl seasons, and, now, those coming through the BCS title game, the Sugar Bowl stands as a historical barometer for the sport.

In fact, it's interesting to note that since the Sugar Bowl was born in 1935, just as many of what would become the major polls and bowls were also moving into place, New Orleans has been nothing less than an incubator for titleholders, 20 (22, if we count the times that, because of the strictures of those eras, both teams left the game with separate but legitimate claims on their championships).

In that same time span 17 national champions have played in the Orange Bowl, and 15 in the Rose Bowl.

The stand-alone title game added to New Orleans' total – and to its niche as a "Cradle of Champions."

To simplify and use the most creditable and recognized sources for the claim, this is how they were determined:

For the 1936 game ('35 season), the Williamson System,

which was in existence for several years before and went on for more than three decades afterward, was used.

• The Associated Press Poll came into being the next season, so from 1937 on, this was used exclusively for the next 14 years.

• The United Press International Coaches' Poll came into existence in 1950, also a legitimate barometer and was used for these tabulations (and, because it has morphed into several different designations through the decades, it is hereafter called "Coaches."

• Four years later, in 1954, the Football Writers Association started naming national champions. Since this is an organization devoted exclusively to credentialed sportswriters covering college football, its opinions were also considered.

• From then until 1998, any of those organizations' final vote on No. 1 was counted. Those, by most reasonable measures, were the most credible and recognized polls.

• But for the last ten years, since the BCS game winner became the quasi-official football champion that was our final determinant of any Sugar Bowl team with a No. 1 claim.

Richard Billingsley, creator of the College Football Research Center, whose computer rankings are part of the BCS rating process, and researcher of his own of a retroactive-national championship system, said this was a reasonable gauge of evaluating No. 1 teams over the course of almost three-quarters of a century.

"To say the AP, Coaches and FWAA (polls) are the bench marks for excellence in college football polling would be an understatement," Billingsley said. "They are truly the royalty of rankings."

CRADLE OF CHAMPIONS

It should be noted that Paul B. Williamson was a member of the Sugar Bowl when it was founded, but his poll came into being three years before the first postseason game in New Orleans and he was not a Sugar Bowl member by the time the first game was played. His poll continued as a respected representation of the collegiate football elite for 31 years until his death.

Billingsley said, "Among the pioneers in that field (early day polling) was Paul Williamson, a geologist who in 1932 created one of America's first power ranking systems. Still today, after more than 75 years, the Williamson System is recognized by the NCAA as a source for national champions."

These are the national champions who played in the Sugar Bowl, and the polls which designated them No. 1.

1.   1936: Texas Christian (Williamson System);
     LSU (Williamson System). Shared title.
2.   1939: Texas Christian (AP).
3.   1940: Texas A&M (AP).
4.   1951: Oklahoma (AP-Coaches).
5.   1952: Tennessee (AP-Coaches).
6.   1959: LSU (AP-Coaches).
7.   1961: Ole Miss (FWAA).
8.   1962: Alabama (AP-Coaches).
9.   1973: Notre Dame (AP, FWAA); Alabama (Coaches).
10. 1976 Pittsburgh (AP, Coaches, FWAA).
11. 1979 Alabama (AP, FWAA).
12. 1980 Alabama (AP, Coaches, FWAA).
13. 1981 Georgia (AP, Coaches, FWAA).
14. 1983 Penn State (AP, Coaches, FWAA).
15. 1990 Miami (AP, UPI, FWAA).
16. 1993 Alabama (AP, Coaches, FWAA).
17. 1997 Florida (AP, Coaches, FWAA).
18. 2000 Florida State (BCS).
19. 2004 LSU (BCS).
20. 2008 LSU (BCS).

The various formulas changed over time. For example, Oklahoma in 1951 and Tennessee in 1952 both lost in the Sugar Bowl, but are still considered the national champions of those years because at the time the final AP vote was taken at the end of the regular season. The changing face of college football began being altered in the late '60s.

After AP changed its policy, Notre Dame won that title after beating Alabama in the 1973 Sugar. Yet, ironically, Bama retained its No. 1 UPI ranking because the coaches' final vote continued to be taken after the last regular season game. That was rectified the following season.

Not taken into consideration or included for this list of No. 1 Sugar Bowl teams were LSU in 1937, Boston College and Tennessee in the 1941 game, Ole Miss in 1959, Alabama in 1978, and several others picked by one poll or another – but not by those rankings universally recognized as the highest level of credibility.

Billingsley placed the Sugar Bowl in proper context when he said, "Although bowl games seem commonplace now, with over 30 postseason games sanctioned by the NCAA, only the names of the 'Big Bowl' games garner the mystique of national championships.

"Among those, the Rose Bowl, with its traditional ties with the Big Ten and Pac-10, may be the 'Granddaddy of them all,' but it's the Sugar Bowl that added the spice to create a 'national' bowl game.

"Historically open to the best teams in America, in addition to the SEC, the Sugar Bowl has matched some of the greatest teams in the history of college football. From Tulane and Temple in 1935 right on through LSU and Notre Dame in 2007, the Sugar Bowl has matched national championship-caliber teams."

LSU 38 Ohio State 24

"We have good news ..."

The calm voice on the intercom intoned: "We have good news ..."

The pilot was informing the Louisiana State University football team, on its way home after winning the Southeastern Conference Championship Game in Atlanta, that the No. 1 team in the country, the University of Missouri, had lost – cracking the door for the Bayou Bengals to get a shot at the national title.

Ecstatic cheers, heavy backslapping and hugs ensued, but the celebration was cut short as the plane took a severe dip and the sounds in the cabin changed immediately to shrieks of alarm. But the plane quickly climbed again to its correct altitude and continued a steady journey back to Baton Rouge with its cargo of happy Tigers, but all tightly squeezing their armrests.

"Man, I was like, 'We need to get off this plane before we start celebrating some team losing,' " Tiger tackle Carnell Stewart sagely said afterward. Yet there would be more rejoicing: When LSU landed there was more news. No. 2-ranked West Virginia also lost, to four-touchdown underdog Pittsburgh, flinging the championship gates wide open for the Bayou Bengals.

The wild plane ride was a precise reflection of the previous four months of college football.

In the craziest season in the almost 140-year history of college football – which opened with an upset of No. 5-ranked Michigan by lower-division opponent Appalachian State, and featured the biggest upset of all-time with 41-point underdog Stanford beating Southern California, ranked No. 1 in the ESPN and Harris polls, used to determine Bowl Championship Series standings;

A season:
• in which Top 10 teams lost to unranked teams an staggering 20 times;
• in which Top 5 teams lost to unranked opponents an unprecedented 13 times;
• in which the No. 1 and No. 2-ranked teams both lost on the final day of the regular season, each a step short of a chance to hoist the Waterford Crystal Ball, emblematic of the BCS title.

And, in the end, after the stunning developments on the last weekend of the Season of the Upset, the last teams standing were Ohio State and LSU – both of which had been previously ranked No. 1 and lost; the Tigers twice.

Just as incongruous, both also lost at home in November, until this zany season a certain killer of high aspirations for elite standing. But when Missouri and West Virginia lost, the Big Ten champion Buckeyes (11-1), then in third place in the BCS rankings, were lifted to the top spot. LSU (11-2), which had dropped to seventh, rose to second, passing five other contenders.

Tiger coach Les Miles thoughtfully offered, "It's as if the Lord wanted these two teams to play."

The Tigers and Buckeyes look to hoist The Coaches' Trophy.

THE COACHES' TROPHY

The apparent reason for LSU's ascension: Missouri (10-2), Kansas (11-1) and Georgia (10-2) failed to win their league championships, the defeat of West Virginia (10-2) at the hands of a pronounced underdog; and the little matter of the 48-7 trouncing of Virginia Tech (11-2) by LSU.

Oklahoma (11-2) and Southern Cal (10-2) could, and would, make arguments that they were as worthy, but LSU's total body of work (a national-best 6-1 against opponents ranked at season's end, and having beaten five teams in the Top 15 while the Trojans defeated none) appeared to be the deciding factor.

The Buckeyes were getting a second chance at redemption. After a 41-14 blowout to underdog Florida in the BCS title game the year before, all Ohio State heard was that it didn't belong on the big stage, that Big Ten teams couldn't compete with the speed of Southeastern Conference teams, that the Buckeye opposition didn't measure up. Even ESPN's Kirk Herbstreit, a former Ohio State quarterback, said the loss to the Gators "set the Big Ten back five years."

This despite the fact that the Buckeyes won the title in 2002, this was their third trip to the national championship game in Coach Jim Tressel's six years in Columbus, and the 2007 Buckeyes had,

statistically, the nation's best defense, featuring All-American linebacker James Laurinaitis, yielding just 225 yards a game.

One holiday gift to the players from the coaching staff was a 10-minute DVD full of the insulting comments, slights and put-downs taken from national television and radio broadcasts made in the aftermath of the humbling defeat. "It's hard to watch," said offensive tackle Alan Boone. "It's tough to see Florida holding up trophy. We hear all the people saying Ohio State is slow, Ohio State is slow, Ohio State is slow."

If the Buckeyes wouldn't be motivated for this game, they never would be.

Just as intriguing was the stage itself, New Orleans, where, since 1935, more national champions appeared in the Sugar Bowl than anywhere else. This was not, of course, truly a Sugar Bowl, but it wouldn't have been played in the Big Easy without the Sugar Bowl. This was properly viewed as "The BCS National Championship Game – as presented by the Sugar Bowl."

And that was fitting, seeing as how the shape of modern postseason college football was largely shaped by Sugar Bowl leadership.

It was Mickey Holmes, then the Sugar Bowl's executive director, who first brought up the notion of a rotating system among the major bowls to host the nearest thing possible, short of a playoff, to a No. 1 vs. No. 2 game. Disgusted after getting torched in the cutthroat behind-the-scenes bowl politics of the time, Holmes sold his idea to his counterparts from the Fiesta, Cotton and Orange bowls. After the 1991 Sugar Bowl, he challenged his cohorts to find the

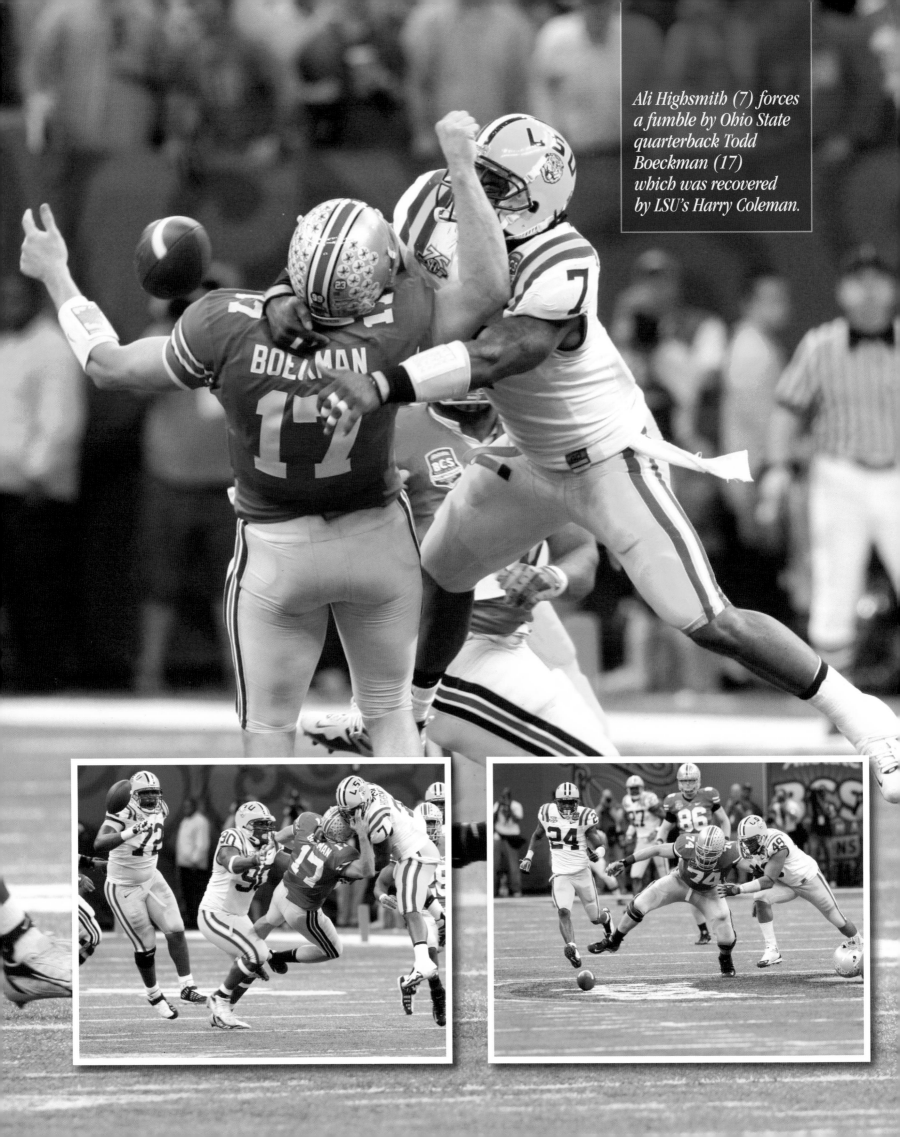

Ali Highsmith (7) forces a fumble by Ohio State quarterback Todd Boeckman (17) which was recovered by LSU's Harry Coleman.

soft spots in his concept. "Cut holes in it, tear it apart, and put it back together again, and then rip it part again," he pleaded.

Two years later a system called the Bowl Coalition went into effect, which morphed into the Bowl Alliance, which, in turn, once the Big Ten and Pac-10 came aboard, evolved into the inclusive Bowl Championship Series.

Then, in 2004, after easier access for BCS conference teams were guaranteed by adding another BCS game, it was current Chief Executive Officer Paul Hoolahan who came up with the brain-storm of "double-hosting," meaning one bowl every four years, such as the Sugar Bowl in 2008, puts on both its regular presentation, then the BCS national title game a week later, thus keeping a model within the four original BCS bowls instead of adding a fifth venue.

"When there was talk of five cities instead of four," Hoolahan said, "we started thinking of the implications and impact it could have for us. Our sponsors did not want to wait five years between championship games," Hoolahan said. "We had to give them fulfillment, and that means return on their investment. Keeping the rotation within four years was the best way to do that."

Interestingly, both coaches in this game were Ohio boys, Miles from Elyria and Tressel from Mentor, and both were tagged with clothing sobriquets: the LSU coach called "The Mad Hatter" for wearing his cap high on his head and a penchant for sometimes taking calculated gambles; the Ohio State coach called "The Vest" for almost always dressing in a sweater vest in Buckeye colors.

LSU had as much to overcome as any team to reach the BCS game in the decade of its existence. Highly rated at the start of the season, a series of injuries to key players – which caused the loss of leading receiver Early Doucet for five games, defensive lineman Charles Alexander for the season, starting quarterback Matt Flynn for two games, and hobbling All-American defensive tackler Glenn Dorsey for the last half of the season – hampered the Tigers from mid-season on.

Still, they kept winning with a hell-bent-for-leather style, overcoming a plethora of obstacles. During the season the Bayou Bengals went for it on fourth down 15 times, and made the necessary yardage an astounding 12 times (80 percent) – including a memorable 5-for-5 night in a win against Florida – while opponents were successful on 4-of-18 (22 percent) fourth downs. The Tigers also went for a touchdown instead of lining up for a relatively safe field goal in the last seconds of a 30-24 victory over Auburn; The morning of the SEC Championship, two hours before kickoff, Miles had to publicly refute an erroneous ESPN report by Herbstreit that he was leaving for the coaching job at Michigan, his alma mater; Defensive coordinator Bo Pelini was named head coach at Nebraska after the regular season, though he would juggle his schedule to handle the LSU defense once last time in the BCS game; the Tigers had to not only win the league title game with its backup quarterback, but one who was also injured when Ryan Perrilloux deeply cut his index finger.

In the end, though, the resilience of Ohio State and LSU carried them through – with just one more curiosity for the last game of this wild season: the No. 1-ranked Buckeyes were a four-point underdog to the No. 2-ranked Tigers.

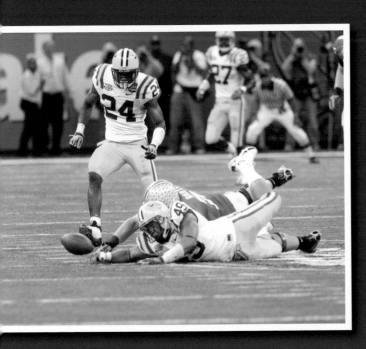

"But you see who's holding the crystal trophy now."

"WaaaaaHOOOOO!"

The whoop of Les Miles interrupted what had been a quiet, polite, press conference with the normally soft-spoken LSU coach reflecting on his good fortune of leading this bunch of football warriors.

In the middle of those introspective thoughts, Miles paused, then gave out his bellow. "Excuse me. Just kind of had to do that," he said, "just one of those things."

Exorcising his emotions was understandable. His Tigers had just earned LSU's second BCS championship trophy in four years, putting an end to a roller-coaster season of blowbacks, comebacks and setbacks, a season in which the sometimes under-appreciated Miles coached the Tigers to victories against five teams ranked in the final Top 15, and, in the process of fighting severe injuries and outside distractions, defeated five coaches with national championship resumes: South Carolina's Steve Spurrier, Florida's Urban Meyer, Alabama's Nick Saban, Tennessee's Phil Fulmer, and, now, Ohio State's Jim Tressel.

Jacob Hester (18) plows in for a touchdown as LSU scored 31 straight points.

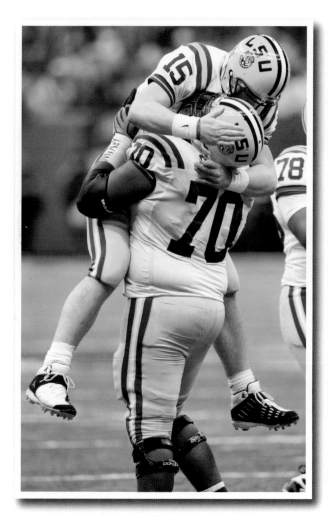

Matt Flynn (15) and Ciron Black (70) embrace
after a touchdown.

Tiger Defensive Coordinator Bo Pelini shows his
excitement in his final LSU game.

That took some doing, which eventually, after the Bayou Bengals' not-as-close-as-the-final-score 38-24 victory over Ohio State, made LSU the first two-game losing champion since Minnesota in 1960. Thinking back on it from his spot on the post-game podium, Miles mused of his team of domination, dramatics and second chances, "It was like divine intervention."

To the Ohio State players, early in the game, it seemed like divine guidance. Sophomore tailback Beanie Wells broke loose for a 65-yard touchdown on the Buckeyes' first possession. On Ohio State's second series, backup Brandon Saine found himself free, courtesy of broken coverage, and caught a 44-yard pass to the LSU 15. Three plays later, Ryan Pretorius kicked a 25-yard field goal.

Things had to look easy at this point for Ohio State, seeing as how the Buckeyes gave up just a nation-leading average of 10.0 points.

This one, to some, must have seemed over.

Think again. LSU had been down by 10 against three other opponents (Florida, Auburn, Alabama) and won them all. "The coaches sat us down and reminded us we've been in big games before," said offensive tackle Ciron Black. "That we've been down before, to just focus and play like we know how to play."

From that point, at 9:12 to go in the first quarter to the half, LSU had:

- 15 of the next 19 first downs;
- 36 of the next 55 plays;
- converted eight of its next nine third downs and stopped Ohio State on four of its next five;
- outgained the Buckeyes 212-101.

The Tigers obviously began solving the Ohio State tendencies. After falling behind by 10, quarterback Matt Flynn drove LSU on a 10-play drive to set up Colt David's 32-yard field goal. The Tigers were showing some signs of life.

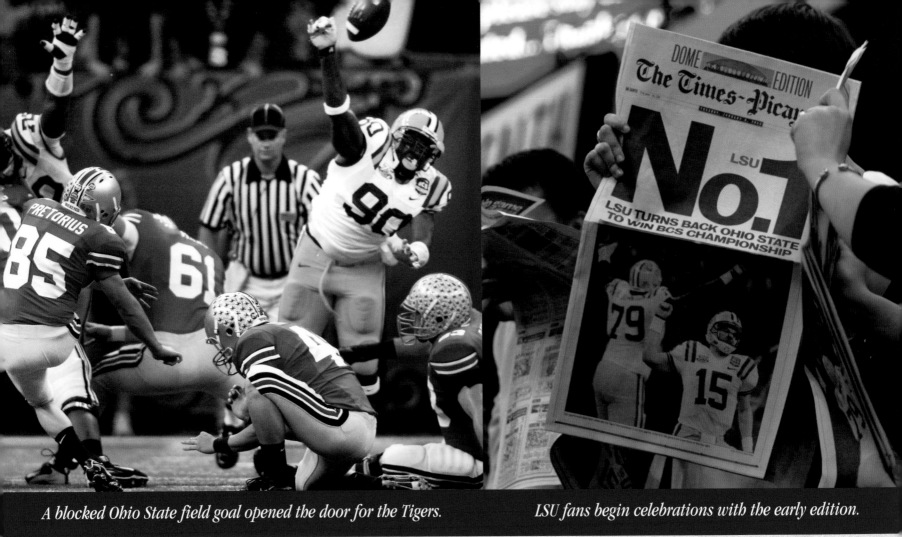

A blocked Ohio State field goal opened the door for the Tigers.

LSU fans begin celebrations with the early edition.

Flynn then drove his team 84 yards – thanks in large measure to two personal fouls on the Buckeyes – to a tying touchdown. Flynn saw Ohio State preoccupied with four LSU receivers bunched to the right and took a quick snap and hit tight end Richard Dickson for a 13-yard score.

That evened the score, and set the stage for a second quarter 21-0 point eruption the likes of which the Buckeyes couldn't have imagined, seeing as how they had given up that many in any game all season only once.

Things conceivably might have been altered, but for the biggest play of the night – by the most unlikely player, but fittingly, considering this unconventional season.

Ohio State got back down to the LSU 21, where Pretorius lined up for a 38-yard field goal. Suspecting a fake, Ricky Jean-Francois hesitated a nanosecond, then roared in, throwing aside a Buckeye lineman, and getting a hand on the ball. Linebacker Darry Beckwith fell on it at the 34. LSU then drove to the go-ahead touchdown – which would never be relinquished – a 10-yard pass from Flynn to sophomore receiver Brandon LaFell.

"They were in position to add three points to their score," Miles said, "and instead we get the short field and come back to get seven. That was really a big play.

Jean-Francois was a sophomore playing in just his second game that season, less 2007 experience of anyone on the field that night. Because of academic issues, he had been suspended and didn't get on the field until the SEC Championship Game, in which he clearly added some muscle in the Tiger defense. Against the Buckeyes, it was Jean-Francois who turned the tide.

Jean-Francois said he spent his time in football exile lamenting his situation, thinking maybe of dropping out of school and going on to something else. He also kept thinking he would make good if he could only get a second chance, a notion fostered by Jean-Francois' support staff – his coaches and teammates – and he kept working hard and practicing, concentrating on school and studying game film. All the time knowing he wouldn't play for a long time, if at all.

"My coaches and the players all kept telling me, 'Keep your head up, you're going to be back.' Once I lifted my head up, I felt like I was on top of the world to go out and play in the national championship game. It was a great thing," Jean-Francois said softly. "Just talking about it brings tears to my eyes."

Les Miles raises the crystal ball to the Tiger faithful.

	1	2	3	4	
LSU	3	21	7	7	38
Ohio State	10	0	7	7	24

Ohio State: Wells, 65-yard run. PAT, Pretorius kick.
Ohio State: Pretorius, 25-yard field goal.
LSU: David, 32-yard field goal.
LSU: Dickson, 13-yard pass from Flynn. PAT, David kick.
LSU: LaFell, 10-yard pass from Flynn. PAT, David kick.
LSU: Hester, 1-yard run. PAT, David kick.
LSU: Doucet, 4-yard pass from Flynn. PAT, David kick.
Ohio State: Robiskie, 5-yard pass from Boeckman. PAT, Pretorius kick.
LSU: Dickson, 5-yard pass from Flynn. PAT, Davis kick.
Ohio State: Hartline, 15-yard pass from Boeckman. PAT, Pretorius kick.

Individual Leaders

Rushing
LSU: Hester, 86 yards, 1 TD.
Ohio State: Wells, 146 yards, 1 TD.

Passing
LSU: Flynn, 19-27-1, 174 yards, 4 TDs.
Ohio State: Boeckman, 15-26-2, 208 yards, 2 TDs.

Receiving
LSU: Doucet, 7-51 yards, 1 TD; Dickson, 4-44 yards, 2 TDs.
Ohio State: Hartline, 6-75 yards, 1 TD; Robiskie, 5-50 yards, 1 TD.

LSU ended up scoring 31 straight points, with a four-yard Flynn pass to Early Doucet early in the third quarter. This game seemed over, and it was, though both teams would trade meaningless touchdowns down the stretch.

Three stats stood out as to what happened: Wells, the leading ground-gainer with 146 yards, got 118 on his first seven carries – then just 28 on his next 13; LSU was 118th in penalties (8.7 a game) throughout the season, second worst. But the Tigers had just four for 36 yards against Ohio State while the Buckeyes had seven for 83 yards; and the Ohio State defense, which gave up just 11 touchdowns to their previous 12 opponents, surrendered five to the Tigers.

As purple-and-gold confetti rained down on the field at game's end, it was left to LSU defensive end Kirston Pittman to put everything in perspective: "We're a team of fight, a team of destiny," he said. "There were people who didn't think we belonged here . . ." Then a big roar went up as Jean-Francois, the game's defensive MVP, held aloft the Waterford symbol of the BCS championship, and Pittman finished, "But you see who's holding up the crystal trophy now."

Thus, in the 20th game in New Orleans that a national champion appeared, LSU became the 22nd team to claim a title.

Therein lies a story . . .

LSU		Ohio State
25	First Downs	17
152	Rushing Yards	145
19-27-1	Passing	15-26-2
174	Passing Yards	208
326	Total Yards	353
3-56.7	Punts	3-50.0
2-0	Fumbles – Lost	3-1
4-36	Penalties – Yards	7-83

Attendance: 79,651.
Teams' remuneration: $36,000,000.
MVPs: Offense – Matt Flynn, LSU quarterback.
Defense – Ricky Jean-Francois, LSU tackle.

HOW IT CAME TO BE...

"I think, the Sugar Bowl I remember best was the first time I sat in the press box high above the west stands and looked across at the double-deck packed with people ... the Tulane-Texas A&M game ... January 1, 1940," said Fred Digby reflectively in 1953. "It looked like a beautiful painting hanging from the heavens."

Digby didn't say he painted that picture, that it's his signature on the canvas. The Sugar Bowl couldn't have emerged without the help of others, but it is Digby's masterpiece.

The New Orleans of that day, in the first half of the 20th Century, was as much Old World as New World, a blithesome town framed in lacy wrought iron. It was and still is, even post-Katrina, a city you visit and then go back to for the rest of your life. Its architecture, exotic airs, musical genius, fine restaurants, and mild weather make New Orleans an extremely attractive town.

It also has been a sports mecca almost from the start. New Orleans was the birthplace of Paul Morphy, the greatest of the chess masters, and the town where dice, or "craps," was introduced by the Count Bernard Mandeville de Marigny. "Gentleman" Jim Corbett knocked out John L. Sullivan in New Orleans in the first heavyweight championship fought with gloves; Clara Baer of Newcomb College wrote the first set of rules for girls' basketball in 1895; fencing was introduced to America in New Orleans; and baseball's rain check and Ladies' Day were originated by Abner Powell of the New Orleans Pelicans.

At one time, New Orleans was the only city in the country with two racetracks running in opposition for 100 weekdays. A third operated on Sundays. It was the site of the first thoroughbred match race, between Lexington and LeCompte; the legendary Black Gold ran his first and last races at the Fair Grounds and is buried in its infield.

Scads of professional baseball players, golfers, and boxers have emerged from the area; and Tulane and Loyola universities in the 1920s were producing excellent football teams with Louisiana State University's Tigers thriving 80 miles away. Fishing is virtually a year-round activity, and in season there is still abundant hunting. The Louisiana slogan "Sportsman's Paradise" is easily understood. The romance of the city and the Mississippi River, the walkability of the Vieux Carre', and the town's very sporting legacy have made New Orleans an ideal place for a showcase football game.

The Sugar Bowl has been a goal and a reward for worthy teams, a laurel of champions, for a half-century; it has been a spectacle for fans; it has paid more than a half-billion dollars to the universities whose teams have played in the game.

Three-quarters of a century ago, the world was snarled in economic collapse, the Great Depression. One of every four Americans lost their jobs. What little money there was went for essentials.

New Orleans, not an industrial center, was spared the dramatic shutdowns of other sections of the country. Nevertheless, the crash of 1929 took its toll on life in the city. Banks closed, businesses failed, and people lost their jobs. Yet, Fred Digby's obsession, the Sugar Bowl, flowered in the most hopeless days of the Depression.

Bowl games were often born, then died within a few months time from the turn of the century to the mid-1930s. Many had the appearance of speculative, flimflam adventures. Others were ill-managed projects of well meaning but incapable civic leaders. The Rose Bowl alone was built on a foundation strong enough to last and to serve as a model for later bowls. Eight thousand curious people watched the first Rose Bowl in 1902 as Michigan defeated host Stanford, 49-0. Stanford literally asked for mercy and Michigan agreed to shorten the game. The lopsided score spoiled the afternoon for almost everyone, and Rose Bowl football lost favor to such holiday diversions as chariot races.

The Tournament of Roses revived its football game in 1916. Its success sparked an alliance between the crusading sports editor Digby and a taciturn New Orleans lawyer named Warren V. Miller. The two of them combined their obsessions to create the Sugar Bowl 18 years later.

Digby was a working-class self-made man who was forced to leave school in order to help his family, but put himself through the Sophie B. Wright night school for needy young men.

While working as an office boy, Digby began writing sports under the nom de plume "Booster." *New Orleans Item* sports editor H.T. McDaniel paid him by the inch for his copy. Digby joined the paper's sports staff full time three years later.

Reserved, quiet, and fiercely independent, he became a sports editor who worked practically every waking hour on projects he saw as for the greater good of the region's populace.

"I worked for Fred 17 years," said Charles L. "Pie" Dufour, "and he was a man of tremendous integrity, a very powerful writer, a reporter who worked like hell. He surrounded himself with people he respected, and people who wouldn't rubber-stamp his ideas. Sometimes I wonder where the Sugar Bowl would be now if everyone around Fred had thought it was such a grand idea in those days."

Warren Miller, five years older than Digby, came from a much more comfortable New Orleans background. He was an exceptional student from grammar school through Louisiana State University, where he studied chemistry, and finished with

Fred Digby

a law degree.

Miller dreamed as a youngster of becoming a professional baseball pitcher but couldn't last more than three innings. Other than writing an LSU fight song, there was little to indicate he would become one of the most influential persons in Louisiana sports history. "I roomed with two football captains at LSU," he once laughed about his athletic background. Where Miller did excel was in civil law and as a civic leader. He ran unsuccessfully for mayor of New Orleans on the Republican ticket in 1930.

"I first got interested in the Sugar Bowl idea when Alabama went to the Rose Bowl in 1926," Miller said. "I thought it would be a fine thing for New Orleans to have such a game." Ironically, that same Rose Bowl also planted the seed in Digby's mind for a postseason game in New Orleans.

Tulane ran up a 9-0-1 record in 1925, and Digby felt the school deserved an invitation to the 1926 Pasadena game. He wrote Warren Brown, a friend and the sports editor of a San Francisco paper, asking about the selection process and if an invitation could be presented to a Southern team. Brown explained that the Pacific Coast representative, in this case the University of Washington, picked its own opponent.

Digby prevailed upon two friends in Seattle to present Tulane's credentials to the Washington officials. Rose Bowl authorities advised Washington to invite an Eastern team. Princeton got the invitation, but then dazed the sponsors by declining. Washington officials called Digby back asking for assurances that Tulane would accept if invited.

Digby expressed confidence that Tulane would accept. A telegram was dispatched to Tulane President Dr. Albert Dinwiddie which read: "Will you accept a Rose Bowl invitation – if invited?" The answer was no. Tulane administrators felt the trip would keep its athletes out of school too long.

Furious and embarrassed, Digby called the unsuspecting Clark Shaughnessy, Tulane's coach, who was on a trip in Chicago. Shaughnessy, in turn, called the University of Washington and recommended Alabama. The Crimson Tide, on that recommendation, became the first Southern team to participate in the Rose Bowl.

Three hundred and seventy-five dollars had been spent in long-distance telephone calls and telegrams in the aborted campaign. Digby felt he owed an explanation to Item publisher James M. Thomson. After a long discussion Thomson approved the charges, then, almost as an afterthought, asked Digby, "Why can't we have a postseason game in New Orleans?"

The torch had been lit.

Digby struggled for a long time attempting to come up with a format and foundation for the game, though he didn't do it publicly. In November of 1928 the subject was broached again, this time by players more than a thousand miles removed from New Orleans. Boston College, en route to a 9-0-0 season, suggested a postseason game with its sister Jesuit institution, Loyola University in New Orleans. Loyola was to host the game, according to the proposal, and Digby used the occasion for his first comprehensive column on a New Orleans bowl game.

"The suggestion from Boston College," he wrote on November 13, 1928, "for a postseason game here with Loyola University in December will get a hearty approval from all football fans. Especially those who have been wondering for years why New Orleans doesn't vie with Los Angeles, Pasadena, and points west for some of the nationwide publicity that such contests secure."

Unfortunately, the suggestion died when it was brought before the authorities at both Boston College and Loyola. "School officials felt it was too long and expensive a trip," explained Joe McKenney, who coached the Eagles in 1928, "and the authorities at BC and Loyola didn't feel it was wise to extend the season."

Twelve months afterward, Loyola did extend its season, and in

New Orleans. It participated in a postseason game sponsored under the auspices of the Young Men's Business Club and the city's dominant newspaper, the stodgy and haughty Times-Picayune.

Loyola of New Orleans and Loyola of Chicago played to a regular season 6-6 tie in what was described by one of the players as a "typhoon" on Armistice Day, 1929. "Players were literally more afraid of drowning than being hurt," Chicago quarterback Corny Collins told Chicago Tribune sportswriter Ed Schneider. "The immediate reaction as a man went down was, 'For God's sake, get those people off him before he drowns!' " said Collins.

The Young Men's Business Club, whose initial experience fueled bigger plans, decided to attempt a "real" college match. The two Loyolas were asked to consider a rematch for the benefit of the Doll & Toy Fund, and both agreed. Tulane Stadium, with a seating capacity in excess of 20,000, would have been the ideal site, but school officials turned down the idea because the game was scheduled for a Sunday. The participating schools then agreed to play at Loyola of New Orleans' home stadium. Despite the game being linked to a rival publication, Digby pushed for its success.

With good weather, the attraction was expected to lure 10,000 fans into Loyola's 15,000-seat stadium. More than 5,000 advance tickets were sold, and prospects of reaching the goal seemed good. But frigid temperatures swept into the South on December 22, the day before the match, and the announced attendance for Loyola of Chicago's 26-6 victory was 6,000. Eight thousand people had seen the same schools play during the regular season, and in equally bad weather.

Most of the principals, considering the circumstances, felt the project was a success. The game — played less than two months after the Wall Street Crash — didn't lose money; it came two days before Christmas; it was played between two teams with less than national mystique; and the weather certainly affected attendance adversely, Clark Shaughnessy, who had left Tulane for Loyola of the South and coached the Wolfpack in the Doll & Toy Fund defeat, agreed. After he became head coach at the University of Chicago, he told Ed Schneider, "That game was really the forerunner of the Sugar Bowl, inasmuch as it opened the eyes of some businessmen in New Orleans to the possibility of a postseason game."

Loyola defeated the University of Detroit 9-6 in the second Doll & Toy Fund game, December 7, 1930, and drew a disappointing 10,000 fans.

Mayor T. Semmes Walmsley earlier in the year sent a delegation headed by Digby to a meeting of the Southern Conference (the predecessor of the Southeastern Conference). They sought approval of a new concept of Digby's — a weeklong carnival of sports climaxed by a football game. It was turned down. "I think the Southern Conference thought this was a fly-by-night deal," said

Pie Dufour. "It doesn't reflect on the judgment of those people; they just weren't going to endorse anything until it was established."

Still, the dream of a New Orleans bowl game wouldn't fade. Months after the proposal was rejected, and two weeks after the second Doll &. Toy Fund game, Mayor Walmsley opened a Southern Conference convention in New Orleans with the suggestion that an annual postseason football game, along the lines of the Rose Bowl, be held in the South. He said New Orleans stood ready to support such an undertaking.

At the same time, Fred Digby was aboard the Crimson Special with Alabama's Pasadena-bound Tide. He was going to get a look at the granddaddy of 'em all. The splendor of the Tournament of Roses and its football attraction only made the sports editor more confident that New Orleans could rival it eventually. What he found that California had — and New Orleans lacked — was simply the willingness to do it.

When he returned, Digby found an ally willing to cooperate. The city's Association of Commerce sanctioned the effort to put together a Carnival of Sports and an intersectional football game. Digby called for a weeklong calendar that could, hypothetically, include a championship fight, an open golf tournament, midwin-

Warren Miller

ter Davis Cup tennis trials, an indoor track and field meet, a special handicap horse race, and the football game.

"What the little city of Pasadena has done with the Tournament of Roses," Digby wrote, "New Orleans can do a hundred times better with a Carnival of Sports."

Weeks, then months, then years went by without any substantive action. It galled the *Item* to realize in the latter part of 1933, two years after the Association of Commerce entered the effort, that Dallas was putting on a postseason game of its own on New Year's Day, the Dixie Classic. Miami had already staged a game in its Festival of Palms attraction and was looking to its second during the holiday season. These were the antecedents of the Cotton and Orange Bowls. Neither had real appeal but were more along the lines of the Doll & Toy Fund enterprises of 1929 and 1930. Centenary and Arkansas competed in Dallas; Duquesne and the University of Miami played in Florida.

The *Item* praised Dallas editorially, and shook an angry finger at New Orleans.

"Dallas and Atlanta," said the paper, "usually do the things that New Orleans ought to do, and get the things that New Orleans ought to get, all the way from Federal Reserve banks to 'football classics.' We sweat at Carnival (Mardi Gras) preparations and fuss with each other over local politics while Texans and Georgians go and get what they want, which is very often what we ought to have. The Tulane Athletic Association, not caring for a postseason game itself, has not cared to show the slightest interest and concern in the enterprise as a matter of municipal comity—though its stadium was built by popular subscription in this city."

Digby had information that at least two teams, Pittsburgh and Nebraska, in addition to LSU and Centenary, were interested in playing in New Orleans had the committee acted promptly. And he admonished Tulane for its lack of support. Part of the difficulty in getting Tulane's sanction was the flimflam image bowls other than the Rose Bowl had at the time. University officials weren't certain the institution should be linked to such an enterprise.

The entire matter seemed to have reached an impossible impasse. There were five noteworthy games on January 1, 1934: the Rose Bowl in Pasadena, the Dixie Classic in Dallas, the Festival of Palms in Miami, the East-West Shrine game in San Francisco, and a charity all-star game in Knoxville, Tennessee. New Orleans had a high school game.

In January 1934, the sports editors of the *Times-Picayune* and the *States*, Bill Keefe and Harry Martinez, with a group of prominent citizens, received the following notice from Joseph M. Cousins, a highly regarded businessman and former president of the New Orleans Athletic Club:

Gentlemen:

Will you please arrange to attend a meeting to be held at my office, 2003 American Bank Building, Monday, January 8, 1934, 12:30 P.M. to discuss plans in connection with the formation of a football league after the regular playing season; also to discuss ways and means of endeavoring to adopt a plan that will mean the staging of a big football game in New Orleans on New Year's Day.

Yours very truly,
J.M. Cousins

Cousins was head of an Association of Commerce group called the Citizens' Committee that had come up with an idea of a semipro football league that would play on Sundays with a championship game on January 1.

At the same time the Co-Operative Club, an organization of executives, had decided to become involved in the formation of a New Year's Day bowl. Both groups, in essence, were anxious to try to get the New Year's Day football concept off the ground. Miller presented his plan to the Item asking for the newspaper's approval. *Item* managing editor Clarke Salmon recommended to Miller that the Co-operative Club unite with Joe Cousins' party.

Fred Digby, of course, was present for the detailing of Miller's plan at the *Item*. Invitations to a meeting with Cousins were sent to Keefe and Martinez because Digby knew full well a venture of this size would need the endorsement of all the papers. Digby was willing to low-key the *Item's* role for the support — at least for a while.

"We passed a resolution in January of 1934 suggesting a New Year's Day game," said Miller of the circumstances leading up to the official meeting in Cousins' office, "and no sooner had the plan been published than we learned that another group was planning to promote a semipro league and wind up with a big championship game for charity on January 1. We talked it over, and they liked the idea of inviting only college teams, so we decided to get the entire city behind the plan."

Dr. Fred Wolfe, Dr. M.P. Boebinger, Francis "Hap" Reilly, Ralph Barry, and T. Semmes Rantlett joined Cousins, Miller, and Digby in the January 8th conference. They were enthusiastic and confident that business, fraternal, and civic associations would unite behind the undertaking. Others weren't quite as sure. The *Times-Picayune* and *States* sports editors didn't attend and Keefe waited four days before commenting; then he said he doubted the Southeastern Conference would approve the game, pointed out the venture had no guarantees against the weather, and recommended instead a boxing carnival, a rodeo, or an indoor tennis match. Martinez didn't write a word about it, pro or con.

Miller's blueprint was simple. A nonprofit organization would be formed, meaning not a cent would be retained above operating expenses — the associations and businesses involved would vol-

An early planning meeting of Sugar Bowl founding members. Front row: Fred Digby, Joseph M. Cousins, Warren V. Miller, Irwin F. Poche, Harry W. Fletcher; Back: Abe N. Goldberg, Dr. Fred J. Wolfe, Albert Wachenheim, Jr., Jacob H. Bodenheimer, Dr. M.P. Boebinger, John Niehaus.

unteer some of their time and labor to the work load of the project; the $30,000 it was estimated necessary to attract top-flight teams would be derived by securing 30 guarantors to pledge $1,000 apiece.

The plan had to be amended because only one of the organizations, the *Item*, whose backing was pledged by James Thomson, was able to pledge the $1,000. A signing of 300 guarantors at $100 apiece — with assurances of only one thing: their money back or its value in tickets — was agreed to be a more feasible plan.

A coalition of individuals and associations began being melded into one athletic front on February 6, 1934, in a preliminary, organizational meeting. Sixteen organizations committed to the undertaking and selected delegates to work on the project and prepare for the drive for guarantors.

Miller, at the expense of the Co-Operative Club, was in Baton Rouge two days later for a Southeastern Conference meeting. Miller wanted the SEC's sanction for the bowl. Another New Orleans group also attended the league talks, seeking permission to hold a New Year's Day all-star game. Since nothing was known of the second group's existence before the gathering, the SEC must have been somewhat confused. But the conference tabled any decision on the bowl plan because it didn't want to commit itself while the movement was still in the process of mobilization. Miller was encouraged. "They didn't say 'yes,' but they didn't say 'no,' " he reported with a smile.

The *Times-Picayune's* reportage came across with a slightly different tone, that the proposal by the New Orleans sports amusement organization had been voted down.

The Mid-Winter Sports Association was officially chartered at the February 15, 1934, meeting at the New Orleans Athletic Club. Forty members of 23 citywide organizations welded together for the purpose of a December-January sports program. According to the charter drawn by Miller, the Association was stipulated to be a "Voluntary, nonprofit civic organization whose members serve without remuneration; there would be no connection with commercial interest or professional sports; there would be no private profit; and any surplus above the required operating expenses or reserve fund must be devoted to 'charitable, religious, or educational purposes.' "

Miller was unanimously elected president, Joe Cousins vice president, T. Semmes Rantlett secretary, and Harry W. Fletcher treasurer.

Miller hinted broadly that evening that the game would have immediate credibility because he was certain a Southeastern Conference team would be in one corner of the inaugural. He noted that no conference member (meaning the Southern Conference from which the SEC descended in 1933) had ever been refused permission to play in a postseason game. Miller was sure a team invited to New Orleans would not be denied.

"I am sure that if we go back to the Southeastern Conference in

November or December with an invitation for one of its teams to play in our game here, that the executive committee will act favorably upon it," Miller said. "We will have no trouble getting a big game for New Orleans every year. What we've got to do is prove to the world that we can put this project over. That job is up to us."

That meant preparing for the hardest part, securing the $30,000 by public subscription. Some still feared it was too steep a task for the times. "We settled that in a hurry," Miller said. "I got Clarence Strauss, who was president of the Co-Operative Club, to try out the plan personally. He went out by himself and got 13 guarantors in 15 visits. We were ready to go ahead then, and soon had guarantees of $32,700."

Miller was next scheduled to attend a convention of Southwest Conference authorities, for there was sentiment the game should be played between the champions of the SEC and the SWC. The visit brought the game's first conference sanction. "We got the approval of the Southwest Conference, providing we had the money in the bank," said Miller. "So we started advertising the game to the world."

Things began falling into place. The Southern Yacht Club agreed to a midwinter regatta, something never attempted in New Orleans previously. Douglas Watters and Allan Smuck, two tennis enthusiasts among the Mid-Winter Sports Association's members, put together an invitational tournament in conjunction with the football game. It wasn't exactly the carnival Digby dreamed of, but it was a beginning.

Tulane remained standoffish to the idea of its stadium being used. Several donors to the private school were close to the bowl project as well. They privately, but anonymously, allowed Tulane authorities to become aware of their strong interest in the success of the bowl. Tulane acquiesced and allowed rent-free use of its stadium for one day a year by the Mid-Winter Sports Association. The decision was a boon for school and bowl. It would play a role in Tulane being able to continue competing with a major college football program years afterward.

The Sugar Bowl was Digby's suggestion as a name for the game. It was ideal and it was adopted. New Orleans is near the heart of Louisiana's mammoth sugar cane industry, and Tulane Stadium is situated on the site of Etienne de Bore's sugar plantation (which covered the tracts that are now the Tulane and Loyola university campuses and Audubon Park). De Bore's plantation was one of the state's first and de Bore, the first mayor of New Orleans, turned from the cultivation of chicory and indigo to the raising of sugar cane in the 17th century, despite the warnings of others that cane juice would not crystallize. The industry de Bore helped found is alive today; and the area of Louisiana just south and west of New Orleans is known as "America's Sugar Bowl."

An elegant piece of silver became the trophy and personality of the Sugar Bowl, giving the Mid-Winter Sports Association a classical tinge even before consummating its purpose. The sterling silver bowl was handmade in England in 1830 during the reign of King George IV by the silversmiths Rebecca Emes and Edward Barnard. It was probably used as a wine cooler or trophy piece. Samuel Waldhorn, a renowned New Orleans antique dealer, obtained the rare piece on one of his yearly European business trips. The bowl formed part of Waldhorn's celebrated antique silver collection. It was spotted by some Sugar Bowl friends of the Waldhorn family who made a fast-talking appeal to Samuel's civic pride. "I don't know how they did it," said Stephen Moses who now runs the antique concern. "They must have been very close friends of my grandfather."

It was decided the striking trophy would be given to the winning football team for a one-year period, then a replica would be donated for permanent possession. Samuel Waldhorn's magnificent generosity gave the Sugar Bowl style from the beginning.

Things were humming until a crisis occurred in October. Paul B. Williamson, whose football ratings service was among the most popular in the country until the wire services began their polls, and Richard Fleming resigned from the Mid-Winter Sports Association, and T. Semmes Rantlett died in the fall of 1934.

A lingering and inaccurate legacy of those formative days is the legend of the "39ers," the 39 men who founded the Sugar Bowl. The loss of three men from the original 40, of course, is 37, though even the listing of the charter members usually totals 39. Two of the three men — and all are mentioned on one list or another—who were unable to continue are added, seemingly to fill the roster.

The combination of circumstances left the Sugar Bowl $5,000 short of $30,000.

"I went out and got Paul E. DeBlanc, new president of the Co-Operative Club, Joseph B. David, and some personal friends to raise the money," Miller said. "In 10 days we collected $5,100 in fresh money and had the $30,000 in the bank when we invited Tulane and Temple for the first game. Ten days later, the guarantors got their money back. Money received from the sale of tickets (was) sufficient to pay the guarantees and expenses of the first game."

With the necessary money in escrow, and Tulane's consent for the rent-free use of its stadium, the Southeastern and Southern Conferences gave the Sugar Bowl their blessings.

Ten years after James Thomson casually asked Fred Digby about the possibility, New Orleans was to host a major postseason football game.

Tulane 20 Temple 14

"We're only here stooging."

The Mid-Winter Sports Association wanted to annually pair the most evenly matched teams, to create the best game possible. Once the Sugar Bowl realized just how far it could reach for quality teams – despite the new Orange Bowl in 1935 and the well-established Rose Bowl – the somewhat popular sentiment for an annual game between the Southeastern and Southwest Conference champions or a North-South format quickly evaporated. The Sugar Bowl's guarantee of $15,000 to the visiting team was a large sum in the midst of the Depression. The "home" team was assured of $12,500, and $2,500 was alloted for the Association's expenses.

From the start, there were mixed feelings about a conference tie-up, with the SEC being the most logical choice. First, there was the assurance of one corner being filled by a quality team with some familiarity in New Orleans, leaving the Bowl free to concentrate on luring big names from outside the South. On the other hand, if the game was open-ended, it might be possible to pair the most evenly matched teams. This was the route Digby favored and the direction chosen. It was understood, however, that if an area school deserved an invitation, it would be extended.

With the necessary funds deposited in a bank by November 1, the Executive Committee concentrated on the caliber of teams across the country. The Sugar Bowl would not allow the home team a say in selecting its opponent as the Rose Bowl did. After contacting the schools and receiving an agreement, the Sugar Bowl's final decision was expected on Sunday, December 2. But no announcement was made. The Committee went back into session at 5 P.M. the following day at the New Orleans Athletic Club. At 9:30 P.M. the pairing was official: Tulane and Temple.

Although Temple was largely an unknown quantity to New Orleans, it quickly became apparent the Sugar Bowl had done its homework and that gave it credibility. Temple was coached by Glenn "Pop" Warner, already a legendary figure, and the Owls were ranked third nationally in the Williamson Poll. Temple was undefeated, though tied twice, and was considered the "Northern Champion." Its roster included a sophomore fullback, Dave Smukler, said to be "better than Jim Thorpe" by Warner, who had coached Thorpe at Carlisle Institute. Tulane was the natural attraction for local fans and an obvious choice for the home berth. The Green Wave was 13th-ranked, with a 9-1 record, and could be expected to draw several thousand additional fans from the immediate area. Tulane, in many ways, was a godsend to the first Sugar Bowl. It was the popular choice of the Mid-Winter Sports Association and of Fred Digby.

"All New Orleans is anxiously awaiting word and expecting Tulane to be invited ... It is inconceivable that Tulane would refuse the invitation since it will offer her an opportunity to provide impetus to an event which the entire city is now supporting with an enthusiasm seldom aroused in an athletic event here," Digby wrote the afternoon of the selections.

Inconceivable or not, Tulane did not want the invitation. School officials did not, players did not. The coaches did. It was later rumored that the Greenies believed they merited Alabama's Rose Bowl berth, or that they wanted a rematch with Colgate, the only team Tulane failed to defeat in 1934. Neither was the case.

Ted Cox's first assistant, Lester Lautenschlaeger, said he was told by Esmond

Tulane's Monk Simons (47) sweeps wide against the Owls of Temple.

Phelps, president of the Tulane board, to call a team meeting and to "have the team vote down the invitation." Lautenschlaeger would have had no difficulty doing that. His task was to get the team to change its mind on an enterprise the Tulane coaching staff felt could become worthwhile.

Barney Mintz, a junior back on the team, insisted there had been no talk about the Rose Bowl, and it had nothing to do with the Green Wave's reluctance. "In fact," he said, "we were surprised when they called us in the team meeting. The Sugar Bowl naturally didn't mean anything to us then. We didn't know anything about it. They called us in and Lester said, 'Look, we have an opportunity to go to the Sugar Bowl, which is the first time it is being held. We think it would be nice, but we're gonna leave it up to you.' The vote was basically unanimous against it."

The coaches apparently had already signaled the Sugar Bowl the bid would be accepted, because they were aghast. "Well, they were shocked," said Mintz, "because they knew what kind of position they were in. Lester got up again and said, 'Now look, let's think it over, maybe we didn't explain it.' We

went through the details, that it was a community undertaking, and that Tulane was in a position ... and should respond." A suggestion was made by a player that they be given $150 a man for playing and was immediately vetoed.

"We took a vote," Mintz added, "and I would guess the vote was not quite enough for a majority. We got a few more. Then Lester got up again and made a really impassioned plea, that we were going to embarrass the university and such and such, etc., you know, the usual thing. I don't know what the vote was, but it was at least one above a majority. We were gonna go out and play." By then, even Tulane President Dr. Albert Dinwiddie was in favor of it.

There was a chemistry working for the Sugar Bowl now. Certainly Temple, with Warner and Smukler, aroused the curiosity of a large block of fans. The hometown Greenies, boasting a ball carrier the equal of Smukler, Claude "Little Monk" Simons, accounted for another segment of fans. What will never be known is how many of the halfhearted were prodded into attendance by the Item's sports staff.

Pie Dufour recalled with a chuckle, "Scoop Kennedy and I would leave the office at lunchtime and go over to the Maison Blanche ticket office, which was downstairs in the men's clothing department. Scoop and I would go stand in line to make it look longer. Then when we'd get to the window, we'd tell the man, 'We're only here stooging.' After that, we'd leave the line, wait a few minutes, then go back in line again. We did that for a week or 10 days to try to stimulate business, make people think this was the damndest demand they ever saw!"

In two days, the Sugar Bowl sold more than $20,000 worth of advance tickets at $3.50 and $1.50 apiece.

Crowds storm ticket counters for 1935 Tulane Temple inaugural.

"No one laid a hand on me."

Tulane starters for the 1935 Sugar Bowl. Lineman, from left, Charles Kyle, Roy Ary, George Tessier, Homer Robinson, Robert Simon, Robert Tessier, and Dick Hardy. Backs, Barney Mintz, Joe Loftin, Claud 'Monk Simmons and John McDaniel.

Claude "Monk" Simons was a Tulane football hero, used to acclaim and applause. But he was the unlikely hero of the first Sugar Bowl.

Dave Smukler of visiting Temple – described by an admiring Pie Dufour as "212 pounds of speed and power who asked nothing more of his own line but that it get out of his way and let him run" – was the pre-game focus. Simons, playing one month after fracturing a shoulder in the act of a game-winning punt-return against LSU, proved every bit the equal of the heralded Smukler. He would eventually ignite the Tulane offense, setting the stage for (A) yet another notable performance by end Dick Hardy and (B) a dramatic victory on that cool, cloudy afternoon.

Wearing a shoulder pad made partly of rubber to protect the injury, Simons sprinkled the first glitter of Sugar Bowl lore into the classic.

Early, though, aided strongly on the bounce of the ball, Smukler and Temple held the upper hand.

Two first half fumbles, on the Tulane 10 and 18, gave Temple two touchdowns, and Smukler had a hand in both – a seven-yard pass to Danny Testa, who eased just over the goal behind a defensive back, Simons; and then Smukler catapulted over center from the 2.

Temple was in front 14-0, having to go a total of 28 yards in six plays for its two-touchdown lead.

"In case you hadn't guessed," Tulane assistant Lester Lautenschlaeger recalled, "we weren't in the best of spirits at the time."

They would pick up with first spectacular play in Sugar Bowl history.

Temple kicked off from within 10 yards of the sideline to keep the return man bottled up on one side. The Wave's Johnny McDaniel took the ball on the 10 and ran up a few yards, drawing most of the Owl coverage to him. Then he lateralled to Simons, five yards behind at the 15 and running in the opposite direction. A pair of defenders were fooled just for a blink, and then gave chase to the speeding ball-carrier.

Unable to shake the pursuing Owls, Simons almost skimmed the sidelines.

Simons vividly recalled a huge cherry-jerseyed figure with outstretched arms that seemed to cover the width of the field and appeared ready to enclose him at the 35. "It looked like he had me pinned to the sidelines," Simons said. But Greenie Stanley Lodrigues came out of nowhere to take the defender out. "That was the biggest obstacle in my path," Simons said. "The rest of the team set up a wall and I simply ran down the sideline. No one laid a hand on me."

By the time he reached the Tulane 40, Monk was in the clear.

It was Simons' 11th touchdown of the season and set the tone for the second half.

Late in the third quarter, Bucky Bryan broke off a breathtaking 28-yard gain to again put the Green Wave in scoring

Dick Hardy makes touchdown catch as
Wilfred Longsderf dives at his heels.

position. From the 11, Bryan flicked a quick pass to Hardy, who leaped high between two Owls and came down with the ball in the end zone, despite one defender still clinging to his back. Mintz' PAT tied the score.

Hardy also gave Tulane the lead – and ultimately the victory – with an impromptu play. At the Owl 48, Horace "Bucco" Mowrey diagnosed Mintz's next attempt perfectly and stepped squarely between passer and receiver, Hardy, at precisely the right instant. But the ball brushed Mowrey's fingers and flew up. Hardy rushed over, took the ball on the run, and raced untouched the remaining 15 yards as Wilfred Longsderf dove desperately and futilely at his heels. It was the third sensational reception of the day for Hardy.

Longsderf kept Temple's hopes alive by blocking Mintz's conversion to keep the score at 20-14, but that's how things would end.

Simons laughed years later that he could still see Smukler at the post-game party, wearing a derby and a seersucker suit and smoking a cigar. Members of both teams were given the suits, then a novelty. "It's a hellava thing," Smukler told Monk, "to come all the way down here and wind up with a pair of pajamas."

Smukler came down for more than that. The attendance of 22,026 allowed the Mid-Winter Sports Association to present each school with a check of $27,800, almost double their guarantee. The quality and derring-do of Temple and Tulane left fans buzzing.

The Sugar Bowl was in business.

	1	2	3	4	
Tulane	0	7	7	6	20
Temple	7	7	0	0	14

Temple: Testa, 7-yard pass from Smukler. PAT Smukler, kick.

Temple: Smukler, 1-yard run. PAT Testa, kick.

Tulane: Simons, 85-yard lateral from McDaniel on kickoff. PAT Mintz, kick.

Tulane: Hardy, 11-yard pass from Mintz. PAT Mintz, kick.

Tulane: Hardy, 48-yard pass from Mintz. PAT blocked.

Individual Leaders

Rushing
Tulane: Simons 9-61; Bryan 3-26.
Temple: Smukler 24-88, 1 TD; Mowrey 12-40.

Passing
Tulane: Mintz 2-6, 53 yards, 1 TD.
Temple: Smukler 3-6, 19 yards, 1 TD.

Receiving
Tulane: Hardy 3-57, 2 TDs.
Temple: Preisser 1-10 yards.

Tulane		Temple
10	First Downs	13
140	Rushing Yards	182
8-16-1	Passing	3-13-1
88	Passing Yards	19
228	Total Yards	201
10-34.5	Punts	12-30.3
3-2	Fumbles – Lost	2-1
2-20	Penalties – Yards	2-7

Attendance: 22,026.
Teams' remuneration: $55,600.

TCU 3 LSU 2

"Duck Hunting and Slingin' Sammy."

Mary Frances Digby remembered her husband coming home the night of January 1, 1935, in a quiet, contemplative mood. "He was very happy," she recalled with a smile. "After a while, he just looked up and said it had been a dream come true."

Almost as soon as the dream of a Sugar Bowl became a reality, it began to build momentum and expand. It was Bill Keefe, noting that general admission tickets weren't put on sale until the day of the game (which put a strain on ticket sellers and forced 2,000 fans away), who called for a 5,000-seat increase of Tulane Stadium. That bit of crusading a couple of days after the Tulane-Temple game must have caused Digby some slight amusement.

Both the Times-Picayune and the States had given the first Sugar Bowl events as much coverage as the Item. The pull of all three influenced the initial wave of popularity that struck as the football game neared.

A February meeting was held to make plans for the following Sugar Bowl. The Sugar Bowl was left with $10,370.61. Half that total was placed in a sinking fund, along with an unsolicited $12,300 already received from eager guarantors for the 1936 game. The other $5,000 was set aside for expenses the Association might need for the coming year.

Also, the Mid-Winter Sports Association became exclusive in 1935. Membership rolls were closed and limited to the original organizers. They had succeeded beyond anyone's belief in less than a year. Four hundred and twenty guarantors put up money for the 1936 game.

Everything the Mid-Winter Sports Association touched at that time was just right. A year after Tulane was the natural selection for the inaugural, LSU emerged as an obvious choice. The Southeastern Conference champions won nine straight after an opening 10-7 loss to Rice and had a flock of exceptional players. They included Abe Mickal, one of the nation's best passers, and Gaynell "Cus" Tinsley, considered the best end in the country. The defensive-minded Tigers had allowed three SEC opponents less than 50 yards from scrimmage.

LSU's probable acceptance was verified belatedly because Athletic Director T.P. Heard returned late from a Tuesday afternoon duck-hunting trip. Heard was asked by a reporter if LSU had a preference of whom it would play. "Our preference is TCU or Nebraska — either would make a great game," said Heard.

Texas Christian was announced as LSU's opponent, and the Sugar Bowl may have backed into its stated goal — the best game possible. TCU was ranked fourth in most polls and had a crowd-pleasing attraction in "Slingin'" Sammy Baugh, whose passing skills had set the Southwest ablaze. The Horned Frogs had finished second to Southern Methodist.

LSU's Rock Reed pulls away from the Horned Frog line.

The TCU and SMU match, each team 10-0-0, was the first Southwest football game to be aired on a nationwide radio hookup. Matty Bell's Mustangs had surrendered only three touchdowns and shut out seven opponents. Dutch Meyer's Horned Frogs averaged three touchdowns a game. This game didn't stir just fans; writers from across the country showed up as did three coaches on a busman's holiday – Dana Bible of Nebraska, Lynn "Pappy" Waldorf of Northwestern, and Bernie Bierman of Minnesota. A dramatic 20-14 SMU victory sent the Mustangs to the Rose Bowl, the only Southwest Conference appearance in Pasadena. TCU was more than acceptable to the Sugar Bowl.

More than $40,000 in tickets had been sold before the pairing was announced. Five thousand dollars more came in the day after, and three weeks before the game only a few hundred tickets remained. It was estimated the alphabetical match of LSU-TCU could have drawn 45,000, but the largest crowd to see a sporting event in Louisiana was already assured, despite slightly higher-priced tickets than for the 1935 Sugar Bowl.

The Mid-Winter Sports Association also reached an agreement with the National Broadcasting Company for a coast-to-coast radio hookup. It would immediately precede the Rose Bowl and introduce another estimated 15 million fans to the Sugar Bowl.

Things were going so well it must have been scary at times. The only possible problem could have been the weather. But Warren Miller and Fred Digby ran a check on New Orleans' New Year's Day weather the year before for the Tulane-Temple match. Cloudy and cool had been the average reading for decades, and it hadn't rained on New Year's in 25 years.

The starting LSU line for the 1936 game: from left. John Mihalic, Paul Caroll, Oscar Matlock, Moose Stewart, Wendell Leisk, Eddie Gatto, Gaynell Tinsley.

"I had a hand in all the scoring."

'Slingin' Sammy Baugh had a hand in all the scoring in the 1936 Sugar Bowl.

It poured the last three days of 1935.

The anticipated passing game – essential component for both the Horned Frogs and the Tigers – went swirling into the gumbo-like surface of Tulane Stadium.

Oddly, the conditions probably hurt LSU more than TCU, whose Slingin' Sammy Baugh was football's proto-type passer. The Tigers' Abe Mickal was also a superb passer. Baugh, though, was more than that. He was one of the best all-around players of the first half of the 20th Century, one who could beat opponents with his blocking, defense and kicking as well as his arm.

Considering everything, the crowd may have witnessed the finest touchdownless game ever played, complete with multiple goal-line stands. The Frogs held the Bayou Bengals six inches from the end zone, and, later, twice from the 2. TCU reached the Tiger 16, though the Frogs could penetrate no further. There was also a kicking duel of heroic proportions: The average of Baugh's 14 punts was 47 yards, and included one of 69 yards; The average of LSU's 13 punts was 45 yards, including one of 65 yards by Mickal and another of 64 yards by Bill Crass.

Those, of course, were no small feats in the best of conditions, let alone with a water-logged ball, though the athletes were themselves also drenched. Equipment at the time added approximately 15 pounds to a player's weight. When the leather helmets, woolen jerseys, and awkward-fitting padding became soaked, as happened early in this game, the load increased dramatically.

Three times the Tigers got inside the TCU 2, and three times the Horned Frogs repulsed them. Baugh, as good a defensive back as he was a passer, made two touchdown-saving tackles. Helping the TCU cause immensely was LSU coach Bernie Moore's stubbornness in going for touchdowns instead of field goals, despite the pleadings of his players.

In the second quarter, the Frogs stopped an LSU drive six inches from the end zone, though the threat did not go unrewarded. Baugh backed up in the end zone on a fake punt. In a play that brought together two future College Football Hall of Fame inductees, LSU end Gus Tinsley came crashing in as Baugh attempted to get a pass off. The ball slipped off his fingers and fell to the swampish end zone turf, in those days an automatic safety.

After the penalty kick, though, Crass fumbled on the LSU 45 and TCU sputtered and splashed its way for 19 more yards.

"We couldn't get anywhere," Baugh said, "so on fourth down, I called for a field goal. I held the ball, and I believe I was more nervous than Taldon (Manton, the place-kicker) was. The kick was from the 26 and, as I recall, it was on the order of a line drive ... at first I thought it might go wide to the right...but it stayed inside the posts."

The points for both teams came within two minutes of each other.

Baugh found a way to win, even with the adverse weather-conditions: defense and kicking. Slingin' Sammy, with two touchdown-saving tackles, two interceptions and his outstanding punting, was the deserved center of attention after his remarkable day in adverse circumstance. He wryly recalled, "Well, I remember doing a little kicking ... and I guess you could say I had a hand in all the scoring."

Baugh's performance, along with that of the gritty TCU defense when its collective back was pressed to the goal posts, caused ripples; as did Bernie Moore's stubborn refusal to go for field

LSU's Pinky Rohm breaks free for a near touchdown against Texas Christian.

goals when LSU had the opportunity; and as did the outcome of another game in Pasadena, Calif.

The Mustangs lost to Stanford 7-0 in the Rose Bowl. Because the Dickinson System closed its tabulations at the end of the regular season, SMU remained its national champion. There is no written history of the Williamson Poll to know exactly what Paul Williamson's post-game reasoning was, perhaps the rationale being the conditions too harsh to truly gauge the participants. But, in any case, in the records of that poll for that season, LSU and TCU are listed as co-national champions.

The Horned Frogs' No. 1 standing made history.

For the only time in the history of the Southwest Conference, two of its member schools could lay claim to the national championship in the same season.

Six inches separated LSU from six game-winning points.

	1	2	3	4	
TCU	0	3	0	0	3
LSU	0	2	0	0	2

LSU: Safety, incomplete pass by Baugh in own end zone.

TCU: Manton, 36-yard field goal.

Individual Leaders

Rushing
TCU: Lawrence 6-54; Baugh 22-45.
LSU: Crass 15-34; Reed 6-29.

Passing
TCU: Baugh 2-7-1, 29 yards.
LSU: Mickal 2-14-3, 36 yards.

Receiving
TCU: Walls, 1-25; Meyer 1-18.
LSU: Barrett 3-59.

TCU		LSU
6	First Downs	9
121	Rushing Yards	120
3-8-1	Passing	3-21-3
54	Passing Yards	59
175	Total Yards	179
14-48.0	Punts	13-44.7
2-1	Fumbles – Lost	3-2
4-20	Penalties – Yards	3-33

Attendance: 35,000.
Teams' remuneration: $59,588.

Santa Clara 21 LSU 14

"Build big for the future."

"The Sugar Bowl has made the most amazing progress of any sports event developed anywhere in recent years," Grantland Rice exclaimed editorially that after two years of existence, Rice also noted that the fledgling game needed more room.

It was plain that football interest had exceeded expectations. After the Tulane-Temple game, Bill Keefe saw the need to add 5,000 seats. Fred Digby envisioned a 60,000-seat stadium after LSU-TCU.

Bob Geasey, the Temple sports information director, had returned to New Orleans for the second Sugar Bowl. He told Digby, "... Remember, you're not building for next year or the year after, but for 10 and 15 years to come. Build big for the future!"

Digby, characteristically, wasted little time in presenting the case for a larger stadium. Two days after the Texas Christian victory he wrote, "Undoubtedly, the most feasible plan is to enlarge the Tulane Stadium. Its capacity can be boosted to 60,000 before next New Year's Day by making a 'sugar bowl' of the structure."

It was readily apparent a larger football facility was necessary, but that matter would have to wait a little while. The major move made by the Mid-Winter Sports Association after the second Sugar Bowl was to a more centrally located office at 722 Common Street. Also, they hired their first full-time employee.

Edna Engert, a brown-eyed, personable young woman whose interest in athletics was minimal until she met her husband, was hired to run the office. It was a significant decision. Edna would leave a mark on the organization.

For its third game, the Sugar Bowl was initiated into bowl politics. The Cotton Bowl went into operation on January 1, 1937, the first year all of the major bowl games were in business. There were also two lesser bowls and a pro exhibition, but the Sugar, Orange, Cotton, and Rose Bowls were clearly special.

LSU, again the Southeastern Conference champion, ranked No. 1 by Williamson and No. 2 in the first Associated Press poll, was the darling of every post-season game committee. The Mid-Winter Sports Association had several options for the 1937 game. An LSU and third-ranked Pittsburgh game would be in keeping with the North-South formula that some favored. Sixth-ranked Santa Clara, ineligible for the Rose Bowl because it wasn't a Pacific Coast Conference member, was considered the best West Coast team. This school would broaden the Sugar's horizon. Then there was the possibility of an

LSU-Alabama match. Only a tie in the conference had kept the Tide from sharing the title with the Tigers in a year when those teams did not meet. LSU-Alabama would have been attractive but sectional.

LSU was the key and high on the Rose Bowl list. Meanwhile, the Rose Bowl pondered an opponent for the University of Washington. But the Rose Bowl bypassed LSU for Pittsburgh, giving the Sugar Bowl the season's plum in a game with Santa Clara. The Item ran a series of nationwide sports editorials ridiculing and laughing at Pasadena. A typical piece was written by John Lardner of the North American Newspaper Alliance, who took some light jabs at the two once-defeated, once-tied schools matched in the Rose Bowl. "For instance," wrote Lardner, "there is the one about the two football teams named Pat and Mike. 'Have you been asked to the Rose Bowl?' says Mike. 'Hell, no,' says Pat. 'I'm undefeated.'"

The Southeastern Conference felt snubbed because two of its teams, LSU and Alabama, were overlooked in California. The SEC hinted that perhaps it and the Sugar Bowl ought to join hands. However, the Sugar Bowl saw the risk of a conference tie-up as the Rose Bowl demonstrated in choosing Washington.

Santa Clara was invited and accepted the Sugar Bowl invita-tion on December 6; at the time, it was the nation's only undefeated, untied (7-0-0) major college team. Sammy Baugh, the hero of the 1936 Sugar Bowl, tarnished the Broncos' unbeaten aspirations with a 9-0 Texas Christian victory on December 12, showing New Orleans the two-edged sword of bowl politics.

Still, Santa Clara, an old mission school founded in the 1700s, brought some glitter. The Broncos were coached by Buck Shaw, who was renowned for developing outstanding lines and was a tackle under Knute Rockne. The team included an All-American quarterback, Nello Falaschi, and an end, Jim "Mississippi" Smith, who gave Santa Clara a down-home flavor.

Five thousand additional seats had to be installed in Tulane Stadium, which brought the capacity to 41,000. It still wasn't enough.

Possibly the only fans unaware of what was building in New Orleans were Californians. "We were extremely happy when we got the invitation," said Al Wolff, a sophomore tackle for Santa Clara. "We had heard of the Sugar Bowl, but not a great deal. The papers on the West Coast concentrated only on the Rose Bowl. But we felt we were good enough to play in a bowl game, against a really good team."

"Find a pair that fits."

Cotton Milner is tripped up by the Bronco defense.

The uniform of this squally day should have included galoshes. Luckily for Santa Clara, Buck Shaw knew where to go to dry things out.

Incredibly, it poured for the second consecutive time on New Year's Eve and continued until just before kickoff. Shaw's team got off to a fast start, but he looked at their soaked, mud-caked togs and cleats practically overflowing with water and, after spotting some familiar faces in the stands, did some fast thinking. He came up with the best strategic move of the afternoon.

But that would have to wait a while.

In a game that was anything but an artistic success, Shaw's best defense may have been the favored Tigers themselves. LSU, which would suffer the most from the weather because of its vaunted passing attack, would turn the ball over an astounding 10 times with six lost fumbles and four interceptions. The only thing that seemed to keep things close was Santa Clara, which had six turnovers itself, four lost fumbles and two interceptions.

Things went bad for LSU from the very start: Nello Falaschi took the opening kickoff at the Santa Clara 17 and returned it to the Bronco 41. Pat Coffee, LSU's best passer, made the tackle but was jarred on the play. He put in only nine minutes the rest of the game. After the Tigers punted from a foot away from their own goal, Santa Clara was in front to stay on a 27-yard pass play from Falaschi to Manny Gomez. Seven minutes after that, the Sugar Bowl was put on ice with a 30-yard fourth-and-nine scoring play from Bruno Pellegrini to Norman Finney.

Eleven minutes after kickoff, the outcome seemed as obvious as the mounds of mud on the uniforms. The best gauge of what was happening wasn't just a glance at the scoreboard. One of the country's most efficient offenses was being dismantled. LSU went 25 minutes without a making a first down. Shaw had trusted center Phil Dougherty to keep LSU off-balance with defensive calls, and the 180-pound junior performed flawlessly.

End Gus Tinsley put LSU back in the hunt late in the second quarter when he caught a 10-yard pass from Bill Crass, then,

Buck Shaw, coach of the Santa Clara Broncos.

seeing the right side overloaded with defenders, reversed field, picked up a convoy and went the distance. The 50-yard play cut the difference to 14-7 at intermission.

Halftime is when Shaw showed his cunning. Early in the game, when he spotted coaches from Loyola University, whose campus was just blocks away, among the crowd, he sent an assistant over to talk to them.

"When we got to the dressing room," recalled tackle Al Wolff, "there were dozens of shoes sent over by Loyola, just scattered around the floor. The coaches said, 'Find a pair that fits and put 'em on.' Then we changed into our practice uniforms for the second half and we were ready to play again."

After an interception, the Broncos' Frank "Mississippi" Smith, who grew up in Picayune, Miss., 60 miles from Tulane Stadium, tried an end around from the LSU 4. With two defenders zeroing in, he tossed the ball straight up in the air. Falaschi made the catch and crashed into the end zone. The PAT snap was botched, but Falaschi dug the ball out of the mud and passed to Smith for a successful conversion, still one point in those days.

With just minutes to go the fourth quarter, LSU blocked a Santa Clara kick and Crass speared Rocky Reed on the dead run for a six-yard touchdown. LSU's fate, however, was sealed.

It added some excitement to a finish radio listeners didn't hear. NBC cut to the Rose Bowl with about two minutes to go. "A lot of people in northern California were furious," Wolff said. "My mother said it seemed forever before it was announced that Santa Clara had won."

	1	2	3	4	
Santa Clara	14	0	7	0	21
LSU	0	7	0	7	14

Santa Clara: Gomez, 27-yard pass from Falaschi. PAT, Pellegrini, kick.

Santa Clara: Finney, 30-yard pass from Pellegrini. PAT, Pellegrini, kick.

LSU: Tinsley, 50-yard pass from Crass. PAT, Crass, kick.

Santa Clara: Falaschi, 1-yard run. PAT, Smith, pass from Falaschi.

LSU: Reed 6-yard pass from Crass. PAT, Crass, kick.

Individual Leaders

Rushing
Santa Clara: DeRosa 11-31; Falaschi 7-15.
LSU: Crass 11-27.

Passing
Santa Clara: Falaschi 4-4, 42 yards, 1 TD.
LSU: Crass 6-14, 95 yards, 1 TD.

Receiving
Santa Clara: Finney 2-39, 1 TD; Gomez 2-30, 1 TD.
LSU: Tinsley 3-67, 1 TD.

Santa Clara		LSU
10	First Downs	7
108	Rushing Yards	44
6-12-4	Passing	7-21-2
74	Passing Yards	125
12-42.0	Punts	13-36.0
182	Total Yards	169
4	Fumbles Lost	6
42	Penalty Yards	0

Attendance: 38,483.
Teams' remuneration: $76,072.

Santa Clara 6   LSU 0

"Let each play and prosper."

Nearly a quarter of a million fans attended football games on the first day of 1937. The Rose Bowl drew 87,000; the Sugar Bowl 41,000; the East-West Shrine game 40,000; the first Cotton Bowl 17,000; the Orange Bowl 12,000; and the Bacardi Bowl in Havana, Cuba, had an attendance of 6,000.

Thoughts of an SEC-Sugar Bowl tie-up rose again with a degree of sheer nastiness when Alabama's Coach Frank Thomas brought up the issue less than a week after the LSU-Santa Clara game. Thomas predicted the South "will choke the Rose Bowl to death if the (Sugar Bowl) situation is handled properly." "Properly" to Thomas meant a tie-up with the SEC and the Southwest Conference, with an agreement to reject any and all invitations to Pasadena. Thomas pointed out that seven of the last 10 visiting teams to the Rose Bowl were from the South.

Thomas was irked because Pasadena had passed up his Crimson Tide; the comments were embarrassing to the Mid-Winter Sports Association, which was not anxious to see the demise of the Rose Bowl. Pasadena was respected for the example of what it had built. Pie Dufour wrote plainly and simply, "Let each play and prosper." Then, too, there was the feeling by the Sugar Bowl that a tie-up would not necessarily help in assuring the best game possible each year.

Fred Digby said he felt the Rose Bowl preferred Eastern teams. "The purpose of the Tournament of Roses," he reminded, "is to interest the rich men of the East and induce them to move out of the snow and ice and into the sunshine of southern California. That was the reason Pittsburgh got the bid over LSU and Alabama." Digby added, "But the Sugar Bowlers shouldn't enter into any agreement like the one the Pacific Coast Conference has with the Rose Bowl. The Sugar Bowlers shouldn't let anyone take control of their classic now that they've put it on a firm foundation after three years of toil."

It was plain almost from the opening kickoff of the first game that the Sugar Bowl would eventually need a larger football stadium. Interest in the game was astounding. The fledgling Sugar had to expand its facility (mainly with temporary arrangements) for each of its first three games. The stadium size would affect the growth of the Sugar Bowl.

There was talk early in 1937 of expanding City Park Stadium, which seated 25,000, to 70,000, and of moving the bowl site there. It was also reported that state authorities were negotiating with the Works Progress Administration for money to erect a 100,000-seat stadium near Lake Pontchartrain. The Mid-Winter Sports Association wanted little to do with either project. Proud that what it had accomplished was free of any political en-

Tulane had tried to obtain WPA funds to make its football facility horseshoe-shaped; efforts failed because of its private status. Sugar Bowl officials, realizing that Tulane was the best site for their attraction, approached university authorities with a deal. Tulane's north end zone wooden seats would be taken out and a steel stand would be erected, pushing the stadium's permanent capacity to 37,000. With the temporary seating, a crowd of several thousand more could be accommodated.

Tulane loved the idea, but there was one slight hitch: The Sugar Bowl didn't have the estimated $180,000 for the project. The Association wanted the university to loan it the money. Tulane administrators were a bit put out by the suggestion. Albert Wachenheim, Jr., a member of the executive board, recalled, "We had to persuade Tulane that it was to their benefit, too."

Tulane was persuaded to loan a total of $164,768.84, for notes that would consist of a $20,000 payment for each of the following eight years, plus five percent interest. Tulane would bear the responsibility of stadium upkeep, and the Sugar Bowl would continue its rent-free status.

Southeastern Conference officials, in a March session in Atlanta, listened to a warning by league President R.L. Menuct of Tulane that bowl games were growing to a "most menacing extent." The SEC then went on record as sanctioning only the Sugar Bowl and the Rose Bowl and "no other so-called 'bowl' games." The move, in effect, said SEC members would be granted permission to play in no postseason games other than in New Orleans and Pasadena. As the Orange Bowl screamed 'foul' and 'politics,' the Sugar Bowl membership had to feel pretty smug. But Miami and the other bowls would have the last laugh on this matter.

Alabama and LSU were again the premier SEC football teams. The Crimson Tide was the conference champion; the Tigers were a notch behind with one loss. There was some argument over which was the best team, but the Sugar wanted 'Bama for two reasons: 1) It was the champion. 2) LSU had been in the game two consecutive years. Pittsburgh, which brought snickers when it was picked for the 1937 Rose Bowl,

The Sugar wanted a match between the Tide and the No. 1 Panthers. But the Rose Bowl flexed some muscle in these pairings. California was the Rose Bowl host of 1938 and stated it wanted to play a school with "comparable academic standards."

Alabama and Fordham were apparently each given the impression they were the Pasadena choice, but the Tournament of Roses made no announcement.

Fred Digby believed the Rose Bowl was trying to embarrass the Sugar Bowl by delaying their own selection and at the same time attempting to keep Alabama and Fordham out of New Orleans. The Sugar Bowl gave those schools 24 hours to make up their minds: Take the Sugar or gamble on the Rose. When time was up, the Sugar extended invitations to LSU and Santa Clara. The Rose had still not made its selection.

Frank Thomas, who 11 months before was talking about the demise of the Rose Bowl, gambled and won. Fordham gambled and stayed at home.

The biggest jolt of December came when Auburn asked for permission to participate in the Orange Bowl. In granting the request, the Southeastern Conference also voted 8 - 5 to rescind the February resolution which looked favorably only on Sugar and Rose Bowl participation.

Digby, whose views certainly reflected that of the Mid-Winter Sports Association membership, was angry. He revealed that a week before, at the suggestion of Alabama and LSU, the Association seriously discussed the advisability of presenting a plan for a definite agreement with the SEC for a tie-up. At the last minute, the Sugar Bowl was asked to hold the plan in abeyance. Obviously, one of the Sugar's guidelines would have been that the SEC would compete only in New Orleans, and the Conference must have known of Auburn's forthcoming request.

Digby wrote that the Sugar Bowl was now free of any obligation — real or imagined — to the Southeastern Conference. It could now look to all corners of the country to fill its berths.

"And that was the way the game was played."

Cotton Milner of LSU carries to the Santa Clara 4 on a fake punt.

LSU may never have had a more frustrating game. The Bayou Bengals out-gained (201-101) and out-first downed (10-4) Santa Clara. The Broncos even returned the favor of their last meeting, losing three fumbles to LSU's none.

With all that, the Tigers spent the day threatening the Bronco goal line – but never getting in the end zone.

"The year before," said junior tackle Al Wolff of Santa Clara, the first undefeated, untied team to play in the Sugar Bowl, "we knew we'd have to play over our heads to beat LSU. But for the 1938 game, we were the better team. Our feeling was LSU would have to play over their heads to stay close to us."

That said, LSU was dominate – and still lost.

LSU put pressure on Santa Clara from the outset, getting a fumble recovery and driving to the Bronco 4, where Wolff prevented a touchdown by dropping Pinky Rohm.

"I was able to save that touchdown because I broke one of our fundamental rules," Wolff said. "Something just told me they were going to try something wide, and instead of penetrating the way we were coached to do, I just ran laterally across the field. As it turned out, I was able to save a touchdown."

And, really, the game.

On three of the five plays, starting with Rohm's jaunt to the 4, Wolff was Santa Clara's sole protector. "I'm convinced," he said, "that series made me an All-American (as a senior). All those sportswriters remembered it the following year when, in all honesty, I didn't have as good a season."

With the Broncos on the Tiger 29, Coach Buck Shaw dug deep into his play-book and came up with a play he had used the year before against LSU.

James Barlow, a substitute halfback, took the ball on what appeared to be a developing sweep to his left. As he reached the end, Barlow wheeled and threw diagonally across the field to quarterback Ray McCarthy. The play covered approximately 50 yards, but the 20 that were officially credited to Santa Clara gave the Broncos a first-and-goal at the LSU 9.

A play later, Pellegrini took the snap and lofted a pass over end Jimmy Coughlan's shoulder in the flat. Coughlan, in almost one motion, made the reception and bounded into the end zone, despite the jolt of being hit by three Tigers. Pellegrini's PAT was wide, leaving the door teasingly open for LSU the rest of the afternoon.

Santa Clara narrowly averted a safety in the fourth quarter, just inches from the goal line. Then Barlow got off a 55-yard punt.

Ultimately, Rohm also went back in kick formation near the Bronco 25, but as his leg arched he handed the ball to Cotton Milner, who raced 21 yards to the 4. In what must have been one of the most vexing days in LSU annals, the last man, John Schiecht, stopped Milner.

LSU eventually turned the ball over at the Bronco 20.

Still, the Tigers would get one last chance when, from the Bronco 29, Santa Clara got off a terrible 16-yard punt with less than three minutes to play.

The rules at the time prohibited anyone but the signal-caller to speak in the huddle. In a bizarre twist, Shaw sent in sub Charles Pavelko on third down. Center Phil Dougherty, who normally called the plays, thought Shaw was sending in a play through Pavelko. Dougherty whispered, "You call the play." Pavelko's eyes got as big as half-dollars. Finally he said, 'We'll punt.' Dougherty said he was shocked. "He could have called anything, but he called for a punt."

There was more. Santa Clara got the ball back, and on fourth and a long four from midfield, Shaw ordered his team to go for it. The play fell short.

On the game's final play, Young Bussey connected with Ken Kavanaugh, who briefly looked as if he were getting away. Bill Gunther brought the big end down at the 23. "We just figured they would go to him," said Wolff. "We were waiting on that play ... but he still nearly did it. And that's the way the game was played all day."

Indeed it was. Despite its statistical superiority, LSU was held scoreless, its first shutout in 50 games. That little stat allowed LSU to become the first school to lose three bowls in successive seasons.

	1	2	3	4	
Santa Clara	6	0	0	0	6
LSU	0	0	0	0	0

Santa Clara: Coughlan, 4-yard pass from Pellegrini. PAT failed.

Individual Leaders

Rushing
Santa Clara: Pelligrini 11-7; Barlow 3-10.
LSU: Milner 13-32; Rohm 14-30.

Passing
Santa Clara: Pelligrini 2-7, 19 yards.
LSU: Rohm 2-5, 22 yards.

Receiving
Santa Clara: Coughlan 2-19, 1 TD.
LSU: Kavanaugh 3-44 yards.

Santa Clara		LSU
4	First Downs	10
34	Rushing Yards	106
5-13-3	Passing	8-21-0
67	Passing Yards	95
14-36.0	Punts	14-32.0
101	Total Yards	201
3	Fumbles Lost	0
30	Penalty Yards	35

Attendance: 40,000.
Teams' remuneration: $87,986.

TCU 15 Carnegie Tech 7

"I'm gonna play in the Sugar Bowl."

It didn't take long for the Sugar Bowl to even up with the Southeastern Conference over their snit. Many choice teams were available during the 1938 season, enough for everyone. The University of Tennessee won the SEC championship with a 10-0-0 record and was the favorite to fill the host berth in New Orleans. Possible opponents from the North were Carnegie Tech, Villanova, and Fordham. Texas Christian and Duke (undefeated, untied, and unscored upon) were more than acceptable, but the Mid-Winter Sports Association seemed to be interested in a North-South game.

Pasadena vacillated between Duke and TCU. The Cotton Bowl panted over the possibility of the No. 2 Horned Frogs, with Heisman, Maxwell, and Camp trophies winner Davey O'Brien, the 5-foot-7 glamour player of the year, as quarterback. All-American center Ki Aldrich and All-American tackle I.B. Hale added more tinsel to the TCU trappings. "If the Sugar Bowl can get Carnegie Tech," wrote Flem Hall of the *Fort Worth Star-Telegram*, "the boys might prefer such an opponent to a beaten California or a twice-beaten Southern Cal team."

The conjecture was startling because it precluded an SEC team, which everyone assumed the Sugar preferred. The Rose Bowl was certainly a strong consideration for the TCU staff and squad. The Cotton Bowl wasn't. "The boys and fans would rather go to New Orleans than Dallas," wrote Dick Freeman of the *Houston Chronicle*. "Get TCU in there with Carnegie Tech and the state of Texas will move to New Orleans."

Carnegie Tech's appeal stemmed from its winning the No. 6 ranking and the Lambert Trophy, symbolic of Eastern supremacy.

Tech was playing a midseason game with Notre Dame in South Bend, Indiana. In the fourth quarter of a scoreless game, with the ball placed near the 50, quarterback Ray Carnelly lost track of the downs. He asked referee John Getchell, who said it was third down. Carnelly ran a play that was stopped short of first down yardage. Getchell — realizing then he had made a mistake and that it was a fourth down play that had just been run — turned the ball over to the Irish. Notre Dame was able to use its field position in the fading minutes to push across the game's only points. Acidly, Carnegie Tech Coach Bill Kem assessed, "It was the biggest bonehead I ever saw pulled by any official. I don't know if he will quit or not, but I know what I'd do in his place." To Tech's credit, it went on to win its next four games. Carnegie Tech finished 7-1-0 and was acclaimed the best in the East. Notre Dame rose to the No. 1 spot nationally after defeating Carnegie Tech.

After TCU defeated Southern Methodist in its final game, the Cotton Bowl extended its invitation, though the Frog staff said nothing official.

George Muha wheels into Texas Christian line.

On November 29 the Sugar announced its pairing, TCU and Carnegie Tech. Duke accepted the Rose Bowl challenge against Southern Cal.

With an excellent Tennessee team expecting bids from the Sugar or the Rose, the SEC appeared shaken by the New Orleans selections. Georgia Tech Coach Bill Alexander told the Associated Press he was "amazed." Joel Hunt, the University of Georgia coach, was quoted by the AP to the effect that the selection "might be a little act of independence." Fred Digby wrote piously that the Sugar Bowl felt free to invite anyone, indicating that getting the best game possible was most important to the Mid-Winter Sports Association. He also subtly chided those who snubbed New Orleans the year before.

The match turned into what Grantland Rice called "The Game of the Year." Southern Cal defeated Notre Dame the week following the selections, which lifted TCU to No. 1. Tech retained its No. 6 spot.

New Year's was bringing to New Orleans the nation's No. 1 team (TCU), the nation's No. 1 player (O'Brien), the nation's No. 1 coach (Bill Kern), the nation's No. 2 coach (Dutch Meyer), and the nation's No. 1 official, Johnny Getchell.

That's right. Getchell was one of the officials submitted to be considered by Carnegie Tech. Shortly after the Notre Dame game, Coach Kern sent a telegram to Getchell which read, "Forget it. It's all in the game. Best regards."

Several questions arose about the game. What in the world was a Skibo (a Tech nickname—the other was Tartans)? Would Ki Aldrich be able to play? The anchor of the imposing TCU line had been hospitalized with an ulcer on the cornea of his eye.

The Skibos, a team of 42 engineering students and 1 musician, were named for Andrew Carnegie's manor, Skibo Castle, in Dunfermline, Scotland. Carnegie, it was said, delighted in being referred to as "The Laird of Skibo Castle." Tech students picked up the nickname.

Aldrich had recurring eye problems after being involved in some freshman-sophomore class horseplay his first year at TCU. He led a group of freshmen up a flight of stairs in a night "raid," but a "guard" at the top of the landing turned a fire extinguisher on the invaders. The spray caught Aldrich in the eye. His screams broke up the prank. For some strange reason, Ki yelled for salt water. When some was obtained, he bathed his eye in it and then was brought to the infirmary. It healed slowly, and from time to time eye difficulties would flare up on the youngster. Between the end of the regular season of his senior year and the Sugar Bowl, he again had to be hospitalized.

However, TCU got an emotional lift on the day the team was to leave for New Orleans. Aldrich's injured eye opened, with his vision restored. Ki jumped into his clothes, ran out, and raced across campus until he spotted Dutch Meyer. "Coach, coach," Ki yelled joyfully, "I can play! I'm gonna play in the Sugar Bowl!"

"And that took care of that."

Davey O'Brien, a 5-foot-7 passing marvel, unloads against Carnegie Tech.

In the late 1930s, "David" of the David and Goliath story was called "Davey."

The smallest quarterback in the land, at 5-foot-7, was himself a Goliath, the biggest name in college football.

In 1938, O'Brien steered Texas Christian to the No. 1 rung in the sport while leading the nation in passing, which, extremely rare for the time, was TCU's standard mode of operation. With a physique more befitting a guard, the 150-pound quarterback – truly the rightful heir to Sammy Baugh – when "David" drew back his arm like a slingshot, he fired footballs with an accuracy and strength that flabbergasted opponents, fans, and even teammates.

"I know that there were a lot of times that I would go out for a pass and look back for Davey – and I couldn't see him. Then all of a sudden the ball would come flying out of nowhere – right into my arms," receiver Don Looney recalled.

They wouldn't raise eyebrows today, but at a time when five pass attempts a game were a lot for most teams, statistics for 1938 show O'Brien completed 94 of 167 passes for 1,509

yards and 19 touchdowns. He led the nation in passing and in total offense (1,847 yards). The year before, O'Brien, ranked second nationally in total offense (1,411 yards), and led the nation in punt returns and passing.

And, while there would be potholes on the road to TCU's 11th victory of the season, O'Brien would be its linchpin.

Not before, however, Carnegie Tech would give the Horned Frogs a run for their money.

A modest early Tartan drive to midfield caused the Frogs to call timeout to talk things over.

"That was the first time," Ki Aldrich said, "that anyone made us do that all season, the first time we had to call time to adjust."

The drive was quickly short-circuited.

After an exchange of punts – including the only one by TCU that afternoon – the Frogs went in for the game's first points – barely. Connie Sparks went over right guard from the 1, and it took several minutes to unravel the writhing mass at the goal line. Finally the officials signaled touchdown. Sparks got in by an inch.

Shockingly, O'Brien, who kicked 28 extra points during the regular season, missed the PAT.

The Tartans came right back, fooling the Frogs on fourth-and-six at its 36, then from the Frog 37 where Pete Moroz backpedaled almost to midfield, waited for George Muha to work his way past O'Brien, a natural target because of his lack of height, and looped a pass. Muha took it in at the 1 without breaking stride and went over.

Muha's PAT made the score Tech 7, TCU 6, marking the first time the Frogs were behind all season.

In the first five plays of the second half the Frogs were back in front to stay. From the Tartan 44, O'Brien flung a darter to Durwood Horner, who grabbed it at the 29, wheeled and went the distance untouched.

"And that took care of that," tackle Allie White said.

Not really. O'Brien again inexplicably missed the PAT, keeping Tech within easy reach.

Davey O'Brien, 1938's Hiesman Trophy Recipient.

In the fourth quarter, when the Tartans held the Frogs at the 1, O'Brien kicked a field goal from the 9 to make the margin 15-7 with seven minutes to play.

Considering his PAT attempts, it could be assumed there was some concern about trying the kick, but Aldrich said no. "The extra points were just one of those things," he said. "Nobody thought Davey couldn't kick the field goal. We had a lot of confidence in Davey. I don't think I even thought he wouldn't make it."

The excitement wasn't over. Muha almost broke the ensuing kickoff for a touchdown before Aldrich caught him from behind, and shortly, O'Brien intercepted a pass at the TCU 21 to put a practical end to the fifth Sugar Bowl.

In the end, gutty Carnegie Tech couldn't cope with the offense of TCU, which finished with a 365-168 edge in total yardage, or with 'L'il Davey,' who, despite a less than perfect outing, was the afternoon's darling with a 17-for-28 passing performance for 225 yards.

As important as anything or anyone, though, TCU left New Orleans as the unquestioned champion of college football because of Aldrich, who nearly didn't make the trip, and who had an eye-opening 19 tackles (13 unassisted) and an interception.

That, as much as anything, allowed for the favorite to win the Sugar Bowl – for the first time.

	1	2	3	4	
TCU	6	0	6	3	15
Carnegie Tech	0	7	0	0	7

TCU: Sparks, 1-yard run. PAT failed.

Carnegie Tech: Muha, 44-yard pass from Moroz. PAT, Muha, kick.

TCU: Horner, 44-yard pass from O'Brien. PAT failed.

TCU: O'Brien, 20-yard field goal.

Individual Leaders

Rushing
TCU: Hall 6-47; Sparks 14-37, 1 TD.
Carnegie Tech: Muha 16-69; Condit 10-31.

Passing
TCU: O'Brien 17-27-0, 224 yards, 1 TD.
Carnegie Tech: Moroz 1-2-0, 38 yards, 1 TD.

Receiving
TCU: Clark 7-81; Hall 5-75.
Carnegie Tech: Muha 1-38; Fisher 1-2.

TCU		Carnegie Tech
17	First Downs	10
142	Rushing Yards	129
17-28-0	Passing	3-8-2
225	Passing Yards	59
367	Total Yards	188
1-40.0	Punts	6-40.0
0-0	Fumbles – Lost	0-0
5	Penalty Yards	20

Attendance: 44,308.
Teams' remuneration: $132,824.

Texas A&M 14 Tulane 13

"Let us strike while the iron is hot."

The original purpose of the Sugar Bowl from the businessmen's standpoint was to fill hotel rooms and restaurants and to stimulate commerce during a traditionally slack period. It was clear after five years that the concept was sound. Texas Christian-Carnegie Tech drew a crowd that spent more money during the four-day period leading up to the game than any group had at any other event or convention in New Orleans for the year, including Mardi Gras.

Mike O'Leary, manager of the St. Charles Hotel, said, "It came in the slump between Christmas and New Year's when every hotel in the country has a slump ... It was just as though Santa Claus filled our stocking with the biggest crowd we've ever seen." Ray Alciatore, proprietor of the world-famous Antoine's restaurant, said his business had prepared 6,012 orders of Oysters Rockefeller in three days. "That's as many as we serve in an ordinary month," Alciatore exclaimed.

As usual, it was Fred Digby who saw beyond the contentment of the present to a cornucopia of the future. After the game, in a column on the front page of the *Item*, Digby sought to enlarge Tulane Stadium to 60,000. He suggested the issuance of debenture bonds to cover the $200,000 project.

Favorable reaction came from far and near, including an endorsement from former World War I flying ace Colonel Eddie Rickenbacker, then president of Eastern Airlines. Louisiana Governor Richard Leche wrote Digby an eight-page letter and promised that the state would take $5,000 of the issuance. Mike O'Leary spoke for many when he declared, "Let us strike while the iron is hot."

After weeks of studying sketches, the Sugar Bowl membership, with Tulane's approval, decided to build the capacity to 70,000 seats backed by $550,000 in debentures, which were to be paid off at the rate of $25,000 a year.

Each purchaser of a $100 bond would be given the option of buying two choice Sugar Bowl tickets prior to public distribution, and two percent interest would be paid after five years. It doesn't sound like much now, but 40 days after the drive began on March 7, the goal was reached.

The contract was awarded to Doullut &. Ewing, Inc., and the firm itself purchased $40,000 in debentures to guard against any contingency that could possibly arise. "We'll have that stadium ready for January 1, 1940," said Jim Ewing to the Sugar Bowl when the company got the contract. "It will be a close fit, but we won't let you down."

The fit was even closer than Ewing thought. Originally, it was thought the enlargement would be of concrete, but the cost would have exceeded the $550,000. So the addition to the bowl and the double-decking of the side stands would be made of steel. The war in Europe threatened to skyrocket expenses in steel, and it became mandatory that

A&M's 'Jarrin' Jawn' Kimbrough jars Tulane with a touchdown run.

the steel needed for the stadium be obtained without delay. This could be done only with a cash outlay above the partial payment already made. It was June when the first piling was driven. Working constantly, except on Saturdays when Tulane played home games, using steel from the Virginia Bridge Company of Birmingham, the contractors Doullut and Ewing met the deadline between the end of Tulane's season and prior to January 1, 1940. Tulane Stadium was now a complete bowl and the largest stadium in the South.

The only problem with expanding a stadium is the filling of it after it is completed. In 1940, the Sugar Bowl was lucky. A three-way tie between Tennessee (undefeated, untied, and unscored upon), Georgia Tech, and Tulane put the Sugar Bowl in fine position.

Texas A&M, the Southwest Conference's second consecutive national champion, was the prime choice for the visitor's berth. Heavyweight competition from the Cotton Bowl was a hurdle which stood in the way of the immediate signing of the Aggies after the regular season.

A&M Coach Homer Norton had an invitation to New Orleans tucked in his pocket right after his final regular season game. Dallas businessmen had put together a package of $170,000, to be split by both teams, as an inducement to A&M for a game with second-ranked Tennessee.

A&M's acceptance was contingent upon Tennessee's appearance. The Volunteers had the inside track on the Rose Bowl but did not want to say anything formally until their last game with Auburn a week later. So Norton let his players vote, and they chose New Orleans. On December 5 it was announced that A&M

would meet fifth-ranked Tulane in the Sugar Bowl. It was the first Sugar Bowl pairing of two undefeated teams. Tennessee spent its holidays in Pasadena.

Getting Texas A&M, as it turned out, was easier than getting Tulane. Just as in 1935, the Greenies were hesitant about playing what amounted to one more home game. Halfback Fred Cassibry told *New Orleans States* sportswriter George Sweeney years after, "(Coach) Red (Dawson) worked us to death during the season. He was a hard taskmaster, but a fair one. He was the type of guy who felt you were at Tulane on scholarship, so you should play your best at all times or he would take that scholarship away. And that meant 100 percent at practice. Some guys just didn't feel like going through three more weeks of practice.

"We wanted some assurance that if we played, we would get something out of it ($150 a man was what the team wanted, Cassibry said later). No one could give us an answer, so we sent word that we didn't want to play in the game. Dr. (Rufus) Harris (Tulane's president) and the coaching staff said that we would always regret it if we turned the invitation down. They would have been right."

The Sugar Bowl was billed as a David (Tulane) and Goliath (A&M) match. Although Tulane was a bigger team physically, the Wave had six tackles ranging from 215 to 240 pounds and standing between 6-foot-3 and 6-foot-5. What brought on the David and Goliath comparison were the measurements of the featured runners—Tulane's 160-pound scatback Bobby Kellogg and A&M's 210-pound fullback John Kimbrough, who had played 60 minutes in every Texas A&M game.

"Gulliver flicking Lilliputians off his coat."

Coin toss before the 1940 Texas A&M-Tulane Classic.

Red Dawson got his wish: John Kimbrough.

Remember the old saw of getting what you wish for?

Dawson, the head coach at Tulane, brought Kimbrough to New Orleans from Texas in the summer of 1937 to work while the Green Wave staff worked overtime in trying to get him in an olive and blue uniform.

He wasn't interested and left in time to enroll at Texas A&M. It was said at the time of his departure that the upset Dawson expressed the fervent hope that someday he would get to coach against his lost recruit.

Now he would.

The crowd of 73,000 had hardly gotten in their seats, the skywriting planes, hired by Louisiana politicians, were still scribbling their messages of the on-going gubernatorial campaign against the clear blue heavens, when reality hit Tulane.

The Green Wave got a dose of what was in store on the first series of the day. On A&M's first series the Aggies got within a foot of the goal line, but Tulane somehow held.

On A&M's second series, the Greenies couldn't hold.

From the Tulane 24, Kimbrough came busting out of the line to bring the ball to the Tulane 16. Two plays later, he hurdled the Tulane line from the 1, his heaving shoulders landing three feet beyond the goal line.

Seven and half playing minutes after the kickoff, Texas A&M led 7-0.

The squads sparred most of the rest of the half, but Bobby Kellogg made Tulane hearts thump harder in the third quarter. Derace Moser quick-kicked from the Aggie 33. Kellogg retreated to handle the punt, which was flat and straight. It bounced high at the 24 while the Aggies bore down on the returner. Kellogg took the ball, sidestepped the first tackler, then took off for the west sidelines. "I came up the middle," Kellogg said, "then cut for the sidelines ... I went right to the Tulane bench. A block by Buddy Banker sprung me loose, and another by Al Bodney cleared the last man in my road ... "I missed some practice because of injuries and when I reached the end zone I was a pretty sick boy."

It was the longest Sugar Bowl run since Monk Simons' dramatic kickoff return in 1935.

Jimmy Thibaut tied the game with his placement.

Shortly afterward Tulane got a chance to take the lead after recovering a fumble on the Aggie 39 as the third period ended. With Fred Cassibry and Monette Butler knifing through the suddenly shaken Aggies, Tulane pressed its way to the 1. Butler scored and the Green Wave seemed totally in command. However, then little Herbie Smith, at 5-foot-8, the smallest man on the field, popped through and blocked Thibaut's PAT. At that juncture, with the Wave energized, the miss didn't appear important.

Starting from its 31, A&M came roaring back in the fourth quarter. After short gains, Kimbrough, taking a snap directly from center, barreled off tackle with Greenies bouncing off at all angles

Tulane's Bobby 'Jitterbug' Kellogg returns a third quarter punt to put Green Wave back in the hunt with Texas A&M.

The decisive play: Herb Smith, the smallest man on the field. blocks Jimmy Thibault's PAT.

and plowed to the Tulane 27. A&M's double-wing offense had shifted to high gear.

Smith latched onto a pass at the 15 and lateralled to the streaking Kimbrough. "Jarrin' Jawn" ran straight into a cluster of Greenies and left them either sprawling or carried on his back to the end zone. New Orleans newspaperman Pie Dufour described the touchdown play thusly: "Kimbrough stormed 18 yards on that last scoring run, brushing off Greenie tacklers like Gulliver flicking Lilliputians off his coat lapel."

Price's PAT put A&M back in front, 14-13. The most routine of all plays in football proved decisive.

Texas A&M completed an unblemished national championship season by the thin margin of one made extra point and one blocked extra point. Wave coach Red Dawson was convinced the Aggies benefited from some crucial non-calls, including one on Kimbrough's winning touchdown run.

"They used the same pass play several times during the game," Dawson stewed. "The ends came across the line and blocked the middle linebacker out of the play. The rule states there can be no blocking downfield before the pass is thrown."

Dawson's last look at Kimbrough was something for him – and the entire crowd – to remember: The Aggie fullback finished with 159 yards on 25 carries, a 6.9 average.

A&M coach Homer Norton had no problem expressing what he thought of Kimbrough, who the next season would be the Heisman Trophy runner-up to Tom Harmon. "He's the greatest football player in the world," Norton said following the Sugar Bowl victory. "And you can put my name on that with a picture."

Tulane takes the lead against Texas A&M on Monettte Butler's one-yard run.

	1	2	3	4	
Texas A&M	7	0	0	7	14
Tulane	0	0	7	6	13

Texas A&M: Kimbrough, 1-yard run. PAT, Price kick.

Tulane: Kellogg, 75-yard punt return. PAT, Thibaut kick.

Tulane: Butler, 1-yard run. PAT blocked (Smith).

Texas A&M: Kimbrough, 18-yard lateral from Smith. PAT, Price kick.

Individual Leaders

Rushing
Texas A&M: Kimbrough 25-159, 1 TD; Connatser 9-31.
Tulane: Butler 10-55 yards, 1 TD; Cassibry 11-42.

Passing
Texas A&M: Price 8-15-1, 62 yards.
Tulane: Kellogg 0-2-0, 0 yards.

Receiving
Texas A&M: Moser 2-17; Connaster 2-12.

Texas A&M		Tulane
18	First Downs	8
244	Rushing Yards	193
8-15-1	Passing	0-4-0
62	Passing Yards	0
306	Total Yards	193
6-44.0	Punts	11-34.0
2-2	Fumbles – Lost	1-0
2-30	Penalties – Yards	2-30

Attendance: 73,000.
Teams' remuneration: $134,526.

Wednesday, January 1, 1941

Boston College 19 Tennessee 13

"That's the way things were then."

In October of 1940 Fred Digby covered a University of Tennessee football game. Immediately after filing his story, he sent a telegram to the Sugar Bowl urging consideration of the Vols. He informed the Mid-Winter Sports Association that no one on its schedule was capable of defeating Major Bob Neyland's squad.

Then, as the year before, there were many good football teams from which the bowls could choose: Boston College, Texas A&M, Nebraska, Mississippi State, or Fordham. All were outstanding.

Tennessee was the key. The Cotton Bowl again considered a Texas A&M-Volunteer match, while in Pasadena there was strong sentiment to invite Tennessee back a second consecutive year.

Neyland's team again finished as undefeated and untied Southeastern Conference champions. Only a loss to Southern California in the 1940 Rose Bowl spotted Tennessee's record over the course of 35 games.

The Tournament of Roses requested that Neyland hold off making a decision until it could decide. The coach saw no reason why he should gamble and take a chance of being shut out. On the evening of November 30, it was announced that Tennessee would play Boston College in the Sugar Bowl.

Boston College, under a 32-year-old firebrand coach, Frank Leahy, had run roughshod over the East and wiped out a 24-game Georgetown winning streak to wind up with a 10-0-0 record, identical to Tennessee's. An early-season 27-7 victory over Tulane in New Orleans first alerted Sugar Bowlers to

Boston College's potential. Neyland was famous for putting his faith in a strong kicking game and defense, but the Vols' offense was extremely potent, having scored 319 points in 1940. Only one team in the country scored more. That was Boston College with 320. Two weeks after the announcement, the Sugar Bowl was declared a complete sellout. Despite the statistics and close rankings, Tennessee opened a touchdown favorite and stayed there.

New Orleans, for the third consecutive year, had come up with the best game possible. The Vols and Boston College were ranked fourth and fifth in the final Associated Press poll. But Minnesota and Michigan were first and third, and their conference, the Big Ten, did not allow bowl participation. Stanford, committed to the Rose Bowl, was second.

Billy Sullivan, then the Boston College publicist, remembers John Drummey, an athletic department treasurer, making the trip. Drummey was not a football fan, as Leahy found out in Bay St. Louis, Mississippi, where Boston College set up its pregame camp at St. Stanislaus High School. Drummey pulled up in the middle of an unusually tough scrimmage while the intense Leahy bombasted the players. Drummey left his car, cheerfully walked to Leahy and said, "Don't worry about it, coach. It doesn't make any difference. I have the biggest

Boston College's Fred Naumetz, left, and Henery Woronicz serve part of the feast at Sugar Bowl party after the 1941 game.

Coach Frank Leahy, standing third from right, and Sugar Bowl Vice-President Joseph B. David, standing far right, introduce Boston College players to Santa Claus.

check we've ever received for a football game."

Leahy turned a cold glare on the accountant and softly said, "John, it's just too bad you don't realize that this may be the greatest mismatch in history. This (Tennessee) is one of the greatest teams in history, the undefeated heavyweight champion. And all you're worried about is a check."

One observer at St. Stanislaus was Louis Montgomery, who knew full well what it would take to beat Tennessee: the best from every man on the Eagle roster. Montgomery's name was on the roster, but he would not be in uniform. He was a reserve running back, and he was black. In the South of the early 1940s, there was never any thought that Montgomery would suit up with his teammates.

"It's embarrassing to talk about it now," said the Rev. Maurice Dullea, S.J., then the faculty-moderator at Boston College. "But the (Sugar Bowl) committee made it quite clear that a Negro would not be allowed to play. It was kind of touchy ... But that's the way things were then ... One of our graduate managers was afraid someone would shoot at Louis from the stands if we even let him on the sidelines with us. ... Certain things didn't go with certain people in certain parts of the country. It was simply reality. Even the United States Army was segregated."

Jerry Nason, who covered the Eagles for the *Boston Globe*, said, "I'm almost ashamed to say it, and I was a guy who didn't mind stirring things up over an injustice, but it was just taken for granted when a team went South to play. I think the attitude was, 'We're gonna play in the South. They are our hosts, and we are their guests. We will play by their rules.' "

Montgomery was at least able to see his teammates in the

Sugar Bowl. A black family in Bay St. Louis, people with ties to Boston College, wired Father Dullea offering a place to stay for the running back. When the Eagles played in the Cotton Bowl the year before, Montgomery wasn't even able to make the trip. For the Sugar Bowl he was given a job spotting for reporters in the press box. Nason and some of Montgomery's teammates were able to see him display his athletic talents a few days later in a black All-Star game played on the Xavier University campus.

Neyland seemed skittish about his opponent, even holding secret practices. His armada of football talent didn't appear as impressed. Bob Suffridge was considered the premier guard in the country, and he overshadowed Ed Molinski only slightly. Bobby Foxx was the backfield scourge of the SEC. These were the sort of specimens that had come to be associated with the image of great football.

George Kerr, a brilliant Greek and Latin student studying for the priesthood, was a standout in the Boston College line. Charlie O'Rourke, weighing about 147 pounds by the time of the Sugar Bowl game, was the Eagles' offensive trigger. End Gene Goodreault made most All-American teams, but even here the gladiator image didn't fit; he had been struck with a form of paralysis as a child. Several relapses nearly killed him. He had heart problems by the age of 11.

Goodreault overcame it all to become an All-American. However, a knee injury threatened to, but did not, keep him out of the Sugar Bowl.

This was not the look of a team to be sent against Neyland's three-deep legions. "We'll be satisfied with anything better than a tie," said Suffridge, who won the Knute Rockne Memorial Trophy as the outstanding lineman of the year, "but I believe we'll win by at least a touchdown."

"But the play O'Rourke scored on was a Tennessee play."

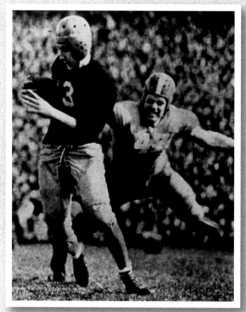

Charlie O'Rouke eludes Ed Cifers (47), left. and starts Boston College's game winning run on a play right of the Tennessee playbook.

The crucial element to Boston College beating Tennessee, it turned out, came straight out of the Tennessee playbook.

"Two days prior to the game," said BC coach Frank Leahy, "we had a live scrimmage, mainly to give our first team a last look at Tennessee's single-wing offense. Our team succeeded in stopping everything except one of General Neyland's bread-and-butter plays ... it was a fake pass-run inside the end. During our final scrimmage it averaged seven yards per try against our first line. It was used approximately seven or eight times. We became impressed to the point where we decided after practice to incorporate the maneuver into our repertoire of plays."

On New Year's Eve, Leahy had the Eagle first stringers work on what they called "shift right, Tennessee Special." Wearing sneakers and sweat clothes they ran through it at the Bay St. Louis School gym. The doors were locked, in fact, the session was so secret that Boston College's trainer didn't know about it.

The Tennessee Special was put away for use at just the right time.

In the first 30 minutes of the Sugar Bowl, the Eagles were hard-pressed to overcome miscues by tailback Charlie O'Rourke, who lost an early fumble and, later, interfered on a Vols' pass play which led to a touchdown.

The score was 7-0 at intermission, and the Eagles were hanging with Tennessee – but it seemed as if they were hanging by a thread.

But very early in the third quarter something took place that was downright rare in southern football: for the first time in seven seasons, Tennessee had a kick blocked.

End Henry Woronicz rushed in as Bobby Foxx attempted to punt from the Tennessee 19. The ball bounced off Woronicz's chest and Joe Zabilski recovered. Mickey Connolly, in for O'Rourke, pulled BC even with a 12-yard sprint.

Center-linebacker Ray Graves, later the head coach and athletic director at the University of Florida, said, "We felt we had 'em beat at halftime. We were ahead 7-0 and pretty much in control. I can still see the guy coming in from the left side. They blocked Bobby Foxx's kick, got the ball, and went in to make it 7-7. After that they were a different ball club and we were sort of in a trance."

If the Vols were in a stupor, it didn't show right away. Tennessee went back ahead on Buist Warren's short run, though the conversion was botched.

Again Boston College came back to tie the score on a 1-yard run by Mike Holovak, who also tried to run for the PAT but was stopped.

All that set the stage for the final minutes. BC, starting from its 20, moved to the Vols' 24. Neyland called timeout and changed his defense to send three men deep.

For BC, it was time for the Tennessee Special.

O'Rourke faded, raising his skinny arm as if to throw. Instead he cut sharply between Tennessee's tackle and end. Like a shadow he glided through a maze of flailing Volunteers and into the end zone. There were two minutes remaining. "I had a clear shot at him and

General Bob Neyland brought two undefeated, untied football teams to the Sugar Bowl and lost both times.

missed," Graves said. "He kept going parallel to the line of scrimmage, but kept coming back toward the sidelines. I had another shot at him – and missed. When he got to the sidelines he turned downfield and scored just inside the boundary line. It really killed the General. We not only had a punt blocked, but the play O'Rourke scored on was a Tennessee play."

Boston College missed the extra point but the game soon ended with an O'Rourke interception. The loss secured a strange Tennessee football fact: In three seasons the Vols had outscored their regular season opposition 807 to 42 in forging a 31-0 record. And, following those three seasons, bowl opponents outscored the Vols 33-30 as Tennessee went 1-2 in the post-season.

The victory made a national name of Frank Leahy and within a month his alma mater, Notre Dame, sought out the coaching wunderkind to lead the Fighting Irish. He would never again coach in a bowl game, due to Notre Dame's prohibition of post-season football. Leahy would, however, coach four national championship teams and six undefeated teams, and forge an 87-11-9 record.

The Sugar Bowl was the fuse to a spectacular career.

"Can you imagine," Graves drawled thoughtfully decades later, "I missed O'Rourke twice, and Frank Leahy has never thanked me for helping him get to South Bend."

James Coleman (31 in light jersey) of Tenneessee is covered on all sides by Boston College's Charlie O'Rourke, Henry Toczylowski (22), Joseph Zabilski (44), Mike Holovak (12), and Chet Gladchuck (45).

	1	2	3	4	
Boston College	0	0	13	6	19
Tennessee	7	0	6	0	13

Tennessee: Thompson, 4-yard run. PAT, Foxx, kick.

Boston College: Connolly, 12yard run. PAT, Maznicki, kick.

Tennessee: Warren, 3-yard run. PAT, run failed.

Boston College: Holovak, 1-yard run. PAT, Maznicki, kick.

Boston College: O'Rourke, 24-yard run. PAT failed.

Individual Leaders

Rushing
Boston College: O'Rourke 7-52, 1 TD.
Tennessee: Fozz 7-41; Thompson 11-40, 1 TD.

Passing
Boston College: O'Rourke 5-11-2, 85 yards.
Tennessee: Thompson 4-9-1, 42 yards.

Receiving
Boston College: Zabilski 2-39.
Tennessee: Coleman 3-49.

Boston College		Tennessee
11	First Downs	13
142	Rushing Yards	124
6-14-3	Passing	9-22-2
106	Passing Yards	121
248	Total Yards	245
6-35.0	Punts	7-36.0
1-1	Fumbles – Lost	1-1
3-25	Penalties – Yards	4-36

Attendance: 68,486.
Teams' remuneration: $142,150.

Fordham 2 Missouri 0

"Japs call home 2 attachés."

Picking the 1941 bowl teams was more of a guessing game than in the preceding few years. Mississippi State and Alabama were the logical SEC candidates; Texas A&M and Texas were the best bets from the Southwest Conference. A late-season loss to Vanderbilt eliminated Alabama. Mississippi State, the conference champion, had a game left with San Francisco after the pairings were to be announced. The Sugar Bowl was afraid to take a chance on the Bulldogs. Neither SEC team finished in the Associated Press Top 10. A similar situation occurred in the Southwest Conference. When the Longhorns upset the Aggies, the Sugar Bowl became interested, but was nervous about inviting Texas due to a late game.

Late Saturday, November 30, the Associated Press ran a story indicating that sixth-ranked Fordham would play in the Rose Bowl opposite Oregon State. But later the Sugar Bowl announced the Fordham Rams would play seventh-ranked Missouri. For the first time, New Orleans had a game without an SEC or SWC team. Public reaction was unfavorable at first, but on New Year's Day the Sugar Bowl was the only game with two Top 10 teams.

The champion of the Third Army and the Pensacola (Florida) Fliers, champions of the Eighth Naval District, were scheduled to meet in Tulane Stadium on January 3, 1942, in a service championship game approved by the War and Navy departments. The day after the announcement was made, however, the front page headline crowning the ominous global news read: "Japs Call Home 2 Attaches From U.S." Less than 24 hours later, the Japanese Empire attacked United States Navy and Army installations at Pearl Harbor. There would be no service championship game in 1942.

The war brought an immediate change in the suddenly inconse-

quential world of college football. Because California was believed to be a danger zone, the military demanded that the Rose Bowl and the East-West Shrine game be relocated. The Tournament of Roses shifted its game to Durham, North Carolina, home of Duke University. The Shrine game was also relocated to New Orleans. Tulane Stadium would be the site of the January 3 East-West Shrine game.

Some foresaw an offensive circus in the 1942 Sugar Bowl. Fordham, a 6-to-5 favorite, had a rock-like defense and a swirling passing game. Ram statistics indicated they had a knack for the big play. The Tigers, with a strong split-T offense and a dynamic backfield, were the nation's best ground-gaining team, averaging 307.7 yards per game. The Tigers' coach Don Faurot said an opening loss to Ohio State led to revamping the offense. "The Ohio State game sold me on the split-T," he said. "We ran 30 single-wing plays and averaged 1.8 yards per try. We ran 10 split-T plays and averaged 10 yards per carry."

Ram Coach Jim Crowley planned to counteract the split-T with a Rockne defense, the Box-and-Seven, a seven-man line. This would allow the Ram ends and linebackers to "wait" for a play to unfold while the guards and tackles rushed. "If the seven-and-box made coaches stop using the T-formation a dozen years ago," Crowley assessed, "it should do it again."

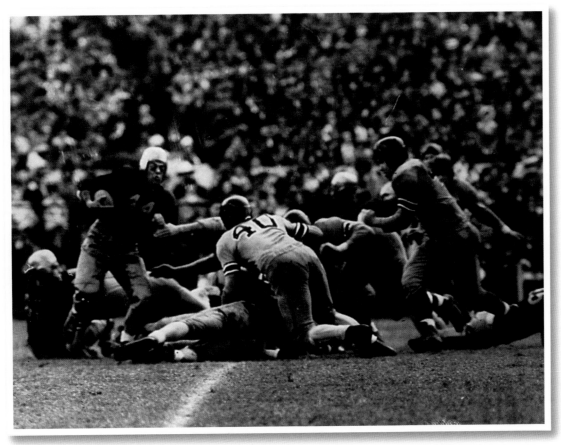

Waterlogged James Blumenstock (44) has precious little room to run against Missouri.

 8TH SUGAR BOWL CLASSIC

"Don't pour it on."

For a locale that boosted its mild winter weather to tourists, this was becoming monotonous: heavy rains again affected the Sugar Bowl.

It come down New Year's Eve, and just before kickoff it began to drizzle again as clouds darkened the field.

Missouri in particular wasn't too concerned about rain because the Tigers had won several games on wet fields during the season. "We were good mudders," said Harry Ice, a 157-pound quarterback. Ice had touchdown runs of 90, 76, 57, 21 and 16 yards during the season and still finished second on his team to Maurice "Red" Wade, who averaged 6.6 yards a carry.

The rain would cripple the Fordham air game, however.

By the time the game's first possession ended a driving rain swept over Tulane Stadium. Ice said of his first punt return, "It was raining so hard, you couldn't see the ball until it was coming down and right on you."

When the Tigers punted again, from their own 31, there was a low snap. Rams' tackle Alex Santilli fired in on substitute kicker Don Greenwood and caught the punt in the chest. The ball bounced crazily back toward the goal line. Fordham end Stanley Ritinski heard the "whomp" of leather against Santilli's soggy jersey and "just reacted to the situation."

James Landing (88) of Fordham hightails it across the soaked Tulane turf.

Ritinsky chased and finally corralled the ball by diving on it in the end zone, then slid off the field. Subsequent photographs indicated Ritinski had control of the ball before he went out, but the referee ruled otherwise and credited Fordham with a safety instead of a touchdown. Coach Jim Crowley said a player on the sidelines turned to him and cracked, "Coach, two's enough. Don't pour it on."

The two points meant different things to different players. Ice said it didn't mean a thing to him at the time. "No bother," Ice recalled. "We had been outplaying them, and had every reason to expect that to continue." Tiger back Bob Steuber had the same reaction. Ritinsky said he was "just so thrilled to get anything on the board ... we felt we had enough defense to hold them."

Missouri showed its vaunted ground game the next time it got the ball. Ice took a lateral and seemed to break clear almost instantly. "I made a crucial mistake," he said. "I cut toward the sideline instead of the middle of the field." That decision allowed Joe Sabasteanski to barely catch Harry's arm from behind 34 yards upstream at the Rams' 47 when he seemed headed to the end zone.

"When Harry went down," Steuber laughed, "I swear he looked like a powerboat sliding across the field."

Missouri never did score then, and later failed on a fourth-and-two at midfield.

Junking their famed split T, the desperate Tigers went to a single-wing, and Ice in the last minutes passed them downfield. Perhaps saving the game, Santilli threw a Tiger for a five-yard loss.

The field goal unit readied for its chance to pull victory out of the quagmire. Ice knelt to hold for Steuber at the 35. The ball was snapped. Steuber got his foot into it, and the ball sailed straight toward the goal.

Steuber and Ice began jumping up and down, hugging each other.

But the ball seemed to die, dipping just under the crossbar, and it was signaled no good. Then the Tigers began to wonder about the cost of the five-yard loss Santilli inflicted just a minute earlier.

Ice steadfastly maintained the field goal was good. Steuber said, "It looked good, but, heck, the official had the best look at it and he said no, and that's the way it was."

Fordham, the passing team, had won a Sugar Bowl without completing a pass. However, it was the weather that got most of the press. *United Press* reporter Henry McLenmore wrote: "At the end of the game, the field was ready for stocking with trout and bream, and tarpon were reported to be leaping in the end zone."

Another writer quipped, "Last time I looked up I saw a Fordham player penalized for doing the Australian Crawl."

"The way was paved."

Dallas was about to change the look of New Year's football — it had always urged a tie-up with the SWC. The Cotton Bowl had lost two stellar Southwest Conference teams, Texas Christian and Texas A&M, to the Sugar for the 1939 and 1940 bowl games. The Cotton Bowl got the SWC champion Aggies in the 1942 game only because the Rose and Sugar didn't extend invitations. Both Texas A&M and Texas were worthy bowl teams for the 1942 games, but A&M's 1941 loss to the Longhorns and a later Texas game made the Sugar Bowl back off.

Until then there was some division among the Southwest Conference officials about whether a tie-up was in the league's best interests. Two of the staunchest opponents had been Coach Dana Bible of Texas and Coach Homer Norton of Texas A&M. However, when those coaches and their schools felt snubbed by the other bowls, they began to listen more attentively to the Cotton Bowl offer.

Fred Digby assessed, "When the Rose Bowlers passed up the Aggies and Longhorns, the Dallas scribes took it as an insult to Southwest Conference football and blasted the Pasadena promoters. That done, they turned their guns on the Sugar Bowl and fired away. Thus the way was paved for a change in attitude by Texas A&M and Texas and the tie-up that is ahead."

So, the Cotton Bowl became the holiday nesting spot of the Southwest Conference champion. It has been a wonderful merger and in many ways the best of the bowl tie-ups.

	1	2	3	4	
Fordham	2	0	0	0	2
Missouri	0	0	0	0	0

Fordham: Safety: Santilli blocks punt; ball rolls through end zone.

Individual Leaders

Rushing
Fordham: Filipowicz 15-58; Anderson 12-49.
Missouri: Ice 15-112; Steuber 9-24.

Passing
Missouri: Ice 2-4, 21 yards.

Receiving
Missouri: Shurnas 1-16; Adams 1-5.

Fordham		Missouri
10	First Downs	8
137	Rushing Yards	148
0-4-0	Passing	2-5-2
0	Passing Yards	21
9-34.0	Punts	6-36.0
137	Total Yards	169
3-1	Fumbles — Lost	3-2
30	Penalty Yards	10

Attendance: 66,154.
Teams' remuneration: $115,118.

Friday, January 1, 1943

Tennessee 14 Tulsa 7

"Lock the door and stack the furniture."

Obviously, the war put a crimp in the sports scene; the quality of competition fell. But the luck of the Sugar Bowl continued. Before the final big week of the 1942 regular season, the Mid-Winter Sports Association was angling for Boston College and either Georgia Tech or Georgia, the best two teams in the Southeastern Conference.

Pasadena flexed its considerable muscle and stepped in with an agreement to take the winner of the Tech-Bulldog fight, snatching a plum right out of the hands of the Sugar. New Orleans then quickly glanced to the Midwest where Henry Frnka's Tulsa Hurricane was blowing over everything in its path. Fourth-ranked Tulsa, the only undefeated team eligible for a bowl and averaging an incredible 42 points a game, would have made an ideal opponent for No. 1-ranked Boston College. Tulsa was invited, and accepted.

Eerie things were taking place at Chestnut Hill, Massachusetts. The program cover of the November 28, 1942, Boston College-Holy Cross game showed a photograph of the schools' captains shaking hands. The Holy Cross captain wore No. 55, the Boston College captain wore No. 12. On that day twenty-six-point underdog Holy Cross drummed the Eagles 55-12. Until Northwestern, a 32-point underdog, defeated Minnesota 31-21 in 1982, this was college football's biggest reversal of form. Boston College instantaneously lost its glitter and national championship aspirations.

The Sugar Bowl appeared to be wiggling on a hook, especially after Boston columnist Bill Cunningham indicated that Boston College might have made an agreement with New Orleans before the game. "So far as I'm concerned," Cunningham said, "the Sugar Bowl is stuck with Boston College. Apparently they can't get out of it, even with that awful drubbing this afternoon."

Cunningham was as close as a reporter could be to the Boston College athletic situation, so his words were taken as an imprimatur. But he was wrong. Seventh-ranked Tennessee received and accepted the Sugar Bowl invitation. It may have been the best thing that ever happened to the Boston College athletic family.

A party celebrating its victory and the Sugar Bowl invitation had been scheduled to follow the Holy Cross game. The crushed Eagles, without victory and without a Sugar Bowl bid, cancelled the af-

54

Vols look for a crack in the Tulsa forward wall.

fair. That night the Coconut Grove, site of the called-off celebration, burned down and almost 500 people were killed.

Tulsa, the Missouri Valley champion, didn't appear to need anything extra in its high-velocity offense, featuring a do-it-all tailback named Glenn Dobbs. The Hurricane had 2,339 yards passing that season, 4,261 yards in total offense, and ranked eighth nationally on defense, surrendering an average of 148.7 yards.

The Hurricane did pick up a lot of what normally would have been neutral fan support in New Orleans. Bill Cunningham, apparently irritated that Boston College had not gotten the Sugar Bowl invitation, wrote that one of the participants was a "fine semi-pro club, peopled with several gents whose eligibility wouldn't pass muster in some of the politer circles." The howl that arose in Oklahoma caused Cunningham to back up and say he was actually speaking of Tennessee, though he seemed to be simply covering his tracks. Tulsa received a great deal of sympathy nationwide for being in the line of fire through no fault of its own. New Orleans went out of its way to show hospitality to the Hurricane.

The game itself had a slightly odd look. Coach John Barnhill had taken over the Volunteer reins for General Bob Neyland. Frnka had been a longtime assistant at Vanderbilt and had crossed swords with Tennessee for years. "I used to scout them so often I sometimes stood up when their band played their alma mater," he laughed.

Tennessee, in the Neyland tradition, emphasized its kicking game and defense. The Vols had a fine running attack and were deep in reserves, accounting for their pick as a three-point favorite. Tulsa, however, was not deep and wasn't a consistent ground threat. "We were a bunch of greyhounds with a lot of heart," said Dobbs. Some felt Tulsa was a little more than that. One sportswriter led off a story with, "Lock the door and stack the furniture because Glenn Dobbs &. Co., otherwise known as the University of Tulsa football team, are in town." Not only was Tulsa exciting, but it had a coach who didn't overlook anything. Frnka brought 300 gallons of drinking water from Oklahoma with the team.

"We aren't taking chances," he explained.

"That ball went straight up in the air."

It was John Barnhill's worst fear.

With Tulsa backed up to its own 14 in the first quarter, the Tennessee coach saw tailback Glenn Dobbs quick-kick a ball 76 yards to the Vols' 9; Then he saw Dobbs drop a kick out of bounds at the Tennessee 14.

"We knew," Barnhill said, "that if we didn't run those kicks back each time for about 15 yards, Tulsa would be camping on our 5-yard line all afternoon."

There was reason to be concerned about that aspect of the Hurricane repertoire. Dobbs was one of the nation's top passers, but the Tulsa running game was nothing to be especially afraid of, making the Hurricane offense one dimensional. But Dobbs was a dangerous punter, able to coffin-kick and able to kick long with three of more than 75 yards during the season. He could really keep the Vols backed up all day.

Of course, Barnhill's own punter, Bobby Cifers, led the nation with a 42.9 average.

Early though, Dobbs was showing his full range. Throwing on every down, he took the Hurricane to the Tennessee 9 as the first quarter ended. From there, moving as if he were running an option, Dobbs pulled up and flicked a pass to Cal Purdin for the touchdown.

The passing drive was a seven-for-seven display by Dobbs.

Notably, he had also completed his last attempt before the drive started and would complete his next, giving him nine consecutive completions.

Tennessee came right back, with Bill Gold slashing into the end zone from the 3. Charlie Mitchell's conversion was wide, leaving Tulsa in front 7-6 at the half.

"We were durned glad to be where we were," Dobbs recalled. "Tennessee had shut down our running game completely ... And we were pretty tired, but (Coach Henry Frnka) didn't tell us anything at the half."

"What we did," explained Tennessee tackle Denver Crawford, "was drop the ends off and rush with four men. Tulsa's running game wasn't tremendous and we concentrated on stopping Dobbs' passing."

In the third quarter, Dobbs dropped into his end zone to punt from the 7. There was a low snap and Crawford roared in, and threw blocking back N.A. Keithley aside. He then felt the sting of the ball on his chest.

"I swear," Crawford said, "that ball went straight up in the air about 70 yards. I thought I was going to be a star and get my first touchdown. I ended up standing in the end zone waiting for that thing to come down. When it did, I tried to jerk it in bounds, but I just couldn't fool that official."

"Why Keithley, the lightest back we had, was back there blocking, I don't know," Dobbs mused of the safety that put the Volunteers ahead for keeps.

Behind now, and with time becoming precious, Tulsa gave up any pretense of running. Dobbs was passing from deep in Tulsa territory, but one attempt was batted in the air by freshman Jim Powell and Dick Jordan picked it off and returned it 11 yards to the 13. In three plays Clyde Fuson went in from the 1. Mitchell again missed the PAT, leaving the score at its final 14-7.

Yet, Tulsa made a gallant last drive to salvage a tie, with Keithley in for Dobbs – who was on the sidelines begging Frnka to let him back in. Keithley got Tulsa to the Tennessee 13, but Powell ended things with an interception on the 5.

The game ended one play later.

The highlight of the ninth Sugar Bowl was the sensational kicking. Ten Tennessee punts averaged 41 yards. Fourteen Tulsa punts averaged 43 yards.

On the other hand, despite Tulsa's 168 yards passing, the Hurricane finished with a minus 39 yards rushing. Quarterback Walter Slater put things in focus, saying, "Tennessee has won a lot of games playing defense," said Walter Slater. "This was one."

That was a major factor, of course but there was more. Barnhill's emphasis on return yardage paid off. Tennessee averaged 17.5 per punt return against Tulsa as the Volunteers became the first Southeastern Conference team to win a Sugar Bowl since Tulane in the inaugural.

	1	2	3	4	
Tennessee	0	6	2	6	14
Tulsa	0	7	0	0	7

Tulsa: Purdin, 9-yard pass from Dobbs. PAT, LeForce, kick.

Tennessee: Gold, 2-yard run. Kick failed.

Tennessee: Safety; Crawford blocked punt out of end zone.

Tennessee: Fulson, 1-yard run. Kick failed.

Individual Leaders

Rushing
Tennessee: Fuson 14-57, 1 TD; Cifer 11-48.
Tulsa: Erickson 1-9.

Passing
Tennessee: Slater 7-15, 88 yards.
Tulsa: Dobbs 11-16, 98 yards, 1 TD; Keithley 6-11, 70 yards.

Receiving
Tennessee: Gaffney 2-30; Hust 2-20.
Tulsa: Judd 8-101; Purdin 5-36, 1 TD.

Tennessee		Tulsa
14	First Downs	10
208	Rushing Yards	-39
7-17-0	Passing	17-27-2
88	Passing Yards	168
10-41.0	Punts	14-43.0
296	Total Yards	129
2-2	Fumbles – Lost	0-0
100	Penalty Yards	10

Attendance: 58,361.
Teams' remuneration: $98,956.

Georgia Tech 20 Tulsa 18

"Rejected, Deferred, Unbeaten."

There was wide speculation during the week following Tulsa-Tennessee that the Sugar Bowl might be scrapped until the end of the war. Fred Digby doubted anything that severe would be done. "They'll do whatever Uncle Sam. thinks best," he wrote. "Two years ago the Sugar Bowlers announced their policy would be to carry on unless the government thought it best to call a halt. To date, the government has not asked anything except that ticket sales be confined to the New Orleans area. This was done, and to the letter."

When the Association met that January, there was no official mention of temporarily suspending the Sugar Bowl other than to refute the idea had substance. President Joseph B. David said, "We held our regular monthly board meeting tonight, and no discussion of the matter was had."

Selecting bowl teams was a chore in the 1943 football season. The best teams were those whose schools were involved in military training, such as the Navy V-12 program, and those on military bases whose participants were still amateurs. Washington and Southern California, both members of the Pacific Coast Conference, were announced early as the Rose Bowl combatants. The reason for the choices was the travel that would be involved for an Eastern or Southern team.

Iowa Preflight and Southwestern Louisiana Institute, a strong team with a military program, appeared the favorites

for one berth in the Sugar Bowl. Georgia Tech, a Navy training school, was the Southeastern Conference champion. It was the choice for the other spot, though badly beaten by No. 1-ranked Notre Dame. Iowa Preflight was eliminated because the Navy had a 48-hour limit on furloughs. The Mid-Winter Sports Association disclosed its pick in late November. Georgia Tech — with the most defeats, three, of any team that had ever competed in the Sugar Bowl — was pitted against the undefeated, once-tied Tulsa.

Receiving and accepting the invitation was a historic occasion for Georgia Tech. It completed Coach Bill Alexander's circuit through the four major bowls. He had taken Tech to the Rose Bowl (1929), the Orange Bowl (1940), the Cotton Bowl (1943), and now the Sugar. Tech became the first school to complete the cycle.

This would not be the same Tulsa team that competed in New Orleans in 1943, although its roster did carry a couple of familiar names. Maurice "Red" Wade, who had played with Missouri against Fordham in the 1942 Sugar Bowl, was now with Coach Henry Frnka's Hurricane. Ed Shedlosky, who had played with Fordham in

Ed Scharfschwerdt scores to put Georgia Tech ahead 20-18 in 1944 comeback against Tulsa.

1942, had also transferred to Tulsa. Only six members were back from the previous Tulsa squad, and 24 of the 40 team members for 1943 were classified 4-F by the draft or had medical discharges. Nine others were 18 years old and expecting draft notices, or under draft age.

Guard Ellis Jones was missing an arm. Another player had one lung. A third had one kidney. Coach Henry Fmka had one athlete who had a large area of scarred tissue, and another who had to play in a special shoe because of a severed Achilles tendon. Red Wade, who suffered an attack of osteomyelitis when he was 13, had back and ankle problems.

This team surprised everyone, including Frnka. Time magazine ran a story on the Hurricane headlined "Rejected, Deferred, Unbeaten." Embarrassed about 'Frnka's 4-Fs', Washington authorities asked for a quiet review of draft physicals.

Eddie Prokop, Joseph B. David, and C.I. Pontius, president of Tulsa University, at 1944 Sugar Bowl party at the St. Charles Hotel.

"Give Me That Ball!"

C-R-R-A-A-K.

That's what Frank Broyles remembers of the turning point in the 1944 Sugar Bowl — though it didn't manifest itself until later.

The crucial play came on Georgia Tech's first series — after Tulsa took a 6-0 lead on a 15-yard pass from Clyde LeForce to Ed Shedlosky — when halfback Eddie Prokop, blocking for Broyles, was rushed by the one-armed guard Ellis Jones. On the collision, Prokop took an accidental crack to the face. "We didn't have big face-guards then," Broyles, who played both halfback and fullback, recalled. "I looked at Eddie, with his bloodied mouth already beginning to swell, and it was plain he was as angry as anybody had ever seen him.

" 'Give me that ball,' he told us. That may have been the biggest play of the game."

It didn't seem so at first, but it was as if a long-burning fuse had been lit.

Tulsa was ahead 18-7 at the half, but Broyles said the Yellow Jackets were still steaming about the shot to Propkop, who began punching out yards at every point of the defense. Tech, though, couldn't sustain anything.

Tulsa's Jimmy Ford faked a pass and then found a hole at right tackle. He veered to the sideline, then went 76 yards with the Tech defense in faint pursuit. It was the longest run from scrimmage in the 10 Sugar Bowl games and staked the Hurricane to a 12-0 lead as LeForce missed his second extra point.

Tech immediately answered with a 12-play drive. Broyles went in from the 1. Prokop converted.

Ford made his presence felt again when, shortly after the Tech touchdown, he launched a 68-yard punt that flew over Broyles and went out at the 'Jackets' 6. Broyles tried to kick it back out of the danger zone, but the weak snap grazed the leg of a blocking back and the ball came to rest at the 1. After a delay penalty, LeForce, who was sent in to kick the PAT before the touchdown was even scored, sliced off tackle for the touchdown.

"I thought (Hurricane) Barney White recovered for a touchdown," a sheepish Coach Henry Frnka said later of the scramble at the 1 for the loose ball. "It looked to me as if one official raised his arms. I sent LeForce in to try the extra point, and I was as much surprised as anyone to see us draw a five-yard penalty for excessive time. Of course, LeForce scored from the 6, but if Tech had held us it would have made us look awful dumb. It was no time to substitute, I'll admit."

When it was time to do what he was originally sent in to do, LeForce missed his third PAT, and the score stood at its half-time margin of 18-7.

Prokop pitched Tech back in it when he arched a pass over the straining fingers of defender Camp Wilson to Phil Tinsley, who made the grab, whirled at the 30, found himself alone and went the 46-yard distance. It was a pivotal play because Wil-

Georgia Tech 's Frank Broyles breaks free against Tulsa.

Frank Broyles about to be roughed getting a punt off against Tulsa.

son came so close to intercepting with a chance of putting the Sugar Bowl out of reach for Georgia Tech. Instead the Yellow Jackets were down just 18-13 after a missed Tech PAT.

"Wilson cried after the game over his failure to intercept," Frnka said. "We have a signal on intercepted passes for the men to form in front of the man intercepting. Wilson actually gave the signal, so sure was he that he had the ball. He must've jumped too soon and missed it coming down. He probably missed it by inches. That's how close it was. We all thought he had the ball."

The momentum had switched. "We began having some injuries," said Jones, "and we weren't real deep to begin with. Georgia Tech was gaining momentum, you could feel it, but we kind of felt we could hold them off."

They couldn't. On a drive highlighted with laterals and scrambles, Prokop moved Tech to the 4. Tulsa held — for three downs. Ed Scharfscherdt went in and Prokop kicked the extra point to put Georgia Tech in front for good.

Ellis Jones was sobbing on a bench in the Tulsa locker room when Notre Dame coach Frank Leahy walked in and shouted to him, "Buck up, boy. You played well enough to win, but didn't. You gave it a good shot, that's all that counts. These things happen in life." Jones said, "I never forgot that."

The man who got the biggest satisfaction of the day was Eddie Prokop, whose number of carries (43), yards gained rushing (199), and total yards (256) were all Sugar Bowl records.

	1	2	3	4	
Georgia Tech	0	7	6	7	20
Tulsa	6	12	0	0	18

Tulsa: Shedlosky, 15-yard pass from LeForce. Kick failed.

Tulsa: Ford, 76-yard run. Kick failed.

Georgia Tech: Broyles, 1-yard run. PAT, Prokop kick.

Tulsa: LeForce, 1-yard run. Kick failed.

Georgia Tech: Tinsley, 46-yard pass from Propkop. Kick failed.

Georgia Tech: Scharfscherdt, 1-yard run. PAT, Prokop kick.

Individual Leaders

Rushing
Georgia Tech: Propkop 29-199; Broyles 19-70, 1 TD.
Tulsa: Ford 14-106, 1 TD; LeForce 5-51; Smith 5-51.

Passing
Georgia Tech: Prokop 3-14, 57 yards; Broyles 1-2, 26 yards.
Tulsa: LeForce 3-6, 68 yards, 1 TD; Ford 2-6, 18 yards.

Receiving
Georgia Tech: Tinsley 2-54, 1 TD.
Tulsa: Shedlosky 3-49, 1 TD.

Georgia Tech		Tulsa
25	First Downs	8
373	Rushing Yards	211
4-16-1	Passing	6-15-1
83	Passing Yards	87
456	Total Yards	298
6-38.0	Punts	7-34.0
3	Fumbles	1
60	Penalty Yards	50

Attendance: 69,134.
Teams' remuneration: $95,956.

Duke 29   Alabama 26

"They're too young to know any different."

The 1945 Sugar Bowl was an almost complete reversal of form from the previous 10 pairings. This one, at first glance, looked to be a pumpkin; but at the stroke of midnight, it was transformed into the princess.

Again, the war made for odd pairings, but Georgia Tech again had a representative team in the South, one in which the Mid-Winter Sports Association was definitely interested. The Orange Bowl made a bold bid and invited the Engineers to Miami for a rematch of the 1944 Sugar Bowl with Tulsa. Tech still had two games to play, including one with Notre Dame.

Tennessee was on its way to an 8-0-1 season but quickly committed to the Rose Bowl, the big winner in the holiday sweepstakes with the only two ranked teams (seventh-ranked Southern Cal and the 12th-ranked Volunteers). The Sugar Bowl was sent scrambling. Alabama, an SEC also-ran with one loss and two ties, was eventually selected. Coach Frank Thomas was surprised when the invitation arrived. The Southern Conference champion Duke, beaten four times, would be the opponent. Duke was also a Navy training team.

Alabama, a civilian school that didn't even field a team the year before and started the 1944 season with only one backfield regular as old as 18, came under some pressure not to accept because it didn't

appear to be an equitable match. Thomas resisted initially but finally accepted.

Thomas, the second coach in two years to complete the major bowl circuit in New Orleans, knew full well what he was getting into. Asked how his team felt, Thomas replied, "They're too young to know any different than they're going to win. I'm not going to tell them any different."

For the first time since Pearl Harbor the Sugar Bowl would be an absolute sellout of 73,000. It may not have been a stellar attraction compared to the other bowls, but a lot of fans wanted to see Alabama-Duke.

Other than the buoyant atmosphere prevalent toward the end of a war, it is hard to see how Alabama-Duke would create much excitement. Purely and simply, it appeared to be a case of men against boys, as the Blue Devils' two-touchdown pick reflected. Alabama's line had only one man who weighted

Alabama passing whiz Harry Gilmer (52) uses his legs as well as his arm against Duke.

as much as 200 pounds — center Vaughn Mancha. Eighteen-year-old Harry Gilmer guided the Crimson Tide offense. In contrast, the older, heavier Duke trainees looked to 23-year-old Tom Davis for leadership. Davis was a Marine lieutenant who had been discharged in September and had returned to school.

Coach Eddie Cameron, who had taken over at Duke while Wallace Wade, also a former Alabama coach, was in the service, realized he could be stepping into a trap. Coach Cameron said the odds were "silly" and read a letter to his team from Colonel Wade, a field artillery officer in France, who wrote that he would be listening and was "setting up a special cheering section over here to help the boys along." In reference to two previous Duke bowl losses, Wade added, "Tell the boys they've got to win this one. We don't want to be three-time losers at anything — especially football."

Thomas, on the other hand would have made the odds higher. The Alabama coach, speaking to the New Orleans Quarterback Club, couldn't contain a gush of praise for his team. Chairman Lester Lautenschlaeger reminded Thomas that it was a bit out of his character to do that before a big game. "I believe in giving the kids the credit they deserve," Thomas reflected. "The boys are young, and are just about the hustlingest team I've had. I wouldn't say it is the greatest team I've coached, but they have more enthusiasm and love to play."

When asked for a prediction, Thomas thought for a few seconds, then answered, "Duke 21, Alabama 6." Lautenschlaeger said, "I understand you told somebody before it would be 21-0." "I did," Thomas admitted with a smile, "but I've become enthused myself since coming to the Quarterback Club and now I think we'll score!"

"You can plainly see him beat the ground."

Grantland Rice, the famed sportswriter, covered many of the biggest sports events of the first half of the 20th Century.

He said he never saw a game the equal of this Sugar Bowl, a game of contrasting styles, a game that changed hands four times, and a game that was in doubt until the last second. Literally.

This game came to a stirring climax exactly 60 playing minutes after the kickoff, with 24 open yards to the end zone in front of a ball-carrier straining to get free of a defender hanging on for dear life as the gun sounded.

As the chilly, golden afternoon began to fade, Rice searched for the precise words to describe what he had just witnessed. He settled on a simple and succinct lead: "The Sugar Bowl classic of 1945 must go down in the book as one of the great thrillers of all time."

At the same time in the Duke locker room, Blue Devil captain Gordon Carver was sighing, "I sure was glad to hear that final whistle."

The civilian kids from the Capstone of Alabama put on a show against the war veterans of Duke. The power-running of Tom Davis and George Clark prevailed over the air-arm of the Crimson Tide's Harry Gilmer. But just barely.

In a game that went off like a Roman candle, Clark broke off a 52-yard run on Duke's first possession, leading to a touchdown.

Then Gilmer lit up the crowd, rearing up and hitting Hal Self, who was stopped by Davis a foot from the end zone. Norman Hodges took it in from there, but the PAT was missed.

It shortly happened again. On a third-and-27 from the Duke 41, Gilmer was chased back again, almost tripping over a defender and nearly in the grasp of two more Blue Devils. Suddenly he broke loose, leaped high, arched his back, and whipped the ball 40 yards to end

Ralph Jones.

"He wasn't supposed to throw to me ... just picked me out," Jones marveled afterward.

Hodges scored on the next play, but Paul Stephanz blocked the PAT.

The first quarter wasn't over yet and three touchdowns were already on the board. Things were heating up.

Gilmer took 'Bama on yet another binge. From the 49, Gilmer, again being rushed by the tormented Blue Devils, leaped on the dead run and duplicated his bulls-eye toss to Jones, this time to the 10. Gilmer then threw over the middle to Jones who then stepped into the end zone from the 2. This time Gilmer kicked the PAT, making the score 19-7, Alabama, and putting the crowd — not to mention Tide coach Frank Thomas — in a frenzy.

Smarting, the Blue Devils struck back, cutting up the Tide defense as it was expected to do before. Cliff Lewis raced 26 yards to the Bama 1, where Davis scored. The half ended with the Crimson Tide ahead 19-13.

The vaunted Duke runners began asserting themselves in the third period with Davis getting 10 straight carries and a one-yard touchdown. The PAT put Duke in front 20-19. Bobby Morrow changed that with a 75-yard interception return for a touchdown.

Duke charged right back, but the gritty Tide stopped the Devils at the 1, then took an intentional safety so Gilmer could kick out from the 20. The strategy backfired when second-string halfback Jim LaRue raced around left end on a reverse from the 39, bounced off a pair of Alabamians, and carried two with him until he went down at the Tide 20.

"The play was run precisely as called and diagrammed," LaRue re-

called. Clark, on a spectacular burst, went off tackle and covered the remaining distance to put Duke in front 29-26 with less than a minute remaining.

Gilmer got the Tide to its 43 with time for one play. He heaved a shot to Jones at the Duke 30. Jones pivoted and had a clearing for an instant. He only had to beat Duke safety Carver and 'Bama was home. Carver managed to grab and hold on to the receiver's woolen stocking and finally brought him down at the 24 as the gun went off.

"The sad thing is that I had another receiver further downfield, Jack McConville," Gilmer said. "I got off a weak pass to Jones, but McConville recognized instantly what to do and turned to block the only defensive back that had a chance of getting Ralph. But when he turned he slipped. On the film you can plainly see him beat the ground."

Rice could scarcely contain his enthusiasm, saying the 18-year-old Gilmer, who rolled up 142 yards passing — almost two hundred yards fewer than Duke's 336 yards rushing — was "the greatest college passer I ever saw."

Gilmer was 8-of-8.

	1	2	3	4	
Duke	7	6	7	9	29
Alabama	12	7	0	7	26

Duke: Clark, 15-yard run, PAT, Raether kick.

Alabama: Hodges, 1-yard run. Kick failed.
Alabama: Hodges, 2-yard run. Kick failed.
Alabama: Jones, 13-yard pass from Gilmer. PAT, Morrow kick.
Duke: Davis, 1-yard run. Kick failed.
Duke: Davis, 1-yard run. PAT, Raether kick.
Alabama: Morrow, 75-yard interception return. PAT, Morrow kick.
Duke: Safety.
Duke: Clark, 20-yard run. PAT, Raether kick.

Individual Leaders

Rushing
Duke: Clark 14-123, 2 TDs; Davis 101, 2 TDs.
Alabama: Gilmer 14-63; Hodges 8-29, 2 TD.

Passing
Duke: Lewis 4-7-1, 40 yards.
Alabama: Gilmer 8-8-0, 142 yards, 1 TD.

Receiving
Duke: Carver 4-35.
Alabama: Jones 4-136, 1 TD.

Duke		Alabama
19	First Downs	8
336	Rushing Yards	102
5-8-1	Passing	8-8-0
47	Passing Yards	142
383	Total Yards	244
4-34.0	Punts	5-35.0
6-1	Fumbles – Lost	1-1
1-5	Penalties – Yards	2-6

Attendance: 68,862.
Teams' remuneration: $126,896.

Oklahoma A&M 33 St. Mary's 13

"I'll be right here for it, too."

A letter from Wallace Wade to Fred Digby after Duke-Alabama cut short the tale of his Sugar Bowl listening post while in the war. Wade wrote he was involved in military operations on January 1, 1945.

Undefeated Alabama was the southern choice of all the major bowls. Little St. Mary's was embarrassing the giants of California. Army was the best team in the country, and there was talk of the Cadets breaking their bowl ban for a holiday in Pasadena or New Orleans.

Army favored a Rose Bowl invitation but was reluctant to decide before the Navy game. The Sugar Bowl pressured Pasadena to extend an early bid. The Sugar Bowl told Alabama to make up its mind or forget a New Orleans trip. Pasadena, with no answer from Army in the offing, was afraid of coming up empty with both the Cadets and the Tide.

Frank Leahy told Fred Digby, "... I have no interest in St. Mary's, nor is Jim Phelan more than an acquaintance; but if the Sugar Bowlers invite the Gaels for their game, I am sure they'll give the fans a show such as they've never seen. I'll be right here for it, too." St. Mary's and Oklahoma A&M were extended Sugar Bowl invitations the following day. Both accepted. The undefeated Aggies, Missouri Valley Conference champions, were the nation's best ground offensive team, averaging 287.7 yards a game. St.

Mary's, a tiny (enrollment under 300) Christian Brothers school in northern California, ran a sleight-of-hand offense and averaged 170 yards passing. A&M's Bob Fenimore, in the era of Glenn Davis and Doc Blanchard, was the nation's leading rusher (1,641 yards), followed by none other than Hawaiian Hurricane Herman Wedemeyer (1,428 yards) of St. Mary's. Both were first team All-Americans. Oklahoma A&M finished fifth and St. Mary's seventh in the final Associated Press poll, giving New Orleans the only major bowl match-up of Top 10 teams.

Ticket demand was incredible. Seventy-five thousand fans, the highest Sugar Bowl attendance in its 12 games, were cramped into Tulane stadium. The governor of Oklahoma strolled into Sugar Bowl headquarters a couple of days before the game, spotted President Sam Corenswet and other bowl committeemen, walked over, and said, "Gentlemen, I'm a man of few words. I want tickets." Corenswet replied, "We're men of few words, too, governor. We haven't got any."

St. Mary's players; Don Adams (24), Leo Verceles (4), and Paul Crowe (39) look on intently.

 12TH SUGAR BOWL CLASSIC

"Too Much Power — Too Much Speed."

Men against boys. Even though the boys were pretty good, so were the bigger, more worldly men.

Oklahoma A&M was a team that started seven war veterans, including fullback Jim Reynolds who flew 52 missions over Germany, and tackle Bert Cole who had been shot down over Yugoslavia and spent months among the Chetniks while making his way back to Allied lines. In contrast, St. Mary's was a lot like Alabama in 1945 with seven 17-year-old starters on a team with an average age of 18 1/2.

Also, A&M, the heaviest team to play in the first 12 Sugar Bowls at a 203-pound average, was man-for-man 15 pounds larger than the Sugar Bowl's youngest team ever.

The Aggies' Bob Fenimore led the nation in total offense for the second straight year. His two-season all-purpose yards average of 212.4 yards was better than those of recent Heisman Trophy recipients Frank Sinkwich, or Tom Harmon or Glenn Davis.

And, to make things worse, St. Mary's was bitten severely by the flu bug four days earlier.

"I remember we went onto the field in just T-shirts and pants with no pads," Herman Wedemeyer – a 21-year-old Honolulu native who then lateralled to guard Carl DeSalvo. The lineman picked up a horde of blockers to escort him the remaining 20 yards. The weary Wedemeyer missed the extra point.

The crowd was mesmerized by the plucky, undersized Gaels somehow staying with the powerful Aggies. "The half ended with us trailing 14-13," Wedemeyer remembered. "The feeling of the entire stadium had changed. Now they all seemed to be rooting for St. Mary's. The Gaels continued playing in that vain, but the Aggies' size and strength began taking over. Fenimore returned a punt 43 yards to the 7, then scored from a yard out on fourth down. Don Schultz blocked the PAT and St. Mary's remained within tying distance, 20-13.

The Sugar Bowl might have remained with a competitive score, or a tie in those days before two-point conversions or overtime, but for a fluke play in the closing minutes. Wedemeyer slipped trying to punt and missed the ball completely, and A&M recovered on the Gaels' 35. Jim Reynolds eventually scored from the 1. Then, on A&M's next possession, from the St. Mary's 20, Reynolds threw deep.

Sugar Bowl president A.B. Nicholas and WWII icon Gen. Jonathan Wainwright before the 1946 game.

would gain even greater fame a quarter-century later with a recurring role on TV's "Hawaii 5-0" – recalled years later. "Bob Fenimore and the big Oklahoma A&M team was already out there. The entire stadium was full. How many were there, 72,000? Well, they all laughed at us. We looked like midgets on the field. No wonder people laughed. But that sort of set the stage for what was to come later."

The Gaels, whose offense was based on deception, started fast with a lateral play that got them to the A&M 46. St. Mary's scored as Spike Cordeiro started wide, then flipped back to Wedemeyer who faded back and waited for Dennis O'Connor to work his way behind Fenimore. He caught it and went in.

The methodical Aggies answered in five plays. Cecil Haskins caught a 29-yard pass from Fenimore, falling into the end zone with Wedemeyer and Cordeiro hanging on.

More of the same was waiting in the second quarter. Quickly, the Aggies put together another drive, culminating in another touchdown, this one of 1-yard by Fenimore.

There was still more to come. Wedemeyer broke loose for 24 yards,

Bob Fenimore turns upfield as St. Mary's defender dives at his heels.

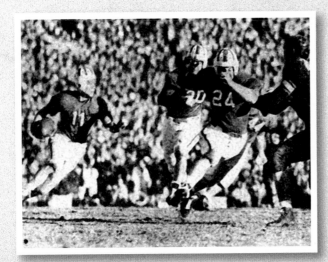

Herman Wedemeyer (11) accounts for two touchdowns but they aren't enough.

Gael halfback Paul Crowe batted the ball into the air, seemingly breaking up the game's last play. Alert Aggie reserve back Joe Thomas grabbed the tumbling ball and crossed the goal.

Oklahoma A&M scored two touchdowns in the final five minutes.

Bob Fenimore was all he was cracked to be, rushing for 125 yards and two touchdowns, and passing for another.

Gaels' coach Jim Phelan, after locking the press out of the locker room for 30 minutes, explained, "Too much power – too much speed. And, above all, too much Fenimore."

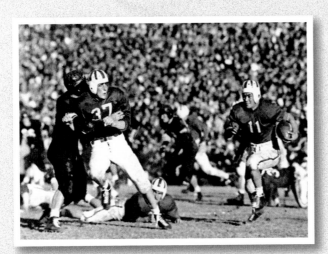

Wedemeyer carries for 'Galloping Gaels' against war-toughened Oklahoma A&M.

	1	2	3	4	
Oklahoma A&M	7	7	6	13	33
St. Mary's	7	6	0	0	13

St. Mary's: O'Connor, 46-yard pass from Wedemeyer. PAT, Wedemeyer kick.

Oklahoma A&M: Haskins, 29-yard pass from Fenimore. PAT, Reynolds kick.

Oklahoma A&M: Fenimore, 1-yard run. PAT, Reynolds kick.

St. Mary's: DeSalvo, 20-yard run. Kick failed.

Oklahoma A&M: Fenimore, 1-yard run. Kick failed.

Oklahoma A&M: Reynolds, 1-yard run. Kick failed.

Oklahoma A&M: Thomas, 20-yard pass from Reynolds. PAT, Reynolds kick.

Individual Leaders

Rushing
Oklahoma A&M: Fenimore 25-125, 2 TDs; Reynolds 14-51, 1 TD.
St. Mary's: Wedemeyer 7-24; DeSalvo 1-24, 1 TD.

Passing
Oklahoma A&M: Fenimore 4-10, 76 yards, 1 TD; Reynolds 2-3, 36 yards.
St. Mary's: Wedemeyer 9-19, 150 yards; O'Connor 2-3, 27 yards.

Receiving
Oklahoma A&M: Haskins 2-48, 1 TD; Armstrong 2-28.
St. Mary's: O'Connor 6-76, 1 TD.

Oklahoma A&M		St. Mary's
15	First Downs	8
217	Rushing Yards	61
4-13-4	Passing	11-24-2
112	Passing Yards	177
339	Total Yards	238
4-47.2	Punts	5-43.0
0-0	Fumbles – Lost	2-2

Attendance: 75,000.
Teams' remuneration: $132,072.

Georgia 20 North Carolina 10

"It would have been interesting."

Notre Dame and Army, two traditional giants respectively with bowl bans, were No. 1 and 2 respectively in 1946. Despite the postseason taboo by both schools, there was some hope the administrations might not be as adamant as before. The Western Conference (the Big Nine), long opposed to bowl games, agreed to a five-year contract with the Pacific Coast Intercollegiate Conference, permitting one of its schools to participate annually in the Rose Bowl.

There was some sentiment in New Orleans for Army, though it was rumored that Army wanted to select its opponent. The Cadets were eyeing Rice, but the Sugar Bowl wanted unbeaten, untied Georgia — the SEC co-champion and No. 3-ranked team. When Sugar Bowl representatives attended the Bulldogs' last game with Georgia Tech, fans unfurled banners which read "Beat Army." Whether it was the selection issue or not, Army turned down all bowl invitations, and so did Notre Dame, which did not have the change of heart its Midwestern brothers did.

Actually, Army, Notre Dame, and Georgia all had claims to national championships. Bulldog Coach Wally Butts wanted Associated Press poll notice to go with his Williamson System No. 1 tag. Army was ranked first by the Helms Athletic Foundation and the Football Thesaurus. Notre Dame was champion in the eyes of AP, the Dunkel System, and the Litkenhous System.

"I was prejudiced," Butts admitted, "but I thought we had the No. 1 team in the nation. Georgia and UCLA were the only teams with perfect records, for Notre Dame and Army had played their famous tie. It would have been interesting to see

(Charley) Trippi competing against Doc Blanchard and Glenn Davis of Army. But neither Coach Red Blaik of Army or Coach Frank Leahy of Notre Dame was interested in playing that Georgia team."

Georgia's firepower was fantastic for the postwar years. Only one team (Alabama) held the Bulldogs under four touchdowns during its 10-game schedule. The Georgia T-formation pulverized its opposition with a 37.2 points-per-game average.

Two of the nation's best backs, Charley Trippi and John Rauch, drove the Bulldog offense. Trippi had a 6.4-yard-per-carry average with 1,366 total yards. Rauch was the country's top-ranked passer, and five Bulldogs were ranked among the top receivers. Defensively, Trippi and Rauch were tied with five players nationally with five interceptions apiece.

Seventh-ranked North Carolina, with legend-in-the-making Charley "Choo-Choo" Justice who had gained 1,213 total yards, was paired with Georgia. It was the Tar Heels' first bowl trip and, despite being Southern Conference champions, 14 points separated the teams in the odds. It was plain most felt Carolina would need luck to stay close to Georgia.

North Carolina Coach Carl Snaveley and halfback Charley Justice, and quarterback Charley Trippi and Bulldog Coach Wally Butts before 1947 Sugar Bowl.

 13TH SUGAR BOWL CLASSIC

"Congratulating you! Ain't that rich!"

The story Harry Wismer relayed to his listening audience on New Year's Day, 1947, the one sportswriters conveyed, and what 73,000 witnessed was incredulous.

The MVP of Georgia's Sugar Bowl victory may well have been the officiating crew with two highly questionable calls which led directly to the Bulldogs' winning margin.

They came in the second half, after Carolina took a 7-0 lead in the first 30 minutes, looking very much the better team.

Leading up to the referring gaffes, a second-quarter interception of an attempted screen by tackle Bob Mitten of Charley Trippi put Carolina at the Bulldog 5. Walt Pupa cut into the end zone as the 'Heels' line leveled everything in his path.

Coach Wally Butts was infuriated by his team's lackadaisical performance in the first 30 minutes.

Georgia's Charlie Trippi.

Charley 'Choo-Choo' Justice (22) follows his blocks against Georgia.

"Why in the dressing room between halves," Butts said, "I told them I found it hard to believe I was seeing what I was seeing. I said, 'Here you boys are getting smacked around and you act like it's all right because those North Carolina boys are patting you on the back, kidding you, and congratulating you after knocking the heck out of you. Congratulating you! Ain't that rich! Those boys are not as gentle and kind as they are trying to make you believe. Junk that congratulations business until after the game. Go on like this and they are going to beat us to a frazzle.' "

Trippi recalled, "We hadn't played against a single wing team all year, and we had a hard time adjusting. We made changes in our line spacing. That got us untracked."

Joe Tereshinski picked off a Pupa pass at the Georgia 25 in the third quarter. Intended receiver Jim Camp recovered enough to turn and tackle Tereshinski as soon as he made the catch. As he was going down, Tereshinski pitched the ball forward to fullback Dick McPhee.

The ball should have been dead at that point, and field judge Gabe Hill appeared ready to mark the spot. Center Dan Stiegam realized he had not heard a whistle and chased down McPhee at the UNC 14. "It was an obvious forward pass, we

thought, and everybody relaxed," Stiegman said.

Charlie Justice remembered arguing so long and loud that he was threatened with expulsion from the game. The end result was a four-yard touchdown run by John Rauch that tied the score.

North Carolina immediately retaliated, driving to within range of the goal posts where Bobby Cox kicked an 18-yard field goal.

On a broken play, the scrambling Trippi finally got a pass off to Dan Edwards, who made the catch at the 50 and outmaneuvered the frantically clutching hands of Justice before zigzagging to the goal line. George Jernigan's PAT was blocked, but the 67-yard Sugar Bowl record scoring pass put Georgia in the lead for good.

The Bulldogs built a cushion in the fourth quarter by driving 80 yards as Rauch picked up his second touchdown on a quick-opener from the 13. North Carolina had a chance to close the gap, but another official's call proved disastrous.

Reaching the Georgia 18, Justice threw to receiver Ken Powell in the end zone. Powell made the reception in front of defensive back Charlie "Rabbit" Smith, who came up to prevent the completion. With Smith hanging on, Powell turned and fell face forward.

Powell was unconscious, apparently the result of a hit by Smith. Head linesman George Gardner threw his flag and interference was called – but on Powell, who was being helped from the field. Gardner ruled Powell instigated the contact before making the catch. The call put a practical end to a 20-10 Georgia victory.

Films later showed Gardner's call incorrect and also that Hill had missed a call on the lateral that resulted in Georgia's first touchdown.

Butts credited his Bulldogs with hanging in when things were going bad. "Carolina completely outplayed us in the first half, but our boys had stickability, and that's what wins games," said Coach Wally Butts, thrilled with Georgia's first perfect record team since 1896.

Still, it was a disappointing afternoon in some ways. The game had little of the anticipated Justice-Trippi juice. Camp, a reserve back, was the leading rusher with 68 yards. Trippi had 54 and Justice a meager 37. Trippi and Rauch played 60 minutes – the last to do so in the Sugar Bowl.

It was also the last Sugar Bowl Fred Digby would cover as a newsman, and the last Warren Miller would see.

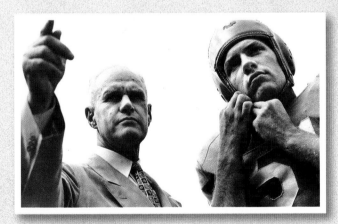

Tar Heel Coach Carl Snaveley gives instructions to "Choo-Choo" Justice.

	1	2	3	4	
Georgia	0	0	13	7	20
North Carolina	0	7	3	0	10

North Carolina: Pupa, 4-yard run. PAT, Cox kick.

Georgia: Rauch, 4-yard run. PAT, Jernigan, kick.

North Carolina: Cox, 18-yard field goal.

Georgia: Edwards, 67-yard pass from Trippi. Kick blocked.

Georgia: Rauch, 13-yard run. PAT, Jernigan, kick.

Individual Leaders

Rushing
Georgia: Trippi 15-56; Smith 8-48.
North Carolina: Camp 8-68; Pupa 14-49; Justice 18-37.

Passing
Georgia: Trippi 2-8, 68 yards.
North Carolina: Pupa 6-10, 95 yards.

Receiving
Georgia: Edwards 1-67, 1 TD.
North Carolina: Powell 3-59.

Georgia		North Carolina
12	First Downs	17
175	Rushing Yards	166
3-14-1	Passing	8-14-1
81	Passing Yards	99
256	Total Yards	265
7-32.7	Punts	6-38.0
0-0	Fumbles – Lost	1-1

Attendance: 68,936.
Teams' remuneration: $139,406.

Texas 27 Alabama 7

"He later realized it was the right decision and he was happy."

It was evident for some time that Tulane Stadium still wasn't adequate for the Sugar Bowl demand. In early 1947, Mid-Winter Sports Association President Sam Corenswet appointed a committee to look into the feasibility of further expansion. Committee Chairman Joseph David presented a plan to extend and double-deck the north end zone stands, which would add 12,241 seats and make Tulane a complete bowl.

The expansion committee was the last Sugar Bowl project for Warren Miller. He suffered a heart attack late on the night of June 21, 1947. The first president of the Sugar Bowl died at 4:30 A.M. the next morning at Touro Infirmary. He was 59.

Herbert J. Schwartz, president of Maison Blanche Co., a New Orleans department store, and Roy Bartlett proposed a memorial to Miller. Schwartz offered to underwrite a substantial sum toward a memorial. It was decided the Most Valuable Player trophy for the Sugar Bowl's outstanding player each year would be named in Miller's honor.

As one pioneer passed from the scene, another was wrestling with his future. The year before, the Sugar Bowl membership asked Fred Digby to become its general manager. The responsibilities had simply become too large for these businessmen to run on a part-time basis.

Digby had been with the *Item* 35 years. Journalism was his vocation and avocation. The Sugar Bowl, at the same time, meant more to him than just some venture; and after he took this position, it became the apex of Digby's fruitful career.

"Leaving the paper was the hardest thing he ever had to do," said Mary Frances Digby. "Finally, I said, 'You'll still be with the same type of people you've always been with, coaches, athletes, etc. I really don't think you'll feel too bad leaving it.' He said maybe I was right. At the time we had two boys in college, and the money sounded good."

Hap Glaudi succeeded Digby as Item sports editor.

"He later realized it was the right decision, and he was happy," said Mrs. Digby.

Alabama had a $50,000 guarantee from the new Dixie Bowl in Birmingham. Alabama's team preferred to play in New Orleans. After the victory over LSU, which secured the Sugar's

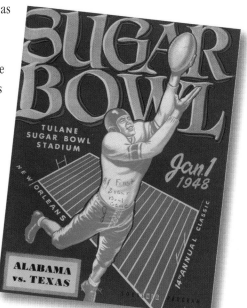

The crowd, including Sugar Bowler Sam Coronswet Jr. (center), settles in before the 1948 Texas - Alabama game.

invitation, the Dixie Bowl offered Coach Frank Thomas a check of $60,000 for the Tide. Thomas went along with his players' wishes.

The Crimson Tide's opponent turned out to be Texas. Texas and Alabama, ranked fifth and sixth nationally, was not a bad attraction. But neither was a champion; it was the first time since 1938 that New Orleans didn't have one. Still, a game between Harry Gilmer, eight-for-eight passing in the 1945 Sugar Bowl, and Longhorn Bobby Layne, 11 of 12 in the '46 Cotton Bowl, promised to be a torrid duel, perfectly suited for a new medium — television.

It was at this Sugar Bowl that America's first woman sportscaster was assigned. Celebrity reporter Jill Jackson did the halftime color. But there was one problem: Women were not allowed in the Tulane press box, and Jackson could not get to the telecasting booth without walking through the press box.

Jackson wrote in 1978, "A meeting was held. It was decreed that Miss Jill Jackson could walk through the press box if she went through before any male member of the press had arrived. Then she must wait until after the game was over, and the press box was cleared of its male content."

"It was the softest landing I had all day."

Harry Gilmer completed his first two passes, meaning after four years and two Sugar Bowls, he was 10-for-10 in the game.

But, like the Justice-Trippi matchup of the year before, the anticipated Gilmer-Bobby Layne aerial display didn't materialize.

After his start, Gilmer misfired. After those two completions, Alabama's offense was virtually finished for the day. And the Crimson Tide was its own worse enemy, committing three critical errors: having a punt blocked, an interception, and a fumble near its end zone. All three resulted in Texas touchdowns.

The combination of Texas' alert defense and the swashbuckling Layne served Alabama its worst defeat in 10 bowl appearances.

Nine minutes and forty seconds after the opening kickoff, Texas scored. Layne drove the Longhorns 85 yards, a drive which included a 44-yard pass to Billy Pyle. The touchdown came on a five-yard pass to Ralph "Peppy" Blount, who was a 21-year-old war veteran and Texas legislator.

"Don't get the idea this was a picnic, despite the score," Blount said. "I made one catch and was knocked out-of-bounds into a pile of photographers on the sidelines. It was the softest landing I had all day."

Playing with its back to the wall almost all day, 'Bama went into the half with a tie after driving to the Texas 8 where Gilmer hit end Ed White. Longhorn Jim Canady almost intercepted as the ball crossed the goal, but White wrestled it away for the touchdown.

But the Longhorns got the winning points when Alabama's Norman "Monk" Mosley attempted a punt from near the Tide goal. George Petrovich broke through to block it, and his roommate Victor Vasicek beat a herd of other Longhorns to the ball in the end zone.

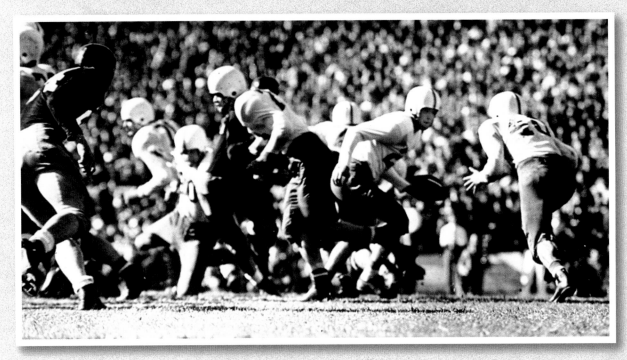

Bobby Layne executes the Texas offense to a T.

Texas quarterback Bobby Layne was recipient of first Miller Memorial Trophy as the Sugar Bowl's MVP.

The worst was yet to come for Gilmer. Lewis Holder anticipated a Gilmer pass from behind the goal line, intercepted at the 20 and returned it for a touchdown. On the next possession, Gilmer, trying to throw from his 20, was tossed for a 10-yard loss and fumbled. Holder recovered at the 5. Layne scored the game's last points on a dive.

"Thing about it," said Gilmer of Layne's 10-of-24 day for 183 yards, "Bobby hit about everything he put up."

Gilmer ended his own sterling college career with his worst statistical performance, three completions on 11 attempts and five yards rushing.

"That was the first year they gave out the MVP award," Blount said, "and I seem to recall walking into Pat O'Brien's (a famed French Quarter night spot) and seeing ol' Bobby drinking Hurricanes out of that trophy." Layne said, "I don't remember that … but I guess it's possible."

Jill Jackson found there was something sacred in the press box after all. It was the passageway to the little room she was allowed to visit, but only after every last man had filed the last word of every story. "Needless to say," she said, "after several hours in that booth, on a cold, cold day, I was a stretcher case when I made it to the other side of the press box. I almost died. It wasn't long after that I relinquished my role as America's only female sports commentator. It has been much easier that way."

	1	2	3	4	
Texas	7	0	7	13	27
Alabama	0	7	0	0	7

Texas: Blount, 5-yard pass from Layne. PAT, Guess kick.

Alabama: White, 8-yard pass from Gilmer. PAT, Morrow kick.

Texas: Vasicek, fumble recovery in the end zone. PAT, Guess kick.

Texas: Holder 20-yard interception return. PAT, Guess kick.

Texas: Layne, 1-yard run. Kick failed.

Individual Leaders

Rushing
Texas: Layne 12-51, Canady 14-24; Pyle 10-22.
Alabama: Noonan 5-20; Tew 7-17.

Passing
Texas: Layne 10-24-0, 183 yards.
Alabama: Gilmer 3-11-1, 45 yards.

Receiving
Texas: Pyle 2-79; Bumgardner 2-52.
Alabama: Davis 1-27; White 1-19, 1 TD.

Texas		Alabama
14	First Downs	7
59	Rushing Yards	41
10-24-0	Passing	4-11-2
183	Passing Yards	62
242	Total Yards	103
5-29.3	Punts	9-38.6
2	Fumbles Lost	1
5	Penalty Yards	15

Attendance: 73,000.
Teams' remuneration: $167,104.
Miller Award recipient: Bobby Layne, Texas quarterback.

Oklahoma 14 North Carolina 6

"But I'm of the opinion."

Dallas apparently was slightly embarrassed. Southwest Conference runner-up Texas pulled down a check from the Sugar Bowl more than $20,000 larger than champion Southern Methodist from the Cotton Bowl game. And SMU had to share its Cotton Bowl receipts with the SWC to help maintain the office of the executive secretary. Texas, because it played in an "outside" bowl, was under no such obligation. What eventually evolved as a result of that situation was the sharing of all SWC bowl revenues with all conference members.

The Sugar Bowl had created an associate membership in 1946 to fill its ranks as death began taking a toll on the original founders. Associate membership, limited to sons, relatives, or sponsorship of extremely close friends, called for two years of service on committee assignments. The first group of associates were given full membership in 1948. Joseph B. David, Jr., Moreau Jumonville, and C. Norman Schwartz constituted the first incoming group. Claude Simons, Jr., (hero of the first Sugar Bowl), Dr. Fred Wolfe, Jr., and Robert Gunsaulus made up the second.

It was tough to select opponents for the 15th Sugar Bowl, the first in the 82,000-seat stadium. Tulane put the squeeze on by unleashing one of its finest teams.

Georgia, Tulane, and Ole Miss were the best of the SEC in 1948; but of these teams, only the Bulldogs were listed in the national Top 10. The Bulldogs were ranked eighth in the nation. The Sugar Bowl wanted a pairing of third-ranked North Carolina and fifth-ranked Oklahoma, led by 33-year-old whiz-kid Coach Bud Wilkinson. Days before the bowl process began to fall into place, Hap Glaudi wrote, "... I'm presently of the opinion that for the Sugar there can be no finer selection than North Carolina and Oklahoma."

This game then would feature Charley "Choo-Choo" Justice in a return appearance, and an Oklahoma team so deep its lines alternated every six minutes.

Jack Mitchell hands off as Oklahoma chips away at North Carolina.

 15TH **SUGAR BOWL CLASSIC**

"I'm Not Allowed To Drive To The Entrance."

The outcome of the North Carolina-Oklahoma game may have been determined three days before when Choo-Choo Charley Justice, the Tar Heels' engine, came down with a virus. For that entire period, a small pre-game steak was all he could eat.

Still, weakened though he was, Justice had North Carolina looking like the favorite it was early, driving to the Oklahoma 7. Then he took the snap from the Tar Heel single-wing formation, started to roll out, stumbled and tried to force a pass in the flat anyway. "I made the mistake of throwing off-bal-

ance," Justice moaned. "He was in the right place at the right time."

Oklahoma linebacker Myrle Greathouse picked it off and brought the crowd to its feet as he picked up three blockers and rumbled 69 yards to the UNC 14 where Eddie Knox tackled him from behind.

Eight plays later, quarterback Jack Mitchell scored from the 1.

The 'Heels got right back in it, taking advantage of a lost

Sooner fumble on the OU 30. A spectacular double reverse on which Bob Kennedy, who had taken the ball from Hosea Rodgers, brought the ball to the 3. Rodgers scored, but Bobby Cox missed the PAT.

North Carolina still had a chance to go into the half in front, going to the 8 in the fading minutes before intermission. But Justice overthrew a pass in the end zone and failed to gain the necessary two yards on fourth down. The Tar Heels didn't get past their own side of the field again until the last stages of the Sugar Bowl.

"North Carolina never used it as an excuse," said OU's Darrell Royal, "but I always felt Charley Justice's strength diminished as the game went along, that his health had a lot to do with it."

On a trick play in the third period, Royal, moving from half-back to quarterback for one snap, threw a long pass to end Frankie Anderson. It was underthrown, but defender Dick Bunting deflected it to the receiver at the 10. Lindell Pearson scored, and then the Sooners concentrated on ball control and defense.

It wasn't a spectacular game, but after Royal planted a kiss on the cheek of Bud Wilkerson in the locker room the young coach mused, "You know, maybe defense isn't a glamorous way to win a Sugar Bowl, but it will win football games and that's what we were down here for, wasn't it?"

Justice, fighting back tears, felt he was the biggest factor in Oklahoma's victory. "I threw that one away," he said, lip quivering.

"I gave them that first touchdown with that bad pass. They've got a great ball club. I lost it. You could say that."

Myrle Greathouse, Oklahoma linebacker, starting back with his 69-yard interception of Charley Justice's pass in the 1949 game.

Jack Mitchell scores first Sooner touchdown in a 14-6 victory over North Carolina.

The deepest cut for North Carolina was yet to come. The Sooners, flushed with victory, showered and dressed quickly, and boarded their buses to return to their hotel. The Tar Heels took their time, letting the sting of the upset fade.

But when the team left the dressing room, the parking area was deserted. The buses assigned to Carolina took Oklahoma's cheering contingent by mistake. After a futile search, Coach Carl Snavely and some team members waved down a passing truck. The team stood in the open back end and the driver brought them to the vicinity of their hotel. "Ya'll have to get off a couple of blocks from the hotel," the driver said. "I'm not allowed to drive to the entrance."

As dark began to envelop New Orleans, the downtrodden Tar Heels slipped unnoticed into a side entrance of the hotel.

	1	2	3	4	
Oklahoma	7	0	7	0	14
North Carolina	6	0	0	0	6

Oklahoma: Mitchell, 1-yard run. PAT, Ming kick.

North Carolina: Rodgers, 2-yard run. Kick failed.

Oklahoma: Pearson, 8-yard run. PAT, Ming kick.

Individual Leaders

Rushing
Oklahoma: Heath 12-58; Thomas 19-51.
North Carolina: Justice 16-84; Rodgers 12-25, 1 TD.

Passing
Oklahoma: Royal 1-1-0, 43 yards.
North Carolina: Justice 6-13-1, 57 yards.

Receiving
Oklahoma: Anderson 1-43.
North Carolina: Weiner 3-35; Kennedy 4-25.

Oklahoma		North Carolina
15	First Downs	12
186	Rushing Yards	128
1-4-0	Passing	8-21-2
43	Passing Yards	82
229	Total Yards	210
5-36.8	Punts	7-38.0
1-1	Fumbles – Lost	0-0
40	Penalty Yards	30

Attendance: 80,383.
Teams' remuneration: $206,162.
Miller Award recipient: Jack Mitchell, Oklahoma quarterback.

Oklahoma 35 LSU 0

"We just don't know very much about them."

In 1949, the Sugar Bowl became the first bowl to work under new National Collegiate Athletic Association (NCAA) guidelines which included: 1) Two representatives from NCAA member schools must be on any noncollegiate or nonconference committee sponsoring a postseason football game. 2) NCAA members cannot take part in more than one such game in the same academic year, or in any game which lacks NCAA approval or doesn't abide by NCAA rules. 3) Competing schools shall agree on officials. 4) The competing schools shall get not less than a third of the seats in the stadium. Each shall get at least one-sixth of them. 5) The competing schools shall get at least 80 percent of the gross receipts. The sponsoring group shall get no more than 20 percent of the gross. 6) The postseason game must be certified by the NCAA's Extra Events Committee.

The 1950 Sugar Bowl pairing took an ironic twist. Second-ranked Oklahoma, which hadn't lost in 20 games, accepted a second consecutive bid. Filling the other spot was more complicated. Louisiana State University was the nation's most-publicized underdog. After losing two early games, the Tigers finished 8-2 and defeated three (Rice, North Carolina, and Tulane) conference champions. The two losses were to Kentucky and Georgia, giving the Tigers a .667 winning percentage in its six SEC games. The SEC rule stipulated a conference school had to win at least 75 percent of its league games to be eligible for bowl competition.

T.P. "Red" Heard, the Tiger athletic director, anticipated victory, and began phoning around the SEC the day before the Tulane game. By 5 P.M. Saturday, LSU had beaten the Greenies and the rule had been thrown out. Digby informed newsmen, "LSU will play Oklahoma."

Gaynell "Gus" Tinsley, the Tiger coach, was the first former Sugar Bowl player to return as a head coach. Tinsley got as much from a team's ability with his 1949 Tigers as any coach ever did. Although ranked ninth nationally (the highest of any SEC team), LSU did not have anyone on the first team all-conference selection. Oklahoma was the country's best rushing team (averaging 320.3 yards a game) and the nation's best defensive team against the rush, giving up an average of 55.6 yards. Tinsley knew he was in trouble. "We just don't know very much about them. We can't find out much either," the coach moaned two weeks before the Sugar Bowl.

There were others who were curious about the Sooners. A resident glanced out a window toward the Biloxi, Mississippi, High School Stadium where Oklahoma was practicing, and noticed someone hiding on a platform in the rear of the residence at 753 Lee Street. Oklahoma officials shortly received a call with the suggestion that someone hide in the yard of the informer and observe the house that adjoined the stadium.

Sooner fullback Leon Heath rambles 34 yards for Oklahoma's final touchdown against LSU.

The next day, a policeman and John "Baby Grand" Scafide, a letterman on Tulane's 1932 Rose Bowl team, closed in on the spy, hidden behind a rigged blanket and ringed with scratch pads and a pair of binoculars. Bill Dennis, a free-lance Biloxi photographer shooting for the Times-Picayune, got a picture as the three flushed out the suspect.

Although his identity wasn't then known, the man photographed was Walter "Piggy" Barnes, a former LSU linesman playing with the Philadelphia Eagles. There was also another person involved, Gustave Adolthus "Goober" Morse, a fan closely associated with the LSU athletic department and who had served in the Navy during World War II with Sooner Coach Bud Wilkinson. Barnes got out of the policeman's clutches and joined Morse on the garage roof where he defied the growing police contingent to come and get him. The police, uncertain as to whether the pair was really guilty of anything or who they were, hesitated. Eventually, Barnes and Morse, buoyed by the uncertainty, climbed down, walked through the police, got into their car, and took off for New Orleans.

"God, they got fighting mad," recalled Morse. "That story just grew and grew all the time we drove to New Orleans until it was front page. Man, we didn't stop until we reached the Roosevelt Hotel. We called Pappy (Art) Lewis (an assistant at Mississippi State about to be named head coach at West Virginia) and asked what he thought we ought to do. 'Well,' he said, 'Your name is M-o-r-s-e, and yours is B-a-r-n-e-s ... tell 'em to make damn sure they don't leave the 'r' out in the spelling.' He was a big help."

Morse insisted to his dying day that he and Barnes were scouting prospects for "Greasy" Neale, the coach of the Eagles. "LSU didn't have a thing to do with it," said Morse. "We just thought it would be a good idea to look 'em over. We could've gone in the main gate, maybe. We didn't exactly scout like we were supposed to. Normally you walk in through the gate and watch 'em work out. So, we didn't do it that way."

It's not a defense most lawyers would be eager to use.

"The coaches were furious," said Sooner quarterback Darrell Royal, "really angry. That gave us additional impetus." Wilkinson was angrily shaking his head, saying, "I can't believe LSU would do such a thing. I just can't believe they'd do us this way."

At a meeting in New Orleans, Wilkinson refused at first to shake Tinsley's hand. LSU officials argued before Bames' and Morse's identities were known that it could have been done by Oklahoma to fire up a complacent team.

Morse chuckled, "Later on, the Atlanta Touch-down Club gave Coach Wilkinson the Walter Barnes-Goober Morse Award, which was a pair of binoculars. Every time I see Coach Wilkinson, we laugh about it now."

But Bud Wilkinson wasn't laughing January 2, 1950.

"I just kept waiting for the bear to jump on him."

Oklahoma Fullback Leon Heath (center) receives the MVP Award from Herbert Benson (left), and Frank Schaub (right).

Harry Wismer and Bud Wilkinson discuss Sugar Bowl for national audience.

Things didn't start the way they finished. Not by a longshot.

"We actually started off well," Tiger back Kenny Konz said later. "We started like we had been playing during the regular season, pretty efficiently. Things at that point were going well."

For 15 minutes the LSU line actually outperformed Bud Wilkerson's alternating units. In two possessions, the Tigers reached the Sooners 15, then the 35.

Sooners quarterback Darrell Royal had to change things up to cope with the LSU defense. "Our drop-back passes were completely useless because they knew exactly what was coming," Royal said. "The passes I did complete were a new set of plays that we didn't practice."

This is how well LSU was playing early against the eight-point favorite Sooners: Nine plays into the second quarter, Royal went to his alternate plan, lateralling to halfback Lindell Pearson, who threw to a wide-open Bobby Goad 40 yards downfield on the 8. The Sooners never did score as LSU held on fourth down inside the 1.

Everything changed in the second quarter with a short drive after an LSU's punt, and a lost fumble. George Thomas going in on a 27-yard pass and a 5-yard run.

Konz seemingly gave LSU a chance to get back in it with a punt that came to rest at the OU 14. Fullback Leon Heath then wheeled out of the Sooner split-T and blazed 86 yards, the longest scoring run of all the previous Sugar Bowls, to effectively end the game.

Armand Kitto, a 157-pound LSU end who chased Heath the

length of the field, said, "... They say on a long run like that, a bear will jump on the runner's back. Well, I just kept waiting for the bear to jump on him and, instead, he jumped on me."

Another lost fumble and interception near the LSU goal led to two more Oklahoma touchdowns, ballooning the score.

In the first 15 games the Sugar Bowl had a remarkable match-making record with an average of seven points separating the opponents. The 1950 game remains the worst scoring differential in Sugar Bowl history. The headline in the *Dallas News* of January 3 read: "Oklahoma Overpowers Minor League LSU Team," ignoring the fact that LSU had beaten both Rice and North Carolina, the Cotton Bowl participants.

Wilkerson graciously understated the SEC's eighth defeat in 12 Sugar Bowls when he said, "If we played LSU a dozen times we'd never play that well against them again, or score that many points. They're too good a team."

This was probably why the Sooners coach didn't take out his regulars until approximately three minutes remained in the game and the score stood at its final 35-0.

	1	2	3	4	
Oklahoma	0	14	7	14	35
LSU	0	0	0	0	0

Oklahoma: Thomas, 27-yard pass from Pearson. PAT, Tipps kick.

Oklahoma: Thomas, 5-yard run. PAT, Tipps kick.

Oklahoma: Heath, 86-yard run. PAT, Tipps kick.

Oklahoma: Royal, 5-yard run. PAT, Tipps, kick.

Oklahoma: Heath, 34-yard run. PAT, Tipps kick.

Individual Leaders

Rushing
Oklahoma: Heath 15-170, 2 TDs.
LSU: West 5-28.

Passing
Oklahoma: Pearson 2-7-0, 74 yards, 1 TD.
LSU: Pevy 5-11-2, 82 yards.

Receiving
Oklahoma: Goad 1-40.
LSU: Baggert 4-50.

Oklahoma		LSU
10	First Downs	8
286	Rushing Yards	38
2-11-2	Passing	9-20-4
74	Passing Yards	121
360	Total Yards	159
7-37.4	Punts	8-33.6
4-4	Fumbles – Lost	4-4
8-40	Penalties – Yards	6-40

Attendance: 82,000.
Teams' remuneration: $238,084.
Miller Award recipient: Leon Heath, Oklahoma fullback.

Kentucky 13 Oklahoma 7

"I still wanted them."

While the conquering Sooners enjoyed a holiday in Cuba after the dismantling of LSU, a question arose concerning LSU's propriety in the Sugar Bowl — but not over the spy incident. The school's Board of Supervisors had approved $250 to each player as an expense allotment, "subject to all rules and regulations of the Southeastern Conference." "That may be questioned," said NCAA President Karl E. Leib at the governing body's annual convention in Chicago, "but only to standardize procedure. We certainly wouldn't quarrel about making up money the boys lost by leaving their jobs to play in the Sugar Bowl and to take care of valid expenses."

Innocent and aboveboard though it was, this sort of action couldn't help but be noticed by critics of bowls (there were 12 games on January 2, 1950) who felt college games were becoming too commercialized. Precisely because of such money-making ventures as bowls, the NCAA at a later meeting in Dallas adopted a recommendation from the previous year. A bylaw was enacted requiring sponsors to give not less than 75 percent of the gross, including such ancillary revenue producers as broadcast, concession, and movie money, to its participating teams. The Sugar Bowl had tried to pay the 80 percent suggested in 1949, but was still paying off the bonds issued for the expansions of Tulane Stadium. The NCAA ruled that bowls with a bond issue before August of 1949 were permitted 20 percent payment toward that debt.

The Southeastern Conference produced two superb teams for the 1950 season — Kentucky, in the fifth year of Coach Paul "Bear" Bryant's five-year plan, and Tennessee. Bryant had already se-

cured the Wildcats' first SEC championship when the Vols and Kentucky played late in the season. An early-season loss to Mississippi State was the only blot on Tennessee's record, and Coach Bob Neyland accepted a Cotton Bowl invitation before the Kentucky game.

Charles C. Zatarain was president of the Sugar Bowl and went to Knoxville to view the second-ranked Wildcats play Tennessee in eight-degree weather with four inches of snow. "It was so bad," said Zatarain, "that at the half I could see the special train just getting fans in. They marched downhill like a troop. It was a miserable day. I went to Knoxville for the purpose of inviting Kentucky, but they lost."

It was a day of reckoning for Bryant, who had held the other bowls off in hope of spending New Year's in New Orleans. "I didn't know where we stood," Bryant said, his hopes of a national championship and undefeated season buried under Knoxville's snowdrifts and his personal jinx against Neyland intact. Bryant was never able to beat the General. "The Orange and Cotton had filled, and I couldn't blame the Sugar Bowl folks if they didn't want us after Tennessee whipped us," said Bear.

Bryant and Zatarain wound up in a hotel room with Kentucky Athletic Director Bernie Shively and Southeastern Conference Commissioner Bernie Moore. "We had a line open to the Sugar Bowl office," recalled Zatarain. "I told them Kentucky was a great team, and that as far as my vote was concerned I still wanted them. The committee talked it over, then came back to tell me to ask Bryant if he'd play if he got an invite. Bear reached out, took the phone, and said, 'If you invite me, I'll beat Oklahoma!'

"If I had gotten shut out of a major bowl after I had passed up several invitations, I would have had a tough time getting back into Lexington," growled Bryant.

The prediction about beating Oklahoma was premature. The Sooners, ranked No. 1 nationally, hadn't been invited yet. It was felt that Coach Bud Wilkinson didn't want to participate in a

Coach Paul 'Bear' Bryant sends Kentucky end Charlie McClendon in against Bud Wilkinson's national champion Sooners.

bowl that year, that he would rather his team retire undefeated after the regular season. His team voted to play in New Orleans a third consecutive year, however, and Wilkinson accepted the invitation. Kentucky dropped to seventh after the Tennessee defeat, but one statistic provides an insight on just how good these teams were: Kentucky and Oklahoma finished their regular season schedules tied for second nationally in fumbles lost with 27. Despite that horrifying stat, there was one loss between them.

Bryant, aware of his promise and the opportunity to atone for the galling Tennessee defeat, tinkered a bit with his defense. Before the game Bryant cleared the locker room of his underclassmen. He turned, stared, and then commanded the seniors in his grumpy, resonant voice, "I want you to give it your absolute all. Play 'til you drop on the field!"

Babe Parilli of Kentucky sets sail for Oklahoma goal.

"They weren't strong enough to move us out of there."

Leon Heath (40) pounds the Kentucky line. Heath gained 121 yards, but Bear Bryant keeps his word as his Wildcats stun Oklahoma, 13-7.

Walt Yowarsky was to get a football baptism against Oklahoma. He was moved to defense – where he had played exactly once before in his life.

Bear Bryant had a plan: to offset Oklahoma's lightning-quick split-T offense, which carried the Sooners to 31 straight victories, he was going to use a multi-look defense, one that often ballooned to a nine-man line.

Four Kentucky tackles were to be incorporated onto the line of scrimmage, including Yowarsky, who was put on the end of the revamped line in the scheme. "Coach Bryant wanted his biggest kids on defense to shoot gaps in the Oklahoma offense," remembered Yowarsky, who was 6-foot-2, 208-pounds.

"That's why, I suppose, I was moved to defense. I think the feeling was that Oklahoma could probably move some on us until they got near the goal, but that they weren't strong enough to move us out of there."

Yowarsky was to go head-to-head with Oklahoma's highly-touted Jim Weatherall, and had specific tasks: Shut down the wide option, consistently harass quarterback Claude Arnold, and, in general, upset the Sooners' offensive precision.

In another bold move, Bryant, ever-mindful of Oklahoma's devastating speed, decided to use an unprotected punter and a line

that did little blocking on punts, believing it was less of a gamble than allowing OU return man Billy Vessels an opportunity to break loose on kicks.

The pressure exerted early paid dividends as Arnold was cracked by Bob Gain behind the line of scrimmage on Oklahoma's first play and fumbled. Yowarsky recovered at the Oklahoma 22.

Quarterback Babe Parilli dropped back on first down, faked a handoff, faked a jump pass, then threw into the end zone for 5-foot-9 Wilbur Jamerson, who out-muscled defender Tommy Gray for possession. Gain kicked the extra point before some of the spectators got to their seats.

After Oklahoma reached the Wildcat 31 in the second quarter, Yowarsky got the ball back for Kentucky by slamming Arnold down for a 12-yard loss. Shortly, Parilli heaved a shot to a streaking Al Bruno, who made an over-the-shoulder reception at the OU 15, then dragged Jack Lockett several yards before going down inside the 1. Jamerson dove over on the next play. Gain missed the conversion.

Kentucky went into the dressing room behind in most of the crucial stats – although, importantly, Parilli was 7-of-9 – but the Wildcats were ahead on the scoreboard 13-0.

On the first Oklahoma possession of the second half, the 'Cats faced their trial by fire. The Sooners got to the Kentucky 4 with a first-and-goal. On third down, from the 2, Yowarsky shot into the line and threw Vessels for a monumental five-yard loss.

"I just knifed through," Yowarsky said. "I don't remember exactly what happened, but I do remember thinking feeling this was a fairly large play."

An incomplete pass ended the series.

With six minutes to go, though, Oklahoma was suddenly again in position to win, when Vessels started wide, drew up and passed 17 yards to Merrill Green for a touchdown.

After Kentucky couldn't move, the Wildcats punted back to the Sooners with plenty of time to score – and steal the victory. Lockett attempted to field the ball on the bounce, but lost control and fumbled. Recovering on the Oklahoma 32 was Yowarsky. That sealed the outcome.

Just as Bryant had blueprinted, Oklahoma won the battle of the stats but fell short on the scoreboard. Two Kentucky statistics may have been the difference: the unprotected punter strategy allowed the Sooners less than a half-yard average on returns, and when the Wildcats needed to control the ball, it did. In the time remaining after Oklahoma's touchdown, only 13 plays were run. The Wildcats wouldn't snap the ball until the game clock was right at its limit – drawing three delay of game penalties.

And there were Yowarsky's contributions: a fumble recovery that led to Kentucky's first touchdown; a touchdown-saving tackle of Vessels at the Wildcat goal line; and his recovery of Lockett's fumble which allowed Kentucky to run off most the clock.

Bryant remembered that game, and the effort his team needed to beat Oklahoma, in his biography. "Early in the game," the Bear related in his biography, "Charlie McClendon came off the field with the side of his face torn off. When I turned to call the trainer and looked around, he was already going back on the field with the defense. His tackling caused three fumbles that day."

McClendon said, "They put cotton on the thing, then froze it. I remember asking the Lord to please 'not let that thing fall down in my eye.' "

	1	2	3	4	
Kentucky	7	6	0	0	13
Oklahoma	0	0	0	7	7

Kentucky: Jamieson, 22-yard pass from Parelli. PAT, Gain kick.

Kentucky: Jamieson, 1-yard run. Kick failed.

Oklahoma: Green, 17-yard pass from Vessels. PAT, Weathersall kick.

Individual Leaders

Rushing
Kentucky: Jamerson 15-58, 1 TD.
Oklahoma: Heath 20-121.

Passing
Kentucky: Parelli 9-12-0, 105 yards, 1 TD.
Oklahoma: Arnold 2-5-0, 21 yards.

Receiving
Kentucky: Bruno 3-57.
Oklahoma: Vessels 2-21.

Kentucky		Oklahoma
7	First Downs	18
84	Rushing Yards	189
9-12-0	Passing	3-8-1
105	Passing Yards	38
189	Total Yards	227
8-41.7	Punts	6-33.4
0-0	Fumbles – Lost	5-5
40	Penalty Yards	30

Attendance: 80,206.
Teams' remuneration: $238,428.
Miller Award recipient: Walt Yowarsky, Kentucky tackle.

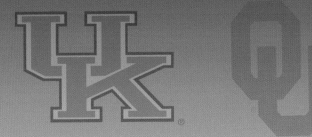

89

Maryland 28   Tennessee 13

"Coach said to vote again."

What the Sugar Bowl had come to mean was put in eloquent perspective with the 1951 Sugar Bowl. After the game, Babe Parilli gave his Sugar Bowl watch to his father. "It was Dad's greatest treasure," said Parilli. "He wore it every day." When Babe's father died at 82, his son fulfilled a final request. "He was buried with the Purple Heart he won in the war and with his Sugar Bowl watch."

Fans, players, and coaches loved the bowls. The major bowls certainly were a symbol of achievement. However, some influential critics did not love the bowls. They thought the bowls fostered crass commercialism and a win-at-all-costs attitude. These critics sought their abolishment and maintained that collegiate sports belonged strictly on campus.

Ironically, in late 1951 it was the Sugar Bowl that gave the critics ammunition and provided the major bowls' defense.

At a September meeting of the presidents of the Southern Conference, the administrators voted to direct their representatives at a scheduled December meeting to vote against allowing any conference school to play in a bowl game that year.

The Southern Conference vote colored the entire bowl scene. Maryland, under Coach Jim Tatum, was clearly one of the premier teams of 1951 and high on all bowl lists. Tatum wanted his third-ranked Terrapins to play on New Year's Day. He told Sugar Bowl President Charles Zatarain he would resign if permission wasn't granted, and he wanted to play the No. 1-ranked Tennessee Volunteers.

Washington, D.C. newspapers predicted Maryland was going to the Cotton Bowl, but in mid-November — with several games remaining — Maryland and Tennessee contracted to play in New Orleans. The early signing seemed to point to increasing competition between the Sugar, Orange, and Cotton Bowls, although the Cotton Bowl vigorously insisted it would not have taken the Terps until Southern Conference permission had been obtained. Maryland had not even taken a telephone poll of its sister schools.

Maryland's defense rested on the fact that any action at the December meeting under the conference constitution would not be binding until September 1953. The Southern Conference bylaws required, however, that the "consent of the conference" be obtained before any member agrees to play in a postseason game. Another bylaw read that all new rules adopted by the conference "shall go into effect the 1st of September, following the annual meeting, or on such a date as the conference may direct." Southern Conference presidents, it seemed plain, intended the bowl ban to go into effect before January 1, 1952.

Clemson, which had accepted a Gator Bowl bid,

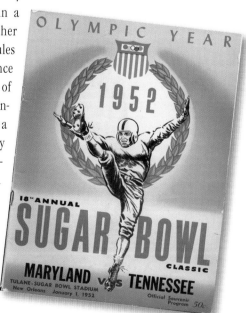

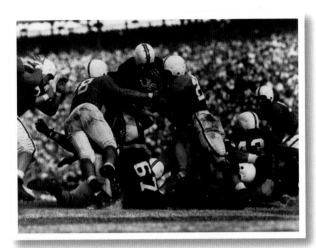

*Maryland battering ram Ed Modzelewski
splinters Tennessee wall.*

and Maryland were placed on a year's probation by the conference. Neither could participate in a football game with another Southern Conference school in the 1952 season. The Sugar Bowl felt this was a family fracas, and it wasn't the concern of the Mid-Winter Sports Association. Of course, if the Sugar or any of the other bowls hadn't extended early invitations, the difficulty would never have arisen.

Aside from its Southeastern Conference and national championships, General Bob Neyland's Tennessee Vols had an additional New Orleans lure. Tennessee's All-American tailback Hank Lauricella had prepped in New Orleans and been overlooked by local colleges. Unbeaten and untied Maryland had a unique brother combination, fullback Ed Modzelewski, who personally had outgained Maryland's regular season opponents (834 yards to 680 yards on a 7.8 average), and Dick Modzelewski, a tackle.

A crowd of several thousand spent the eve of the Terrapin-Vol announcement standing in an icy wind waiting to get tickets. The match, as Zatarain had said, was the one everybody wanted. Not until it was over did anyone realize Tatum had convinced his team to take a shot at the No. 1 team — over a stack of cowboy hats.

Although the Cotton Bowl said it wouldn't invite Maryland until the Southern Conference granted permission, it apparently did. An anonymous Terp confided to Hap Glaudi, "We came damn close to not playing in the Sugar Bowl. We had invitations from the Cotton and Sugar Bowls because Dave Cianelli, the Maryland co-captain, asked us to vote where we wanted to go. We had been talking about it among ourselves

and decided we would like to go to the Cotton Bowl. We knew fellows who played in the Cotton Bowl came home wearing those big cowboy hats and boots. We weren't worried about the team we would play. So they voted for the Cotton Bowl, and Dave went to tell the coach the vote."

Dave returned and told them Coach Tatum said to vote again. If they voted for the Sugar Bowl, the coach said he would buy them all the cowboy hats they wanted. They knew the coach really wanted to play Tennessee, so they voted this time for the Sugar Bowl.

The dispute over the value of bowl games had silenced many university employees, including coaches, not wishing to publicly argue with the academicians. The silence generated a sentiment that perhaps the critics were right, that bowls helped foster a win-at-all-costs attitude and contributed to moving college football from a campus activity to a big business. Timed to coincide with a special NCAA meeting, and virtually the only voice heard in defense of the four major bowls, the Mid-Winter Sports Association issued a statement with a list of 15 contributions the New Year's Day games had made to college football. It ended by laying, "We would cease our program at once if we thought we were doing anything harmful to collegiate sports."

No one seriously doubted the integrity of the major bowl sponsors. The Sugar, like the three other major bowls, had always conducted its activities on the highest collegiate plane. When the NCAA tentatively set up a code of conduct for post-season football, the Sugar Bowl immediately and voluntarily adopted it. The 1950 and 1951 games were conducted under that code.

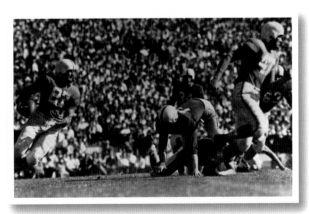

*Hank Lauricella (27) searches for running room
against giant-killing Maryland.*

"Lord, what a day that was."

"The closer it gets, the scareder I get," quipped Jim Tatum, whose coaching role model was General Bob Neyland – and who fully appreciated the capabilities of the Tennessee single wing offense and fundamentally sound defense.

He changed the Maryland defense alternately to four and five-man lines with three linebackers up front in order to cut off Hank Lauricella's wide runs and to put additional pressure on the passer. The changes also upset Tennessee's blocking schemes.

"Coach told us over and over that Tennessee's offense was (really) on the ground," said Terp center Bob Ward. "He told us the Tennessee team had been overpowering teams all season long – four yards, three yards, five, and four again. So we dug in and did our best to stop the running."

Ed Modzelewski, called "Mighty Mo" to distinguish him from his brother Dick "Little Mo," said the Maryland offense was pared to a fairly simple operation. "Our plays were designed to gain three or four yards at a time," he said. Tatum targeted Tennessee All-American guard Ted Daffer as the point of attack. "We decided to slant our offense at Daffer," said Tatum. "He's built pretty much like Bobby (Ward, who would play on Daffer), about 190 pounds and extremely fast for a lineman. But a study of game pictures showed Daffer couldn't handle plays run straight at him. He could make tackles all over the field, but when a play was run straight at him he couldn't handle it."

Neyland's 6-2-2-1 defense was rigged to stop the option and wide plays – all taylor-made for Tatum and his very confident line-buster Mighty Mo. Trying to emphasize the quality of an opposing lineman, a Terrapin assistant told Modzelewski this was biggest, strongest, quickest, and smartest lineman he'd ever face. "Don't worry," Mighty Mo replied. "After I hit him a couple of times he'll be as dumb as I am."

Tennessee's Hank Lauricella, a hometown boy who didn't make good in the 1952 Sugar Bowl.

It was a Terrapin day from the start. Midway through the first quarter, after Modzelewski paved the way, Ed Fullerton scored from the 2.

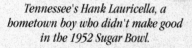

Tennessee cheerleaders poke fun of the Terps before Maryland gets the last laugh.

That was the last time the game was close.

On the ensuing kickoff Lauricella was sandwiched, the ball popped loose, and Maryland was back in business at the Tennessee 13. Fullerton tossed a halfback pass to Bob Shemonski in the end zone.

Maryland, a seven-point underdog to the national champions, was an astonishing two touchdowns ahead with the second quarter barely under way.

Fullerton had his hand in a third Maryland touchdown by intercepting a Lauricella pass and returning it 46 yards for a score.

"Lord, what a day that was," moaned Lauricella, who finished his collegiate career in his hometown with his poorest day as a Tennessee Vol. He had one-yard rushing, fumbled the kick that led to Maryland's second touchdown, and threw three interceptions in five attempts.

Hal Payne finally got Tennessee moving in the latter stages of the half, and put the Vols on the scoreboard with a 4-yard pass to Bert Rechichar.

Modzelewski picked up 46 yards in the third quarter before quarterback Jack Scarbath sneaked in for the last Terp touchdown. That pushed Mighty Mo's rushing total for the day to 153 yards – 72 more than the entire Tennessee team, helping offset Maryland's incredible 120 yards in penalties.

A crushed General Neyland wouldn't even meet with the press; he simply sent out a release praising Tatum and the Terrapins.

For the second consecutive year, a national champion left its bones on the Sugar Bowl field.

	1	2	3	4	
Maryland	7	14	7	0	28
Tennessee	0	6	0	7	13

Maryland: Fullerton, 2-yard run. PAT, Decker kick.

Maryland: Shemonski, 6-yard pass from Fullerton. PAT, Decker kick.

Maryland: Fullerton, 46-yard interception return. PAT, Decker kick.

Tennessee: Rechichar, 4-yard pass from Payne. Kick failed.

Maryland: Scarbath, 1-yard run. PAT, Decker kick.

Tennessee: Payne, 2-yard run. PAT, Rechichar kick.

Individual Leaders

Rushing
Maryland: Modzelewski 28-153.
Tennessee: Payne 11-54, 1 TD; Kozar 9-29.

Passing
Maryland: Scarbath 6-9-0, 61 yards, 1 TD.
Tennessee: Payne 7-14-1, 61 yards.

Receiving
Maryland: Shemonski 3-19, 1 TD.
Tennessee: Rechichar 3-27, 1 TD.

Maryland		Tennessee
18	First Downs	12
289	Rushing Yards	81
7-13-1	Passing	9-19-4
62	Passing Yards	75
351	Total Yards	156
8-38.8	Punts	7-43.0
7-3	Fumbles – Lost	2-2
12-120	Penalties – Yards	2-20

Attendance: 80,187.
Teams' remuneration: $252,464.
Miller Award recipient: Ed Modzelewski, Maryland fullback.

Georgia Tech 24 Mississippi 7

"That made us nationwide."

While the recommendations of the 10 university presidents on the American Council of Education committee were being studied, the NCAA ordered member institutions not to make bowl commitments beyond January 2, 1953. The Southern Conference made its antibowl position official, and punished Maryland and Clemson for their appearances by barring them from participating in Southern Conference regular season games for a year. The Big Seven Conference took an antibowl posture, apparently putting Oklahoma out of the holiday picture. One of the maddest bowl scrambles of all time was the result.

Most observers thought Georgia Tech was heading to the Orange Bowl for a return engagement. However, Fred Digby made a trip to Atlanta and on November 4, an unusually early signing date, Tech surprisingly committed to the Sugar Bowl. Bobby Dodd's Engineers were ranked third in the United Press poll at the time, 6-0-0 with four games remaining.

Dodd, it seems, grabbed the Sugar because of an offer of 14,000 tickets (1,500 more than the SEC requirement) for Tech supporters. That story was printed and denied by both parties. Before the denial, however, Dodd was quoted as saying, "I wanted as many tickets as I could get because I don't want Tech fans saying we let them down. We want as many fans as can go with us."

For an opponent, the Sugar waited for either Maryland or Oklahoma to indicate an interest, despite their respective confer-

ence stands. Another possibility was Mississippi, tied twice in early season games but undefeated since then.

Ole Miss took matters into its hands and forced the bowl to make a decision. Coach Johnny Vaught's Rebels pulled off what was acknowledged to be 1952's college upset of the year by beating Maryland, 21-14. The victory, probably the most important in Ole Miss history, jumped the Rebs to No. 7 in the national polls. It was the school's first Top 10 ranking, and it earned them a Sugar Bowl berth. This was Ole Miss' first major bowl invitation since a 1936 Orange Bowl appearance.

"Bowl fever killed us," said Coach Jim Tatum of Maryland. "We wanted to go to the Sugar badly."

So did Ole Miss, who after its ticket allotment was gone was left with 65,000 supporters still trying to get in. It would-n't be quite as trying for these fans as it was for those who didn't get tickets in past years, though. For the first time, the Sugar, Cotton, and Orange Bowls would be telecast nationally. The Rose Bowl, in populous southern California, a

Georgia Tech Coach Bobby Dodd checks in hotel with assistant Ray Graves.

Little Leon Hardeman (11) swings past Ole Miss defender in first all-SEC pairing.

media center, had already gone national the year before.

Television depended then on coaxial cable, but it didn't yet reach New Orleans. Sugar Bowl President Irwin Poche had a friend, Basil O'Connor, who was president of the national March of Dimes. Poche suggested to O'Connor early in 1952 that a large portion of the proceeds be donated to the March of Dimes when the Sugar Bowl was carried on national TV. O'Connor hit on the idea of asking AT&T to extend the coaxial cable to New Orleans as its donation to the March of Dimes. It may have been a coincidence, but the cable was in place for the 1953 Sugar Bowl.

The Sugar Bowl had received $50,000 for its 1952 telecast, which was carried locally on WDSU-TV and then sent to other cities. On December 10, 1952, the Sugar Bowl and ABC completed arrangements for its national coverage. "That made us nationwide," said Charles Zatarain. "That was the difference between national television and the radio." The network paid $100,000 ($25,000 of which was earmarked for the March of Dimes for the length of the contract) for a combined TV-radio package.

It was a huge step forward, but it was not without additional headaches. ABC was the new network and, because of limited outlets in comparison to NBC and CBS, its largest sponsor withdrew. ABC had to depend on local sponsorship in the cities where the Sugar Bowl was piped. But it was a start.

Coach Bobby Dodd seemed to have a lot more to worry about than mundane things like television, despite his Yellow Jackets being a 7-point favorite. Tech finished the season as undefeated SEC champion, ranked No. 2 nationally. In the last few games, however, his team had incurred numerous injuries, including those of running backs Leon Hardeman (ankle) and Bill Teas (collarbone). This threatened to curtail their playing time, if indeed, they could play at all.

"I see you've still got your watch and chain."

If football really is often a game of inches and close calls, this would be Exhibit A.

Rebel quarterback Jim "King" Lear wasted no time in staking Ole Miss to the lead, sending Wilson Dillard into the end zone eight plays after the kickoff.

Then Georgia Tech, traditionally a slow-starting outfit, fumbled at the Yellow Jacket 19, and quickly the Rebels were at the goal again with two downs to get in. Dick Westerman gained a yard, and then Dillard carried again on fourth down. Players were piled up at the edge of the stripe; when they were untangled, Dillard was ruled an inch short of a touchdown and the ball went over to Tech.

Coach Johnny Vaught protested later, "That ball was over, but they pushed it back two inches!" Yellow Jacket linebacker Larry Morris thought the call could have gone either way.

Another fumble, this one by Lear as the second quarter began, eventually had the 'Jackets camped on the Rebel 9 with a first down. The ball popped loose as Glenn Turner hit the line, but he caught it in midair and gained four yards. Bill Brigman sneaked over from the 2.

Instead of a two-touchdown lead, Ole Miss was all even with Georgia Tech.

The Rebels, though, charged right back with a drive to the 'Jackets' 3. But four plays gained one yard and no points.

"That's where we won the game," said Tech coach Bobby Dodd. "Those goal line stands won the game."
Also, for the first time, Tech was beginning to control the Ole Miss offense. Frank Broyles, a Yellow Jacket assistant who nine years before starred in the Sugar Bowl, explained, "We changed the play of our tackles. All season long we have been crashing our tackles straight ahead on pass plays. There's not but one quarterback in 50 who can get out of the pocket we form that way. Lear was that one in 50. So we changed the angle on them. Instead of charging straight, we sent them crashing out at an angle toward the sidelines."

Leon Hardeman and Billy Teas began finding holes in the line, and soon Tech was at the Ole Miss 5 where Franklin "Pepper" Rodgers kicked a 22-yard field goal to give the Yellow Jackets a 10-7 halftime lead.

"When we went into the locker room I remember Coach Dodd sitting on a table, swinging his legs and drinking a Coke," said George Morris, who was recruited for Tech right out of the Rebel stronghold of Vicksburgh, Miss. "He said, 'Well, boys, it

Leon Hardeman spins away from a Rebel lineman to score a six-yard Georgia Tech touchdown.

looks like we got 'em on the run.' Our reaction was that Coach Dodd wasn't watching the same game we were."

A third Rebel fumble on their 18 led to a six-yard touchdown by the 5-foot-6 bowling ball Hardeman. Ole Miss argued – to no avail – that Hardeman's knee had touched at the 3.

Another controversial call occurred in the third quarter when Lear punted to Bobby Moorhead on the Tech 24. As three blue-shirted Rebels zeroed in on the returner, he gave a last-second motion that was described as "something like a wave to his girl friend." The ball was knocked loose and Ole Miss recovered on the 21. But the officials ruled the faint fair-catch signal had given the coverage enough time to back off, a decision derided by the press.

Tech was in the clear by then, although Rodgers threw a 24-yard touchdown pass to Jeff Knox in the fourth period.

Statistically, little separated the Yellow Jackets and Rebels, but the stats were deceiving. In the first half Ole Miss gained 164 yards. In the second half the Rebels had 123 yards against the revamped Tech defense. Ninety of those second-half Ole Miss yards came after Tech's 24th point.

None of that was the topic of conversation afterward, though. "Three of the four officials who worked in the Sugar Bowl live in Georgia." *Times-Picayune* sports editor Bill Keefe couldn't resist noting. "Two are from Atlanta. Mississippi Governor Hugh White sent letters to George Gardner, president of the SEC Officials Association, and to Bernie Moore, SEC commissioner, saying he had "witnessed the worst officiating I have ever seen."

A Rebel fan spotted Ole Miss President Dr. John Davis Williams walking from the stadium and said, "Well, Doc, I see you've still got your watch and chain, so maybe we're lucky."

	1	2	3	4	
Georgia Tech	0	10	7	7	24
Mississippi	7	0	0	0	7

Mississippi: Dillard, 4-yard run. PAT, Lear kick.

Georgia Tech: Brigman, 1-yard run. PAT, Rodgers kick.

Georgia Tech: Rodgers, 25-yard field goal.

Georgia Tech: Hardeman, 6-yard run. PAT, Rodgers kick.

Georgia Tech: Knox, 24-yard pass from Rodgers. PAT, Rodgers kick.

Individual Leaders

Rushing
Georgia Tech: Hardeman 14-76, 1 TD; Turner 20-56.
Mississippi: Dillard 17-39, 1 TD; Westerman 7-36.

Passing
Georgia Tech: Brigman 5-7-1, 39 yards; Rodgers 4-9-0, 55 yards, 1 TD.
Mississippi: Lear 8-19-3, 122 yards.

Receiving
Georgia Tech: Hardeman 2-24; Marks 2-14.
Mississippi: Slay 1-45; Bridges 2-25.

Georgia Tech		Mississippi
16	First Downs	15
194	Rushing Yards	137
10-18-1	Passing	11-23-3
101	Passing Yards	150
295	Total Yards	287
6-41.8	Punts	7-35.4
5-2	Fumbles – Lost	5-3
5-42	Penalties – Yards	6-60

Attendance: 80,206.
Teams' remuneration: $257,260.
Miller Award recipient: Leon Hardeman, Georgia Tech halfback.

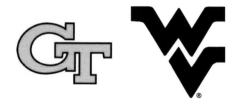

Georgia Tech 42 West Virginia 19

"You taught me too well."

The NCAA Extra Events Committee voted unanimously, January 9, 1953, to continue postseason bowl games that it sanctioned (the recommendation of the 10 presidents of the American Council on Education committee having fallen on deaf ears).

Maryland's acceptance to play in the 1952 Sugar Bowl and Clemson's participation in the Gator Bowl had dramatic results in the spring of 1953. Maryland and Clemson, along with North Carolina, North Carolina State, Wake Forest, Virginia, and South Carolina, broke from the Southern Conference and formed a new league, the Atlantic Coast Conference.

The ACC first approached the Sugar Bowl on the feasibility of a tie-up. The Sugar Bowl would not commit to a tie-up, but assured the ACC if it produced a good team they would receive an invitation. The fledgling conference wanted more, and secured an Orange Bowl tie-up several months later. Miami also tied up the Big Seven, which rescinded its bowl ban. This meant that five of the eight berths in the major bowls were filled automatically. It also meant that the choice of quality football teams for New Orleans had diminished greatly, considering that most of the conference-bowl agreements allowed only the designated representative (not necessarily the champion) to participate.

General Manager Fred Digby wrote that the Sugar Bowl and the Southeastern Conference unsuccessfully discussed a tie-up on several occasions. The Sugar Bowlers were reluctant to tie up be-

cause they had been successful without such an agreement.

In 1954, the Sugar Bowl openly wooed unbeaten West Virginia and the Southern Conference. The conference's executive committee was empowered to lift its bowl ban for one year, but only if a member received a bid.

Several attractive Southwest teams were available, including Texas, Baylor, and high-scoring, colorful Texas Tech. With the SEC championship up for grabs, Alabama, Georgia Tech, Auburn, and Ole Miss all looked promising. At breakfast in Birmingham the morning of the Tech-Alabama game, Irvin Poche, the president of the Sugar Bowl committee, extended an invitation to Engineer Coach Bobby Dodd. With three games remaining and not wishing to put a bowl in a difficult position, Dodd declined, saying he was uncertain about the outcomes of the 'Bama and Duke games. He did promise to contact the Sugar Bowl before accepting another bid.

Alabama defeated Tech, but the colorful Yellow Jackets were still a prime contender. The Cotton

Pepper Rodgers directs devastating attack against West Virginia.

Bowl put out a feeler and the 'Jackets voted to go to Dallas; however, this was with the stipulation that if they were invited to the Sugar Bowl, the team could vote again. Poche told the press November 24 that the Sugar Bowl would wait until that weekend's games were completed before making its selection. Then Dodd called saying he had a Cotton Bowl invitation. An emergency meeting was hurriedly called. Tech players revoted for the Sugar, and Georgia Tech was extended an invitation.

West Virginia's stock had slipped considerably with a 12-7 squeaker against VPI and a 14-20 loss to South Carolina, but the Sugar Bowl chose them to play Georgia Tech. Many thought this was a mismatch, one made because Dodd was allowed to handpick his opponent and the Sugar Bowl didn't want to disappoint the Southern Conference it had been playing to most of the season.

Clark Nealon, sports editor of the *Houston Post*, blistered the Sugar saying it buttered Texas and Baylor "on a contingency basis, then forgot it all and made its mind (up) in one session. The question is: Did Bobby Dodd operate with the "ax"

of having the Cotton Bowl bid in his pocket when he started negotiations with the Sugar Bowl? And did he close with the Sugar Bowl with the understanding he would play West Virginia? ... From what we have cause to believe Dodd dealt within a finger snap of final closing with the Cotton Bowl, then, when news leaked out in the Southeastern area and the Sugar Bowl beckoned, closed with the Sugar Bowl with the understanding he name his own opponent."

Everyone connected agreed the story was too ridiculous to comment on and most of the New Orleans press sugarcoated the situation.

Fred Digby's protégé, Hap Claudi, refused to drop the matter and unrelentingly mocked the selection, referring to the game as the "Lemon Bowl." The situation caused a breach between Digby and Glaudi, who tried to explain to his old mentor, "I only did what you would have done. You taught me too well."

Georgia Tech, fifth-ranked and weighing an average of 12 pounds less than the ponderous 10th-ranked Mountaineers, was made a 12 1/2-point favorite.

"It got them off to a bad start."

West Virginia tackle Sam Huff.

Be careful what you plan for is a paraphrase of an old maxim, but in this case it truly applied to West Virginia coach Art "Pappy" Lewis.

Lewis put in an 8-3 defense in order to shut off Georgia Tech's wide plays, and hopefully force the Yellow Jackets into the Mountaineer line, which averaged a mammoth for the day 228 pounds.

And Tech coach Bobby Dodd seized on what turned into a golden opportunity.

Lewis was a good coach. Dodd was one of the great ones – and especially in bowl games. He coached the Yellow Jackets to a 165-64-8 record, and to nine victories in 13 postseason

games. The unorthodox Dodd simply didn't believe in working his squad very hard, which made him popular with his athletes. "During the fall we did not scrimmage once the season began," Dodd once explained, "You get your players hurt, tired out, and mentally depressed. So I didn't do it, and if it worked during the season, it should work in a bowl game ... the players had confidence in our system. I convinced them that they could have fun and (still) win."

And Dodd was expert at deciphering opponents. All-American linebacker George Morris said succinctly, "We just knew Coach Dodd was smarter than the other coach."

Not any particular coach, mind you. *Any* opposing coach is what Morris meant.

It sort of worked out that way in the Sugar Bowl, where Dodd's teams would have fun three times in a four-year span – and never lose.

As it turned out, the Mountaineers' defense did shut down Tech's running game but opened the airways for quarterback Franklin "Pepper" Rodgers, who hit on passes of 20, 15, 9, 11 and 24 yards and a touchdown on Tech's first possession.

That's pretty much the way rest of the afternoon went, too.

On Tech's second series, Rodgers threw another touchdown pass, two-yards to Jimmy Durham.

Despite its dismal start, West Virginia didn't run up a white flag. Tommy Allman took a pitch-out sweep and went 60 yards for an apparent TD. The Mountaineers, though, were called for holding, and the touchdown was brought back. Danny Williams did get in the end zone with a five-yard run following a 70-yard drive, though Larry Morris blocked Jack Stone's PAT.

And back came the Mountaineers right afterward, recovering a fumble on the Tech 25 and inching 20 yards. But end Cecil Turner threw quarterback Freddie Wyant for a 16-yard loss, and an opportunity to climb within a point of Georgia Tech was lost on fourth down when Joe Marconi dropped a Wyant pass in the end zone.

"Won't say it demoralized them," Lewis said of Allman's called-back run and Marconi's drop, "but it got them off to a bad start."

Rodgers again passed the Yellow jackets downfield, and Henry Hair caught a 2-yard throw to inflate the halftime score to 20-6. At intermission Tech had a record 233 yards passing to 13 for West Virginia, and the Sugar Bowl was sealed.

Rodgers, who finished with 16 completions in 26 attempts for 195 yards, was clearly the dominant player and was named recipient of the Miller Memorial Trophy.

The West Virginia locker room was numb. Lewis said, with eyes glistening, "We thought we'd get beat, but not by that much." Guard Sam Huff couldn't express himself, at least not with the emotion of Wyant who spat out, "They ain't so good!"

But Tech was now 2-0 in Sugar Bowls.

	1	2	3	4	
Georgia Tech	14	6	9	13	42
West Virginia	0	6	0	13	19

Georgia Tech: Hensley, 24-yard pass from Rodgers. PAT, Rodgers kick.
Georgia Tech:: Durham, 2-yard pass from Rodgers. PAT, Rodgers kick.
West Virginia: Williams, 5-yard run. Kick failed.
Georgia Tech: Hair, 5-yard pass from Rodgers. Kick failed.
Georgia Tech: Rodgers, 18-yard field goal.
Georgia Tech: Hardemann, 23-yard run. Kick failed.
West Virginia: Marconi, 1-yard run. PAT, Allman kick.
Georgia Tech: Ruffin, 43-yard run. Kick blocked.
West Virginia: Allman, 1-yard run. Kick failed.
Georgia Tech:: Teas, 9-yard run. PAT, Turner kick.

Individual Leaders

Rushing
Georgia Tech: Ruffin 3-58, 1 TD; Teas 9-32, 1 TD.
West Virginia: Anderson 13-57; Moss 5-36.

Passing
Georgia Tech: Rodgers 18-26-2, 195 yards, 3 TDs.
West Virginia: Wyant 4-15-2, 29 yards; Anderson 3-3-0, 49 yards.

Receiving
Georgia Tech: Hensley 4-73, 1 TD; Davis 4-33; Hardemann 3-37.
West Virginia: Papetti 3-51; Hillen 2-14; Allman 2-13.

Georgia Tech		West Virginia
19	First Downs	19
170	Rushing Yards	233
20-35-2	Passing	7-16-2
268	Passing Yards	76
438	Total Yards	301
1-36.0	Punts	2-28.5
3-1	Fumbles – Lost	5-4
7-45	Penalties – Yards	5-35

Attendance: 71,666.
Teams' remuneration: $289,338.
Miller Award recipient: Franklin "Pepper" Rodgers, Georgia Tech quarterback.

Navy 21   Mississippi 0

"That streetcar down in New Orleans."

After the debacle of the 1954 game, the Mid-Winter Sports Association felt obligated to reestablish itself as the premier bowl. The Sugar went hunting in new territory: the service academies. Army and Navy still had college football glitter, and both were excellent football teams. Either one would be a bowl coup.

In the Deep South, fate played a hand in the Sugar Bowl's 1955 pairing. Ole Miss ran away from the SEC field with a 9-1-0 record. The Rebels led the country in total defense and were fifth in offense, although some critics pointed to a "patty-cake" schedule. Arkansas, the only nationally ranked team Ole Miss played, defeated the Rebs, 6-0. However, Mississippi played exciting football and won the SEC championship.

Coach Johnny Vaught was asked how a Sugar Bowl invitation would be received in Oxford after his squad whipped LSU. Vaught replied he would like to return "because I'm still unhappy over the thing that happened down there two years ago (Georgia Tech's 1953 victory)." Rebel players weren't concerned about a game played two years ago. They wanted a Cotton Bowl invitation for another shot at Arkansas. Razorback Coach Bowden Wyatt slammed that door in Ole Miss' face by telling Dallas officials he saw no reason why he should give a regular season opponent a repeat game.

Army wasn't interested in Sugar Bowl "feelers." However, Navy was, and the Cotton Bowl also moved into the picture. Navy had lost two close games to Pittsburgh (19-21) and Notre Dame (0-6) but was a colorful and courageous squad. Coach Eddie Erdelatz, after a particularly satisfying win, likened his team "to that streetcar down in New Orleans, the one they call Desire." Thus, Navy became the "Team Named Desire."

Fullback Joe Gattuso felt certain, because of the rumors swirling around the Naval Academy during the week, that if the Midshipmen could defeat Army they would be allowed to participate in a bowl. End Ron Beagle, the Player of the Year, didn't believe it. But at halftime of a dogfight with the favored Cadets, it was confirmed. "At the half of our game with Army — we were leading 21-20, you know — Coach Erdelatz asked for our attention," said Beagle. "He told us, 'Go out and finish the job. Beat Army today and you're in

A streetcar named Desire and its namesake Navy squad before the 1955 Sugar Bowl.

the Sugar Bowl game!' That's all we wanted to know. We wanted to beat Army real bad, and we wanted to go to the Sugar Bowl, too. We went out and got both."

After beating Army, 27-20, Navy was selected as the first service academy to play in a bowl since the 1924 Rose Bowl. Navy's bowl opponent was Mississippi, who beat Mississippi State 14-0 in its last game.

According to Sugar Bowl mythology the nation applauded Navy, but realistic odds-makers looked upon the Middies as lambs about to be sacrificed to the lordly Rebels. Before the game opened, Navy was picked as a three-point favorite, a fact that irritated Vaught. "It makes no difference if Navy is the favorite," said a miffed Vaught. "I saw pictures of Navy's games with Notre Dame and Army and I'm sure we're going to win." But before the game started, Navy halfback Bob Craig came down with tonsillitis and tackle Jim Royer sustained a hip injury and both were unable to play. Noting those losses against an opponent that was 15 pounds heavier, with much deeper

reserve strength and more experience, Ole Miss' stock with the odds-makers climbed. By New Year's Eve, they were a point-and-a-half favorite.

A blast from the frigid winds of social change made a mark on the 1955 Sugar Bowl. Clarence Mitchell, a member of the National Association for the Advancement of Colored People in Washington, protested to Secretary Charles R. Thomas that Sugar Bowl tickets read they were for use by whites only and that others were subject to ejection. Actually, blacks had been attending the Sugar Bowl from its inception, although they were seated in segregated areas.

Secretary Thomas replied to Mitchell by telegram, stating the Navy Department had distributed its 13,000 tickets without regard to racial restrictions, "and will be so honored regardless of any printing thereon." "The Navy statement speaks for itself," said Bernie Grenrood, then Sugar Bowl president. "No other comment is necessary."

"If you think you can make it, go for it."

Joe Gatuso of Navy high-steps through Ole Miss' vauted defense.

Quarterback George Welsh stepped into the Navy huddle. All he heard was his teammates pleading for a play, not a punt.

It was fourth down with a foot to go at Navy's own 39, against Ole Miss' imposing defense – and on the game's first series.

"The fellows all said, 'C'mon George, we can make it. Let's try it." Welsh related. "So we had (Joe) Gattuso slant off tackle."

Gattuso gained four yards. Mythology of this memorable game says this call spurred the Midshipmen to its victory. Actually, Ole Miss was offsides and, in fact, Navy accepted the five-yard penalty. But the play seemed to prick the poise and pride of the Rebels. "The coach tells us only one thing," explained Navy second-string quarterback Dick Echard. "If you think you can make it, go for it. Because if you believe you can, then you will."

"When I saw them do that," said Coach Eddie Erdelatz, "I knew we were going to play a whale of a game."

Welsh ran options for short, but surprisingly consistent, gains, sending a flanker to one side, then running the play the opposite way. It led to a Gattuso touchdown of three yards. John Weaver, who had a 24-yard gain in the drive, kicked the extra point.

Navy's bug-sized defense, using 14 different looks, played head-to-head with the fearsome Rebel offense the remainder of the quarter. In the second period, it was Navy who again threatened, going from its 40 to the Ole Miss 8. Three plays at that point produced nothing. On fourth down Welsh threw a pass to Ron Beagle, who made a flying catch right on the goal line. It was originally called a touchdown, but head linesman Charles Wood, who was in better position to judge, overruled it. Wood said that while Beagle's feet were in the end zone, he fell just outside when he made the catch. Film revealed it to be a highly questionable call.

Navy probably secured the victory in the third quarter when Gattuso broke through right tackle, going 17 yards to the Ole Miss 17. On fourth down, after picking up one yard, Weaver

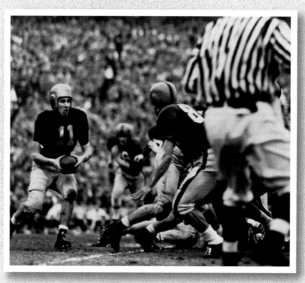

Georgia Welsh (11) directs the 'Team Named Desire agaiat Ole Miss.

Middle bench in a brief moment of concern during Navy's 21-0 cruise over Ole Miss.

eased into the end zone and Welsh threw straight into the Rebel coverage. Weaver, with Billy Kinard's arms around his neck and Eagle Day practically inside his jersey, went up and made a miraculous catch.

Day, one of the nation's outstanding quarterbacks, gave the outplayed Rebels a sliver of hope with a 72-yard punt to the Navy 7. If Ole Miss could hold them, or force Navy to make a mistake, the Rebels might turn the tide. Instead, Navy ran off four successive first downs, one on a 22-yard run by Gattuso and another on a Gattuso fumble that bounced 14 yards up-field to be recovered by teammate Wilson Whitmire. Then Weaver raced 21 yards around right end. Gattuso scored from two yards out on his third consecutive carry from the 5.

Gattuso (111 yards) and Weaver (106 yards) each outrushed the Ole Miss offense, which had just 78 yards rushing and 43 passing.

"The difference," Erdelatz told the press, "was desire." The coach asked the media to move from the center of the locker room, saying he wished to speak to his team. "Men," he said simply, "you were terrific today. Let's get down on our knees and thank God." A moment of silence was offered by the grateful Midshipmen who knew full well what they had accomplished.

Then Erdelatz leaped up, fist in air, and shouted, "Now let's go raise hell in Noo Awleans."

	1	2	3	4	
Navy	7	0	14	0	21
Mississippi	0	0	0	0	0

Navy: Gattuso, 3-yard run. PAT, Weaver kick.

Navy: Weaver, 16-yard pass from Welsh. PAT, Weaver kick.

Navy: Gattuso, 1-yard run. PAT, Weaver kick.

Individual Leaders

Rushing
Navy: Weaver 16-106; Gattuso 16-111, 2 TDs.
Mississippi: Cothen 7-24.

Passing
Navy: Welsh 8-14-0, 78 yards, 1 TD.
Mississippi: Day 2-9-0, 16 yards; Patton 3-6-0, 27 yards.

Receiving
Navy: Beagle 3-19.
Mississippi: Muirhead 2-16.

Navy		Mississippi
20	First Downs	5
295	Rushing Yards	78
12-28-4	Passing	5-18-0
147	Passing Yards	43
442	Total Yards	121
4-33.8	Punts	9-36.1
1-0	Fumbles – Lost	3-1
1-15	Penalties – Yards	6-50

Attendance: 80,190.
Teams' remuneration: $320,000.
Miller Award recipient: Joe Gattuso, Navy fullback.

Georgia Tech 7   Pittsburgh 0

"The South stands at Armageddon."

Something was amiss. As fine as the Ole Miss-Navy pairing was, something of the old Sugar Bowl matchmaking magic was gone. Not since the 1951 Kentucky-Oklahoma game had a Sugar Bowl been close, and this from an organization, which took extraordinary pride in its thrillers. To be sure, the task was more difficult because of all the tie-ups by the other major bowls: the Orange with the Big Seven and the Atlantic Coast Conferences, the Cotton with the Southwest, and the Rose with the Big Ten and Pacific Coast Conferences.

The Mid-Winter Sports Association still felt it could get the best game possible by remaining "open," but it was also feeling a certain amount of self-imposed pressure to produce the kind of exciting, close games that had become a Sugar Bowl hallmark.

West Virginia, despite the debacle in New Orleans two years before, and Navy were high on the Sugar's checklist for the 1956 game. Mississippi and Georgia Tech were the most desirable Southeastern Conference teams. Paul DeBlanc and Claude Simons scouted the West Virginia-Pittsburgh game for the Sugar Bowl. The sixth-ranked Mountaineers had an 11-game winning streak broken, 26-7. Although it had lost three games, two to highly ranked Oklahoma and Navy, Pitt greatly impressed the scouts and newsmen Hap Glaudi and Steve Perkins.

An invitation was extended to Pittsburgh with the worst

record (7-3) of a Sugar Bowl team since 1945 – and it was accepted. Georgia Tech would be the opponent.

Then began a period of stormy controversy. Fifteen years after Louis Montgomery watched from the press box as his Boston College teammates achieved one of their school's most stirring moments, a Sugar Bowl team's roster (Pittsburgh) again included the name of a black player, fullback Bobby Grier.

Georgia Governor Marvin Griffin focused a spotlight on Grier and the Sugar Bowl, and the national press made the game a cause celebre. New Orleans was caught in a no-win situation, although mixed athletics were not new to the city. Loyola University competed against blacks in basketball and, indeed, days before Grier would set foot in Tulane Stadium, a 6-foot black sophomore named Al Avant would play for Marquette in the Sugar Bowl basketball tournament.

The flap roared across national front pages when Griffin said in a telegram to Regent Chairman Robert O. Arnold, "It is

Fred Digby points to a dream come true.

my request that athletic teams of units of the university system of Georgia not be permitted to engage in contests with other teams where the races are mixed on such teams or where segregation is not required at such games ... The South stands at Armageddon."

Arnold indicated the board had no control over university athletic policies, and Pittsburgh announced that Grier would be on the Sugar Bowl squad and he would "travel, eat, live, practice, and play with the team." A school spokesman added, "If Grier regains his midseason form he will be our starting full-

back. Heck, he intercepted the pass (against Penn State) that put us in the Sugar Bowl."

In Atlanta, Tech was mightily trying to ignore the governor. A Georgia Tech spokesman said, "Our boys voted to play in the Sugar Bowl, and we will not break our contract, especially since Georgia and Tech have played against Negroes before and there has been no criticism."

Security around the governor's mansion had to be increased at night, as it became a rallying area for torch-carrying throngs of protesting Tech students. The Southern press, for the most part, joined Georgia Tech professors, students, alumni, and players in the disagreement with Griffin.

The individuals, whose opinions on the matter should have counted most, the Georgia Tech athletes, were finally asked what their thoughts were. Quarterback Wade Mitchell said he considered the entire situation "silly." Mitchell went on, "I personally have no objection to playing a team with a Negro member on it, and, as far as I know, the rest of the boys feel the same way."

The Georgia Board of Regents voted 10-1 to allow the team to participate, although there was a soothing rider attached for the segregationists. It barred future games in the state of Georgia between Georgia colleges and integrated teams.

Pete Neft (18) shows air-arm while on the run behind blocker Bobby Grier (38) in the Pitt-Georgia Tech war.

"You don't really believe that, do you."

Don Ellis reaches for the ball as Bobby Grier goes down in the biggest, and most controversial, play of 1956.

From the Pitt 32, where Tech recovered a fumble, quarterback Wade Mitchell lofted a soft pitch to right end Don Ellis near the goal.

The ball sailed over both the heads of Ellis and defender Grier.

Interference on Grier was called.

"I was outside in what we called an 'Eagle' defense," said Grier. "I went back with the player and when I turned to look up and see where the ball was, I got pushed in the back. The ball was over his head and I was lying on the ground, then he (back judge Frank Lowry) threw a flag and said I pushed him ... with me lying on the ground, looking up and the ball over both our heads."

Ellis said, "I got behind him. Then, when I turned around to look for the pass, he shoved me in the stomach, knocking me off stride. It was a fine pass, and I think I could have caught it."

Realizing a teammate was going to be under a tremendous strain, the Pittsburgh players tried to keep things light.

"At first, we were offended," said guard Hal Hunter, one of the Panther co-captains.

"Then, to loosen him up and try to take the pressure off him, we played practical jokes on Bobby during practice for the Sugar Bowl."

But things turned pretty grim quickly once the Sugar Bowl began.

As the game began, the Tulane Stadium clock malfunctioned – which would have ramifications throughout – and an immediate controversy involving Bobby Grier flared up.

The film was inconclusive, but indicated Grier may have been out of position, stumbled, and fell a few yards in front of Ellis. A roar of protest erupted from the stands as the ball was placed on the 1-yard line. Immediately the reporter sitting next to New Orleans sports writer Buddy Diliberto began typing a bulletin that read, "Bobby Grier, the first Negro to play in the Sugar Bowl, was roundly booed by a crowd of 80,175 spectators today in Tulane Stadium."

"You don't REALLY believe that, do you?" shouted the incredulous Diliberto. "They're booing the call, not Grier!"

After Pitt was penalized a half-yard for offsides, Mitchell followed the surge of his line and made into the end zone by inches. He then added the extra point.

The Panthers took complete control in the second quarter, allowing the Yellow Jackets just five plays. With time being kept on the field, a 79-yard drive put Pitt at the Tech 1 with time running out in the first half. Franklin Brooks and Allen Ecker stopped what appeared to be a hurried quarterback sneak on fourth-and-goal. "Corny" Salvaterra, the Pitt quarterback, said he thought there was plenty of time to at least get a play off.

Pittsburgh had two opportunities to score in the third quarter, driving to the Tech 16, with a 26-yard crowd-pleasing run by Grier that almost went all the way, where an interception ended the threat; and to the 7, where a fumble killed the drive.

In the fourth period, third-string quarterback Darrell Lewis lit a fire under the Panthers, and would have scored himself on a sweep but for a last-second tackle that sent him pin-wheeling out-of-bounds at the 10.

Before going to the huddle, Lewis asked an official how much time remained and he said he was told two minutes and 39 seconds. Hunter also asked and said he was told only 39 seconds. In either case there was enough time for several plays. Ralph Jelic gained five yards on a power play. As Pitt lined up again, the officials began waving their arms, signaling the game's end. "I thought we could get off another play easily," Lewis protested.

Time has a way of affecting memory, particularly in a game like this where Pitt had all the stats and Georgia Tech had the scoreboard. Both Hunter and Lewis felt the loss was racially motivated, pointing to a "crew of Southern officials." It may or may not have been competent, but it was not a crew of Southern officials. It was a split crew, and one agreed to beforehand by Pittsburgh.

In a sort of coda, it should be noted Grier finished as the Sugar Bowl's leading ground-gainer with 51 yards.

The game was a distinct landmark in Sugar Bowl history. From its inception the Mid-Winter Sports Association strived for intersectional pairings. But after the 1956 game, the Sugar Bowl was forced to retrench because of the political climate of the times, and the Louisiana Legislature. For the next decade the Sugar Bowl would have great teams and great games. But not a single team would come from outside the Southeastern, Southwest, or Atlantic Coast conferences.

	1	2	3	4	
Georgia Tech	7	0	0	0	7
Pittsburgh	0	0	0	0	0

Pittsburgh: Mitchell, 1-yard run. PAT, Mitchell kick.

Individual Leaders

Rushing
Georgia Tech: Owen 7-29; Mattison 7-27.
Pittsburgh: Grier 6-51; Cimarollo 11-37.

Passing
Georgia Tech: Mitchell 0-1; Vann 0-2.
Pittsburgh: Salvaterra 4-9, 50.

Receiving
Pittsburgh: Walton 4-54; Glatz 2-48.

Georgia Tech		Pittsburgh
10	First Downs	19
142	Rushing Yards	217
0-3-1	Passing	8-18-1
0	Passing Yards	94
142	Total Yards	311
6-33.8	Punts	4-38.7
2-0	Fumbles – Lost	4-2
1-15	Penalties – Yards	8-72

Attendance: 76,535.
Teams' remuneration: $304,000.
Miller Award recipient: Franklin Brooks, Georgia Tech guard.

Baylor 13 Tennessee 7

"Some kind of Dixie championship only."

In the mid 1950s, the federal government began moving in earnest to guarantee equality in all phases of American life, but southern state governments began passing segregation laws as restrictive as any before. Louisiana passed more than a dozen segregation laws in 1956, some designed to limit interracial social and athletic activity. The crux of Act No. 579, vigorously fought by the Mid-Winter Sports Association but signed into law by Governor Earl K. Long, was a prohibition of racially mixed athletic events.

The Sugar Bowl, well aware that such a law could make its events backyard triflings, voiced the only opposition to the legislation. Noticeably silent were Tulane, LSU, and Loyola, all of which had games scheduled with integrated teams.

Long signed the law and three of the teams – Notre Dame, Dayton, and St. Louis – scheduled for the basketball tournament withdrew. The Sugar then fought for a plan to exempt cities over 100,000 from the legislation. If passed, the bowl planned to work around the segregated stands problem by having no restrictions on the tickets sent to visiting schools, but every other section would be segregated. It was a well-thought-out plan, designed to please every faction. But the bill did not pass.

Most felt like Shirley Povich of the *Washington Post*, who wrote, "For the Sugar Bowl, the upshot is that it will be known henceforth merely as a sectional contest to settle some kind of

a Dixie championship only." DeBlanc said wearily, "That's the law and we will try to live under it."

It was a law that obviously couldn't stay on the books for long, but the Sugar was apprehensive about becoming a small regional contest before the prohibition was rescinded. Already there were problems with television. The contract with ABC was up and the network had reservations about renewing because the newly enacted law (Act 579) bothered prospective national sponsors.

With its boundaries greatly diminished, the Sugar Bowl went looking in 1957 for the best game possible. As it happened, the most desirable non-SEC teams were also ineligible. Oklahoma, the nation's No. 1 squad, couldn't participate in the Orange Bowl because of the Big Seven's no-return rule; Texas A&M, the champion of the Southwest Conference, wouldn't be able to play in the Cotton Bowl because it was on NCAA probation, as was sixth-ranked Miami—the Sugar's favorite.

The spot usually reserved

Johnny Majors (45) flying into the Baylor line.

for a Southeastern Conference team figured to be no problem because second-ranked Tennessee and Georgia Tech were both exceptional teams.

Digby was still working miracles. His deep friendship with Athletic Director Bob Neyland helped land Tennessee. Then Baylor became Digby's focal point. The Bears were a good, solid football team (although unranked) that wasn't going to a major bowl because of midseason losses to Texas A&M and Texas Christian by a total of seven points. The Sugar must have looked pretty good to Baylor, too. The match was made.

A coast-to-coast television and radio coverage agreement finally was made between the Sugar Bowl and ABC when General Motor's Oldsmobile Division consented to sponsorship.

With the third- (Iowa) and tenth- (Oregon State) ranked teams, the Rose Bowl drew the quality New Year's pairing of 1957. Considering the circumstances, the Sugar didn't do badly with second-ranked Tennessee.

Del Shofner (27) sweeps behind the blocking of Larry Hickman (38) and quarterback Bobby Jones (12) in Baylor's 13-7 upset of Tennessee.

"Mister..."

Cheerleaders awaiting the Tennessee Vols.

This was a bright day, but a dark Sugar Bowl.

On the football front, after studying the Tennessee films, what the underdog Baylor Bears feared most was not the Vols: it was overconfidence.

"Tennessee, with its single wing offense, is going to get about as far as our ends let 'em," crowed Bears right end Jerry Marcontell beforehand. Second-string fullback Larry Hickman said afterward, "We knew they were good, but we also knew we could muscle with them. We knew we could win."

The Bears did, but with a backdrop of a hideous on-the-field incident, one which overshadowed Baylor's major accomplishment of beating the previously unbeaten Vols.

That, though, wouldn't occur until the second half.

Right off the Bears seemed in control, driving to the Vols' 4 to start the game, and where the Tennessee band, directed by an Elvis Presley imitator in a cerise jacket, blared the strains of "Hound Dog" at the Baylor team as a missed field goal ended the threat.

In the second quarter, Del Shofner, flanked to the right on the 12, went down and in on a pass pattern, taking the defensive back with him. Marcontell went down and out, found himself open, grabbed the ball on the goal line and fell in for the touchdown. Barry's conversion was wide, but at the half stats verified Baylor's dominance: The Bears had 186 yards rushing to Tennessee's 82.

Johnny Majors, though, had the Vols smoking to open the second half, returning a punt to the Tennessee 46. After a roughing penalty put the ball on the 39, Majors carried on nine of 11 plays, overcoming a 15-yard penalty in the process, and scored around end from the 1. Sammy Burklow kicked the PAT and Tennessee was in front 7-6.

Everyone braced for the exciting finish that appeared to be developing ... when the Sugar Bowl took a sinister turn.

Tennessee guard Bruce Burnham and Baylor guard Charley Horton got into a scuffle on the ground. Burnham got in a couple of punches. Seeing that, Hickman rushed in and kicked Burnham in the face.

The defenseless Vol lay sprawled on the field quivering, ribbons of blood covering his features. "I thought the boy would be gone before we got him off the field," commented a physician on the scene. "There's no way anyone could excuse what I did," Hickman reflected decades later. "I think I was so keyed up ... In my mind I saw him doing something he shouldn't, and I guess I just flashed temper."

Hickman was banished from the game and Burnham was

Baylor flag-wavers at the Sugar Bowl.

taken to Touro Infirmary. For the rest of the Sugar Bowl, Hickman sat on the Baylor bench, head in palms, sobbing.

The Bears turned a fourth-quarter opportunity into the winning points. Majors took a Shofner punt at the Vols' 6, raced out to the 15 where he was smacked by Bill Glass, the ball popping out. Ruben Saage recovered for Baylor. Buddy Humphrey – one of four quarterbacks used by Baylor – sneaked over six plays later.

Most of the post game talk centered not on a magnificent upset, but on the kicking incident. Burnham had a concussion and broken nose, but it seemed he wasn't in nearly so much pain as Hickman, who stood in a corner of the Baylor locker room still crying. When approached by Tom Fox of the *New Orleans Item* Hickman again buried his head in his hands and "quivered like a child. Once he raised his head and again tried to speak. 'Mister' was all he was able to say before he burst into tears again."

Baylor's victory represented the third Sugar Bowl loss in 16 years for a Tennessee team that entered the game undefeated and untied.

Hickman visited the recovering Burnham the next day at the hospital to apologize personally. The night before at a Sugar Bowl post-game party, the 20-year old stood before the Volunteer team and softy said, "I hope someday that boy and you Tennessee players can find it in your hearts to forgive me for what I've done. I'm sorry, truly sorry."

Volunteer do-it-all back Majors.

	1	2	3	4	
Baylor	0	6	0	7	13
Tennessee	0	0	7	0	7

Baylor: Marcontell, 12-yard pass from Jones. Kick failed.

Tennessee: Majors, 1-yard run. PAT, Burklow kick.

Baylor: Humphrey, 1-yard run. PAT, Berry kick.

Individual Leaders

Rushing
Baylor: Shofner 14-88.
Tennessee: Majors 15-59, 1 TD; Bronson 8-56.

Passing
Baylor: Jones 2-4-0, 19 yards, 1 TD.
Tennessee: Majors 1-7-2, 16 yards.

Receiving
Baylor: Marcontell 3-24, 1 TD.
Tennessee: Urbano 1-16.

Baylor		Tennessee
13	First Downs	10
275	Rushing Yards	146
3-11-0	Passing	1-10-1
24	Passing Yards	16
299	Total Yards	162
8-32.6	Punts	5-41.6
0-0	Fumbles – Lost	1-1
60	Penalty Yards	55

Attendance: 78,084.
Teams' remuneration: $310,984.
Miller Award recipient: Del Shofner, Baylor halfback.

Mississippi 39 Texas 7

"We weren't that good of a football team."

Even the Southeastern Conference began putting the squeeze on the Sugar Bowl. With northern and western teams virtually unobtainable for New Orleans, Auburn emerged in 1957 as the New Year's most desirable trophy.

The undefeated, untied War Eagles were the season's national champion but were ineligible for bowl competition because of NCAA probation. Mississippi, which missed a share of the SEC title because of a final game tie with Mississippi State, was a solid second choice. Ole Miss was still embarrassed over its previous Sugar Bowl appearances against Georgia Tech and Navy, and wanted a New Orleans stage again.

"Jimmie-nee! I have a special desire to win this one. That's what we're going down there for – to try to win," said Rebel Coach Johnny Vaught.

Getting a suitable opponent was a man-sized job. From the season's beginning, Texas A&M was in the comer of every bowl's eye. Bear Bryant's Aggies started fast and finished slow while young Darrell Royal's Texas Longhorns came off a disastrous 1956 and a slow 1957. The Longhorns rode a season-ending surge that battered A&M on national television, as well as Cotton Bowl-bound Rice and TCU. The Sugar then took Texas, which finished 6-3-1 and wasn't in the Top 10.

Royal later said, "We shouldn't have been in a bowl to begin with. We were kind of a Cinderella team even with that record. The year before we were 1-9, so we received a lot of notoriety. But the truth of the matter is we weren't that good of a football team."

Ray Brown, who quarterbacked the sixth-ranked Rebels and led the team with a better than five-yard-per-carry average, was the story of the 1958 Sugar Bowl. Ole Miss had a superb defense, headed by Gene Hickerson, and a top-ranked offense. But it was Brown who was the team's soul.

When Brown was a child, a small friend pulled a wagon from under him. "We thought it was just another fall," said his mother, "but Ray ran a high fever ..." Doctors in Memphis diagnosed osteomyelitis; they had to operate and scrape the bone. It looked doubtful that he would walk again.

"They used tractions on my right leg," ... said Ray. "That saved me from being crippled...after I showed doctors I could walk, well, then I started running ... and then I went out for high school football ..." He kept going until he became the ignition of Vaught's high-octane offense.

Crew of WDSU-TV, a pioneering television station in New Orleans, covers the Sugar Bowl.

  24TH SUGAR BOWL CLASSIC

"Lateral, Ray, lateral."

That chilly, 47-degree afternoon, was a day to be remembered, for the Sugar Bowl, for Ray Brown.

The diagnosis of fourteen years before was hard to believe at the Sugar Bowl, where Brown was a starting quarterback-defensive back.

Ken Kirk recovered an early Texas fumble at the Longhorn 33, leading to a one-yard Brown touchdown; In the second quarter he threw a three-yard scoring pass to Don Williams; coffin-cornered a kick out at the Texas 7, then intercepted a pass at the 20 which led to another Rebel touchdown

It was 19-0 at the half, and things seemed to get worst for the Longhorns, falling under a 26-0 deficit.

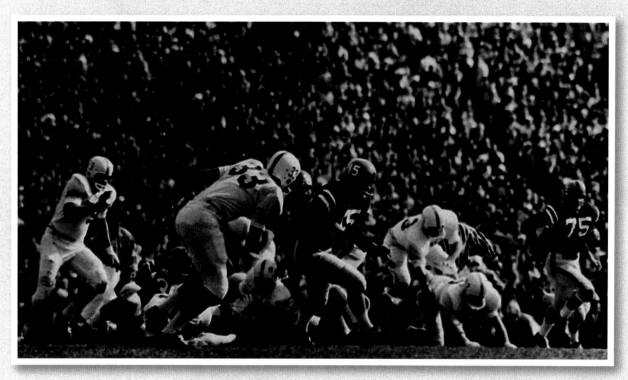

Ole Miss' Ray Brown (15) wiggles free against Texas.

As the game wound down, ballots were passed out in the press box for the vote on the Most Valuable Player. All 116 media voters placed Brown as their choice for his quadruple-threat performance. Raoul Carlisle, an Arkansas newspaperman who had covered every Sugar Bowl, commented to Pie Dufour as Brown dropped into his end zone to punt, "He's the greatest performer in Sugar Bowl history." Pie noncommittally answered, "He certainly is one of the best."

As they talked, Brown took a high snap and, before he could boot the ball, saw a Texas end boring in unopposed. Brown bolted, circled right end and began steaming for the Longhorn goal 103 yards from where he had been standing. "I was weary, so weary that I thought about asking for a replacement to do the punting," Brown said. "I told the fellows, 'I don't know if I can kick that ball 20 yards I'm so tired.

You'll have to get downfield in a hurry ... I didn't know I was in the clear 'til I looked back near midfield and saw all those blue shirts around me. And I kept hearing (teammate) Jackie Simpson yelling, 'Lateral, Ray, lateral.' I knew if he wanted the ball there wasn't anyone else around but us Rebels."

"That proves Brown's the best," Carlisle was screaming in Dufour's ear to make himself heard over the din of the crowd. Ole Miss scored another, meaningless, touchdown after a Texas fumble with 12 seconds remaining.

But everyone, Rebel and Longhorn alike, was aware they had witnessed a special individual performance. Brown's 92-yard run from scrimmage had pushed his rushing figures to 157 yards on 15 carries, a 10.5 average. Several of his passes were dropped in the cold, but he completed three of eight for 24 more yards. He averaged 34.7 yards on four punts, specializing in out-of-bounds rolls.

He scored two touchdowns, passed for another, and was brilliant on defense with three interceptions. Brown also saved an early touchdown by catching George Blanch after the Longhorn had galloped 46 yards.

Coach Johnny Vaught chuckled about the long run and insisted, "We called that one from the bench." The 6-foot-1, 190-pound Brown was elated when he was awarded the Miller Memorial Trophy, then being informed he was the first unanimous selection.

"Say, if nobody has ever won it that way before," he said with emotion, "that means I have a chance to make the all-time Sugar Bowl team. Oh, man, I'd like that."

A rousing halftime show at 1958 game.

	1	2	3	4	
Ole Miss	6	13	7	13	39
Texas	0	0	0	7	7

Mississippi: Brown, 1-yard run. Kick failed.

Mississippi: Williams, 3-yard pass from Brown. PAT, Khayat kick.

Mississippi: Lovelace, 9-yard run. Kick failed.

Mississippi: Franklin, 3-yard run. PAT, Khayat kick.

Texas: Blanch, 1-yard run. PAT, Lackey kick.

Mississippi: Brown, 92-yard run. Khayat kick.

Mississippi: Taylor, 12-yard pass from Brewer. Kick failed.

Individual Leaders

Rushing
Mississippi: Brown 15-157, 2 TDs; Franklin 9-64, 1 TD.
Texas: Blanch 11-58, 1 TD; Allen 8-43; Fondren 8-39.

Passing
Mississippi: Brown 3-8-0, 24 yards, 1 TD.
Texas: Lackey 2-5-2, 14 yards.

Receiving
Mississippi: Taylor 2-20, 1 TD; Williams 2-15, 1 TD.
Texas: Ramirez 1-3.

Mississippi		Texas
18	First Downs	13
304	Rushing Yards	192
7-16-0	Passing	2-11-4
71	Passing Yards	14
375	Total Yards	206
7-34.7	Punts	5-38.2
5-2	Fumbles – Lost	7-4
9-95	Penalties – Yards	6-30

Attendance: 77, 484.
Teams' remuneration: $320,006.
Miller Award recipient: Ray Brown, Ole Miss quarterback.

LSU 7 Clemson 0

"I'd like to see once more."

Fate occasionally takes strange twists. It was a little unbelievable to those who built it, but the Sugar Bowl would be celebrating its silver anniversary game on New Year's Day, 1959. Twenty-five years had passed since Warren Miller and the Co-operative Club had initiated a bold plan to make a New Orleans postseason football game a reality. The current Sugar Bowl's president was Claude "Monk" Simons, whose football exploits made Tulane the winner of the inaugural game. After a quarter of a century, the Sugar Bowl exceeded the stature and prominence that even Fred Digby envisioned.

Time brought other changes. Miller and nine other original members of the Mid-Winter Sports Association were deceased. *The Item*, which had been the project's incubator, was sold to the Times-Picayune Publishing Co. and merged with the *States*.

On September 12, 1958, two days before the *Item* slipped under the waves, sports editor Hap Glaudi reprinted Digby's column of October 31, 1947 (the last day he served as the paper's sports editor). Two days later, in the final *Item* editions, Digby's byline again appeared on the *Item's* sports pages, along with that of his protégé and that of his staff, each in his own way saying good-bye. Digby recounted some of the most memorable events and people he had covered in a piece headlined "I'd Like To See Once More..." Less than two months after the *Item* died, and less than a month before the Sugar's silver anniversary game, Fred Digby passed away.

"We knew he was ill," said Mary Frances Digby, "but we didn't know he was as sick as he was. He was on a fishing trip with A.B. Nicholas in August when he took sick. He looked like death then. I called our doctor, a longtime friend, and he told me to get him to the hospital as fast as I could. After he took X rays he called us in and told us this was the hardest thing he ever had to do, as much as he thought of Fred. But he had cancer of the liver, that he could operate but he didn't hold much hope."

Digby was allowed to go home where he continued to work with the Mid-Winter Sports Association on plans for the festivities of the 25th game and on his piece for the *Item*. He had to return to the hospital on October 21.

The evening of the November 2, 1958, he listened from his hospital bed to the broadcast of the LSU-Mississippi football game. Both teams were high on the Sugar Bowl checklist. Digby was visibly moved when announcer J.C. Politz passed along the good wishes of himself and of the schools. The next day, with his wife at his bedside, Fred Digby died. An outpouring from the high and mighty as well as the humble of collegiate sports, and from newspapermen far and near, engulfed the Digby family and his monument, the Sugar Bowl.

Joe Carter, who had covered every Sugar Bowl as sports

Billy Cannon releasing the touchdown pass.

editor of the *Shreveport Times*, summed up the feelings of those involved with the Mid-Winter Sports Association in a touching piece just before the 1959 game. "They are going to stage the 25th annual Sugar Bowl football classic in the Tulane University stadium this Thursday afternoon, New Year's Day," Carter wrote. His words conveyed the riot of color, the carnival atmosphere and hysteria of 80,000-plus football-frenzied fans — the parade of bands, the dancing and prancing of beautiful cheerleaders, and the color-bearers.

"Even the familiar cry of the hucksters as they ply their trade both on the inside and the outside of the huge stadium will be there," Carter wrote, "but in the press box far above the maddened crowd will be a vacancy. It will be the spot where Fred Digby, general manager of the Mid-Winter Sports Association, sat every New Year's Day game and watched the dream of a lifetime unfurled. A spot from where he saw his master handwork put into reality."

Lawrence diBenedetto, another original Sugar Bowl member and the person who coordinated the Association-sponsored track meets, died several days after Digby. Adding to the melancholy circumstances, James M. Thomson, the former *Item* publisher and the man who offhandedly made the first suggestion of a New Year's Day game in New Orleans, died in September of 1959.

LSU, en route to the national championship, was obviously the first choice of the Mid-Winter Sports Association. After a late-season squeeze past Mississippi State, the eventual signing of the Tigers was a simple formality.

When young Cadet assistant coach Paul Dietzel took the LSU job some four years before, he suggested to Digby he match his team and Army in the 1958 Sugar Bowl. Army, of course, was out in 1959 because of the segregation problem, and Dietzel would later leave LSU to coach the Army team.

Most New Orleans fans preferred to match LSU with SMU, with its spectacular quarterback Don Meredith.

From the available teams of Clemson, North Carolina, SMU, Southern Mississippi, and Air Force, Clemson was picked for two reasons: The Tigers were champions of the Atlantic Coast Conference with an 8-2 record; also, Dietzel, LSU's coach, thought his lightning-quick team could easily handle them.

Clemson Coach Frank Howard realized he was sitting in a gap with practically all the New Orleans sports pages centering on the home-state Tigers and the lukewarm sentiment for Clemson's selection. "The fans can think what they want," snapped Howard, before adding to the overconfidence of LSU supporters. "My boys play like a bunch of one-armed bandits," Howard said in comparison to the LSU defensive team, the Chinese Bandits.

LSU was a 14-point favorite. Howard was privately confident his Tigers could blow holes in the light LSU line and that no third-string unit like the Chinese Bandits could stop his offense. Howard commented, "You can tell them for me, they're gonna have to be No. 1 to beat us ... that's the way our boys feel about this game."

"It went off with a prayer."

A riled Howard was fully prepared and motivated to knock LSU from its pedestal – as were most of the South Carolina contingent on the chilly, overcast New Year's Day, 1959.

"They (the press) keep telling us we're not worth a darn," the tobacco-chewing coach of the 11th-ranked Carolina Tigers drawled. "I don't know, maybe we're not. But you keep telling a feller that long enough and it begins to get under his hide."

Clemson decided to train its offensive weapons on LSU guard Charles Strange, a 210-pound sophomore.

It was, however, the quicksilver Bayou Bengals that put in the early bid for points, driving to the Clemson 22 late in the first quarter before a fumble thwarted the march. When Clemson couldn't move, Charlie Horne dropped back to punt. He got a bad snap and, under a strong rush by Max Fugler, hooked the ball straight up and out-of-bounds for a minus two-yard punt at the 29.

"When he saw me coming in, he tried to kick it off to the side," Fugler said. LSU inched to the 12, but came up empty again when quarterback Warren Rabb missed on four straight passes, including one on a fourth-down fake field goal.

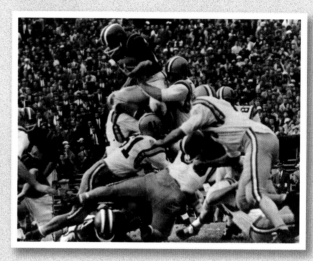

A Clemson back vainly tries to breach LSU's 'Great Wall of China.'

Later in the second period, Rabb ignited another drive, running for 33 yards but suffered a broken hand on the tackle. "I didn't know it was broken until I came out before the half," he explained. "I think it got hit with a helmet." Rabb continued to pilot the drive, completing a 24-yard pass to end Mickey Mangham and guiding the Bayou Bengals to the 1. Brodnax crashed into the end zone but fumbled. Doug Cline recovered for the Clemson touchback. "I thought I was over," Brodnax said with insistence afterward.

LSU had muffed three scoring opportunities in the first half, and lost its quarterback in the process, changing the game plan.

"I was glad, in a way, the first half ended the way it did ... I felt certain they thought they had us," Dietzel said.

That's what it seemed in the third quarter when Clemson, which posed no serious threat in the opening half, pounded its way to the LSU 20 – where George Usry was hit by Red Hendrix and fumbled.

Mickey Mangham clutching the pass that allowed LSU a 7-0 victory.

Strange, fighting off every Clemson thrust, recovered for LSU on the play.

Tommy Davis boomed a 52-yard punt, and when Clemson failed to move again, it appeared the two sets of Tigers were settling down into trench warfare. A reserve center, Paul Snyder, was in during this series. As it happened, when Clemson tried to punt, Synder's snap went awry and bounced off the leg of kicker Doug Cline. LSU tackle Duane Leopard fell on the loose ball at the Clemson 11.

On third and nine, Cannon took a pitch-out, rolled to his right, then shot a pass to end Mickey Mangham, who was clear in the end zone. The play was not run as diagrammed. "I didn't throw it, the Lord did," Cannon said later. "I looked for (halfback) Johnny Robinson, and they had him covered ... then I spied Mickey and let go ... I wasn't sure it would get to him until he grabbed it ... It went off with a prayer."

Behind with time becoming critical, quarterback Harvey White started a drive from the Clemson 17 and whipped his unit to within sight of the Bengal goal. Dietzel sent in his rested Chinese Bandits.

At the 25 the Chinese Bandits threw up one of their patented stands. Gaining one yard in three plays, White then flipped a screen pass to Usry, who appeared to have running room. The left halfback started to run before he had complete possession and dropped the ball. Howard was certain Usry "would have gone all the way," had the pass been complete. "It was the perfect play," he added. "All the downfield blockers were in position to clear the road to the goal."

Less than two minutes remained to play at that point.

Howard admitted his strategy didn't work out the way he figured and said in his opinion Strange, not Cannon, deserved the MVP award, dismissing the Tiger halfback's touchdown pass, his PAT, his 51 yards rushing out of LSU's total of 114, and being in on several key tackles. "We figured we could drive Strange back 10 yards a crack – and planned our offense to run right at him," Howard said. "But, as it turned out, he was the toughest man on the field."

Because he was, LSU finally won a Sugar Bowl game – and in the process became the first national champion to do so since 1940.

	1	2	3	4	
LSU	0	0	7	0	7
Clemson	0	0	0	0	0

LSU: Mangham, 9-yard pass from Cannon. PAT, Cannon kick.

Individual Leaders

Rushing
LSU: Cannon 13-51; Davis 2-17.
Clemson: Hayes 17-55; Usry 1-29.

Passing
LSU: Rabb 2-7, 33; Cannon 1-1, 9, 1 TD.
Clemson: White 1-3, 21.

Receiving
LSU: Mangham 2-33, 1 TD; McClain 1-26.
Clemson: Cox 1-12; Anderson 1-11.

LSU		Clemson
9	First Downs	12
114	Rushing Yards	168
4-11-0	Passing	2-4-0
68	Passing Yards	23
182	Total Yards	191
6-41.7	Punts	6-32.8
4-2	Fumbles – Lost	3-2
5-35	Penalties – Yards	2-20

Attendance: 80,331.
Teams' remuneration: $320,006.
Miller-Digby Award recipient: Billy Cannon, LSU halfback.

Mississippi 21 LSU 0

"The game would be a natural again."

Jim Cartwright, a Tennessee player, proved to be the most influential figure in the bowl makeup of 1960. But before Mr. Cartwright stepped into the picture, LSU and Mississippi played the season's "Game of the Century" on Halloween night, 1959. The Tigers, still unbeaten and No. 1-ranked, were losing a game of field position and defense to the No. 3-ranked Rebels until Billy Cannon cut loose with a fourth-quarter superhuman 89-yard punt return for a touchdown. LSU prevailed, 7-3.

It was a Southeastern Conference classic. Fred Russell of the *Nashville Banner* wrote, "For its suspense, and competitive team performance, Louisiana State's 7-3 throbber over Ole Miss was the fullest and finest football game I've witnessed in 31 years of sports reporting." Mercer Bailey of the Associated Press wrote two days after the game, "Maybe the Sugar Bowl folks should go ahead and invite Louisiana State and Mississippi for its New Year's Day extravaganza. If tense, exciting football is what they want, they could hardly improve on a rematch of the national champion Tigers and those classy Rebels."

The wheels were set in motion for the rematch the following weekend by Tennessee's Jim Cartwright. LSU was running wild against the Vols, but had scored only one touchdown by the third quarter. Quarterback Warren Rabb threw to wide-open halfback Johnny Robinson; and Cartwright, who had been blocked from Rabb's line of vision, made a leaping interception and ran unmolested 59 yards for: the tying touchdown. Cartwright became the first man to cross the Tiger goal line in 40 quarters and changed the entire complexion of the game. LSU, which had three backs individually out-rush the entire

Volunteer team, lost 14-13 and dropped from its No. 1 perch.

Within seven days, Ole Miss tore apart the same Tennessee team 37-7 and moved to No. 2 in the national polls, one spot ahead of LSU. The Rebels were considered the SEC's "Team of the Decade" and were leaning toward the Cotton Bowl until the Sugar promised to help bring about Mercer Bailey's dream game, a rematch with LSU. Coach Johnny Vaught unofficially committed to the Sugar Bowl right after the Tennessee victory.

However, some felt a rematch would be too sectional to suit the taste of television. "Not so," said Tom Gallery, NBC's sports director. "NBC would be most happy if the Sugar Bowl was able to land LSU and Ole Miss. The game would be a natural again, as it was the first time."

LSU was not as enthusiastic. The Tigers would be placed at a severe psychological disadvantage playing a team they had already defeated. Also, LSU was a weary, wounded football team at season's end.

The other bowls were rapidly filling. Syracuse, which took over the No. 1 position after LSU's loss to Tennessee, was paired with Texas in the Cotton; fifth-ranked Georgia,

Rebel quaterback Bobby Franklin looks for a receiver in 1960 rematch with arch-rival LSU.

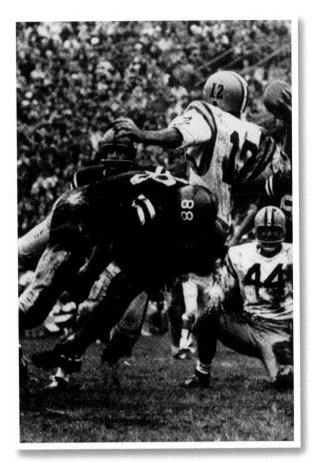

Larry Grantham (88) brings down Warren Rabb (12) in the 21-0 avenging of a regular season defeat to LSU.

which won the SEC championship after the LSU-Tennessee-Ole Miss round robin, was matched with Missouri in the Orange. If the Tigers wanted a bowl game, it would have to be either in the Sugar against Ole Miss or in Houston's Bluebonnet in another rematch with a defeated opponent, Texas Christian.

Dietzel polled the team informally and a full third voted to sit out the bowls altogether. Dietzel and the Tigers wanted to choose a bowl after a December 5 game between Syracuse and UCLA. If Syracuse lost the game, it would mean LSU could be playing for at least the Football Writers of America's version of the national championship, which was awarded after the bowl games. If Syracuse won, then LSU would stay home. Dietzel said, "If an honor (a bowl invitation) becomes a chore, then perhaps it is best left undone."

The Tigers took an official team vote, considering both the Sugar and Bluebonnet invitations as well as sitting out the bowls, on November 23 with a battalion of newspapermen sitting outside. Tension began to mount as the session stretched into a half hour and then an hour. Seventy minutes after the voting started, Carl Higgins, LSU's sports information director, burst into the waiting room and announced, "They voted to

play." Billy Cannon walked in with a slight grin and said, "It was a unanimous vote. So I guess it will be Ole Miss again." Dietzel described his reaction as "shell-shocked"; he thought the team would call it a year.

As it happened, Syracuse walloped UCLA 36-8. Then on December 22 at practice, halfback Johnny Robinson broke a hand. Things were definitely not going well for LSU.

It didn't matter to the fans. The game, of course, would be televised, the first bowl to be telecast in color from coast-to-coast, but tickets were being swapped for used cars and refrigerator repairs. Four tickets went for a 14-foot fiberglass boat; 60 tickets went for a 1952 Cadillac and 4 new tires. The sizzle of the rematch had the fans steaming. It was estimated the Sugar Bowl had over a quarter of a million requests for tickets.

Ole Miss had given up only 21 points during the entire season, the lowest for a major college in 20 years—since the 1939 Tennessee Vols went undefeated, untied, and unscored upon. LSU gave up only 29 points. The rivals were ranked one-two nationally on defense. LSU allowed an average of 2.5 yards per play to the opposition; Ole Miss gave up an average of 2.8 yards.

"Go everywhere he went."

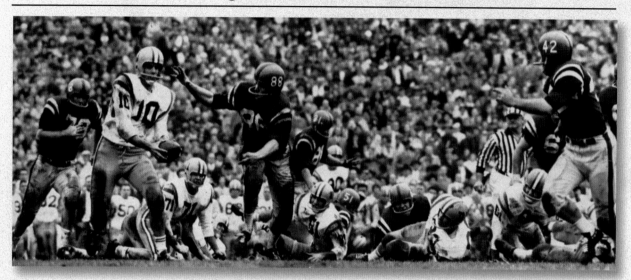

Chinese Bandit quarterback Darryl Jenkins (10) has no protection against the rampaging Rebels.

Before the rematch, an Ole Miss fan said unsmilingly to a newsman, "We'd rather beat LSU than be president."

Coach Johnny Vaught gave his constituency a victory in a landslide. Vaught, criticized for his conservative approach in the 7-3 regular season Tiger win, gave the Rebels the green light to "go for broke." He wasn't going to hold anything back.

Warren Rabb, the LSU quarterback, was still hobbled from a knee strain from the Tennessee game more than a month before. Further complicating matters for LSU was halfback Johnny Robinson, who started with a protective covering over his fractured hand. He would not carry a single time in the Sugar Bowl, nor did another halfback, Wendell Harris, whose injuries kept him completely sidelined. It all meant the Ole Miss defense could zero in on LSU's only threat, Billy Cannon.

"We did something I don't think we had ever done before," said Rebel safety Billy Brewer. "We went to a man defense in the secondary because we knew LSU wouldn't be a passing threat. My assignment was to stay with Cannon, go everywhere he went."

Murky, damp weather made the field muddy in spots, and a cold wind lowered the temperature to 49 degrees at kickoff, opening a half in which the seven-point favorite Rebels put

constant pressure on the Tigers, who were saved by an interception at the LSU 5, a missed field goal from the 18, and at the 11 where the Tiger defense held.

Despite its problems, LSU kept the Rebels even on the scoreboard. Then, with 38 seconds left and Mississippi on its 42, the Tigers were assessed a 15-yard personal foul penalty. Ole Miss' Jake Gibbs, who led the SEC in total offense, received instructions from the bench. He took the snap, started to roll out, and pulled up behind tackle. Delaying for an instant while Ole Miss' other receivers flared to different areas, taking the deep defenders with them, James "Cowboy" Woodruff raced downfield behind end Larry Grantham and cut slightly to the center where Gibbs' pass was arching down.

No Tiger was within 15 yards of the receiver.

"I don't think there's any question that the touchdown pass just before the end of the half broke our backs," Paul Dietzel said. "It might have been a different game if we had gone into halftime 0-0."

Grantham caught an 18-yard touchdown pass from Bobby Franklin in the third quarter, then Franklin threw a nine-yard fourth-period TD pass to George Blair. Those touchdowns were a striking illustration of just how dominant Ole Miss was: The touchdown pass just before the half was the first passing score against LSU in 14 games, and against the Rebels the Tigers yielded three in one afternoon.

Ole Miss held an awesome edge in statistics, 363 yards to 74, the lowest offensive total in Sugar Bowl annals; the Tigers gained 49 yards rushing but lost 64 for a net gain of minus 15 yards. The longest Tiger gain of the day was eight yards by Darryl Jenkins of the Chinese Bandits – the defensive unit. It had taken LSU more than 25 minutes to get its initial first down – and that was the only one the Tigers were credited with in the first half. Cannon made eight yards in six carries.

Vaught was magnanimous in victory, pointing out the injuries that decimated the Tiger team that beat the Rebels in the regular-season. "Don't forget LSU lost three pretty good football players," he said. "Rabb wasn't at his best, Robinson was of little use offensively and Harris didn't dress out. Those are three mighty fine football players."

Most Ole Miss people didn't want to hear anything that might take the edge off their win.

In the satisfied Rebel locker room, Woodruff sighed, "I always thought we had a better one (team), and I kind of feel we proved it today."

Billy Cannon (20) and Tiger Coach Paul Dietzel look on in dismay as Rebels completely dominate LSU.

	1	2	3	4	
Mississippi	0	7	7	7	21
LSU	0	0	0	0	0

Mississippi: Woodruff, 43-yard pass from Gibbs. PAT, Khayat kick.

Mississippi: Grantham, 18-yard pass from Franklin. PAT, Khayat kick.

Mississippi: Blair, 9-yard pass from Franklin. PAT, Khayat kick.

Individual Leaders

Rushing
Mississippi: Flowers 19-60; Blair 8-26.
LSU: Cannon 6-8.

Passing
Mississippi: Franklin 10-15-1, 148 yards, 2 TDs; Gibbs 4-10-1, 65 yards.
LSU: Rabb 4-15-0, 36 yards.

Receiving
Mississippi: Flowers 4-64.
LSU: Cannon 3-39; McClain 3-31.

Mississippi		LSU
19	First Downs	6
140	Rushing Yards	-15
15-27-2	Passing	9-25-1
223	Passing Yards	89
363	Total Yards	74
6-37.5	Punts	12-34.3
4-2	Fumbles – Lost	2-0
7-65	Penalties – Yards	4-30

Attendance: 81,141.
Teams' remuneration: $330,000.
Miller-Digby Award recipient: Bobby Franklin, Ole Miss quarterback.

Mississippi 14 Rice 6

"You are going too, aren't you?"

From the beginning the Mid-Winter Sports Association seemed to have been conceived under a providential star. Even the strangulation of the segregation law hadn't damaged its string of successes.

A young New Orleans state legislator, Maurice 'Moon' Landrieu, believing the race laws clearly put the Sugar Bowl in jeopardy, tried to convince Louisiana Governor Jimmie Davis. Davis listened and never got back to Landrieu. Landrieu tried to buttonhole members of the Sugar Bowl for a plan to fight the legislation, but by then the Association was unwilling to take on both state government and public opinion.

The air began seeping from the balloon with the 1961 Sugar Bowl. It wasn't a dramatic occurrence perhaps, but in looking back, it seems obvious that the Sugar Bowl's fortunes altered slightly.

Mississippi, which had participated in two of the last three Sugar Bowls, was head and shoulders above the rest of the Southeastern Conference. Because there was no championship berth attached to a New Orleans invitation, the No. 2-ranked Rebels understandably wanted to play elsewhere during the holiday season. It would have been pleasing to New Orleans fans, too, because they wanted new blood in the game. But Ole Miss was the best team in the area, and the Sugar Bowl really didn't want to take a hand-me-down.

The Rebels, who were prohibited by Mississippi state law from competing against teams with black athletes, were coveted desperately by the Sugar, Gator, and Bluebonnet Bowls. Reports filtered out of Houston that Ole Miss had unofficially accepted an invitation to play in that game. Coach Johnny Vaught and Lou Hassell of the Bluebonnet selection committee both denied a deal had been struck.

Ole Miss eventually signed to play in the Sugar Bowl again. Apparently the Rebels gave the Bluebonnet an indication that they were interested. When the Sugar realized it was losing the No. 2 nationally ranked team, it went to work on the warm friendship the bowl and school had enjoyed for years.

To its credit, the Sugar Bowl didn't have only Mississippi in its sights. It made long-shot attempts at No. 1-ranked Minnesota (the Big Ten contract with the Rose Bowl had lapsed), and was briefly interested in No. 4-ranked Navy, although it is hard to see how a service academy could have gotten around the segregation issue. Sugar Bowl President George Schneider told the New Orleans Quarterback Club that the Association had tried to get Minnesota.

"It's our understanding that although the Big Ten pact with the Rose Bowl has been concluded, a Big Ten team can only play in the

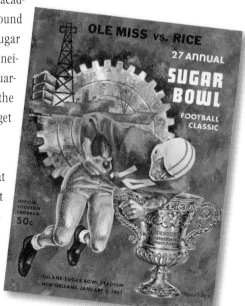

Captains of Ole Miss and Rice watch intently as ref flips coin before 1961 Sugar Bowl.

Rose Bowl this year." It was reassuring to realize that the Sugar Bowl would still reach out.

For whatever reasons, the Sugar Bowl was far more serious about Duke, Baylor, and Rice. After a 7-6 Duke loss to North Carolina, New Orleans eyed the season-ending Baylor-Rice game. Baylor dropped out of the picture before the game was played by accepting a Gator Bowl invitation. So the Sugar Bowl more or less pinned its hopes on the Owls, who could move into a tie with Arkansas with a win. An 8-2 co-champion would have suited New Orleans just fine. Instead, the Bears won 12-7 in the fading minutes, a finish that would characterize future Sugar Bowl selections. Rice dropped into a second-place SWC tie and put an unranked team with three losses in the Sugar Bowl.

Thrice beaten or not, Rice was no pushover. It had an excellent pass defense, intercepting 17 passes over the course of the season and holding its opponents to a 44 percent completion average. Its defensive middle was good; offensively it ran a sound attack that boasted of 10 backs who carried at least 25 times each, nine gaining 100 yards or more over the course of the season. Its 74 pass receptions were spread over 14 receivers. All Rice lacked was a little luck.

Ole Miss could be awesome. Jake Gibbs, by consensus the finest quarterback in the country, completed passes at a 60.6 ratio and directed his offense to a perfectly balanced 18 rushing touchdowns and 18 passing touchdowns. Another was added by an interception return. Rice Coach Jess Neely as-sessed, "They tell me Ole Miss can beat you up the middle, but humiliate you outside." He had heard right, and the Owls were immediately made a 10-point underdog — biggest of the major bowls.

The only thing that appeared to concern Ole Miss was the rankings. The final Associated Press and United Press International polls came out, placing the Rebels second and third respectively. Students made "AP" and "UPI" dummies, hung them from the Union Building, and burned them while chanting, "We're No. 1, to hell with AP and UPI."

Times-Picayune columnist Buddy Diliberto noticed how unconcerned the Rebs seemed about Rice and wrote the game would be closer than the betting line. Ole Miss, he analyzed, was in the same position LSU was in for the 1959 Sugar Bowl against Clemson. It had no reason to get 'steamed up.' "The Rebs can't prove anything by winning," said Diliberto.

Vaught had a very difficult time turning his team's thoughts to the capable Owls. While the Rebels prepared in Oxford, one of his reserve backs, Frank Halbert, asked Vaught if he knew what time the team would arrive in New Orleans. The boy's family wanted to greet the squad and the anxious sub inquired, "So what time are we going to get there?" The traveling squad hadn't yet been made up, and Vaught responded with, "What do you mean, 'we?' " Halbert was taken aback. He hesitated, then innocently asked, "Well, coach, you are going too, aren't you?"

"Once I straightened up I had blockers infront of me."

Buddy Diliberto was right. Ole Miss wasn't razor-sharp for Rice, though not a person in the crowd of almost 80,000 would have believed it in the opening three minutes and 20 seconds.

Jake Gibbs, Ole Miss' "Rifleman," put up the first points of the day in that span. In a short 52-yard drive, Gibbs, faking a pass at the 8, rolled out around end and scored.

It was an awesome, almost effortless, drive that darkened the festive mood in the Rice section of the stands. Rufus King, an Owl guard, said, "I think we were trying too hard the first time they had the football. We were a little tense ..."

Coach Jess Neely found a remedy for the tenseness. He took out most of his starters. So did Rebel coach Johnny Vaught, although Vaught made the move to give his regulars a rest after their drive.

From that point until the fading moments, Rice starters and subs played Ole Miss on better than even terms. In fact, six inches in another direction on one play of a 78-yard drive might have changed the outcome. Randy Kerbow guided Rice to the Rebel 27 when, on fourth-and-one, he crossed the Rebels up by sending 163-pound halfback Butch Blume wide on a power sweep to the right. "I got some good blocks and

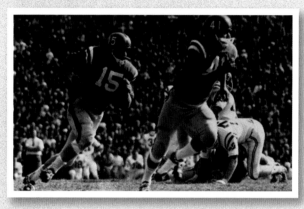

Glynn Griffing (15) runs for first down against Rice.

made the turn," Blume explained while demonstrating with a two-step. "I was moving down the sidelines when my foot went out by no more than six inches. If I had just a little more running room I could have walked in."

Blume's run gave Rice a first down at the 10, but two plays later Allen Green intercepted a Kerbow pass at the Rebel 9.

Rice shortly threatened again, but this time Blume's halfback pass was picked off at the Ole Miss 17.

In the second half, Billy Cox led an impressive 18-play Rice drive. It took four downs to get it in from two and a half yards out, but Blume went around end with four Mississippians on his back to finally get the Owls on the boards.

Max Webb missed the extra point, leaving Ole Miss with a precarious 7-6 lead.

Another interception of the Owls gave Ole Miss possession on the Rice 11. The rejuvenated Owls threw the Rebs back to the 17. There, almost arrogantly, the Rebels again passed up a field goal attempt that could have clinched the victory. Ole Miss was stopped on a running play and Rice took over.

Gibbs finally pulled Ole Miss together. In 10 plays, primarily on the strengths of runners Jim Anderson and Art Doty, Mis-

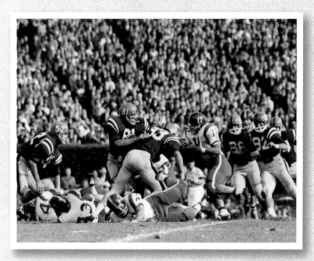

Owl quarterback Billy Cox (11) on a keeper against Rebs.

Ole Miss' Jake Gibbs, rolls out for a first down against Rice.

sissippi went 42 yards to camp at the Rice 1. There the Owls fought the Rebels to a standstill for three downs.

Gibbs lined up his teammates – who hadn't gained a foot since reaching the apron of the goal line – took the snap, stumbled, and then raced wide. He was hit at the goal by two defenders, barely slipping in and losing the ball in the process. It was ruled Gibbs had already crossed the line before the fumble.

"I almost fouled up on that last touchdown – and we needed it," Gibbs said. "I came out too fast and slipped. But once I straightened out I had blockers in front of me and knew I'd go in for six." Ole Miss held a 14-6 lead with five minutes and 16 seconds remaining. That was enough.

Rice out-gained the Rebels 281-186, had a 19-13 advantage in first downs, and ran 81 plays to Ole Miss' 60. As New Orleans columnist Charles "Pie" Dufour put it, "Rice left too many men on base." Although the Owls held Gibbs to 15 yards rushing, 11 of those yards accounted for both Rebel touchdowns.

Probably the most memorable part of the game for gallant Rice, after the sting of defeat wore off, was sophomore Ray Alborn wobbling off the field after being cracked on a particularly tough play. He walked on legs of jello to the Ole Miss bench to have a seat. "I don't remember any of it," Albon said, "but some teammates came to get me and bring me over to our side of the field. They knew they couldn't win without me ... We did win, didn't we?"

No, and to point out how important that fact was, Minnesota didn't win either, losing to the University of Washington in the Rose Bowl. Because of that, Ole Miss, who won its bowl game in less than impressive fashion, found itself atop one poll. In its final ballot, the Football Writers of America ranked the Rebels No. 1.

	1	2	3	4	
Mississippi	7	0	0	7	14
Rice	0	0	6	0	6

Mississippi: Gibbs, 8-yard run. PAT, Green kick.

Rice: Blume, 3-yard run. Kick failed.

Mississippi: Gibbs, 3-yard run. PAT, Green kick.

Individual Leaders

Rushing
Mississippi: Anderson 15-59; Doty 4-25.
Rice: Blume 7-54, 1 TD.

Passing
Mississippi: Gibbs 5-15-0, 43 yards.
Rice: Cox 11-20-1, 143 yards.

Receiving
Mississippi: Crespino 2-21; Blair 2-18.
Rice: Webb 3-31.

Mississippi		Rice
13	First Downs	19
143	Rushing Yards	103
5-15-0	Passing	14-28-4
43	Passing Yards	178
186	Total Yards	281
5-42.4	Punts	3-34.0
1-1	Fumbles – Lost	2-0
2-10	Penalties – Yards	6-30

Attendance: 79,707.
Teams' remuneration: $330,058.
Miller-Digby Award recipient: Jake Gibbs, Ole Miss quarterback.

Alabama 10 Arkansas 3

"The boys voted to go to the Sugar Bowl."

Since 1956, when the segregation edict went into effect and as civil rights became the overriding domestic political issue, the Sugar Bowl was fighting a war with one arm tied. It was winning the war, but only because two backyard schools, LSU and Ole Miss, were enjoying some of their finest seasons. One or the other had participated in four consecutive Sugar Bowls. It was fortunate that those teams were available at the time, but the feeling began to grow that LSU and Ole. Miss were becoming crutches for the Sugar Bowl.

It was an ideal situation for New Orleans: Pencil in one of those popular teams and automatically fill one berth with a high national contender. Then all the Mid-Winter Sports Association had to do was look for another team that wouldn't be offended by segregated seating.

Both schools were in their accustomed elite positions in the 1961 national rankings, along with a newcomer, Alabama, ranked second behind Texas. The crutch was rudely knocked from under the Sugar when in mid-November Tiger Coach Paul Dietzel informed the Mid-Winter Sports Association that under no circumstances would the Tigers accept a Sugar Bowl invitation. Although LSU came under some heat from home-state fans, the Tiger position had some merit. An 80-mile bus trip from Baton Rouge to New Orleans the day of the game

wasn't a big reward for a job well done – particularly since, unlike the Cotton, Orange, and Rose Bowls, participation didn't automatically establish championship status of the "home" team. Also, Dietzel was still irritated by the corner he was painted into for the 1960 rematch with Ole Miss, when the Sugar Bowl insisted he make a decision before the LSU hierarchy really wanted to.

For the 1962 game, the Sugar Bowl wanted a match between No. 2 Alabama and the No. 4 Tigers, two SEC schools who had not played in the regular season. A committee from the Mid-Winter Sports Association visited Baton Rouge to meet with Athletic Director Jim Corbett and Dietzel and offer an invitation. Corbett met with the committee. Dietzel refused, telling Corbett in effect, "If you want this team to play in the Sugar Bowl, you'll have to take 'em."

Ole Miss was already unofficially committed to the Cotton Bowl, and Alabama was no guarantee either. The

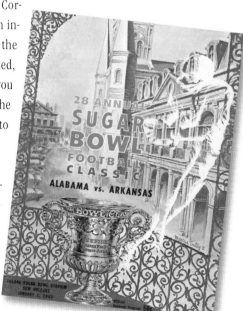

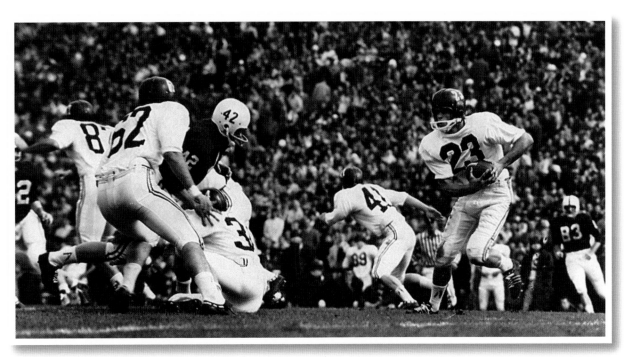

The nation's No.1 all-purpose runner of 1961, Lance Alworth (23), shifts into gear against Alabama in the 1962 Sugar Bowl.

Big Ten contract with the Rose Bowl had still not been renewed, and Pasadena was flirting with Alabama and LSU. Alabama had far more tradition in Pasadena than in New Orleans, winning five of six California appearances before the Rose Bowl closed on both ends. Tide Coach Paul "Bear" Bryant saw a Rose Bowl invitation as a dramatic way of reasserting Alabama football, which had fallen on desperate times before he returned in 1958.

A poll of Southern California sportswriters favored Alabama and LSU in that order for the 1962 game. Fred Neil of the *Los Angeles Herald Express* wrote, "The sportswriters' No. 1 choice is Alabama because everyone thinks they have a better team. I think they (the Rose Bowl) will look favorably on LSU. The Big Ten teams under consideration are dull, and there's a little reaction to our going to the Big Ten with hat in hand and begging them to play us."

LSU took itself out of the California picture by accepting an Orange Bowl invitation to play Colorado, but 'Bama continued to wait. There was some sentiment on the West Coast against a southern team because of the segregation issue, although Alabama obviously had no qualms about playing an integrated team.

Ohio State, the Big Ten champion, was tentatively offered the Rose Bowl bid November 28. Shockingly, the school's faculty council rejected it. Reporters quickly got in touch with Dr. Frank Rose, president of the University of Alabama, who said his school should not be considered a Rose Bowl candidate. "If we win Saturday (the season finale against cross-state rival Auburn) our team is to go to the Sugar Bowl," said Dr. Rose. "The boys voted to go to the Sugar Bowl if invited, and I think they will be invited."

During the bowl chess match, Texas Christian had upset Texas and Alabama had moved up to No. 1. A 34-0 victory over Auburn solidified Bryant's first national championship.

The Sugar Bowl then grabbed the next most attractive team available, No. 9 Arkansas, the Southwest Conference co-champion. New Orleans had somehow come up with a stellar attraction ... again.

"It might have been my praying."

Mike Fracchia hammers Arkansas line with MVP form.

Part of the self-styled mythology of Bear Bryant is how football saved him from a hard life of plowing the fields of his native Arkansas.

"If I hadn't been lucky I'd still be out there somewhere plowing," he liked to say.

As it was – more than a decade after begging his way into the Sugar Bowl, and coaching Kentucky to its remarkable victory over Oklahoma – his newest team was plowing through Southern football fields.

Coaching now at his alma mater of Alabama, Bryant's first national championship was college football's equivalent of the providential immovable object. This team gave up a total of 22 points in 10 games, none in the last five ("They played like it was a sin to give up a point," Bryant assessed after the season."), they led the NCAA in three defensive categories and set 10 school defensive records.

Arkansas coach Frank Broyles knew his team had its work cut out, though he also felt the Razorbacks could move on anybody's defense. They had a weapon no one had been able to neutralize: halfback Lance Alworth, one of the nation's most dangerous ball carriers, running, receiving or returning kicks.

It took the Tide six plays to score. "We noticed something a little different in their defensive alignment," Alabama tackle Billy Neighbors said, "so we made a slight adjustment." The adjustment sent running back Mike Fracchia scurrying past a defender who penetrated into the backfield, past another just beyond the line, and racing down the sidelines 43 yards to the Arkansas 12. On the next play, quarterback Pat Trammel faked a pass and then, around left end, ran it in.

A pleased but perplexed Neighbors said later, "We ran that doggone play about six more times and never did do anything with it again."

Though the Tide kept pressure on the Hogs, Bama got no more points until late in the half when Butch Wilson intercepted Arkansas quarterback George McKinney and returned the ball 17 yards to the 20. Eventually, kicker Tim Davis, who had missed one earlier, was waved back into the game. This time he kicked true and Alabama led 10-0 with four minutes to go.

That very nearly was enough time for Arkansas to get to the dressing room just a field goal behind. The main thrust of the Razorback offense had been to the inside, but, from the Tide 48, Paul Dudley swung out to the short side of the field and, as his blockers mowed down defenders, made his way to the 10 where Tommy Brooker collared the runner.

"I should have gone the distance," Dudley said. "Billy Moore threw the key block that got me past the line, and Jim Collier cleared part of the path downfield. After Collier threw his block I cut to the inside . . . I could see daylight, but before I could resume my regular course down the sideline I was hit from the side."

The threat ended with a missed field goal.

In the second half, Razorback kicker Mickey Cissell had two more early chances. One of his field goals was blocked, the other was good, recording the first points against Alabama since October. Now the score was 10-3, and Arkansas was back in the hunt.

In the final minutes, McKinney began opening up, hitting Alworth with a 31-yard pass to the Alabama 43, where the ball was fumbled, a 37-yard completion to Collier at the Tide 40, and another pass that tantalizingly grazed Alworth's fingertips in the end zone.

Wilson deflected another pass, then intercepted it and stepped out of bounds no more than four inches from the Alabama goal, but essentially ending the game.

Bryant, who said he had "nine heart attacks out there," revealed he was prepared to give the Razorbacks a safety on fourth down if time had not run out.

"We were in it on the scoreboard, but were never in it on the field," a glum Broyles assessed afterward.

Alabama had won its first Sugar Bowl by allowing the Razorbacks only four real chances at the end zone, and holding Alworth to 15 yards rushing.

As the coaches met at midfield, Broyles had to cut his congratulations short. His players were trying to claim the game ball. "Give them the ball," he yelled to his squad. "They won it. It belongs to them!"

Bryant growled at his own players. "Let 'em have it."

It was the only thing Alabama gave up all day.

	1	2	3	4	
Alabama	7	3	0	0	10
Arkansas	0	0	3	0	3

Alabama: Trammel, 12-yard run. PAT, Davis kick.

Alabama: Davis, 32-yard field goal.

Arkansas: Cissell, 23-yard field goal.

Individual Leaders

Rushing
Alabama: Fracchia 20-124; Trammel 18-69, 1 TD.
Arkansas: Alworth 10-15; McKinney 6-14.

Passing
Alabama: Trammel 4-10, 20 yards.
Arkansas: McKinney 2-10, 55 yards.

Receiving
Alabama: Oliver 2-13; Clark 2-7.
Arkansas: Alworth 2-55.

Alabama		Arkansas
12	First Downs	7
234	Rushing Yards	113
4-10-0	Passing	2-12-3
20	Passing Yards	55
254	Total Yards	168
6-23.5	Punts	7-33.8
3	Fumbles Lost	1
53	Penalty Yards	34

Attendance: 82,910.
Teams' remuneration: $340,000.
Miller-Digby Award recipient: Mike Fracchia, Alabama fullback.

Mississippi 17   Arkansas 13

"The number is listed."

Johnny Vaught's Mississippi Rebels, in those halcyon days of Southeastern Conference football, appeared to be suffering a bit of an identity crisis. Over the course of a decade, the Rebels were consistently the SEC's premier team. Yet since 1951, Tennessee, Auburn, LSU, and Alabama had all won consensus national championships. Ole Miss had only been presented the Grantland Rice Award by the Football Writers of America as the country's No. 1 team after its 1961 Sugar Bowl victory, though that did not carry the weight of the wire service voting.

Vaught seemed determined to show the doubters just how good his program was during the 1963 bowls. On the eve of the LSU-Mississippi football game, the Sugar Bowl tendered an invitation to Vaught, contingent upon a victory over the Tigers. The Rebels were on their way to the school's first unbeaten, untied season. At the same time the Sugar Bowl extended an invitation to Alabama, 3rd-ranked and unbeaten in 25 games.

The South was anxious for a match-up between two SEC teams which had not played each other during the season. 'Bama Coach Paul "Bear" Bryant, because he had played in the Sugar Bowl the year before and then returned to New Orleans to play Tulane in September, wasn't interested.

Quoting unnamed sources almost daily, a few New Orleans writers kept the Ole Miss-Alabama brew stirred, but nothing substantial materialized. Then Vaught, in a telephone interview with Associated Press reporter Ben Thomas, seemed to try to challenge Alabama in the same manner in which LSU had been pressured into the 1960 game. Thomas asked Vaught if he had a bowl preference. The Rebel coach laughed and replied, "Yeah, but I can't say it." Thomas asked specifically if Ole Miss wanted to play Alabama. Vaught answered that it would be the best of the bowls. "It would match two of the finest teams in college football," he said. "We'll play anybody, I don't care who they are."

Bryant responded, "We've got three more teams licking their chops to get at us, starting with Miami. When they get through with us, if they (Ole Miss) still want us, the number is listed." That week, after a game in Florida with the University of Miami, Bryant, who saw no logic in risking his national ranking against a team from his own conference, committed to the Orange Bowl.

This all meant the Sugar Bowl was sent scrambling for the next best match-up it could find. Frank Broyles' Arkansas Razorbacks, with a loss only in the final 36 seconds to Texas, was a strong prospect with the Gator, Bluebonnet, and Liberty Bowls. Broyles wanted a quick answer

The Hogs' Billy Moore (10) rushes for a short gain against Mississippi.

from the Sugar Bowl or he would commit to another bowl.

The Sugar answered with an invitation to play Ole Miss. He accepted – contingent upon Texas winning the Southwest Conference title and the Cotton Bowl berth.

Mississippi and Arkansas had been longtime rivals whose series had been terminated by Broyles in 1962. Since Broyles took over in 1958, Arkansas enjoyed its finest football moments. But he was unable to beat the Rebels in four tries. "It's easier to change coaches than change teams," said Broyles at the announcement of the series termination.

"You know," Broyles said after accepting the conditional invitation, "when people chided me about canceling the series, I told them that we'd play Mississippi in a bowl game. Now look. And here we are again."

Third-ranked Mississippi, 27-1-1 over the last three seasons, won its Southeastern Conference championship with the league's best offense, the nation's best defense, and a versatile quarterback named Glynn Griffing. Sixth-ranked Arkansas led the Southwest Conference in rushing and total defense in going unbeaten for nine games.

The game didn't have the lure of the Rose Bowl, which for the first time in bowl history had a No. 1 (Southern Cal) and a No. 2 (Wisconsin) team, but it was a good selection.

Texas upheld its end by beating Texas A&M 13-3 on Thanksgiving Day to take its SWC title. That score held Sugar Bowl interest as much as any during the 1962 season, because if Texas had lost, Arkansas would have been the SWC champion and in Dallas on New Year's Day. But Texas would not have turned to New Orleans. It would have been in the Bluebonnet Bowl.

"I wanted to kiss him."

Johnny Vaught, left, and Frank Broyles renewed the Ole Miss-Arkansas rivalry faster than anyone could have thought.

A weak punt gave the Hogs possession at the Rebel 27 – and the first shot at points. But, in a preview of what was to come, Ole Miss' viselike defense didn't allow an inch, and a 43-yard field goal fell short. In the second period, the Rebels' Billy Carl Irwin made a 32-yard field goal to give Ole Miss the lead.

With six minutes left in the half, on third-and-nine from the Arkansas 19, sophomore reserve quarterback Billy Gray dropped back and spotted wingback Jerry Lamb 10 yards behind the Rebel secondary. Lamb slowed to catch the arching pass near midfield, then stumbled as he turned for the unguarded end zone. Lamb fought to keep his balance for 10, 20, 30 yards more when Buck Randall came flying out of the afternoon sun in a desperate dive. He just grazed Lamb's back and heel. It was enough to cause the staggering receiver to fall at the 13.

"I don't know how I caught him ... I wanted to kiss him for falling down," Randall said. The play covered what was then a Sugar Bowl record 68 yards, leading to a 30-yard field goal by Tom McKnelly to tie the score.

For an instant it appeared Arkansas would get more points. Dave Jennings fielded the kickoff in the Ole Miss end zone, started to run it out, couldn't make up his mind and started to step back, then took a knee. "The official signaled it was a safety," Broyles said. "I thought we had two points ... the official quickly reversed his decision, so I guess Jennings didn't step out of the end zone."

Frank Broyles made the succinct assessment: "The difference," the Arkansas coach said, "was Glynn Griffing."

The Ole Miss quarterback completed 14 of 23 passes for 242 yards, and broke two records (passing yardage and total yardage).

Just as imposing, though, was a Herculean performance by the Ole Miss line, which may have been the biggest factor in the outcome by flushing the Razorback quarterbacks from the pocket and into the unprotected open field.

Backup Jim Weatherly immediately started up another drive, but Griffing came in and finished up. Louis Guy shook off two Razorbacks, turned, and took a 33-yard pass over his shoulder for a touchdown.

Three plays into the third quarter, Randall had his team in trouble again, fumbling and losing the ball at the Rebel 18. Billy Moore rolled out from the 5, and dropped a soft pass into the cradled arms of Jesse Branch to again tie the score.

*Billy Gray (11) goes over the top against
onrushing Ole Miss.*

Stung, Griffing brought the Rebels right back, driving 80 yards in 10 plays, largely on 23-yard and 35-yard receptions by Guy. Griffing sneaked in from the 1.

Scrappy Arkansas fought back, making another series threat against all odds. Randall may have saved the game when he broke through to tackle Moore at the 4. The Razorbacks kicked another field goal.

Broyles would be severely second-guessed for going for three points at that juncture, but Vaught agreed with the strategy. "I would have done the same thing," he said. "He thought he'd have another chance."

Vaught did not give Broyles another chance. Ole Miss threatened three times in the fourth quarter, driving to the 3, 8, and 9 without scoring. Arkansas did not get another sniff of the Rebel goal.

The Rebels had been only a slight favorite, and the score indicated the odds-makers were on-target. But Arkansas, which averaged 241.2 yards rushing during the regular season, had 47 against Ole Miss; and Arkansas, whose defense led the Southwest Conference by giving up an average of only 200.1 yards of total offense, surrendered 429 to the Rebs. Ole Miss had three times as many first downs and two-and-a-half times as much yardage as the Hogs.

Arkansas had stayed in the game with a superior opponent about as well as anyone ever had.

	1	2	3	4	
Mississippi	0	10	7	0	17
Arkansas	0	3	10	0	13

Mississippi: Irwin, 30-yard field goal.

Arkansas: McKnelly, 30-yard field goal.

Mississippi: Guy, 33-yard pass from Griffing. PAT, Irwin kick.

Arkansas: Branch, 5-yard pass from Moore. PAT, McKnelly kick.

Mississippi: Griffing, 1-yard run. PAT, Irwin kick.

Arkansas: McKnelly, 23-yard field goal.

Individual Leaders

Rushing
Mississippi: Jennings 9-39; Weatherly 9-36.
Arkansas: Branch 7-21.

Passing
Mississippi: Griffing 14-23-1, 242 yards, 1 TD.
Arkansas: Moore 5-10-0, 55 yards, 1 TD.

Receiving
Mississippi: Guy 5-107, 1 TD; Morris 5-62.
Arkansas: Lamb 3-107; Branch 3-16, 1 TD.

Mississippi		Arkansas
22	First Downs	7
160	Rushing Yards	47
18-28-1	Passing	6-18-2
269	Passing Yards	123
429	Total Yards	170
2-36.0	Punts	4-38.2
2-1	Fumbles – Lost	2-0
4-40	Penalties – Yards	2-13

Attendance: 82,096.
Teams' remuneration: $340,000.
Miller-Digby Award recipient: Glynn Griffing, Ole Miss quarterback.

Alabama 12   Mississippi 7

"I remember a time like this."

Seven Sugar Bowls had been played since the segregation issue had encased the Mid-Winter Sports Association in an insular, provincial cocoon. Almost miraculously, the damage was minimal because 1) Many Southern schools followed similar policy and law, and the Southeastern Conference was then the finest collegiate football league in America, and 2) Sheer good fortune. The situation was bound to change.

The segregation obstacle began to dissolve, although few realized it in June of 1963 when a suit seeking integration of seating arrangements and other facilities at New Orleans' Municipal Auditorium was taken under advisement by a special three-judge federal court. Horace Bynum, vice-president of the New Orleans chapter of the National Association for the Advancement of Colored People, filed the suit after the city denied it use of the building for a 1962 rally featuring such speakers as Thurgood Marshall.

According to Assistant City Attorney Ernest Salatich, closed meetings and religious assemblies could be held on a desegregated basis. Open meetings were segregated under Louisiana law. The court was asked to declare unconstitutional the state's statute requiring segregation at entertainment and athletic events.

It would take time for the court to reach a decision, but on the football front things were unraveling. In 1964, the Sugar Bowl wanted Navy and Mississippi. Roger Staubach had transformed Navy from an Eastern also-ran into a glamorous, exciting, and undefeated football team. Whether the segregation issue would

have been an insurmountable barrier will never be known because No. 2-ranked Navy only had eyes for Dallas, where No. 1-ranked Texas was scheduled for a New Year's bout.

Other than Texas, the Southwest Conference did not have a strong team; there was not one in the Atlantic Coast Conference; and because of the conference contract with the Orange Bowl, the Big Eight runner-up was not allowed to play in another bowl.

The third and only alternative was an all-SEC game between Mississippi and the winner of the Alabama-Auburn game. It looked feasible because this year — unlike the previous — Ole Miss was the higher ranked team. Bryant, with two strong teams left to play, wanted a no-strings-attached invitation. He received one from the Bluebonnet Bowl in Houston and tried to use it as a lever with the Orange Bowl. Miami, who could use backups in Pitt, Syracuse, and Penn State, wouldn't bite.

When the Sugar tested the waters, Bryant laid it on the line: Either he would get a no-strings invitation, or he would accept the bid from the Bluebonnet Bowl. Auburn appeared willing to wait, but the Plainsmen seemed a longer shot than the Tide. Bryant got his invitation on

his terms. Auburn accepted an Orange Bowl bid. So for the first time, when Auburn and Alabama met, two teams already committed to rival New Year's Day bowls met in the regular season. Auburn won 10-8.

This would be Alabama's 17th bowl game, pushing it ahead of Georgia Tech as the all-time bowl entrant.

Despite a season-ending 10-10 tie with Mississippi State, seventh-ranked and unbeaten (7-0-2) Mississippi appeared as formidable as ever to Bryant.

Eighth-ranked Alabama and the Rebels hadn't played since 1944. The Crimson Tide hadn't been an underdog since 1960, but Ole Miss opened a 7 1/2 -point favorite.

Joe Namath, a young quarterback whose rubber-band right arm had the South buzzing, directed the Tide offense. Then in early December, Namath was suspended for the remainder of the season (including the Sugar Bowl), because of a team infraction. The Sugar was turning sour.

Bryant couldn't have known it but his first recruiting trip in 1936, as an Alabama assistant would play a role in the 1964 Sugar Bowl. He signed Alvin Davis from Arkansas, who later became a prep coach in Tifton, Georgia. His son Tim was a quarterback but hurt a leg. Tim remembered his dad said, "Son, there's no reason you can't be a college kicker. But be sure to go to a school that always has a strong line." At first,

Paul 'Bear' Bryant is surrounded by his Crimson Tide before doing battle with Ole Miss in the snow.

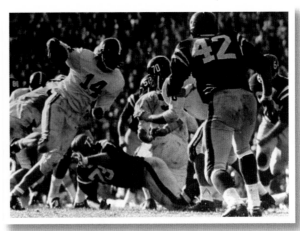

Steve Sloan (14), subbing for Joe Namath, hits the Ole Miss line.

Tim's knee didn't respond, but "... my dad kept Coach Bryant informed on my progress and he stuck with me." When the time came to choose a college, Tim chose Alabama over Georgia Tech. "Coach Bryant's colorful personality swung me," he said. Thus, Alabama acquired a talented athlete who was to determine the 1964 Sugar Bowl.

Nothing matched the snowfall of New Year's Eve, 1963. More than three inches of snow fluttered down on New Orleans, the most snow in the city since 1895. A crew of 25 workers from the police department's House of Detention worked with Tulane Stadium Superintendent Nolan Chaix until midnight clearing the tarpaulin and the seats. The crew was brought back at 5 a.m. "It looked pretty hopeless," said Chaix. "We just weren't prepared to cope with anything like we got Tuesday. The snow was still coming down when we started about 3 p.m. (Tuesday), but we had to go to work."

It seemed much more hopeless to Bryant. Alabama had given up more points (88) and more yardage (216.5 yards per game) and had been victimized with more long-scoring plays than any team Bryant coached since 1958.

"This is not the best time for us to be catching Mississippi," assessed the Bear. "They come at you in a big wave, all of them. And if we can't block Miami, and we didn't, how in the world can we block Ole Miss?" Reflecting, he added, "I remember a time like this — in 1958. We'd scratch and claw and quick kick ... and we won games we had no right winning.

"I saw you take your eyes off the ball."

Tulane Stadium was like an icebox, cold and damp.

But in the midst of snow banks, with players bothered by frosted fingertips, Tim Davis was hot.

Or, at least, his toe was.

There had been Sugar Bowls won by field goals before – the 1936 game being won by a kick, the only points the winning team could manage. To show how much the game has changed, Sammy Baugh's boot in that one was the first of just nine before this in what was then the Sugar Bowl's three-decade history.

Tulane Stadium really did resemble a huge sugar bowl on the first day of 1964, with snow banks flanking the field. The moist 45-degree temperatures was said later to have played a critical role in the outcome, causing a total of 17 fumbles, 11 by the losing team, and bringing on an incredible for-the-time four field goals – including the longest ever kicked in any bowl – by Davis, three coming after bobbles, which provided the ultimate difference.

Playing with a second-string quarterback, 18-year-old Steve Sloan in place of suspended Joe Namath, and against the nation's best run defense, Bear Bryant figured he was in for an

Rebelettes perform in the snowy, sunny South on January 1, 1964.

iffy afternoon.

On 'Bama's first series, though, Sloan took the Crimson Tide on an impressive quick-hitting, between the tackles drive that netted five straight first downs. Ole Miss, which led the nation in rushing defense, finally were able to stop the Tide at the Rebel 15. Davis came in and kicked a 31-yard field goal.

Following the kickoff, quarterback Jim Weatherly, in for Perry Lee Dunn, set the tone for a frustrating Rebel day by losing the ball with no one around him as he attempted to pass. Butch Henry recovered at the Ole Miss 31, and Davis eventually came back in to boot a 46-yard field goal. Two years before, against Arkansas, Davis kicked a 32-yarder that was then the Sugar Bowl record. Tim broke his own record.

After yet another lost muff at the Rebel 37, Davis, in for his third play of the game, attempted a 50-yard field goal, but it was wide to the right. "I ought to beat you with a stick, you rascal," admonished the Bear with a smile. "You should have had that other one, too. I saw you take your eyes off the ball."

Another lost Rebel fumble at the 16 gave Davis another chance. With 16 seconds left until intermission Davis kicked a 22-yarder that gave Alabama a 9-0 halftime lead.

"I'm not taking anything away from Alabama," reflected Rebel end Joe Wilkins. "We played under the same conditions. Our game, though, I feel, was much more affected by the weather than theirs. We had a much more open offense, handled the ball more than Alabama, which ran basically a simple quick-hitting offense. The main thing was the snow put more moisture in the air. The field was slick as glass ... With our roll-out offense, it just seemed a little more difficult for us."

Dennis picked up 11 yards on the first play of the second half, registering Ole Miss' initial first down. Two plays later, Frank Kinard dropped the Rebels' eighth fumble, bringing Mississippi Governor Ross Barnett to his feet, saying, "Why is it the boys can't hold onto the football?"

Two series after that, Davis kicked a 48-yard field, at that time the record for any bowl.

Ole Miss crossed midfield for the first time in the fourth quarter, and Dunn eventually hit Larry Smith with a five-yard touchdown pass. The Rebels, outplayed most of the day, were now in position to win. And soon they were knocking on the door again, but on a fourth down at the 4, Dunn was stopped at the 2. Bryant would say later, "If I remember right, we (Kentucky) stopped Oklahoma in almost the same spot in the '51 game."

Ole Miss, hot now, made a last bid, getting to the 19 where end Joe Pettey caught a pass in the numbers and near the sideline. Fittingly, he couldn't hold the ball as he was tackled. 'Bama recovered at the 9 to seal the victory.

It was difficult to believe that a game with 17 fumbles, 11 by Ole Miss – both all time bowl records – could be so exciting at the finish.

Davis, of course, was the postgame story. He credited the snow with his performance. "I think being off the day before the game was the answer," he theorized. "I just had more zip in my kicks. I could see when I was warming up before the game. If the snow hadn't forced us indoors Tuesday, I would not have been so strong and accurate."

Bear Bryant offers thanks with his Crimson Tide after the 1964 Sugar Bowl.

	1	2	3	4	
Alabama	3	6	3	0	12
Mississippi	0	0	0	7	7

Alabama: Davis, 31-yard field goal.

Alabama: Davis, 46-yard field goal.

Alabama: Davis, 22-yard field goal.

Alabama: Davis, 48-yard field goal.

Mississippi: Smith, 5-yard pass from Dunn. PAT, Irwin kick.

Individual Leaders

Rushing
Alabama: Sloan 16-51; Nelson 16-47.
Mississippi: Dennis 7-37; Dunn 6-24.

Passing
Alabama: Sloan 3-10-1, 29 yards.
Mississippi: Dunn 8-10-0, 125 yards, 1 TD.

Receiving
Alabama: Stephens 1-15.
Mississippi: Wells 4-76.

Alabama		Mississippi
14	First Downs	9
165	Rushing Yards	77
3-11-1	Passing	11-21-3
29	Passing Yards	171
194	Total Yards	248
5-36.8	Punts	4-44.0
6-3	Fumbles – Lost	11-6
3-15	Penalties – Yards	5-45

Attendance: 73,024.
Teams' remuneration: $340,000.
Miller-Digby Award recipient: Tim Davis, Alabama kicker.

LSU 13 Syracuse 10

"Attractiveness and individual stars."

Seven days after the Alabama-Ole Miss football game, the United States Supreme Court ruled that the Louisiana statute requiring racial segregation of public entertainment and athletic events was unconstitutional. Ernest N. Morial and A.P. Tureaud, who argued the case for Horace Bynum, were the winning attorneys. Both were trailblazers in the civil rights' years and Mortal, 14 years later, would become the first black mayor of New Orleans.

That decision removed a barrier that had hindered the Sugar Bowl from being the national game it had been before 1957. There was no reason New Orleans shouldn't pick up the bowl tempo again.

Meanwhile, the Orange Bowl, in one of the most farsighted moves any postseason game ever took, changed its kickoff from early afternoon to prime television time—in the evening. The Rose Bowl, because of the time difference, had always started later than the other three bowls. That, combined with the tie-up between two of the country's most populous areas, had given Pasadena control of the ratings and a much larger TV contract than the others. Miami, no longer bound to the Big Eight, would now also be unopposed. Eventually, the money would be an inducement to help the Orange Bowl get the games it most desired. This was the real start of the television age for the bowls.

Hearts across the nation quickened when it was rumored Notre Dame might break its long-standing bowl ban. Irish Athletic Director Ed "Moose" Krause ended such banter by stating, "We're not going to any bowl game." He couldn't have been more definitive. Alabama, who would finish as the national champion, had no-strings-attached invitations from the Sugar, Cotton, and Orange Bowls. Coach Bear Bryant said he wouldn't consider any of them until after his Georgia Tech game.

It was known, however, that he favored the Cotton Bowl, a game he had not been to since his coaching years at the University of Kentucky. But the Orange Bowl lured Bryant from Dallas to Miami for a titanic confrontation with fifth-ranked Texas. Undefeated Southwest Conference champion Arkansas was scheduled against Nebraska in the Cotton. Both were excellent pairings. The Sugar was left with a solid, if not quite as flashy, hand.

Sam Corenswet, Sr., of the Mid-Winter Sports Association was asked what he looked for in bowl matches. "Attractiveness and individual stars," he said.

That left a great deal of leeway in the 1964 season. *States-Item* columnist Peter Finney and his *Times-Picayune* counterpart Buddy Diliberto felt one team filled both bills for the Sugar Bowl: Syracuse — the East's best team — featured an incredible running tandem in fullback Jim Nance and halfback Floyd Little. The two accounted for 1,779 yards

Doug Moreau streches for a reception as LSU catches Syracuse 13-10 in 1963.

and 25 touchdowns.

The problem was the Orangemen had two defeats and one game to go before the Bowl invitations would be extended. Finney and Diliberto continued to plug for Syracuse. "For one thing," said Diliberto, "we thought it would be a dramatic way to end the segregation thing. Secondly, there was talk beginning then that New Orleans might be in line for a National Football League franchise. If there was any doubt about racial problems in the city, it could have endangered that move."

"The East vs. the South competition," wrote Finney, "as far as I'm concerned has more postseason appeal than the SWC vs. SEC or all-SEC matches we've been getting."

Louisiana State University had an iron defense and an exceptional flanker-kicker. The kicker had set a national record with 13 field goals during the regular season. LSU was a logical SEC choice since Alabama was going to the Orange Bowl. Seventh-ranked LSU, however, also had a loss and a tie with a game with Florida remaining.

The Sugar took a chance and invited both. Ninth-ranked Syracuse lost its last game to West Virginia. LSU was beaten by Florida, setting up a New Orleans match with the most combined losses since 1945.

"Finney and I were sitting in the press box when the results of the Syracuse-West Virginia game began coming in by quarters," laughed Diliberto. "Man, you should've seen the looks the Sugar Bowl people were giving us. We just kind of ducked our heads and talked to each other. No one else would. But, considering everything, it was still the right choice."

Syracuse Coach Ben Schwartzwalder gives instructions to quarterback Walley Mahle.

"I-26-wide-and-go."

Odd how things come around. Doug Moreau vividly remembers as a sports-minded kid in Baton Rouge hearing on the radio about the segregated seating issue before the 1955 Sugar Bowl, and about the flap over Bobby Grier, the first African-American to play in the Sugar Bowl a year later.

The thought that raced through Moreau's 10-year-old mind was: "That's sounds silly."

To add to the circumstance a decade later, the only football Moreau ever kicked before he entered LSU was over a telephone line hanging across his backyard. When an assistant coach asked members of the Tiger freshman team who wanted to kick, though, Moreau raised his hand.

"There just wasn't any high priority on kickers (then)," Moreau said of the offensive weapon that was little more than an afterthought in those days.

It was LSU's good fortune that Moreau wanted to kick. He kicked a then-NCAA record 13 field goals in 1964, and combined with his pass-receiving duties, scored 73 of the Bengals' 115 total in the regular season, fully 63 percent of the LSU total.

Clearly, at crunch-time, LSU looked to the junior Moreau – bringing him to this point, in a socially-significant Sugar Bowl: lining up a 28-yard attempt against Syracuse with 3:48 to play, with victory, defeat, or most likely a frustrating tie, depending on his left-footed kicking accuracy.

Orangemen running backs Floyd Little and Jim Nance were the first African-Americans to appear on Sugar Bowl rosters since Grier of Pittsburgh in 1956, and were by far the most nationally known figures in the game, having scored 25 touchdowns between them, 14 more than LSU scored as a team in that era when defenses dominated the sport.

But Moreau turned out to be the central figure of the game – just as he was for LSU's season as a whole.

Not many would actually see it. If East versus SEC was the perfect vehicle for ending the segregation era, it was not a good

way to fill the stadium. A crowd of 60,000, the smallest for a Sugar Bowl since 1939, sat in the stands. The teams' records and the smallest ticket sale (1,300 by Syracuse), more than any political consideration, kept the crowd down.

But what a game those that came witnessed! It went back-and-forth, and the only kind of scoring it lacked was forfeiture.

There were field goals, a safety, touchdowns coming on a blocked punt and a long pass, and a two-point conversion. The Tigers, 5½ point favorites, down 10-2 in this topsy-turvy game at intermission, knew they were in for battle to the wire.

On the first possession of the second half, at the Tiger 43, substitute LSU quarterback Billy Ezell stepped into the huddle and called "I-26-wide-and-go." The play would send Moreau out as a lone receiver. He would run downfield, fake a cut to the sideline and then head for the end zone. In the first quarter Moreau had cleanly beaten defensive back Will Hunter by 15

*Joe Labruzzo (22) of LSU is wrapped up by
the Orange defense.*

yards on the same play, but Ezell overthrew him. This time Ezell pumped once and lofted the ball to Moreau at the 25. Moreau said of the second-and-16 play, "When I broke straight, there was the ball." The touchdown covered 57 yards.

A two-point conversion pulled LSU even at 10.

That's where things stood until the game moved into the latter stages of the fourth quarter when starting quarterback Pat Screen eased the Tigers to the 8. Coach Charlie McClendon called on Moreau to try to nail his 14th field goal of the season.

"The kick felt good when it left my shoe," Moreau said of the field goal, "then, before I looked up, Billy (Ezell, the holder) screamed, 'It's good!' "

In a game eerily similar to LSU's season as an entity, Moreau not only was responsible for the winning play, but scored nine of the Tigers' 13 points.

Jim Nance gained 70 yards and Little gained 48 in something of a collapse of the Syracuse offense. Charlie McClendon became the first former Sugar Bowl player to come back and coach a team to a Sugar Bowl victory.

It was the city of New Orleans that was the big winner, though. Syracuse was happy with its treatment. Nance exuded without solicitation, "I'm going to tell everyone about the splendid treatment we received down there."

The game marked the end of an era in football, too. The following year Charlie Gogolak of Princeton broke Moreau's record with 16 field goals, and from then on the field goal became an indispensable part of virtually every offense.

Doug Moreau kicks a 28-yard field goal to beat Syracuse in final minutes.

	1	2	3	4	
LSU	2	0	8	3	13
Syracuse	10	0	0	0	10

Syracuse: Smith, 23-yard field goal.

LSU: Rice tackles Little in end zone for safety.

Syracuse: Clarke returns blocked kick 28-yards. PAT, Smith.

LSU: Moreau, 57-yard pass from Ezell. PAT, Moreau kick.

LSU: Moreau, 28-yard field goal.

Individual Leaders

Rushing
LSU: Schwab 17-81.
Syracuse: Nance 15-70; Little 8-46.

Passing
LSU: Ezell 2-5-0, 67 yards, 1 TD.
Syracuse: King 6-15-0, 41 yards.

Receiving
LSU: Moreau 2-55, 1 TD; Labruzzo 2-45.
Syracuse: Cripps 2-18; Mahle 3-15.

LSU		Syracuse
11	First Downs	10
161	Rushing Yards	151
6-15-1	Passing	8-20-1
114	Passing Yards	52
275	Total Yards	203
9-36.2	Punts	6-37.5
4-0	Fumbles – Lost	3-1
4-46	Penalties – Yards	5-55

Attendance: 60,322.
Teams' remuneration: $280,000.
Miller-Digby Award recipient: Doug Moreau, LSU flanker.

Missouri 20 Florida 18

"You find another ginmill."

Less than two weeks after Jim Nance endorsed New Orleans, an American Football League All-Star game was moved from the city to Houston because of discrimination charges. This civic embarrassment stemmed from black players being refused cab service and admittance to French Quarter nightclubs.

There was no problem whatsoever with the better establishments. Indeed, the New Orleans hotel, restaurant, and motion picture associations agreed to accommodate all citizens and visitors. Players were welcomed into places like Al Hirt's, where Buffalo end Ernie Warlick was introduced and applauded. It was some less-fashionable spots that were in question, a detail that steamed the ire of Orleanians. The black professionals voted 13-8 to pull out, and AFL Commissioner Joe Foss complied.

New Orleans suffered a huge black eye, one that would affect the next Sugar Bowl, and one that the northern press predictably emphasized. Only Dick Young, the respected sportswriter of the *New York Daily News*, peeked beyond the obvious for eastern readers. Young wrote: "... What I mean is, you don't judge an entire town by some slob cab driver because there are a lot of good cabbies, and you don't say an entire city stinks just because some guys in a lousy ginmill insult you, because there is something about a ginmill that makes it very easy to be insulted, whether you're black or white, and when that happens you either fight your way out of the joint or you find another ginmill ...

"There were many fine places in New Orleans willing ... Some AFL Negroes stayed away from Bourbon Street. They ate in the Blue Room of the Roosevelt Hotel, and in Antoine's, and in other swank, respectable places, and apparently they were well-treated ..."

The walkout was to play a role in the 1966 bowls, and New Orleans was made to pay further. The rules were changed in the 1966 postseason jousting tournament. Because so many outstanding teams were still in the running, the Associated Press decided to name its national champion after the bowls so the top teams were looking for the match that would best help their chances. Alabama-Nebraska was the match-up for which both of the "open" bowls (Orange and Sugar) were angling. The Cotton Bowl, with No. 2-ranked Arkansas, had the highest-rated team either 'Bama or the Cornhuskers could play in their quests for the national championship. Razorback Coach Frank Broyles, however, wasn't interested in putting his team's long winning streak on the line against either one.

Largely due to the effect of the AFL walkout, Nebraska wasn't coming to New Orleans.

Intrigue characterized the bowl cast after it became apparent Alabama and Ne-

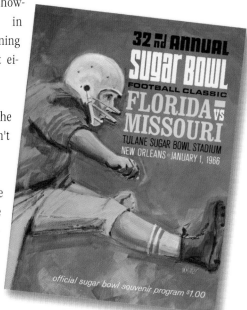

Missouri's Earl Denny (45) swoops down on the Gators.

braska were to play in Miami. Southeastern Conference Commissioner Bernie Moore became the middleman in providing SEC teams for the Sugar and Cotton Bowls. Missouri, who lost a 16-14 heartbreaker to Nebraska and held only a 5-2-1 record with Oklahoma and Kansas remaining to be played, had moved into the Sugar Bowl picture.

It appeared that Kentucky would host the Sugar Bowl, and Florida was headed for the Cotton. But Kentucky had beaten Missouri and agreed to accept a Cotton Bowl bid if it defeated Houston. (It did not.) Florida, meanwhile, agreed to take the Sugar Bowl bid if it beat Tulane (which the Gators did). LSU, with a 7-3 record, eventually filled the spot for the desperate Cotton Bowl. And Florida later lost to Miami, also falling to an unexciting 7-3 record. Florida under Ray Graves, who had played for Tennessee in Boston College's monumental 1941 upset, had a spectacular passing combination in quarterback Steve Spurrier and receiver Charlie Casey. Missouri, with a horde of pro prospects, was a more conservative but very

steady team offensively and defensively. But in some ways the 1966 Sugar Bowl was the lowest point of the Mid-Winter Sports Association.

Steve Spurrier (11) throws into the teeth of the Missouri defense during an awesome fourth quarter performance.

"Yep, it was pretty impressive all right."

This could have been the Mother of All Comebacks.

Didn't quite make it, but it was a rousing display – a two-minute drill that lasted 15.

Down 17-0 at the half, 20-0 in the third quarter, junior quarterback Steve Spurrier and the Florida Gators made the fourth quarter a sparkler.

"We figured," Spurrier recalled of Florida's late strategy, "we could only score three times in the last quarter. What we had to do was keep Missouri from getting a touchdown. But they might have gotten close enough for (another) field goal, which would have given them 23 points. So, to win, we would need 24 points."

For a team that could manage almost zero offense to that point, and would finish with minus two yards rushing, that was a mighty tall order.

Early, overcoming Florida's offensive and defensive units must have looked relatively simple to Missouri coach Dan Devine, at least on the blackboard. The Tigers utilized a wide tackle – or an eight-man line – to put pressure on Spurrier.

Should the Gators withstand the increased Missouri rush, the task of stopping Spurrier would fall to secondary coach Clay Cooper's unit, which was formidable with safety Johnny Roland roaming the perimeter.

The Tigers felt that eventually the Gators offensive line would give way under the hammering Missouri assault. "It couldn't have worked better," Spurrier reflected later. "For a while I couldn't breathe out there."

Two long drives in the first quarter were one of Missouri's best weapons. On its lone series in the period, Spurrier hit on a 9-yard pass, but two running plays lost a yard and the Gators had to punt. That was Florida's offense for the quarter.

Gary Lane, a methodical craftsman, put the Tigers ahead with a 59-yard drive. Charlie Brown, a 5-foot-8, 185-pound halfback who looked more like a professor than a student, dove into the end zone inside the flag on a 10-yard play. Missouri took definite command after converting a fumble recovery at the Gator 11 into a touchdown. Devine rushed in Roland who executed a perfect halfback pass to Earl Denny, who was open at the goal.

"It wasn't a usual play," Cooper said. "Roland had been an offensive back until last year, and we used the play during the regular season. We just caught 'em asleep, I guess."

Before the half was over, Bill Bates also kicked a 37-yard field goal for a 17-0 lead. Even with that cushion, however, Devine sensed his team weakening, both from following the game plan and from the 78-degree heat.

Florida changed things in the locker room. The offense, and its non-existent running game, was modified by placing a halfback wide as a receiver. If Florida was going to win, it would be by air, and Spurrier was instructed to roll away from the pressure and to look for targets in the flat.

First, though, Missouri added to its lead with a 34-yard field goal.

That's when Spurrier went to work.

Scrambling away from the Tiger pressure points, Spurrier took his team downfield, completing six passes in six attempts, culminating with a 22-yard touchdown to Jack Harper just inbounds in the end zone. Coach Ray Graves sent in instructions to go for two points, but the pass was off target.

A Missouri fumble on the ensuing kickoff at the Florida 10 gave the Gators heart. "That looked like manna from heaven," said Spurrier, who ran in from the 2. Harper threw an incomplete halfback pass on the attempted two-point conversion. A simple kick would have put the Gators just seven points back.

"Looking back on it," Spurrier reflected, "I wish we had done something different."

After forcing a Missouri punt, back came the Gators going from their 19 to the Tiger 21. There, on third down, Spurrier spotted Charlie Casey in the end zone and tried to float a pass to him. Defender Gary Grossnickle came up and covered Casey perfectly, deflecting the ball. In a tremendous effort, Casey dove headlong and caught the ball just off the ground.

For the third consecutive time Florida's two-point attempt went astray. Given up for dead at the start of the fourth quarter, the Gators trailed just 20-18. But there was just 2:08 remaining. The Tigers ran out the clock.

In the last period, the junior Florida quarterback swept his team to three touchdowns in barely 11 minutes of play. He completed 16-of-23 passes for 198 yards and two touchdowns, and scored another himself. To put it in perspective, the Sugar Bowl completion record for an entire game had been 17, set by Davey O'Brien in 1939.

"Yep, it was pretty impressive, all right," said Clay Cooper. "They were a real good team, and we knew that sooner or later they would hit a couple on us. They hit more than a couple, but you noticed who won the game? ... Missouri."

	1	2	3	4	
Missouri	0	17	3	0	20
Florida	0	0	0	18	18

Missouri: Brown, 10-yard run. PAT, Bates kick.

Missouri: Denny, 11-yard pass from Roland. PAT, Bates kick.

Missouri: Bates, 37-yard field goal.

Missouri: Bates, 34-yard field goal.

Florida: Harper, 22-yard pass from Spurrier. Pass failed.

Florida: Spurrier, 2-yard run. Pass failed.

Florida: Casey, 21-yard pass from Spurrier. Pass failed.

Individual Leaders

Rushing
Missouri: Brown 23-121, 1 TD; Lane 19-76.
Florida: Poe 2-11.

Passing
Missouri: Lane 4-13-1, 39 yards.
Florida: Spurrier 22-45-1, 352 yards, 2 TDs.

Receiving
Missouri: Phelps 2-11.
Florida: Casey 5-108, 1 TD; Brown 9-88; Harper 4-66, 1 TD.

Missouri		Florida
18	First Downs	18
257	Rushing Yards	-2
5-14-1	Passing	27-46-1
50	Passing Yards	352
307	Total Yards	350
5-44.0	Punts	6-32.5
2-2	Fumbles – Lost	1-1
2-30	Penalties – Yards	3-25

Attendance: 61,346.
Teams' remuneration: $382,000.
Miller-Digby Award recipient: Steve Spurrier, Florida quarterback.

Alabama 34 Nebraska 7

"This is the only time I feel like a success."

As an artistic endeavor, the 1966 Sugar Bowl was a smashing success. But by other measures it served only to show how far behind the other major bowls the Sugar had fallen. It attracted 67,421 fans, only a couple of thousand more than the dismal attendance of the 1965 game. And with the Associated Press balloting coming after the bowls, the Sugar Bowl was the only New Year's Day game that had no direct bearing on the national championship. LSU defeated No. 2 Arkansas in the Cotton, UCLA upset No. 1 Michigan State in the Rose, leaving Alabama to outslug Nebraska 38-28 in the Orange and take its long-shot national crown. The almost unbelievable domino effect made for excellent reading the following week in Sports Illustrated, the foremost sports magazine in the country. No one would read about Missouri-Florida, though. It wasn't covered.

The Sugar Bowl appeared to be on a merry-go-round it couldn't control. As good as its luck was in earlier days, the reverse seemed to be true in the mid 1960s. LSU-Syracuse was a good match for the 1965 game — until both lost their last games. Florida-Missouri was blemished by a late Gator loss.

States-Item columnist Peter Finney correctly wrote, "Check these Sugar figures (national rankings) for the last 10 games and you'll probably come to the same conclusion I did. You can't beat national ratings or a match between Southern teams when it comes to putting people in the ball park." Among other problems the Sugar Bowl now confronted was

the growing feeling that its membership was too restrictive. When no one else stepped forward in 1934 to help launch the project, the Mid-Winter Sports Association limited the organization to the founders, their offspring, close relatives, and special, sponsored individuals. Thirty-three years later, the founders were getting old and many of their sons simply weren't as interested — or as capable — as the fathers. The image of the Sugar Bowl had become one of a snobbish exclusive fraternity, which didn't matter much as long as its product remained one of quality. But it was plain the product had slipped.

The Sugar Bowl's Executive Committee began mulling over possible candidates to join the Association. They wanted people who were hardworking and upstanding, had made a positive mark on the community, and had the ability to get things done.

New associate members selected were John U. Barr, Aruns Callery, Henry Zac

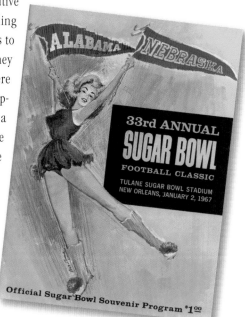

Paul 'Bear' Bryant, the Sugar Bowl's winningest coach and its patron.

Carter, William J. Childress, Harry M. England, Robert J. Fabacher, Charles C. Glueck, Richard L. Hindermann, and Richard H. Nelson.

In other business the Sugar finally saw the wisdom in an Orange Bowl move – a local television blackout should the attraction not sell out.

Nineteen sixty-six was a wondrous year for college football. Three exceptional teams dominated the sports pages: Notre Dame, Michigan State, and Alabama. All had legitimate claims to the national championship, but the Irish were proclaimed No. 1 even after a 10-10 tie with the Spartans. Undefeated, untied Alabama was insulted, and Coach Paul Bryant maintained for years afterward that this was the best team he'd ever coached.

Notre Dame did not compete in bowl games then, and Michigan State could not go to the Rose Bowl because of the no-repeat rule, leaving Alabama the highest-ranked team in postseason competition.

Bryant and Bob Devaney, coach of the fourth-ranked, undefeated Nebraska Cornhuskers, had decided to try to play each other in an "open" bowl. This would be the Sugar, because Alabama had played in Miami two consecutive years and Bryant liked to have his teams enjoy all the postseason sites. Both coaches also knew a victory over the other would give either

of them a slight chance to win the MacArthur Bowl, the National Football Foundation's version of the national championship.

Alabama and Nebraska signed for the Sugar Bowl; then the Cornhuskers, in what was becoming a Sugar Bowl tradition, lost its last game to Oklahoma. Alabama upheld its end, coming in unblemished in a 10-game schedule and providing a rare glimpse of the soul of the man who would rule the Southeastern Conference with a crimson-colored fist. "This is the only time I feel like a success," Bear Bryant said of the undefeated season.

Devaney's team was formidable, built along the lines of the other Midwest giants, Notre Dame and Michigan State. It was very big but also slow. Alabama, which would be outweighed by 35 pounds a man, was a remarkable team – one known for its defense but which featured notables like quarterback Ken Stabler and receivers Ray Perkins and Dennis Homan.

Perkins, however, had pulled a hamstring and wasn't expected to play. "Nothing was going to keep me out," said Perkins. "That game meant everything to us. We felt we had to win, and win convincingly. Coach Bryant felt sure we'd win the MacArthur Bowl with a big win. I even told Stabler I was going to beat him out of the MVP trophy."

Devaney said he wouldn't be surprised if Stabler didn't throw to Perkins on the first play of the game. Then Devaney, noting 'Bama's eight-point favoritism and the huge weight advantage his team enjoyed, said he was going to pray for rain.

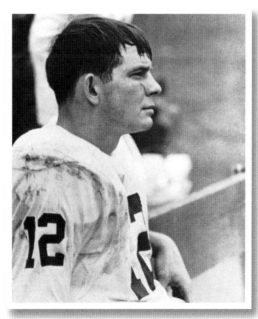

Ken Stabler takes a breather.

"That really gave us a lift."

Quaterback Ken Stabler (12) fires into the heart of the Cornhusker secondary.

In prayers and predictions, Bob Devaney, outstanding coach that he was, batted a thousand.

Rain swept the city for two days before the Sugar Bowl. A steady, light shower finally stopped an hour and half before kickoff, but the field remained in good condition – with the exception of one spot at the 10-yard line on the north side.

As Devaney predicted, on the game's first play from scrimmage, at the Alabama 28, Ken Stabler faked fullback Les Kelley into the line, stepped back and lofted a pass to Ray Perkins at the 49. Perkins made the catch and slithered down to the Nebraska 27 for a 45-yard gain. "We wanted to give them a set we would use the first time we got the ball," Coach Bear Bryant said. "We wanted to throw long to Perkins and see what defense they were in. If Ray was covered, Kenny Stabler was to overthrow him. Perkins got behind his man, though, and that really gave us a big lift."

Perkins, who in 1983 succeeded Bryant as coach of the Crimson Tide, said the completion was no big surprise. "We felt it would work because we were pretty certain our receivers could get open on their defensive backs. They were kind of slow."

Seven plays afterward, Kelley scored from the 1. That, for all practical purposes, ended the game.

Stabler took the Tide on a 71-yard drive, then went around end from the 14 as the 'Huskers appeared to be grabbing at a ghost. Steve Davis' PAT made the score 14-0 with 7:28 left in the opening quarter. The weight advantage Devaney expected to be one of his chief allies wasn't working out. "We couldn't do the things against them we did against other teams," Devaney offered.

Davis, brother of Tim, the kicking machine of the 1964 Sugar Bowl, came in to boot a 30-yard field goal with 28 seconds left in the first period. Bryant had used 35 players in digging Nebraska's football grave in that 15-minute swirl of offense.

Only the final score was in question by this time. Bryant, had his team gobbling up real estate at a staggering 295-112 yard advantage in the opening 30 minutes. "Well, we were pretty confident at the half," Perkins said, "but we felt we had to win convincingly."

Ray Perkins (88) breaks free against Nebraska.

	1	2	3	4	
Alabama	17	7	3	7	34
Nebraska	0	0	0	7	7

Alabama: Kelley, 1-yard run. PAT, S. Davis kick.

Alabama: Stabler, 14-yard run. PAT, S. Davis kick.

Alabama: S. Davis, 30-yard field goal.

Alabama: Trimble, 6-yard run. PAT, S. Davis kick.

Alabama: S. Davis, 40-yard field goal.

Nebraska: D. Davis, 15-yard pass from Churchich. PAT, Wachholtz kick.

Alabama: Perkins, 45-yard pass from Stabler. PAT, S. Davis kick.

Individual Leaders

Rushing
Alabama: Stabler 9-34, 1 TD; Morgan 10-37.
Nebraska: Davis 10-37, 1 TD; Wilson 4-24; Gregory 4-24.

Passing
Alabama: Stabler 12-18, 218, 1 TD.
Nebraska: Churchich 21-34, 201; Weber 1-4, 12.

Receiving
Alabama: Perkins 7-178, 1 TD; Homan 5-36.
Nebraska: Richnosky 6-48; Penny 6-42.

The Bear has a few choice instructions from the bench.

The victory extended an unusual accomplishment.

It was Alabama's 23rd consecutive game without a holding penalty. But the 34-7 blowout also made the results of the MacArthur Bowl presentation even more disappointing. Notre Dame won that, too.

"The hardest part about that whole season," Perkins recalled, "is that we were never recognized. They gave us the national championship the year before and we probably didn't deserve it with a loss and a tie. But in 1966, with an 11-0-0 record and beating a good team soundly in a bowl game, I think we did deserve some recognition. It was disappointing."

Devaney was also disappointed, although he immediately knew where he went wrong. "Sure, I prayed for rain. But that was a mistake," he admitted. "I should've prayed for a driving rain."

Alabama		Nebraska
19	First Downs	16
157	Rushing Yards	84
15-26-1	Passing	22-38-5
279	Passing Yards	213
436	Total Yards	297
4-35.0	Punts	5-39.0
3-1	Fumbles – Lost	5-2
1-15	Penalties – Yards	2-30

Attendance: 82,000.
Teams' remuneration: $472,000.
Miller-Digby Award recipient: Ken Stabler, Alabama quarterback.

LSU 20 Wyoming 13

"Its the biggest thing since statehood."

The Sugar Bowl, still basking in the glory of 1967's outstanding game, felt it could get one of football's storied names into the 1968 classic. Army, 5-1 at the time, had indicated an interest in breaking its bowl ban in either the Sugar or the Gator Bowl. New Orleans would have loved it, even taking into account that Army was more of a curiosity piece than a proven commodity. Army hadn't beaten a single winning team and lost 10-7 to five times beaten Duke.

If West Point had any such notion, it disappeared as soon as the story came out in the open. Secretary of the Army Stanley Resor stated officially, "It is concluded that accepting any invitation to play in a postseason game would tend to emphasize football to an extent not consistent with the basic mission of the academy, which is to produce career Army officers."

The host spot would also be hard to fill because Tennessee, the Southeastern Conference champion, let it be known early that its first preference was Miami, and Bear Bryant was guiding his 8-1-1 Alabama team to Dallas for the first time since 1954.

Circumstances painted the Sugar into what was becoming its usual wait-and-see position. On the second-to-last weekend of the regular season, it was decided that 1) If Ole Miss beat Tennessee, the Rebels would be invited; 2) If Ole Miss lost

and Auburn beat Georgia, Auburn would be invited; 3) If both Ole Miss and Auburn lost and North Carolina State beat Clemson, North Carolina State would receive the invitation; 4) If all three lost, Penn State would be considered the visitor; 5) In case Ole Miss lost, an alternate possibility was LSU, then a precarious 4-3-1 but impressive enough in its final two games to merit a bid. Wyoming, then 9-0-0 and seventh-ranked, but like Army somewhat of a curiosity, couldn't be counted out of the visitor's corner because of its impressive record. However, the Western Athletic Conference was an unknown quantity, and the Sugar Bowl had not scouted the Cowboys. The results rolled in: Tennessee 20, Ole Miss 7; Georgia 17, Auburn 0; Clemson 14, N.C. State 6.

Penn State defeated Ohio University 35-14 to save what appeared to be a snakebitten Sugar Saturday. That night LSU waxed Mississippi State 55-0, and Wyoming completed a perfect season with a 21-19 edging

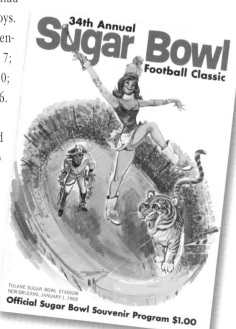

Jim Kiick (21) evades Johnny Garlington (89) behind a block.

of Texas Western. The Sugar jumped at an LSU-Penn State match, but the Nittany Lions wanted to hold off any firm decision until after their game with Pittsburgh the following week. Sight unseen and reminiscent of the early days, the Cowboys were contacted and asked if they'd be interested. Wyoming most certainly was.

The Cowboys led the nation in rushing defense (42.3 yards) and total defense (185.2 yards) and was 10th in passing offense (207.7 yards). It had not lost in 14 consecutive games and was unbeaten in one Gator and three Sun Bowl appearances. According to one fan, the reaction to the Sugar Bowl invitation by Wyoming's 330,000 inhabitants was, "It's the biggest thing since statehood."

LSU, an old bowl hand, took things as a matter of course. Despite its 5-3-1 record and unranked standing, LSU was an excellent football team and one that stood only 10 points away from a perfect season. Each of its losses and the tie could be traced to its placekicking game. "I've never seen more losses in one season stemming from the place-kick," said Tiger Coach Charlie McClendon. "If we would have made all our placekicks, we'd be on top."

With only arch-rival Tulane left to play, LSU looked like a shoo-in for a 6-3-1 record. At the half the Tigers were ahead

28-0. In the second half Tulane picked up the fight and cut the difference to 34-27 in the fourth quarter. With Tulane driving for a possible tying or winning touchdown, an ill-looking Sugar Bowl President Sam Corenswet, Jr., forced himself to his feet and told *States-Item* columnist Peter Finney he was going to search for a place to jump out of the stadium. "Try the press box window," advised Finney. "That's high enough so that if they go for two and miss you'll have enough time to pull the rip-cord."

Fortunately for Corenswet, matters didn't come to that. LSU won, 41-27.

The chase is on after LSU's Sammy Grezaffi blocks Wyoning's Jerry DePoyster's field goal attempt.

"I don't know if I can run that fast again."

Nelson Stokley (14) finally lights LSU's fire against Wyoming.

This was one of those Games of My Life – an unexpected performance by an unexpected player at an unexpected time, and one never equaled again.

Nobody knew much about third-string sophomore tailback Glenn Smith, except high school aficionados in New Orleans who remembered him from prep powerhouse Holy Cross.

Wyoming coach Lloyd Eaton was much more concerned about the cold, damp and soggy Sugar Bowl turf under drizzly skies. Eaton said on New Year's Eve, "I believe the weather could be an important factor. The team with the best runners and pass receivers, and the heaviest linemen, would have the advantage on a wet field."

Everyone agreed that on all accounts those conditions favored LSU. "We were limited in that we had a sparse club," said Eaton, whose 47-man club was a six-point underdog. "Charlie McClendon would use 55-60 players routinely. We just didn't have that kind of depth, and I knew by the fourth quarter our boys would be leg-weary."

Obviously, the best thing Eaton could hope for was to be far enough ahead after three quarters to withstand a fourth-quarter assault.

It very nearly worked out that way. LSU, which hadn't played particularly well in any of its previous seven Sugar Bowl appearances, showed signs of that malaise again. Dominating the first half, the seemingly much more animated Cowboys finally got points when Jim Kiick went over on the first play of the second quarter. Jerry DePoyster added to the lead with a 24-yard field goal with 2:58 remaining in the half, then got another one – a Sugar Bowl record 49-yarder – with one second to go.

Eaton's troops not only had a 13-0 lead, but had 11 first downs to LSU's 1. The Cowboys had outrushed the Tigers 130-33, and outgained LSU in passing yardage 85-5.

"We were very worried by the half," said Tiger center Barry Wilson, who had been a high school teammate of Smith. "The field turned up a little sloppy, and it upset our plans to block Wyoming low. Because we weren't able to get solid footing, they merely pushed us off and got to the ball-carrier. They were also able to put a lot of pressure on (quarterback) Nelson (Stokley). At halftime we decided to take advantage of their pursuit by starting to the outside and then running back against the grain."

Also, after DePoyster barely missed a 46-yard field goal, Smith was inserted into the lineup.

Flying out of the backfield, Smith took a pass over his shoulder and sloshed his way down the middle to the 26 for a 39-yard gain – LSU's first real sign of life in the game. Smith went in from the 1, and Roy Hurd's PAT cut the margin to 13-7.

With Stokley throwing medium passes and running the option, and Smith constantly picking his holes and cutting back, the Tigers threatened again. "Glenn was great at (running to daylight)," Wilson said. Tommy Morel out-jumped two defenders for an eight-yard touchdown, but Hurd missed the PAT, leaving the score tied with 11:39 to play. Following an interception, Stokley rolled out from the Cowboy 14, spotted a wide-open Morel at the 1 and threw for LSU's go-ahead points.

With 1:37 left, Wyoming made for a wild finish. From his 18, Paul Toscano dropped and threw to a more than adequately covered George Anderson. One of three Tigers converging on the ball reached up and tipped it – right into the tight end's hands. Anderson was suddenly racing, alone, for points. "When I saw Anderson take off with the football," said cornerback Barton Frye, "I started running for my life. I don't know if I can run that fast again." He caught and brought down Anderson 54 yards downfield, at the LSU 18.

It happened again. With one second left, Gene Huey cut across the secondary from left to right and Toscano went to him at the 5. He was immediately nailed by defensive back Gerry Kent.

"I would have given half a year's salary for 10 more seconds," moaned Eaton. "Just 10 more seconds."

Depth, the very factor Eaton most feared, was the difference. Smith, with little more than a quarter's playing time, finished with 74 yards rushing and caught one pass for 39 yards to be named the game's MVP.

Smith had a different perspective on the biggest Sugar Bowl comeback since Tulane fell behind Temple 14-0 in 1935. "If Wyoming had beaten us," Smith, who never did start a game at LSU, said, "I wouldn't have been able to go home."

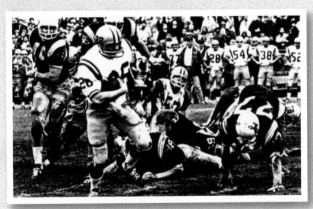

LSU tailback Glenn Smith (26) breaks away from the Cowboy defense in key play of Tiger comeback.

	1	2	3	4	
LSU	0	0	7	13	20
Wyoming	0	13	0	0	13

Wyoming: Kiick, 1-yard run. PAT, DePoyster kick.

Wyoming: DePoyster, 24-yard field goal.

Wyoming: DePoyster, 49-yard field goal.

LSU: Smith, 1-yard run. PAT, Hurd kick.

LSU: Morel, 8-yard pass from Stokley. Kick failed.

LSU: Morel, 14-yard pass from Stokley. PAT, Hurd kick.

Individual Leaders

Rushing
LSU: Smith 16-74, 1 TD; Allen 16-41.
Wyoming: Kiick 19-75, 1 TD; Williams 16-64.

Passing
LSU: Stokley 6-20, 91, 2 TDs.
Wyoming: Toscano 14-23, 239; Kiick 1-0.

Receiving
LSU: Morel 4-38, 2 TDs; Smith 1-39.
Wyoming: Anderson 3-100; Toscano 4-70.

LSU		Wyoming
12	First Downs	20
151	Rushing Yards	167
6-20-1	Passing	14-24-4
91	Passing Yards	239
242	Total Yards	406
9-37.1	Punts	4-49.0
0-0	Fumbles – Lost	1-1
3-25	Penalties – Yards	5-65

Attendance: 72,858.
Teams' remuneration: $430,000.
Miller-Digby Award recipient: Glenn Smith, LSU halfback.

Arkansas 16 Georgia 2

"Someday I will."

North Carolina lost a heartbreaker to Georgia in the 1947 Sugar Bowl. It's doubtful, though, that the game meant any more to the participants than to 14-year-old Vince Dooley from Mobile, Alabama. A neighborhood friend and his father asked him to accompany them to the game. Young Dooley received his allowance, one dollar, from his father and was permitted to go. "I thought I could buy a ticket," Dooley recalled, "but when we got there, all I could see was people holding tickets up and offering two for $100. It was harder to get in then than now."

The boy sat on a curb outside the stadium and listened to the crowd cheer the exploits of Charley Trippi and Charley Justice for a heartbreaking half. Eventually he made his way downtown and into a bar. "No one questioned my age," said Dooley, "in fact, I don't think anyone even noticed me. Everyone was involved with the game ... I recall a TV in the place, but I know that was before television so I guess it was a radio everyone was huddled around."

"That was my first Sugar Bowl, but I remember while I was sitting outside the stadium a policeman asked me what was the matter. I told him 'I didn't get in. But someday I will!' "

Twenty-two years later Vince Dooley did return, as head coach of Georgia's unbeaten Bulldogs. It took some doing to get Georgia in the 1969 Sugar. Early indications were that the Orange Bowl gambled and packaged a Penn State-Kansas game, which was a fine pairing. After the Jayhawks lost to Oklahoma, though, it lost some of its appeal. On the surface, Georgia was still the pick of both the Orange and Sugar. The Bulldogs, leaders in total offense and defense for the SEC, were atop the standings with an undefeated but twice-tied record.

The Sugar Bowl was not an object of Georgia affection. Bulldog officials and fans felt Georgia, not LSU, should have been asked to the 1968 game. But while the Orange Bowl said it wanted to await the outcome of the Georgia-Auburn game, the Sugar Bowl offered Georgia a no-strings-attached invitation which was accepted.

35th Annual Sugar Bowl

Missouri was the first choice for the visitor's berth, but a loss to Oklahoma forced the Sugar to look at the Southwest Conference. Texas and Arkansas were tied for the conference lead. An expected Longhorn victory over Texas A&M and a Razorback win over Texas Tech would put Texas in the Cotton Bowl and send Arkansas to New Orleans. The reverse

A pair of young lions: Coach Vince Dooley of Georgia and Frank Broyles of Arkansas pose before 1969 Sugar.

would put Texas in the Crescent City. However, it worked out as planned.

The eigth-rankcd Hogs had given up a very noticeable 187 points during their 9-1 season. Dooley immediately explained Arkansas' success, "Overall, I believe the Arkansas defense recovered 22 fumbles and made 20-odd interceptions. To put it simply, they did an exceptionally good job of getting the football for their offense."

Coach Frank Broyles relished the role his seven-point underdog Hogs took against the fourth-ranked Bulldogs. "You know, it's not cricket for an underdog to talk about the favorite," he grinned. "They are favored, and a year older and stronger across the board." Broyles' 80-year-old mother was going to be at the game, and even she knew not to believe everything a coach says before a game. "She hasn't missed one of our bowl games," laughed Broyles. "I remember in 1945, when

we (Georgia Tech) played Tulsa in the Orange Bowl, my father couldn't make the game so mother put an ad in the paper saying, 'I'm Frank Broyles mother. I need a ride to the Orange Bowl.' " Needless to say, she got it.

Georgia's SEC-leading statistics in total offense (391.7 yards), total defense (235 yards), scoring offense (28.2 points), and nation-leading scoring defense (9.8 points) brought reminiscences from Broyles.

"I'd like to thank the Sugar Bowl for being so nice to us," said Broyles. "This is our third trip here. Our first two opponents were Southeastern Conference champions (Alabama in 1962, Ole Miss in 1963) and both led the nation in scoring defense. This year we're playing Georgia, another SEC champion, and they had the best defensive average this year. Why pick on us?"

"I couldn't believe I was past him."

No one had to tell the Arkansas Razorbacks their defense was suspect. Their coach, Frank Broyles, had been saying it all season.

As Vince Dooley observed, the Hog defense earned its keep with its adeptness at forcing turnovers.

For Arkansas to be able to stay with Georgia, Broyles felt he had to be able to find some way to exploit the Bulldog defense, and that his own defense would have to find ways to pry the ball away from the Dawgs.

Part of the plan was to bring on a personal duel between Georgia All-American safety Jake Scott and Arkansas' Chuck Dicus, then a 171-pound sophomore and an outstanding pass receiver.

When Georgia went to a slot formation, where the split end, flanker and tight end were lined up on the same side, Scott would cover whoever was in the slot. Quarterback Bill Montgomery said, "The idea was to get Scott one-on-one with Dicus." The other part of the plan was for the Razorback defensive backs to delay the Georgia receivers. Broyles also put

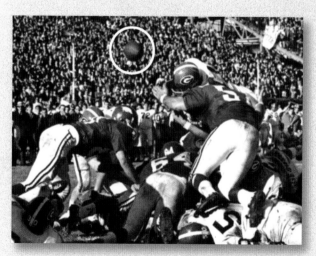

The ball flies from Brad Johnson's grasp and Vince Dooley realizes things couldn't have been nearly as bad in 1947 as in 1969.

in a blitz package, the idea being to pressure quarterback Mike Cavan into hurrying his plays, perhaps forcing turnovers, and preventing the receivers from getting deep before the pressure could be applied.

A game plan has seldom worked as successfully as this one, particularly early.

In Georgia's first six possessions the Bulldogs lost the ball four times with three fumbles and an interception. The problem for Broyles was that Arkansas fared only slightly better, with Montgomery throwing seven incompletions and one interception as well as being sacked once before his first successful pass, a one-yarder.

On the first play of the second quarter, though, Dicus faked a down-and-out, then blew downfield on a post pattern and made an arms extended, fingertip grab at the goal line for a 27-yard touchdown. "I had been running the down-and-out with some success," said Dicus. "I think Scott had gotten to where he was anticipating it, so we changed to the post. I couldn't believe I was past him."

Later, after a clipping penalty put Arkansas back to its 6, tailback Bill Burnett started a sweep. But end David McKnight broke through and dropped the runner for a safety.

Montgomery, who had to be administered a nerve shot at the half, the result of a spinning tackle, took the Hogs on a long drive after a lost Georgia fumble – in the process tying Glenn Dobbs' 26-year-old record of nine straight completions – to a 24-yard field goal by Bob White.

Georgia no sooner came out in the second half when it was in threatening position again. After Cavan took the Bulldogs to the Razorbacks 3, Brad Johnson tried to hurdle the line.

Arkansas' Bill Burnett skips past Georgia defender.

Defenders Dick Bumpus and Lynn Garner sandwiched the runner and the ball jettisoned from Johnson's arm straight out of the end zone for a touchback.

"It was about then that I realized how much better off I might have been 22 years before," Dooley said, "when I was a kid sitting on the curb outside the stadium." Broyles added, "You could almost feel the lift that gave us. And it had to take something out of them."

Two fourth-quarter Arkansas field goals of 24 and 31 yards by White put the game out of reach for Georgia.

With just 40 yards rushing, it was obvious Broyles' aerial plan was essential. It produced only one touchdown but Dicus caught a Sugar Bowl record 12 passes for 169 of Arkansas' 183 air yards.

The Arkansas defense was striking, slicing Georgia's 397-yard per game average in half, and the Hogs recovered all five of Georgia's fumbles and picked off a pass. It wasn't pretty, but Broyles handicapped the game perfectly.

Noting those stats and that Cliff Powell had eight unassisted tackles and was in on seven others, that Guy Parker had 10 solos, and that defensive back Jerry Moore had two interceptions, broke up two passes, and was in on four tackles, lineman Gordon McNulty had one question for his coach in the locker room: "Coach," he asked, "is the defense still suspect?"

Broyles returned the grin.

	1	2	3	4	
Arkansas	0	10	0	6	16
Georgia	0	2	0	0	2

Arkansas: Dicus, 27-yard pass from Montgomery. PAT, White kick.

Georgia: Safety, Burnett tackled in end zone.

Arkansas: White, 34-yard field goal.

Arkansas: White, 24-yard field goal.

Arkansas: White, 31-yard field goal.

Individual Leaders

Rushing
Arkansas: Burnett 2-31.
Georgia: Johnson 12-45.

Passing
Arkansas: Montgomery 17-39-1, 185 yards, 1 TD.
Georgia: Cavan 9-22-1, 103 yards.

Receiving
Arkansas: Dicus 12-169, 1 TD; Peacock 3-15.
Georgia: Whittemore 5-56; Lawrence 3-54.

Arkansas		Georgia
13	First Downs	13
40	Rushing Yards	75
17-39-1	Passing	11-31-3
185	Passing Yards	117
225	Total Yards	192
10-33.6	Punts	10-38.5
4-2	Fumbles – Lost	5-5
4-31	Penalties – Yards	4-25

Attendance: 82,113.
Teams' remuneration: $480,000.
Miller-Digby Award recipient: Chuck Dicus, Arkansas flanker.

Mississippi 27 Arkansas 22

"Hee-haw, hee-haw."

In a roundabout way the seeds for the 1970 Sugar Bowl pairing were planted in a magazine article. Nineteen sixty-nine was a season that would bring one of the most dramatic changes in the bowl scene, and one in which the Mid-Winter Sports Association would deliberately select a lesser-ranked team over a stronger possibility.

Rumors began circulating in November, 1969, that Notre Dame, because of expected projects in the athletic department, would consider breaking the school's 45-year-old bowl ban. Coach Ara Parseghian told the Chicago Football Writers, "In all previous five seasons I've coached at Notre Dame, we've received a bowl invitation every year. And every year our board meets to review and consider these invitations, and every year the board turns them down. I'm sure, if we can win the rest of our games this year, we'll probably get another invitation, but I have no reason to believe the policy will change. Maybe somebody knows something that I don't know."

As the football season moved toward the middle of November the bowl scene seemed to be falling easily into line. No. 1-ranked Texas held the almost certain home spot in Dallas; Tennessee seemed headed for the Orange Bowl; the Sugar looked well-fixed with a possibility of either Auburn or LSU. Joe Paterno's excellent Penn State Nittany Lions were the top priority as the opposition for all three bowls. Texas Coach Darrell Royal tried to talk Paterno into a Dallas New Year's because this fine pairing would have given the Cotton Bowl the foremost game of the day.

Second in line for Dallas was LSU — truly an exceptional team that allowed only 38 yards a game rushing and 91 points for the season while scoring 349 points, a modern school record. It translated into a 9-1 record and an eighth place in the polls. Las Vegas odds-makers considered only Ohio State and the Longhorns better than the Tigers on a neutral field.

When Penn State declined its offer to play Texas, LSU was rarin' to prove its mettle in Dallas. With only a three-point loss to Ole Miss on its record, the right set of circumstances and a victory over the No. 1-ranked team would catapult the Tigers very high in the final voting, which again would take place after the bowls.

But that three-point loss would prove an insurmountable obstacle. Mississippi started the season as the odds-on choice to win the Southeastern Conference championship. Early losses to Kentucky and Alabama and a later defeat to Houston made the Rebels a disappointment. With the most exciting quarterback in the country, Archie Manning, a scrambling, tackle-slipping shadow, Ole Miss

Archie Manning (18) of Ole Miss searches for a receiver.

was one of the nation's most entertaining offensive shows — one that left a mark on SEC and national standings. Georgia was unbeaten and ranked sixth when it played the Rebels. Ole Miss won 26-23.

The week Mississippi was to play unbeaten and 3rd-ranked Tennessee, things started cracking. Rumors of Notre Dame breaking its bowl ban grew stronger. Then there was the matter of Tennessee linebacker Steve Kiner's quotes in Sports Illustrated. "I don't think they're that tough," Kiner said of the Rebels. The reporter said, "But they have a lot of horses down there." Kiner snorted, "A lot of people go down on the farm and can't tell the difference between a horse and a mule."

Ole Miss beat Tennessee, 38-0. When the score reached 31-0, Confederate flag-waving Rebel fans in Jackson's Memorial Stadium began braying at the Vols, Kiner in particular, "Hee-haw, hee-haw ..." Tennessee's eye-catching loss knocked it from the Orange Bowl.

Then Notre Dame agreed to meet Texas in the Cotton Bowl. The Orange Bowl quickly secured Missouri to play Penn State. The Sugar Bowl would seem to have found a diamond with LSU. A breakdown in communications, however, left the Tigers home for the holidays.

"We thought we had the Cotton Bowl locked up," said one person in the LSU athletic department. "We handled the thing all wrong. We waited all day for word from the Cotton Bowl, but they never called. LSU didn't handle it right, and neither did the Cotton Bowl for that matter."

The Sugar Bowl, miffed because its home-state team seemed far more interested in playing Texas than playing in New Orleans, bypassed what looked to be an obvious choice and selected Ole Miss. Tiger fans immediately began saying the Sugar should go for an LSU-Rebel rematch, like the 1960 game into which they felt they had been cornered. Dr. Fred Wolfe, president of the Sugar Bowl, reminded Tiger supporters, "We did invite LSU, but to my knowledge they wanted to go to the Cotton Bowl."

Arkansas, 3rd-ranked with a fiery offense featuring junior quarterback Bill Montgomery and receiver Chuck Dicus, was to be Ole Miss' opponent. The Hogs had an outside chance at winning the national championship, though the Rebels' 7-3 record took some gilt off the game.

In the final analysis the Sugar Bowl's choice of Ole Miss was a vote for the most exciting player in America — Manning. Coupled with Arkansas' fire-power in a game that couldn't touch the other bowls in ranking, the Rebels would give New Orleans a game the others couldn't match in spectacle.

"We were just a hot football team."

"That was an exceptional year in college football," Archie Manning recalled. "There were a lot of real good teams all across the country. But I honestly felt, despite the loss to Texas (which may well have decided the national championship), that we had drawn the best team anywhere in the Sugar Bowl. Arkansas was one heck of a football team."

At the end of the day most observers would say the Sugar Bowl had drawn two of the very best.

The spotlight was temporarily taken from superstar Manning, a mild-mannered, red-haired quarterback who also may have been the best in the country, when work-horse fullback Bo Bowen took a pitch and sideswiped defenders 69 yards to the end zone.

Arkansas missed a chance – and a field goal – by driving to the Rebel 23. Six plays later, Ole Miss was in front 14-0.

In a display of Manning's hell-bent-for-leather style, on fourth-and-one at the 18, he hightailed it around right end, ran over two Hogs at the 15, then slashed through several more before high-stepping into the end zone.

Bill Montgomery, an outstanding quarterback in his own right, answered with an 81-yard 13-play drive. Bill Burnett, taking a pitch at the 12, got outside containment, split a couple of Rebels at the goal and scored. Bill McClard's PAT was wide, leaving the score at 14-6.

Back came the Rebels, and shortly Cloyce Hinton kicked a Sugar Bowl record 52-yard field goal. "I'll tell you, we were just a hot football team," said Manning. "Everything was working for us."

That was a good thing for Ole Miss, because every point would ultimately prove precious.

There were just under five minutes remaining until the half when Hinton made his kick. When Arkansas was held to a three-and-out, the door was opened for another Ole Miss score. From the Rebel 30, Manning eased his offense downfield, and when two Razorback defensive backs went with tight end Jim Poole across the middle, receiver Vern Studdard was open at the 15. He grabbed Manning's pass and went in untouched. "Archie rolled away from the direction I took, and I started downfield, stopped, and came back for the pass. The backs had gone across to stop Archie and I was all alone," Studdard said.

In the two-and-a-half minutes remaining, Montgomery furiously lashed the Razorbacks 80 yards to get back in the game. Dicus caught a 47-yard touchdown pass when the Ole Miss secondary got twisted up in its assignments. With the score at 24-12, Broyles elected to go for a two-point conversion, which failed.

"You know, we had 260 yards offense at the half," Mont-

Elusive Archie Manning slips loose from Razorback defense.

gomery said, "So we couldn't be disappointed with that aspect. We just didn't score enough points."

Hinton added to the Ole Miss margin with a 36-yard field goal in the third quarter, but McClard answered with a 35-yarder for Arkansas.

A pair of fourth period interceptions put the Hogs back in the hunt. Glenn Cannon, who was having a spectacular days in the Rebel secondary, picked off Montgomery in the end zone after he drove Arkansas to the Ole Miss 11.

Dennis Berner returned the favor – and the ball back to the 11 – by picking off Manning. The upshot was that in three plays Montgomery had Arkansas within five points of the Rebels. Montgomery rolled right, was hit hard by Hap Farber, and still managed to get the ball to fullback Bruce Maxwell. That cut it to 27-22.

In the final minutes, it was left to Cannon to preserve the victory for Ole Miss breaking ups several passes. With less than two minutes to play, and Arkansas at the Rebel 40, Montgomery found Dicus at the 25, who made the catch but fumbled when Cannon hit him. The defender recovered. "I just hit Dicus," Cannon said, "and when I saw the ball jump loose, I hopped on it ... I knew it was over then."

Ironically, the pass that Dicus fumbled was his sixth catch for 171 yards, breaking his own receiving yardage record from the 1969 game by two yards.

Ole Miss, in what had to be in some ways its most frustrating season, had upset its fourth Top 10 opponent. The Rebels and Arkansas each broke three Sugar Bowl records in amassing a whopping total of 954 yards. If not the most important game played that day, it was the most entertaining.

Unfortunately only a few more than the stadium crowd of 82,500 would know just what a spectacle the 1970 Sugar Bowl really was. The game drew a television rating of 8.3.

Since records had been kept, going back to 1964, it was the worst rating for any major bowl.

	1	2	3	4	
Mississippi	14	10	3	0	27
Arkansas	0	12	3	7	22

Mississippi: Bowen, 69-yard run. PAT, King kick.
Mississippi: Manning, 18-yard run. PAT, King kick.
Arkansas: Burnett, 12-yard run. Kick failed.
Mississippi: Hinton, 52-yard field goal.
Mississippi: Studdard, 30-yard pass from Manning. PAT, King kick.
Arkansas: Dicus, 47-yard pass from Montgomery. Pass failed.
Mississippi: Hinton, 36-yard field goal.
Arkansas: McClard, 35-yard field goal.
Arkansas: Maxwell, 6-yard pass from Montgomery. PAT, McClard kick.

Individual Leaders

Rushing
Mississippi: Bowen 12-94, 1 TD; Manning 13-39, 1 TD.
Arkansas: Maxwell 8-108, Burnett 17-59, 1 TD.

Passing
Mississippi: Manning 21-35-2, 273 yards, 1 TD.
Arkansas: Montgomery 17-34-1, 338 yards, 2 TDs.

Receiving
Mississippi: Studdard 5-108, 1 TD; Reed 2-22.
Arkansas: Dicus 6-171, 1 TD; Maxwell 9-137, 1 TD.

Mississippi		Arkansas
21	First Downs	24
154	Rushing Yards	189
21-35-2	Passing	16-34-2
273	Passing Yards	338
427	Total Yards	527
6-37.6	Punts	2-30.5
0-0	Fumbles – Lost	1-1
11-101	Penalties – Yards	3-22

Attendance: 80,096.
Teams' remuneration: $698,792.
Miller-Digby Award recipient: Archie Manning, Ole Miss quarterback.

Tennessee 34 Air Force 13

"I've already been bombed."

For 12 years, since the death of Fred Digby, the Mid-Winter Sports Association had basically been run by committee. Edna Engert, the secretary hired by the organization in 1936, carried out the day-by-day duties of the office, and the various committees of the membership made the hard-and-fast decisions. The Sugar Bowl had realized for some time that it needed an executive director.

Navy Captain Joseph T. Katz, a native New Orleanian, was retiring. His last tour of duty in a 28-year military career was as head of public relations and special projects for Vice Admiral Tom Connolly. On July 27, 1970, Joe Katz was appointed executive director.

The pickings for bowl eligibles outside the South were slim in 1970. Nebraska, Notre Dame, and Air Force, in that order, were the obvious choices to fill the 1971 berths. At an early date it appeared that Notre Dame and Nebraska would meet in the Orange Bowl, though the Irish had a late-season game with formidable LSU. The Sugar Bowl wanted either of those teams or, in lieu of the Southeastern Conference champion, the higher-ranked SEC runner-up Tennessee Volunteers.

Voting for the Associated Press national champion would again be done after the bowls, and this situation added some spice to postseason games. When the champion was picked before the bowls, the higher-ranked teams seemed to look more for the easy mark and a good time.

The No. 3-ranked Cornhuskers wanted the No. 6-ranked Irish because Notre Dame was viewed as Nebraska's stepping-stone to the national championship. It was reported that some Orange Bowl officials wanted Notre Dame win, lose, or draw against No. 7-ranked LSU; others wanted the Irish-Tiger victor.

Texas, with a No. 1 ranking, was a huge attraction for the Cotton Bowl, and it was also keenly interested in the LSU-Notre Dame winner.

As it turned out, Notre Dame won a somewhat controversial 3-0 victory over the Tigers and accepted a Cotton Bowl invitation. The snubbed Orange Bowl was then left with a choice of LSU or Arkansas. Any chance the Sugar had with LSU may have been dashed the year before when the Mid-Winter Sports Association opted for Ole Miss.

LSU accepted a provisional invitation from Miami that stipulated the Tigers had to defeat its final two opponents, Tulane and Ole Miss. At the same time, the Sugar invited No. 8-ranked Tennessee, which in most years would have been a

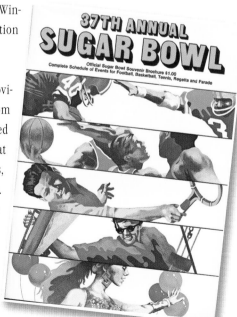

Captain Joe Katz, second executive director of the Sugar Bowl.

prime bowl target, and No. 10-ranked Air Force, an exciting offensive team, though both had difficult games remaining.

The Vols handled their assignments well, defeating Vanderbilt 24-6 and UCLA 28-17 and rose to 4th in the polls. Air Force did not do as well, beating Rose Bowl-bound Stanford 31-14 but getting drubbed 49-19 by Colorado in its final game.

Charles Zatarain represented the Sugar Bowl at the Air Force-Colorado game, trying to keep a smile on through the darkest moments of the ordeal. An officer came to Zatarain's seat and informed him there had been a crank call about a bomb planted in the press box. "Don't worry about me, Colonel," smiled Zatarain, casting an eye toward the scoreboard. "I've already been bombed."

So, while the Cotton Bowl and Orange Bowl had the earmarks of No. 1 shoot-outs, the Sugar and Rose Bowls had only outside shots at one of their teams becoming the national champion.

Still, New Orleans would be getting an interesting contrast. Air Force averaged 423.6 yards in offense, third best in the na-

tion. The Vols were second nationally in defense, surrendering a miserly 88.4 yards a game.

The pragmatic Sugar Bowlers made a concession to realism for this game. New Orleans and Dallas, the only bowls that competed in the same approximate time slot, had been inflicting damage on each other's television ratings. The Cotton Bowl had come out the better in recent years. With No. 1 Texas and an attention-grabber like Notre Dame, the Sugar realized there was no way anybody was going to top the Cotton Bowl's viewer interest. The Mid-Winter Sports Association moved its kickoff to noon, which gave it an hour jump on Dallas. It was also realized that the move would hold the Sugar viewers until just about the half.

Tennessee, under 29-year-old Coach Bill Battle, opened a 10-point favorite. Battle, who felt that a bowl trip was a reward, worked his team hard in practice but allowed the squad freedom to enjoy the city. On the other hand, Air Force Coach Ben Martin appeared grim and determined to make up for the Colorado defeat. Writers, noticing this and Tennessee's mediocre 6-10 bowl history, began picking the Falcons.

"We had the momentum going."

It was over quickly, if not painlessly. Making the shortest work of any Sugar Bowl foe, Tennessee virtually put an end to Air Force's hopes nine minutes after kickoff.

The Falcons threw up an eight-man line, in an attempt to slow down the Vols' potent running game. Quarterback Bobby Scott neutralized that strategy and outguessed the blitz threat as the Vols steamed 59 yards on Tennessee's first possession for a touchdown. Two minutes and 45 seconds were gone in the first period when Don McLeary took a pitchout, cut behind a block by Curt Watson, and scored from the 5.

"We had the momentum going," said Scott.

They sure did.

After recovering an Air Force fumble, George Hunt kicked a 30-yard field goal for Tennessee.

Then the Vols applied the coup de grace to the flyboys. After Air Force punted to the Tennessee 42, Scott, rolling right, zipped a pass to Lester McLain at the 20. McLeary took a handoff, found a hole on the left side, broke a tackle and cut to his left. Another defender slipped off, and McLeary scored his second TD of the afternoon.

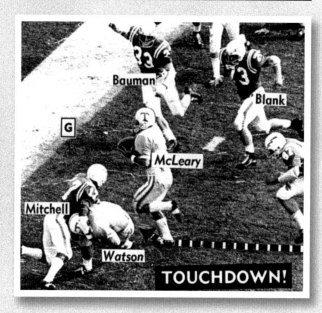

Don McLeary cuts behind a block to score Tennessee's first touchdown against Air Force.

Yet another Air Force fumble gave the Vols possession at the Falcon 24. Four plays later, Scott passed to Gary Theiler at the 5 and he stepped the rest of the way into the end zone.

In four possessions, Tennessee scored four times and led 24-0 with 3:12 to go in the first quarter.

This one was all over but the weeping for the Falcons.

Air Force finally saw the other side of the 50 in the period's waning moments with a pass interference call at the Vols' 45. That was followed by the day's most exciting moment, though it nothing to do with football. A dog raced on the field and held up the game for more than ten minutes. "I tried to chase him off," said Tennessee split end Joe Thompson, "and he almost bit me."

So much for exciting moments – the time the dog spent running around the field represented the longest first-half span that Tennessee did not score.

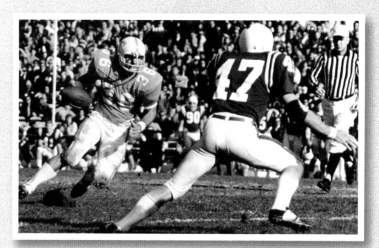

Don McLeary (36) of Tennessee turns on the afterburners while Air Force's Cyd Maattala (47) moves in.

Scott Hamm punted out on the Tennessee 8, which turned out to be one of Air Force's most effective plays. Scott fumbled the next snap, and ran back to pick up the ball at the 1. There he was knocked into the end zone and fumbled again. Darryl Hass fell on the ball to slice the margin to 24-7.

"I tried to pick it up," Scott said, "and knock it out of the end zone. But a Falcon grabbed my arm and Air Force fell on it for a touchdown."

A 57-yard punt return by Bobby Majors the first time Tennessee touched the ball in the third quarter added to the Vols' total. Majors fielded the ball, stepped to his left, picked up a convoy and headed for the faraway goal line. Hamm, the kicker, had the last chance at stopping Majors at the 30, but the runner whizzed past. "After I caught the punt," Majors said, "I looked downfield and right away (Jackie) Walker got the first man and I saw a lane there. The punter had a shot, but I sidestepped him and turned it on."

Each team scored again, but the final score, convincing as it was, didn't reflect the Vols' mistakes. Tennessee, which cut down the Air Force rushing game to minus 12 yards, came up empty on six other legitimate scoring opportunities; (1) a lost fumble on the Falcons 17; (2) a missed 32-yard field goal; (3) a missed 30-yard field goal; (4) a lost fumble on the Air Force 14; (5) a missed 42-yard field goal; and (6) an interception in the end zone from the Falcons' 21.

The Vols defense, though, was more than impressive in the mismatch. Linebacker Jamie Rotella had eight solo tackles and an assist, recovered two fumbles and broke up a pass. Fellow linebacker Ray Nettles had nine tackles, three assists and one sack.

Nettles said, "I didn't like them (Air Force). They said things on the sidelines and seemed awful cocky."

	1	2	3	4	
Tennessee	24	0	7	3	34
Air Force	7	0	6	0	13

Tennessee: McLeary, 5-yard run. PAT, Hunt kick.

Tennessee: Hunt, 30-yard field goal.

Tennessee: McLeary, 20-yard run. PAT, Hunt kick.

Tennessee: Theiler, 10-yard pass from Scott. PAT, Hunt kick.

Air Force: Haas, fumble recovery in end zone. PAT, Barry kick.

Tennessee: Majors, 57-yard punt return. PAT, Hunt kick.

Air Force: Bassa, 27-yard pass from Parker. Kick failed.

Tennessee: Hunt, 33-yard field goal.

Individual Leaders

Rushing
Tennessee: Watson 14-57; McLeary 14-39, 2 TDs.
Air Force: Bream 16-16.

Passing
Tennessee: Scott 22-40-2, 288 yards, 1 TD.
Air Force: Parker 23-46-4, 239 yards, 1 TD.

Receiving
Tennessee: Thompson 9-125.
Air Force: Bassa 10-114, 1 TD; Bolen 6-60.

Tennessee		Air Force
24	First Downs	15
86	Rushing Yards	-12
24-46-2	Passing	23-46-4
306	Passing Yards	239
392	Total Yards	227
5-31.4	Punts	8-34.5
7-3	Fumbles – Lost	7-4
6-74	Penalties – Yards	0-0

Attendance: 75,087.
Teams' remuneration: $659,668.
Miller-Digby Award recipient: Bobby Scott, Tennessee quarterback.

Oklahoma 40   Auburn 22

"Now we had invited another one."

The switch in the Sugar Bowl kickoff time to noon had exactly the anticipated effect: The ratings were fine – for a half. As soon as Texas-Notre Dame got under way the viewers changed channels. Tennessee-Air Force went into four million homes with a 8.3 rating, the same as 1970. Texas-Notre Dame was beamed into 20 million homes. The wipeout caused ABC to start thinking of a radical change in time – a New Year's Eve game.

It was strange, this merry-go-round the Sugar Bowl had boarded. Because of something out of its control – the segregation legislation of the 1950s – the Sugar Bowl entered an era of essentially regional games. Because of it, and some extraordinary bad fortune when race was no longer an issue, its television ratings were weak. The Orange and Cotton Bowls had, conversely, gotten stronger with television. It added up to this: The Dallas and Miami games received more television money because of ratings. New Orleans didn't do as well but could hardly do better since its network, ABC, was reluctant to provide more money, money that could be used to attract better teams for the higher ratings.

What ABC wanted, beginning with the 1972 game, was a Monday night, prime-time attraction. In this case, ABC was talking about January 3. The Mid-Winter Sports Association was opposed, though it realized its $500,000 contract was up for renewal and that outcome could depend upon the ratings of the next Sugar Bowl.

The parties compromised. The Sugar Bowl stayed on New

Year's Day, but agreed to move its kickoff back to 11 a.m. where most of the attraction would be unopposed.

The Big Eight Conference, where Nebraska, Oklahoma, and Colorado held sway, lorded over the 1971 polls. Alabama and cross-state rival Auburn were the standard-bearers in the South. Penn State was the best in the East, and Notre Dame held its usual magic in the rankings. It was the Big Eight and SEC teams that were most coveted. The only question was the match-up. Nebraska, ranked No. 1 all season and leaning to New Orleans, and No. 2 Oklahoma would play in the regular season finale for the Big Eight championship. Also undefeated. No. 4 Alabama was to play No. 5-ranked Auburn for the SEC title in their last game.

Of course, the selections would have to be made before those outcomes. The Orange Bowl wanted the schools to put off committing to the bowls until the championships were resolved; then the Nebraska-Oklahoma and Alabama-Auburn winners would be welcomed to Miami, and the losers to New Orleans. The Sugar wouldn't agree to this and neither would the schools. Miami had to take its chances, too.

ABC wanted to pair Alabama and Penn State. For sheer glamour and business, Alabama-Oklahoma was the people's choice.

New Orleans' prospects were excellent. On a motion by the Executive Committee, Aruns Callery was sent to Tuscaloosa the weekend of the bowl selections. He was to invite Alabama and consult with Bear Bryant on an opponent. After Alabama's Saturday afternoon game, Bryant asked Callery to meet him at his office at 6 a.m. Sunday.

Bryant told Callery that he had made a decision and wanted to go to the Sugar Bowl. Assured the bowl most certainly wanted him, Bryant said, "I think I'll call Chuck (Fairbanks, the Oklahoma coach) and see if we can't have a national championship game for New Orleans," said Bear to a startled Callery. And Fairbanks agreed. The only thing Bryant asked of Callery was to wait until noon Monday to announce it.

On the phone with the Sugar Bowl at noon, Callery told the committee members things were looking good, but Bryant didn't want to say anything until noon the following day. He couldn't be more explicit than that. The rest of the afternoon Callery was out of phone reach, driving to Birmingham and then flying to New Orleans. And while Callery was traveling, Auburn Coach Ralph "Shug" Jordon was putting the squeeze on the Executive Committee. Jordon wanted his team invited to the Sugar Bowl and if he didn't get an immediate invitation, he would not wait until Monday. He wouldn't play in New Orleans — win, lose, or draw.

Auburn was undefeated, untied, 5th-ranked, and readying for an SEC championship game. It had a Heisman Trophy-winning quarterback in Pat Sullivan and was an excellent, exciting offensive football team.

In an emergency meeting Sunday afternoon the Executive Committee of the Sugar Bowl agreed to accept Auburn.

"When I got home," Callery remembered, "1 had a message to call Bernie Grenrood immediately. Bernie asked me to meet him at his house. 'I have terrible news,' he told me when I arrived. 'The committee called an emergency meeting at 4 o'-clock this afternoon and picked Auburn.'

"I was just frozen when I heard," said Callery. "We had, in essence, already invited two teams that morning — Alabama and Oklahoma. Now we had invited another one. I had to pour myself a couple of drinks before I called Coach Bryant. It must have looked like I was a fraud. You can't print what Bryant said when I told him. He did tell me to tell the Sugar Bowl that he was going to beat the hell out of Auburn."

And he did. Alabama walloped Auburn, 31-7, and Nebraska edged Oklahoma 35-31 in a game matching two of college football's all-time teams. Those results set up a national championship game for Miami and a runner-up game in the Sugar. It was just what Miami was angling for, but this time New Orleans kayoed itself.

Auburn-Oklahoma wasn't a bad match, pairing an awesome Sooner ground game against a devastating Auburn aerial display. The Sugar could have been in far worse shape. But it was still a runner-up game.

Oklahoma quarterback Jack Mildren (11) pops through Auburn line.

"We had the momentum going."

*Joe Wylie (22) leaves Tigers in his wake in
71-yard punt return.*

This should have been a spectacle.

Oklahoma, averaging 566 yards a game in a 10-1 season, was the most efficient offense in NCAA history. The Sooners were so potent they punted only 26 times in those 11 games. Auburn was no slouch either, averaging 393 yards.

Whereas Oklahoma inflicted most of its damage on the ground, with its devastating wishbone offense, the Tigers were air-minded. Quarterback Pat Sullivan passed for 2,012 yards and 20 touchdowns that season, and Terry Beasley, a superb receiver, caught 12 of those TD passes.

If the luster of a 9-1 record was smudged by the 31-7 defeat to Alabama, Auburn coach Ralph "Shug" Jordan expected that to be a psychological weapon for the Sugar Bowl. "We have a chance to redeem ourselves," said Jordan, whose team was a 10 point underdog.

But there would be no redemption for Auburn, and only Oklahoma was spectacular.

Like the 1971 Tennessee-Air Force game, the suspense in the 1972 Sugar Bowl ended shortly after the coin toss.

On the night's first play from scrimmage, quarterback Jack

Mildren gained 17 yards on a keeper and the Sooners, as they say, never looked back.

On the 13th play of the 77-yard drive, six minutes removed from the kickoff, Leon Crosswhite scored from the 4.

Sullivan misplaced a handoff onto the hip of a tailback, and Ray Hamilton recovered for Oklahoma on the Auburn 41. In eight plays, with the OU offense humming near-perfectly, the Sooners were back in the end zone. Faking to Crosswhite, who took the Tiger defense with him, Mildren went in from the 5. John Carroll, who missed the first, made the PAT to lift the score to 13-0.

Joe Wylie was the next Sooner to touch the ball. David Beverly punted to Wylie at the Oklahoma 29. Joe gathered in the kick, slipped through two onrushing Tigers and headed down the right sideline. Mark Driscoll chopped down the last man with a chance of catching the runner, and Wyle skipped into the end zone.

"It was as if we had put it on the drawing board," Wyle laughed. "It was perfect ... I ducked behind the wall. I thought I could go all the way when the wall formed."

*Jack Mildren of Oklahoma dashes in with the first of his record
three touchdowns against Auburn.*

	1	2	3	4	
Oklahoma	19	12	3	6	40
Auburn	0	0	7	15	22

Oklahoma: Crosswhite, 4-yard run. Kick failed.
Oklahoma: Mildren, 5-yard run. PAT, Carroll kick.
Oklahoma: Wylie, 71-yard punt return. Pass failed.
Oklahoma: Mildren, 4-yard run. Run failed.
Oklahoma: Mildren, 7-yard run. Pass failed.
Oklahoma: Carroll, 53-yard field goal.
Auburn: Unger, 1-yard run. PAT, Jett kick.
Oklahoma: Pruitt, 2-yard run. Kick failed.
Auburn: Cannon, 11-yard pass from Sullivan. PAT, Jett kick.
Auburn: Unger, 1-yard run. PAT, Beck run.

Individual Leaders

Rushing
Oklahoma: Mildren 30-149, 3 TDs; Pruitt 18-95, 1 TD; Crosswhite 17-78, 1 TD.
Auburn: Unger 6-38, 2 TDs; Lowry 5-12.

Passing
Oklahoma: Mildren 1-4-0, 11 yards.
Auburn: Sullivan 20-44-1, 250 yards, 1 TD.

Receiving
Oklahoma: Chandler 1-11.
Auburn: Beasley 6-117; Unger 5-36.

Oklahoma		Auburn
28	First Downs	15
439	Rushing Yards	40
1-4-0	Passing	20-45-2
11	Passing Yards	250
450	Total Yards	290
5-35.4	Punts	5-48.6
5-2	Fumbles – Lost	5-1
3-12	Penalties – Yards	0-0

Attendance: 84,031.
Teams' remuneration: $742,878.
Miller-Digby Award recipient: Jack Mildren, Oklahoma quarterback.

Sooner Coach Chuck Fairbanks, left, greets Ralph "Shug" Jordan after 40-22 Oklahoma victory.

As nobody could catch Wylie, at this point, with a three-touchdown lead and the first quarter not even over, nobody was going to catch Oklahoma either – despite the Sooners missing on five after-touchdown conversions.

"I just started playing bad," Sullivan offered afterward. "As big and strong as they were, I knew they were going to score a lot, and we were just going to have to out-score them. We just weren't able to."

There were many reasons why things got out of hand for Auburn. Sullivan may have found the best one when he sighed, "If there is a team in the country better than Oklahoma, I'm sure glad we don't have to play them."

The only balm for Auburn was the Orange Bowl. Alabama played a better team than Oklahoma and Nebraska ground up the Crimson Tide in another game that was over pretty quickly.

Oklahoma 14 Penn State 0

"They got that idea from Monday Night Football."

The noon kickoff, a time change that for all practical purposes excluded West Coast television viewing, was a disaster. The ratings for the Sugar Bowl were only slightly higher than those for regular season NCAA telecasts (14.6 to 14.0), and it had the smallest audience of the major bowls. ABC, whose sports operation was headed by Roone Arledge, decided drastic measures had to be taken and began pressing for a New Year's Eve game over the objections of most of the Mid-Winter Sports Association membership.

"They (ABC) got that idea from 'Monday Night Football,' " said Sugar Bowl member Charles Zatarain. "On a night when people are planning to go out to celebrate, it didn't seem logical that a football game would keep them home that extra couple of hours. And in New Orleans it sure wouldn't work. This is a party town, so we were going to lose people in the stadium because of New Year's celebrations. The thing was a network decision. They wanted it, and, of course, they were buying it and we went along with it."

For going along with it, ABC increased its yearly payment to the Sugar Bowl from $510,000 to $575,000 and spent an additional $100,000 improving the Tulane Stadium lighting. For a New Year's Day game, ABC would have paid $300,000.

The NCAA granted the Sugar Bowl permission to move the date of the game. A Sugar Bowl was scheduled for New Year's Eve, 1972, for 8 p.m. instead of the more logical 7 p.m. because the network didn't want to preempt its popular series, "The FBI." They pointed out that the Orange Bowl had been hurt during the opening 30 minutes the year before while "All in the Family" was being telecast in opposition to the Nebraska-Alabama national championship match.

New Year's Eve, 1972, would also break another tradition. The game would be played on a Sunday. All the major bowls historically sidestepped Sunday games and played on January 2 in those years when New Year's fell on the Sabbath. "We kind of expected protests from the churches and religious groups," said Joe Katz, of the Sugar Bowl committee, "but nobody made anything over it at all."

Of the events important to the Sugar Bowl in 1972, none may have been bigger than the retirement of the last bonds indebted by the Mid-Winter Sports Association. Now it was free and clear of debt.

Bear Bryant held the keys to the makeup of the bowl games that season. Practically everyone agreed that for pure talent Nebraska had the best team in the country. But the Cornhuskers, playing their last season under Bob Devaney, had a loss and a tie on their record. Undefeated Southern Cal was ranked No. 1, making also unbeaten and 2nd-ranked Alabama the team every bowl wanted and the team any national championship contender would have to play in order to have a chance at the title.

Devaney had a no-strings-attached invitation to New Orleans that he seemed to relish, but he wanted to play Alabama. Bryant hinted early that he would play in either the Sugar or the Cotton Bowl, but let it be known if he played in New Orleans he wanted to play Penn State. Notre Dame was interested in the Sugar if it did not have to play Nebraska. The team preferred to play Alabama, Penn State, or Louisiana State. LSU was the second SEC choice (Alabama, the first) for the Sugar's host spot, and the Tigers wanted Penn State.

Bryant accepted a bid to the Cotton Bowl. With its only chance for a national championship gone, Nebraska went to the Big Eight's port of call. LSU, thinking Penn State was out of the Sugar Bowl picture, accepted a Bluebonnet Bowl berth. But the Sugar took 6th-ranked Penn State and, with its two SEC favorites no longer on the scene, went for 4th-ranked Oklahoma. Notre Dame ended up as Nebraska's Orange Bowl partner.

Oklahoma still had a game to play — with Bob Devaney's dreadnought — but the Sooners had an outside chance at No. 1, with a potential 11-1-0 season.

Upset coaches began sniping at Bryant. Devaney complained, "He got three shots at me when I was unbeaten, and he won two of them. Now he won't play me." Notre Dame's Ara Parseghian criticized Alabama for taking on Southwest Conference champion Texas instead of Nebraska, or presumably Notre Dame. "From everything I've read, and by their own admission, Alabama took the easy way out," said Parseghian. "They were in the driver's seat, being undefeated, and their decision dictated the structure of the other bowls."

Bryant responded, "I just can't see playing a team in a bowl that has lost two games. We would be honored and privileged to play Notre Dame at any time except at this time."

Oklahoma made Nebraska's chance at No. 1 academic when, on Thanksgiving Day, the Sooners, a 2-touchdown underdog, scored 17 points in the final 17 minutes to beat the Cornhuskers 17-14.

Charles "Tinker" Owens, a Sooner freshman receiver, added

Freshman Tinker Owens (11) makes touchdown grab on '346-S-Post.'

excitement to the first Sugar Bowl in 23 years without an SEC team. He was the brother of former Oklahoma Heisman Trophy winner Steve Owens.

The coach of the 10-1 Nittany Lions Joe Paterno — a man whose .838 winning percentage (64-12-1) was the best in the country and who had never lost (3-0-1) in a bowl — was in a reflective mood when he met the press in New Orleans.

Paterno spoke about his team, a talented offensive unit featuring quarterback John Hufnagel, the school's total offensive leader, and John Cappelletti, who gained 1,117 yards at running back. The potent Lions averaged 32 points a game. Paterno also spoke of Oklahoma, which averaged 478 yards and 37 points a game — the nation's best. Befitting a 6-point underdog, Paterno said, "There are only two great teams in college football today — Oklahoma and Southern California. Sure, there are several good teams ... Texas, Ohio State, Tennessee, Alabama, but only two great ones.

"When you talk about what makes a great team, you must consider its size, speed, balance on offense and defense. That's Oklahoma!"

Taking his mind off the awesome Sooner wishbone, though, Paterno spoke of his first Sugar Bowl on January 1, 1952. He was then a 26-year-old assistant who wanted to see the Tennessee-Maryland game and bought a scalper's ticket to do so.

"I can still see Ed Modzelewski ripping into Tennessee's wide-tackle-six," he reminisced. "I drove down from Penn State with two friends, drove all night to see that game, my first trip to New Orleans. I paid twenty bucks for my ticket. My friends sneaked in with the Boy Scouts. "It was one of those trips I'll never forget. We left New Orleans early the next morning — after doing the town — and we turned the car over on the way home."

"It didn't bounce at all."

Trivia question: Exactly who won the 39th Sugar Bowl?

On the field, the answer is Oklahoma. The official outcome would be questioned afterward.

But that was months later.

Before kickoff, a virus struck the Penn State team, and bad health news hit Oklahoma.

Joe Paterno learned the day of the game he would be without much of his ground attack – John Cappelletti, who had rushed for 1,117 yards during the regular-season, had a 102-degree fever and was out of the Sugar Bowl. The Penn State coach had the flu himself, but refused to have his temperature taken so no one could command him from the sideline.

Chuck Fairbanks, coach of the Sooners, decided hours before kickoff that the knee of starting split end John Carroll still hadn't recovered sufficiently. It was a major decision because much of Paterno's pre-game concern centered on Carroll. Just before the game, freshman Tinker Owens was told he would start.

Oklahoma was stymied until the Sooners started hammering the Nittany Lions in the middle. "That's where most of our success came from," said OU quarterback Dave Robertson. It opened up the passing lanes.
After 10 consecutive running plays used five minutes of the clock in the second period and put Oklahoma at the 27, OU put the first points up. "We called what we referred to as '346-S-Post,' said Owens. "It was a fake dive and I would go down field. Penn State was playing me man-to-man and really watching for Joe Washington to get the ball."

Owens made an over-the-shoulder catch at the 7 between two defenders, worked himself loose and went over. "It was funny," Tinker said. "I didn't even think I would catch it. The ball was right there, but it was over my shoulder and I had to look up and back. After I caught it, I just kept running and the guy on me slid off."

Penn State defense rises to stop Oklahoma.

The half ended with the same 7-0 score, and it was obvious that without Cappelletti, Penn State was seriously hindered. The Sooners concentrated on a stopping a suddenly one-dimensional offense.

Two minutes into the fourth quarter, Gary Hayman dropped an Oklahoma punt and Ken Jones recovered on the Lions' 33. After a couple of plays, Joe Wylie unleashed a halfback pass in the highlight (though disputed) of the night. "I ran a post pattern again," Owens said, "and the ball was a little underthrown. I dove for it and caught it between my elbows. It didn't bounce at all."

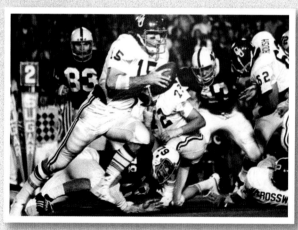

*Oklahoma quarterback Dave Robertson (15)
flashes past Nittany Lions.*

Penn State Coach Joe Paterno.

The Penn State contingent, and some reporters, felt the reception at the 1 was trapped. The film was unclear. Owens maintained it was a catch. "I caught it," he said. "I knew I had it then, I know I had it now."

Leon Crosswhite went in two plays later and, after Rick Fulcher's kick, Oklahoma led 14-0 with 9:46 to go.

Owens, in his third starting assignment, had five receptions for 132 yards, which resulted in one touchdown and set up another. He would receive the Miller-Digby Trophy.

Three months later there was a question of having to change the score: A joint investigation by the University of Oklahoma and the Big Eight Conference revealed that the high school transcripts of freshman quarterback Kerry Jackson and center-linebacker Mike Phillips had been tampered with. As a result, Oklahoma voluntarily forfeited every game in which the pair participated, including the Sugar Bowl.

Penn State coach Joe Paterno refused to change the outcome. "It's a shame that a great effort by an Oklahoma football team has to be marred by an inexcusable recruiting violation such as this incident," Paterno said in a prepared statement. "However, irrespective of what action Oklahoma or the Sugar Bowl would take in regards to the forfeit, our players and the Oklahoma players know who won the game."

Penn State-Oklahoma was a treasure trove for trivia buffs: it was the first Sugar Bowl ever played on a Sunday; it was the first time two Sugar Bowls were played in the same calendar year (Jan. 1, 1972 and Dec. 31, 1972); one team, Oklahoma, won two Sugar Bowls in the same year; and for the first time a freshman was the game's MVP.

	1	2	3	4	
Oklahoma	0	7	0	7	14
Penn State	0	0	0	0	0

Oklahoma: Owens, 27-yard pass from Robertson. PAT, Fulcher kick.

Oklahoma: Crosswhite, 1-yard run. PAT, Fulcher kick.

Individual Leaders

Rushing
Oklahoma: Pruitt 21-86; Crosswhite 22-82, 1 TD.
Penn State: Huffnagle 10-22; Addie 7-18.

Passing
Oklahoma: Robertson 3-6-0, 88 yards, 1 TD.
Penn State: Huffnagle 12-31-1, 147 yards.

Receiving
Oklahoma: Owens 5-132, 1 TD; Pruitt 2-43.
Penn State: Scott 3-59; Bland 3-39.

Oklahoma		Penn State
20	First Downs	11
278	Rushing Yards	49
7-12-0	Passing	12-31-1
175	Passing Yards	147
453	Total Yards	196
8-32.8	Punts	10-42.9
8-5	Fumbles – Lost	6-4
3-55	Penalties – Yards	3-15

Attendance: 80,123.
Teams' remuneration: $763,482.
Miller-Digby Award recipient: Tinker Owens, Oklahoma flanker.

Notre Dame 24 Alabama 23

"I just have players."

A series of events, some reaching back to the opening days of the decade, had a deep effect upon the Sugar Bowl in 1973. The Mid-Winter Sports Association had opened its membership and taken in a select group of capable, civic- and sports-minded individuals in 1966, but immediately thereafter slipped back into comfortable insulation. Though the intention in 1966 was to consider and sponsor new members periodically, new people were not admitted for six years.

A coalition of primarily younger members, realizing the organization had to expand itself in order to regain its former stature, began pressing for new admittances at the start of the 1970s. Moon Landrieu, newly elected mayor and the most progressive New Orleans government head in a decade, urged that the Sugar Bowl admit blacks to its membership.

"Because it had come to mean so much to the city and region," reflected Landrieu, "because its membership included names of individuals that meant something in business, government ... meant something to New Orleans, the Sugar Bowl had become almost a 'quasi-public' organization. It was an organization that served exceedingly well, but also one that did business each year with schools that had more and more black representation while the Sugar Bowl had none."

For three years of Landrieu's first term nothing was done by the Sugar Bowl. In August of 1973 several black groups represented by an Ad Hoc Committee put together by Carl Galmon, (a New Orleans member of the Southern Christian Leadership Conference) charged the Mid-Winter Sports Association with racial discrimination. The Ad Hoc Committee, identifying itself as composed of members of the National As-

sociation for the Advancement of Colored People, the Urban League, the Southern Media Coalition, the Modern Organization for Dynamic and Effective Leadership, and the Community Organization for Urban Politics, requested that NCAA President Alien J. Chapman conduct an investigation into Sugar Bowl operations. They asked that the NCAA approval of the Sugar Bowl be lifted if discrimination was found in its operations, but this question was out of NCAA's jurisdiction.

Unquestionably, there was a lingering hold from the past on some Sugar Bowl members, as there seemed to be on a large segment of American society. The feeling remained that the Sugar Bowl was, after all, a private organization and as such was entitled to choose its makeup. A significant portion of the Sugar Bowl membership, particularly the younger people, disagreed. Finally, a group of 11 men were invited to join the Sugar Bowl. Six of them were among the most influential people in the black community. They were: Xavier University President Dr. Norman C. Francis; Dr. Leonard Bums; educator Elliot Willard; banker Sidney Cates; newspaperman Jim Hall; and Juvenile Court Judge Ernest N. Morial.

The 11 new members were asked to serve on a 23-man advisory committee called "Ambassadors" for one year before being considered for full membership. The usual probation period was two years. All the blacks declined, feeling the

Bear Bryant and Ara Parseghian chat before New Year's Eve, 1973, classic of classics.

offer was made to placate them rather than to provide meaningful participation. After the Sugar Bowl talked with all parties concerned again, the six blacks were elected to associate membership on December 10. Five others, Louisiana Lt. Gov. James E. Fitzmorris, Jr., Richard Gaiennie, Lloyd F. Gaubert, Ronnie J. Kole, and 24th Judicial District Court Judge Thomas C. Wicker, were also elected to membership.

On November 8, Alabama's Coach Bryant announced in what was described as a sugarcoated challenge that his team wanted to play Notre Dame in New Orleans. The key words were "in New Orleans" because Alabama-Notre Dame was a match anyone would have loved.

The 5th-ranked Irish, with a week to think about the prospects, had to consider the $100,000 or so more the Orange Bowl would pay, no small sum to an independent that doesn't have to share with conference members. Coach Ara Parseghian, speculating on what would happen, said, "We will select the competition first and the site second ... it doesn't take too much intelligence on the part of anybody to figure what will happen."

Bryant had hinted this could be his best team. Parseghian had done the same. The thought of Alabama and Notre Dame, titans of the college football world, meeting was exhilarating. "Look at the possibilities," wrote Dave Lagarde in the *Times-Picayune*, "Alabama undefeated and untied; Notre Dame undefeated and untied; North against South; Catholic against Protestant; Parseghian against Bryant; the Bear against the Pope."

There was another dimension to add to the excitement. Alabama had risen to No. 1 and Notre Dame to No. 3. Oklahoma was the No. 2-ranked team, but it was on NCAA probation and ineligible for bowls. This meant the Alabama-Notre Dame game would probably be played for the national championship. "This will be one of the biggest moments in Alabama's history," said Bryant in anticipation. "We've talked about this game for years," Ed "Moose" Krauss, the Irish athletic director said. "There's no question that this could be the most important game ever, certainly since Ara Parseghian has been here. We have a chance to go undefeated and win the national championship and become one of the greatest teams in the history of this school ... and there have been some great ones."

While the football world awaited the game, political currents continued to swirl around the Sugar Bowl. After the appointments of the six blacks to the Mid-Winter Sports Association membership, the Ad Hoc Committee asked that four more blacks be appointed. They wanted at least 33 percent blacks involved in meaningful participation by 1975 and an agreement in writing for an affirmative action program before the Alabama-Notre Dame game on December 31.

Asked if he had discussed the situation with his black players, Bryant shot back, "I don't have any black players and I don't have any white players. I just have players."

The winner, both coaches agreed, would be the defense that could control the other's offense. It would be 'Bama's odd-man front defense against the Irish wing-T with motion and misdirection. And the Irish even-odd defense would face the Tide wishbone. Notre Dame gave up only 201.2 yards a game during the season—the second best in the nation. Alabama, on the other hand, averaged 366 yards offensively — the country's second best. The Irish averaged 350 yards offensively while the Tide defense gave up 244.8 yards.

ABC, in a gesture of sportsmanship to the New Orleans fans, lifted the local blackout. Alabama entered the game a 6-point favorite, but the words of Southern California Coach John McKay should've kept Crimson Tide feet on the ground. "Now listen, Paul," McKay advised Bryant, "you're going to look at films and you're going to write them (Notre Dame) off. Don't, because they're faster than they look and are even bigger than the program says they are."

"Oh, (bleep), this is one I better not miss."

Notre Dame's Tom Clements (2) lets fly from his end zone for the victory — and the national championship.

This one didn't go for a touchdown, stop a touchdown, lead to a touchdown – or points of any sort.

This was for a first down.

Moving the chains was never more dramatic.

With a national title on the line and time running out, a quarterback dropped into his own end zone and threw – to his second option, a receiver who hadn't caught a pass all season. Football doesn't get more theatrical than this.

Of the eight decades of the Sugar Bowl, and the thousands of plays run in that time, this one first down is indelibly etched into the chronicles of the game.

In a game charged with as much electricity as filled the New Orleans skies with a fierce thunderstorm hours earlier, there was a Sugar Bowl record 93-yard kickoff return by Notre Dame's Al Hunter, and a 25-yard Alabama touchdown pass from quarterback Mike Stock to quarterback Richard Todd on a trick play that put the Crimson Tide in front 23-21 with 9:33 left in the fourth quarter. 'Bama kicker Bill Davis missed the extra point attempt.

All the scoring ended with 4:12 remaining in the game when

Notre Dame kicker Bob Thomas put the Irish ahead 24-23 with a 19-yard field goal.

A series after Thomas' field goal, Greg Gantt boomed a punt that was downed at the Notre Dame 1-yard line with less than three minutes remaining.

The Irish faced third-and-six with 2:12 left. Coach Ara Parseghian told quarterback Tom Clements to go with a long count in hopes of drawing Alabama offsides. Instead, Irish tight end Dave Casper was the one who jumped, pushing Notre Dame back almost to the 2, and making the situation third-and-nine.

Parseghian gave Clements the next play, one which took the signal-caller aback. Parseghian called Power-I-right, tackle-trap-left. "There were two options on the play," Parseghian said. "Clements could bootleg the ball around the left end or throw to Casper, the primary receiver, who would cross the middle of the field from right to left."

"I do remember asking him, 'Are you sure?' " Clements said. "He said, 'Yeah.' I said, 'OK, let's go.' "

Parseghian said decades later a pass out of his end zone wasn't that much of a gamble. "Circumstances prevail there," he said. "I knew we could get beat by a field goal if we didn't maintain possession. Being so close to the goal line, we would have to punt out of our end zone. We tried to lead them into thinking we were going to run the ball by coming out in a two-tight end formation and a stacked backfield. We made it look conservative."

Alabama fell for it.

"I was the outside linebacker on the play, and we were completely fooled by it," said Mike Dubose, who later became head coach at Alabama. "It caught us off guard. Third-and-nine in 1973 wasn't exactly the way it is now, as easy to pick up.

In that situation in 1973, you're thinking 'Run.' It was a great call on their part."

Trouble was, the player who was supposed to catch the pass, Casper, got hung up in the middle of the field by the Tide defense, forcing Clements to look for his second option, Robin Weber, who hadn't practiced in two days because of a knee injury and who hadn't caught a single pass all season.

An Alabama defensive back, expecting the run, froze. Weber blew past him and suddenly was all alone. Cutting diagonally, Weber saw Clements let loose with the pass and thought, 'Oh (bleep), this is one I better not miss."

He didn't, and Notre Dame had a new set of downs at the 38, from where the Irish were able to run out the clock.

Bryant said he missed the crucial play because he was busy getting the punt return team ready for the anticipated fourth-down kick.

"We were going to rush and try to block it," said the Bear. "Two points would have won the game, or three on a field goal. When we had them backed up like that, if I had been a betting man, I would have bet anything we were going to win. I think Notre Dame is a great team. But I wouldn't mind playing them again. In fact, I'd like that."

This was a game of historical proportions. Two "national champions" came out of this Sugar Bowl, just as in the 1936 game.

The UPI poll continued to vote for its No. 1 team at the end of the regular season. This year it was Alabama. The AP, of course, voted after the bowls, and Notre Dame, as expected, leapfrogged Alabama in that ballot.

The embarrassment caused UPI to amend its practice the next season, while Alabama continues to proclaim its No. 1 standing in that poll, ignoring the defeat.

Still, more than three decades after it was played, Parseghian, whose team inflicted the only Sugar Bowl defeat of Bear Bryant's career, assessed it by saying evenly: "There were no losers in that game."

True enough. This was one for the ages.

	1	2	3	4	
Notre Dame	6	8	7	3	24
Alabama	0	10	7	6	23

Notre Dame: Bullock, 6-yard run. Kick failed.
Alabama: Billingsley, 6-yard run. PAT, Davis kick.
Notre Dame: Hunter, 93-yard kickoff return. PAT, Demmarle pass from Clements.
Alabama: Davis, 39-yard field goal.
Alabama: Jackson, 5-yard run. PAT, Davis kick.
Notre Dame: Penick, 12-yard run. PAT, Thomas kick.
Alabama: Todd, 25-yard pass from Stock, Kick failed.
Notre Dame: Thomas, 19-yard field goal.

Individual Leaders

Rushing
Notre Dame: Bullock 19-79, 1 TD; Clements 15-74.
Alabama: Jackson 11-62, 1 TD; Billingsley 7-54, 1 TD.

Passing
Notre Dame: Clements 7-12-0, 169 yards.
Alabama: Rutledge 7-12-1, 88 yards.

Receiving
Notre Dame: Casper 3-75; Demmerle 3-59.
Alabama: Pugh 2-28; Jackson 2-22.

Notre Dame		Alabama
20	First Downs	23
252	Rushing Yards	190
7-12-0	Passing	10-15-1
169	Passing Yards	127
421	Total Yards	317
7-35.8	Punts	6-46.3
4-3	Fumbles – Lost	5-2
5-45	Penalties – Yards	3-32

Attendance: 85,161.
Teams' remuneration: $900,412.
Miller-Digby Award recipient: Tom Clements, Notre Dame quarterback.

Nebraska 13 Florida 10

"The Sugar Bowl means everything to me."

Notre Dame-Alabama was a spectacular success and immediately ranked among the finest collegiate games ever played.

A very respectable 25.3 television rating, the highest the Sugar had received since records began being kept in 1964, was gratifying. It was also third behind comparatively weak attractions in the Rose and Cotton Bowls. The inescapable conclusion was if a game like this didn't rank higher than third on New Year's Eve, no game ever would. Returning the Sugar Bowl to its natural spot – New Year's Day – seemed inevitable after Notre Dame-Alabama.

Everyone, of course, wanted a duplicate of the Irish-Tide match the following season, setting off an early scramble for those teams. New NCAA rules allowed the bowls to set up matches as early as possible, though there was a gentleman's agreement among the various committees not to firm up anything until November 16. Word seeped out of Miami two weeks before that Alabama, then ranked 3rd, and the Irish, ranked 8th, would have a rematch in the Orange Bowl.

Coach Paul "Bear" Bryant's Crimson Tide had played in Dallas and New Orleans the previous two years. As the story went, Bryant allowed Notre Dame Coach Ara Parseghian to select the site of their showdown since Bear chose the Sugar Bowl the previous year. The Orange Bowl was paying approximately $100,000 more than the Sugar.

Oklahoma, the No. 1 team, was again ineligible for postseason football because of NCAA probation, but the Sugar had several options. ABC-TV wanted to put on a Penn State - Nebraska telecast because of the eastern audience the Nittany Lions would draw. Also, the Cornhuskers (ranked No. 6) appeared to have a legitimate chance of beating Oklahoma.

Florida (7-1), Auburn (7-1), Texas A&M (7-1), and Texas (6-2) were also in the picture with the Cornhuskers (6-2) and Penn State (7-1). Nebraska-Auburn figured to be the best draw in terms of bringing fans to the game. When the Cornhuskers played Alabama in the 1967 Sugar Bowl, 16,000 fans followed Nebraska. When Auburn played Oklahoma, 18,000 fans followed the War Eagles. When Penn State played Oklahoma, it brought only 8,500 fans. And just 6,000 Gator fans followed Florida to New Orleans in 1966.

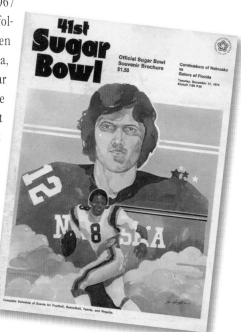

In terms of rankings, the best bet the Sugar seemed to have was Penn State-Florida, and both teams seemed capable of winning the remainder of their games. Penn State, although the Sugar didn't know it at the time, was already spoken for — by the Cotton Bowl. The Sugar took the best it could from this assorted grab bag: Florida and Nebraska.

Later, Florida missed on a two-point conversion in the final 12 seconds and lost to Georgia, 17-16. A week later the Gators lost to Kentucky, 41-24. By the end of the season Florida was barely in the Top Twenty. Both the Gators and the Cornhuskers, 8th-ranked after a 28-14 defeat to Oklahoma, were 8-3 entering the Sugar Bowl.

As a footnote, the Alabama-Notre Dame rematch soured somewhat, too, though those teams were 2nd and 9th entering the Orange Bowl. Southern California waxed the Irish 55-24, removing the luster.

An offensive game was anticipated in the Sugar Bowl. Nebraska averaged 32 points and 412 yards a game. Florida averaged 22 points and 371 yards. A closer glance at the opponents, though, was intriguing. In one corner was bowl-tested and tradition-steeped Nebraska. Alabama defeated the 'Huskers in the 1967 Sugar, but that was the last time Nebraska had lost a bowl game. A victory in the Sugar Bowl would be Nebraska's sixth straight and would tie it with Georgia Tech for the national record.

The Cornhuskers hadn't lost often in recent history. In the decade from 1965 to 1974, Nebraska finished in the Top Ten seven times. On the other hand, Florida, though it had a program on the upswing, astoundingly had never finished in the Top Ten. The 18th-ranked Gators felt they had an outside

Nebraska Coach Tom Osborne.

chance at breaking that barrier with a victory over Nebraska.

Florida brought some tradition in the form of Ray Graves, a distinguished Sugar Bowl alumnus. Graves was the starting center on the Tennessee team that was upset by Boston College in 1941. He later returned as a Georgia Tech assistant in 1953, 1954, and 1956, then as the head coach of the Gators in 1966. His return as athletic director made Graves the first person to compete on all levels in the Sugar Bowl. Unfortunately, his school had little of that kind of background.

The odds-makers felt strongly that this Gator team would not be the one to crack the Top Ten. Nebraska was a 12 1/2-point favorite, a line that obviously reflected a lack of respect for the angered Gators. "You hear so much about Nebraska and how we're a 12-point underdog," fumed linebacker Glenn Cameron, "but I don't think Nebraska is a super team. I ask this question: Who has Nebraska played this year? They played Oklahoma, one of the greatest teams this year, and lost. But, who else have they played this year? When people start talking about Nebraska they are talking about the Nebraska team of three years ago that won the national championship."

Lee McGriff wasn't as belligerent. He wore his heart on his sleeve as he summed up the game. "Being a senior," said the wingback, "the Sugar Bowl means everything to me. It's my last game in a Gator uniform. We have a chance to finish in the Top Ten, and a chance for the seniors to go out with the feeling we gave something to this university. It's everything we ever dreamed of boiled down to one night."

Crisp play between Nebraska and Florida on New Year's Eve, 1974.

"It had that famous Coyle hook on it."

Mike Feltz (72) has Gator quarterback Don Gaffney hangin by a thread.

Seldom has a game turned so completely on one play.

The underdog Florida Gators were camped on the Nebraska 1, about to put the Cornhuskers away.

With a 10-0 lead in the third quarter, and the Husker offense sputtering against the aggressive, swarming Gator defense, a Florida touchdown at that point would have been monumental – a touchdown, it should be added, that probably should have been counted two plays before.

On third-and-four from the Nebraska 18, tailback Tony Green took a pitchout from Don Gaffney and bolted for the end zone. Knocked off balance, Green went the final five yards sideways while trying to stay inbounds. He reached the end zone, but the officials ruled he stepped out at the 5. Films later showed he had not.

Gaining just four yards of the necessary five on the next three plays, Gator coach Doug Dickey waved off the field goal team and had his team go for it. Gaffney pitched to James Richards – who slipped, then was dropped by defensive back Jim Bur-

row (a former walk-on at Ole Miss, where he was told he was too small).

Dickey didn't really feel the situation was that much of a gamble. "I thought maybe (even) if we left the ball there (at the 1)," the coach said, "we're going to get it back and kick the field goal anyway."

Huskers' coach Tom Osborne, however, made a critical change in strategy: he benched quarterback David Humm, normally a feared passer but who the Gators harnessed (at that juncture, Humm had two completions in 14 attempts – and four interceptions) and sent in reserve Terry Luck with orders to junk the passing game and use the runners.

Nebraska began worming its way out of the shadows of the goal posts as Don Westbrook, Monte Anthony, and Tony Davis consistently gained ground – short gains, maybe, but steady yardage. By the end of the third period, the Huskers were planted on the Gator 12. Anthony bounced into the end zone two minutes later to cut the lead to 10-7.

The 18-play, 99-yard drive consumed eight minutes and 50 seconds of playing time.

There was more the next time Nebraska got the ball. Luck's unit came to a fourth-and-two at the 49. Osborne signaled "Go for it" and Anthony gained three yards. The drive eventually slowed, but Mike Coyle's line-drive field goal of 37-yards tied the score with 7:12 to play.

The dynamics of the game had completely changed. Florida again could not move and the Huskers got the ball at their 25 with four minutes to go. Davis put Nebraska in position for the victory when he broke off a 40-yard gain to the Gators' 31. The last minutes wouldn't have been an issue except that defensive back Alvin Cowan brought Davis down when no one else could.

That tackle could have salvaged at least a tie for the Gators. But with 2:22 left, Coyle came back for Nebraska, facing a fourth-and-one at the Florida 22. It was close, but his 39-yard field goal was true. "I didn't think that last one was good," he said, "but it had that famous Coyle hook on it."

Nebraska had somehow pulled itself not only from defeat but also from humiliation.

The Florida locker room was steamy and somber afterward. Dickey spent a lot of time talking individually with his warriors. Preston Kendrick, who was absolutely superb on the field with two interceptions, eight solo tackles and four assists, couldn't look up.

In another corner, defensive back Randy Talbot stopped taking his jersey off, looked around, then expressed what everyone else seemed to be thinking: "I'll tell you what, I'd like to play them again."

Don Gaffney (8) has 'Husker defense running in circles.

	1	2	3	4	
Nebraska	0	0	0	13	13
Florida	7	3	0	0	10

Florida: Green, 21-yard run. PAT, Posey kick.

Florida: Posey, 40-yard field goal.

Nebraska: Anthony, 2-yard run. PAT, Coyle kick.

Nebraska: Coyle, 37-yard field goal.

Nebraska: Coyle, 39-yard field goal.

Individual Leaders

Rushing
Nebraska: Davis 17-126; Anthony 15-64, 1 TD.
Florida: Dubose 17-84; Green 14-73, 1 TD.

Passing
Nebraska: Humm 2-12-4, 16 yards.
Florida: Gaffney 5-10-1, 97 yards.

Receiving
Nebraska: Westbrook 2-16.
Florida: McGriff 2-52; Darby 1-32.

Nebraska		Florida
18	First Downs	13
304	Rushing Yards	178
2-14-4	Passing	5-10-1
16	Passing Yards	97
320	Total Yards	275
4-37.0	Punts - Yards	6-32.5
3-1	Fumbles – Lost	3-1
1-17	Penalties – Yards	5-41

Attendance: 68,890.
Teams' remuneration: $961,112.
Miller-Digby Award recipient: Tony Davis, Nebraska fullback.

Alabama 13 Penn State 6

"I think we ought to consider it."

It had been demonstrated that ABC's New Year's Eve experiment was failing. The Nebraska-Florida game, at least as attractive as the Penn State-Baylor Cotton Bowl, was overwhelmed (25.3 to 16.0) by 3rd-place Dallas in the ratings. The Notre Dame-Alabama Orange Bowl, a rematch without nearly as much sizzle as the previous year's Sugar Bowl, pulled a much higher audience. There was simply no question that New Year's Day was a stronger date than New Year's Eve for bowls.

Other factors that could change the entire bowl structure were coming into play. The Big Ten and Pacific Eight were about to break their traditional Rose Bowl-only affiliation. Champions from those conferences, of course, would continue to play in Pasadena, but runners-up and others would be free to participate in other postseason games. Also, the Orange Bowl, which had expressed interest in the Southeastern Conference but was turned down, was close to resuming its tie-up with the Big Eight after a hiatus of several years.

Those changes would have an effect on the SEC. The SEC, which on occasion had sent as many as seven of its teams to bowls in one year, would have stiff competition for minor bowl berths as the number of available quality teams increased. And with the Miami tie-up, a New Year's Day berth would be gone. Theoretically, the SEC champion, under the right set of circumstances, could be shut out of a New Year's Day game.

For years, as the Sugar Bowl's fortunes nosed downward, the Mid-Winter Sports Association concluded that a tie-up could rejuvenate an ailing bowl. The arguments of past decades against such an arrangement were no longer valid.

It seemed to become an annual ritual: The Sugar Bowl would inquire about the feasibility of a tie-up with the SEC, and the SEC would politely decline. New Orleans began pressing harder in 1973.

Things were now different. Realizing that shortly the Sugar Bowl again would be the only New Year's Day game without a tie-up, and that the SEC champion could be shut out of a New Year's Day game, some members began to perceive the situation differently. For New Orleans to host a No. 1 game without the SEC champion would require a highly ranked independent or a rare national contender that was not a champion of the Southwest, Big Eight, Big Ten, or Pacific Coast Conferences. For the first time, there seemed to be a mutual need by both parties.

Sugar Bowl President Cliff Kern, Sam Corenswet, Jr., and Charles V. Cusimano drove to Baton Rouge in the spring to talk with Louisiana State University Athletic Director Carl Maddox. Maddox would chair the athletic directors' meeting at the SEC convention in December, and the delegation wanted the chance to make a definite proposal. Maddox promised to get them on the docket.

Conference Commissioner Boyd McWhorter was contacted for advice. "I gave them the proper procedure," said McWhorter. "They would have to get the athletic directors to approve of it, and to make that recommendation to the conference presidents. Personally, I did not think at the time it would pass because the conference simply had not shown any tendency toward tying up with any bowl."

McWhorter advised the Sugar Bowl that the possibility of a tie-up would be greatly enhanced if there was a financial guarantee.

The Mid-Winter Sports Association went to work. "We put together a group that had very close relationships with the athletic directors around the conference," said Kern. "A.B. Nicholas was very close with Johnny Vaught at Ole Miss and Bob Woodruff at Tennessee. So he contacted those gentlemen. I was about the only one in the group that knew Clay Stapleton at Vanderbilt very well, so I got in touch with him. John Boebinger was good friends with Joel Eaves at Georgia. Charles Cusimano was on the Board of Supervisors at LSU. And Aruns Gallery contacted Bear Bryant."

Pete Fountain and his famed clarinet charm an audience of attentive football players.

Bryant was the fly in the ointment. He had only one vote, but his stature was such that no one would seriously try to tell him where his team was to play over the holidays. Bryant had made Alabama into the most glamorous bowl team in the region, if not the country, and in the process had become something of a kingmaker. Alabama was so coveted as a bowl commodity that frequently it was only when Bryant decided where and who he was to play that the year's bowl pairings fell into place.

Bear told Callery he would not consider a tie-up, that he could go where he wanted and felt it was in the best interest of the University of Alabama. This put a practical end to the matter.

Months later, Bryant called Callery and thoughtfully said, "I have to think about the rest of the conference, too." Callery knew the Sugar Bowl was about to change.

Sports in New Orleans was approaching a new age with the completion of one of the world's unique buildings, the Louisiana Superdome. It was the most multifaceted building ever designed. The Battle of Gettysburg conceivably could have been fought within its walls. A 25-story structure could fit under its roof, which spans 9 1/2 acres. It took two years and nine months to complete, with 800 construction workers swarming over the 13-acre site on any given day. The scope of the Superdome was so vast that its architect, Buster Curtis, concedes that no single man could have put it together on paper — computers did it. It is a ludicrous statistic, but the Superdome has 125 million cubic feet of space and was built at a cost of $163 million.

Bryant wanted to coach in the first Superdome Sugar Bowl and asked to be considered. Who could have turned him down? After a season-opening loss to Missouri, the Crimson Tide tore through its schedule and was on the verge of another Southeastern Conference championship. Bryant also winked at the Cotton Bowl where he might have the opportunity to play a higher-ranked team.

There was no question he could play a higher-ranked team in the Orange Bowl. Either 2nd-ranked Nebraska or 6th-ranked Oklahoma would be waiting there. But not only was Alabama refusing to play either of those schools in Miami, but the Tide

Joe Paterno, left, and Bear Bryant toast each other with café brulot at Antoine's.

wouldn't play them in New Orleans either. The Sugar Bowl was informed that should Bryant play in the Sugar Bowl, he would like to play Penn State. Eleventh-ranked Penn State was a fine ball club, but was not of the same caliber as Oklahoma or Nebraska. "This is a helluva note," stormed Oklahoma's Barry Switzer. "It would have made no difference if we were 10-0 like Nebraska. The Sugar Bowl still wouldn't have taken the loser of our game, even though that would have guaranteed them at least one 10-1 team." "Tell that son of a buck not to duck us," an angry Nebraska Coach Tom Osborne told Sugar Bowl official John Barr.

"I want to make it clear that we want to play in the best bowl against the best team," Osborne went on. "Any team that doesn't feel that way doesn't belong in competitive athletics. I know that's a pretty strong statement, but it's time this thing is brought out in the open."

"We have no apologies to make to anyone," retorted Bryant in Birmingham. "If the Big Eight wanted to play Alabama, why did they sign with the Orange Bowl?" It was a weak response, and the whole situation was ironic since a strong argument against a tie-up in the early days was the possibility a team might want to call the shots on its opposition.

There were two reasons why Bryant would have been interested in Penn State. The first was obvious. Alabama, for all its success, had not won a bowl game since the 1967 Sugar against Nebraska. There were some who were saying Bear

had quit eating soup because he couldn't handle the bowl. While this Penn State team was capable and deserving, it did not have the weapons of the Big Eight contenders. Second, Penn State seldom used its entire allotment of tickets. Alabama fans could never get enough. A Penn State - 'Bama bowl gave Bryant an excellent chance at victory and more tickets for his legion of supporters.

An indication of the ticket pressure at Alabama was illustrated one Sunday morning at Birmingham's St. Paul's Cathedral. Aruns Callery, who had been following the Tide, attended early Mass attired in his Sugar Bowl blazer. As he went for a seat, an usher with whom he'd become friendly handed Callery a folded church pledge card. Callery put it in his pocket. After church Callery found a $20 bill attached to the card with a note requesting two Sugar Bowl tickets.

After Bryant's turnabout concerning the tie-up, he joined with Ole Miss' Johnny Vaught in buttonholing their fellow athletic directors in the cause. The proposal probably would have failed without them. Bryant felt he could deliver three votes, which left seven for Vaught. "I guess part of the reason we were able to do it," said Vaught, "is because Bear and I went to so many bowls. We were kind of the dominant teams as far as the bowls were concerned, and I think the other athletic directors recognized that if we stood behind it, it had some merit."

Vaught, who lobbied vigorously and successfully, said he had never been for tie-ups per se, and that if he could he would abolish them all. "I have a lot of friends with the Sugar Bowl," he said, "but I pushed for it because it seemed like the thing to do. If we hadn't tied with the Sugar Bowl we eventually would have had to tie up with another bowl. If we were going to go that way, I think we were better off with the Sugar Bowl."

In the meantime, Sam Corenswet, Jr., and other members of the Sugar Bowl were negotiating with ABC. This would be the final game of the television pact and since the Sugar Bowl wanted to guarantee the SEC a payment, those talks were as important as the conference vote in Birmingham.

Cliff Kern, Executive Committee Chairman Marshall David, A.B. Nicholas, Aruns Callery, and Charles Cusimano went to Birmingham for the November 30 SEC meeting and were prepared to offer a $750,000 guarantee. The reception was warm. "I think we ought to consider it," Tennessee's Bob Woodruff. "It would be a fine thing for our conference." Apparently the groundwork laid by the Sugar Bowlers, Bryant, and Vaught was solid. The SEC athletic directors voted unanimously to recommend to the university presidents a tie-up with New Orleans.

"I stood aghast when the vote came in," recalled SEC Commissioner Boyd McWhorter. "I wasn't disappointed, just surprised at the unanimous vote."

There was no way of knowing it at the time, but the Orange Bowl's matchup of Oklahoma and Michigan influenced the Sugar Bowl's proposal. McWhorter and others throughout the SEC were concerned that a tie-up would have the effect of limiting it to one team in a major bowl. "But right after that," recalled the commissioner, "the Orange Bowl invited the runner-up from another conference (Michigan). So I thought if a runner-up from that conference can get it, all of us can get it."

The SEC presidents would have to make the final decision, but after 42 years and many attempts, the SEC and the Sugar Bowl were engaged.

On the football front, things were not moving smoothly for

Bryant. Quarterback Richard Todd, a two-time All-SEC athlete from Mobile, sliced the middle finger of his right (throwing) hand Christmas Day and required two stitches.

"If it had to happen I'm glad it happened yesterday and not the day before the game," Todd said. "If we had to play tomorrow night, I don't think I could take a snap. But I'm gonna play in the game unless I break my leg."

Some thought was given as to whether Todd would play. Twenty-three Alabama players, including Todd, were anywhere from 15 to 90 minutes late returning to their hotel after a Saturday night on the town. This happened to the coach that once suspended Joe Namath before a Sugar Bowl game. But Bryant tried to be understanding, calling the incident "no big thing." Then more players were late coming in Monday night, and Bryant stripped two of their starting assignments.

Captains of Alabama and Penn State meet at midfield.

Todd, meanwhile, was gaining a healthy respect for the Nittany Lions. He and Penn State linebacker Greg Buttle sized each other up in a press conference. Todd listened attentively as the 6-foot-2, 228-pound linebacker joined a New Orleans barbershop quartet for a song. When asked what he thought of Buttle, Todd laughed, "Well, the way he sings you can smell his breath from here. I hope he doesn't get that close during the game."

"Lordy, it sure didn't come easy."

Bear Bryant was typically downplaying his chances, even against a preferred opponent, one that figured to be 13 ½ points behind Alabama at game's end, even with an injured Crimson Tide quarterback. "I think we'll win," Bryant said, then hastily added, "if I don't overcoach 'em."

It was the classic Bryant style — laid back, understated and homespun. But the Bear wanted badly to break his bowl skein. He walked out for the kickoff without his trademark houndstooth hat. Bryant would say later he was taught never to wear a hat indoors. But he was searching for something that might bring his team good luck — and a victory. That was the reason he let wife Mary Harmon Bryant ride on the team bus to the Superdome.

Todd came out with his finger bandaged, and Penn State literally dared him to throw. Overloading the line and hoping to force 'Bama into mistakes, Penn State paid an early price. Joe Dale Harris, a starter just because of the curfew violations, ran a simple turn-in pattern that Todd got off just before being engulfed by the defense. There weren't enough Lions in the secondary to take all the receivers, and Harris was free, turning the short yardage pass into a 54-yard gain.

That play eventually was converted into a 25-yard field goal by Danny Ridgeway and a 3-0 Alabama lead that held up to the half.

Chris Bahr tied things with a 42-yard field goal in the third quarter, but Todd brought the Tide roaring back, though admittedly he was never really sure of what he was doing against the ever-changing Penn State defense. At his 35, Todd called a time-out. "There were times that I didn't know who

to read or who to give the ball to," he said. "I called the time-out because they shifted to our tight end side, right where we wanted to run a play. I went over to the sideline and Coach Bryant sort of winked at me. He called the pass. We felt they'd be single-covering Ozzie (Newsome)."

Freshman Bill Crummy was inserted in the Penn State secondary in the first period when Tommy Odell suffered a rib injury. Crummy had played well, but on this play he took Todd's pump fake and Newsome broke back to the sideline and caught the pass 30 yards upstream, being brought down on the 10.

Todd lost four yards recovering a fumble, but Mike Stock swept into the end zone behind a ferocious block by Newsome.

Bahr cut the margin to 10-6 with a 37-yard field goal in the fourth quarter, but Ridgeway answered with a 28-yarder. With 3:19 left, Penn State got one last chance. The Nittany Lions inched out to their 39, where, on fourth-and-one, they went for it. Alabama held with 1:15 to go, and Bryant's bowl skein was broken.

"Lordy, it sure didn't come easy," grumbled Bear, who took special care to note that Penn State had dropped his backs for losses nine times. "We beat a helluva football team tonight," he said. "Anyone who doesn't think that is an idiot."

Todd, with his bandaged throwing hand, completed 10 of his 12 passes for 210 yards and in the process probably prevented a Nittany Lions upset. "Believe it or not," said standout linebacker Kurt Allerman of Alabama's lean but effective air

	1	2	3	4	
Alabama	3	0	7	3	13
Penn State	0	0	3	3	6

Alabama: Ridgeway, 25-yard field goal.

Penn State: Bahr, 42-yard field goal.

Alabama: Stock, 14-yard run. PAT, Ridgeway kick.

Penn State: Bahr, 37-yard field goal.

Alabama: Ridgeway, 28-yard field goal.

Individual Leaders

Rushing
Alabama: Shelby 8-45; Davis 12-32.
Penn State: Geise 8-46; Taylor 12-36.

Passing
Alabama: Todd 10-12-0, 210 yards.
Penn State: Andress 8-14-1, 57 yards.

Receiving
Alabama: Newsome 4-97; Harris 2-69.
Penn State: Cefalo 2-18; Petchel 2-13.

Bear Bryant gives one of his players a well-earned pat.

game, "we wanted them to pass. But they mixed up their passes well, and they executed them exceptionally well. They executed the big play and had no turnovers – what more can you say?"

Before the first snap, Todd was unsure how the injury would affect him. "I don't throw a spiral when I have a good hand," he cracked afterward. "It didn't hurt any."

It only hurt Penn State, and Coach Joe Paterno, who came into the Alabama locker room where Todd was surrounded by newsmen. "I want to congratulate you on a great game," said the Nittany Lions coach. When he learned Todd was next planning on going to the Senior Bowl, Paterno quipped, "I'd like to recommend you for that one. It's the least I can do since Bear recommended me for this one."

Alabama		Penn State
14	First Downs	12
106	Rushing Yards	157
10-12-0	Passing	8-14-1
210	Passing Yards	57
316	Total Yards	214
5-40.8	Punts	4-48.5
1-0	Fumbles – Lost	1-0
3-22	Penalties – Yards	0

Attendance: 74,331.
Teams' remuneration: $1,000,000.
Miller-Digby Award recipient: Richard Todd, Alabama quarterback.

Pittsburgh 27 Georgia 3

"We think it will be a very popular move."

Bear Bryant, as unselfish as he was in helping weld the support necessary for the SEC-Sugar Bowl tie-up, made a last plea after the Penn State game to open all the bowls, to let them all compete for the best match. His argument was parallel to the one the Mid-Winter Sports Association had made for years. But no one really listened. "What I'm for is all bowls to open up for everybody, nobody have a tie-up," said Bryant, who was also opposed to the voting of national champions after bowls. "If we are going to stay with the polls," he stated, "take it out of the bowls. It puts too much pressure when bowls are used for it. It takes all the fun out of the bowls."

Voters would continue to decide the national champion after postseason games because the general public enjoys seeing grand matches with something riding on the outcome. Instead of decreasing the number of bowl tie-ups, there would be an increase. The SEC presidents, after studying the Sugar Bowl's proposal, approved it.

On March 3, 1976, after 42 years of infatuation, spats, and courtship, the SEC and Sugar Bowl were finally hitched. "We think it will be a very popular move," said Harry M. England, who had succeeded Cliff Kern as Sugar Bowl president. "We recognize that the SEC has been a very contributing factor in the Sugar Bowl for many years. Unofficially it has been almost a partner."

With what England called the Sugar Bowl's "new arsenal of weapons" – the tie-up and the Superdome – the Mid-Winter Sports Association also believed it was time to call an end to the experiment with a New Year's Eve playing date. The December 31 date was a failure because the traditional celebrations interfered and further, there was a drop-off in eastern press coverage because of early deadlines on newspaper holiday runs. ABC agreed, and the Sugar Bowl petitioned the NCAA for a return to its New Year's playing date. "We hope it will be a mere formality," said England. "We tried New Year's Eve for four years and found it was not the best time to hold a football game."

The NCAA approved the request, not only putting the Sugar Bowl back on New Year's Day, but also creating two questions for sports trivia buffs: What year was there not a Sugar Bowl? The answer is 1976, since the December 31, 1975, game would be followed by a January 1, 1977, game. The companion question is, of course: In what year were there two Sugar Bowls? The switch to New Year's Eve had made possible a game on January 1, 1972, and another on December 31, 1972.

These significant changes were taking place without Joe Katz, who resigned as executive director of the Mid-Winter Sports Association shortly after the Alabama-Penn State game. Katz wanted to pursue other business ventures. A search committee was formed to find his successor, the third director of the Sugar Bowl.

The 1976 SEC season was wild and woolly, and there was a certain irony in that the first year of the tie-up, after an unyielding five-year hold on the throne by Alabama, the conference had a horse race. This was also evident elsewhere; as late as Novem-

ber 1 it appeared that of the nonaligned bowl berths, only 2nd-ranked Pittsburgh in the Orange Bowl looked definite.

Pittsburgh, on the other hand, was also the team New Orleans wanted and, for the first time in a long while, all the Sugar Bowl's resources were going to be used to get a favored team. Coach Johnny Major's Panthers were more than just very good. Pittsburgh featured an extraordinary runner, Heisman Trophy winner Tony Dorsett. He was college football's all-time ground gainer with 6,082 yards. The Panthers also had an underrated but suffocating defense. Uppermost in Majors' mind was playing the best opponent he could find, an opponent whose defeat would push the Panthers to No. 1, or solidify that position if it were achieved beforehand.

ABC helped overcome the difference in money between the Orange and Sugar Bowls by putting the Panther-West Virginia game on regional television, which was perfectly legal and ethical, though some other bowl officials squirmed. It wasn't as if Pitt didn't belong on TV. "The opponent is more important than the money," said sources at Pitt. "The main goal is the best way of getting No. 1."

Pittsburgh rose to No. 1 after Purdue defeated Michigan early in November. A week later, Iowa State assured the Orange Bowl of a host with at least two losses when it whipped Nebraska and put the Big Eight in a five-way first-place tie. At the same time, 4th-ranked Georgia emerged as the Southeastern Conference champion and the highest-ranking available opponent for the Panthers. The Panthers voted to play in New Orleans against the 10-1 Bulldogs.

Georgia won the SEC championship on the merits of a ball-control offense and an effective defensive unit called the "Junkyard Dogs." The dedication of the defense was reflected in a supreme sacrifice of the 1970s – shaved heads – a symbol that so inspired Georgians that Coach Vince Dooley shaved his head, too. Ironically, Majors built Pitt from a 6-5-1 team to 11-0 in four years, and the first game his seniors had played was a 7-7 tie with Georgia.

"The winner of the Rose Bowl (between USC and Michigan) is the national champion," said Trojan Coach John Robinson of his 2nd-ranked team, "and the hell with the rest of them. If we win, we're going into the dressing room and declare ourselves unanimous national champions." His Rose Bowl rival, Bo Schembechler of the No. 3 Wolverines, chimed in, "I can hardly believe that Pitt could beat Southern Cal, and if we beat them we're going to claim the national championship."

Majors was incredulous, pointing out that USC's 21-point loss

Greater love hath no man ... Georgia Coach Vince Dooley wears the trademark of his defensive unit. (Right) Dooley watches practice intently.

to Missouri was a pretty wide margin for a national contender. "That's the most ridiculous farce ever perpetrated," said Majors. "If Georgia beats us, they'd have more of a claim than Michigan or Southern Cal."

Pitt raised two questions in the public's mind, neither of which had anything to do with its ability. The first was how the loss of Coach Majors would affect the Panthers' bowl effort. Bill Battle resigned from the University of Tennessee, and Majors leaped at the opportunity to return to his alma mater after this last game. The second question was how Majors' treat-'em-like-men attitude would hold up.

Majors gave his team of mostly seniors run of the town until just a couple of days before the game. He wouldn't have done it, he said, with a less-mature team. This team could handle it. The gesture was in keeping with the coach's personality.

Twenty years before, when Majors' fumble was instrumental in Baylor's 13-7 upset of Tennessee, Johnny recalled, "I went out and partied. I wasn't feeling too good, but I knew back then you'd always have to take the bad with the good. I remember I stayed up all night, drove to Mobile, and was at practice for the Senior Bowl the next afternoon."

While the press wondered about the Panthers prowling the French Quarter, Dooley fretted about them prowling the Superdome. A lot of attention was given Dorsett, who gained a single-season record 1,948 yards as a senior; but the Georgia coach knew that in order to stop Dorsett he had to contain multitalented quarterback Matt Cavanaugh. If the Georgia defense was on the field too long, Dooley knew he was in trouble.

"Well I guess they're drinking Bloody Marys."

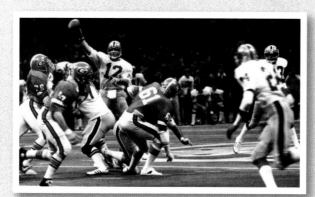

Pitt's Matt Cavanaugh (12), Pitt's decisive 1977 Sugar Bowl weapon, rears up and fires at Georgia.

This, at least in the early stages, was a classic example of winning a battle but losing the war.

The Georgia defense was determined to stop Tony Dorsett, and did – but just for a while.

The run-conscious Bulldogs threw up a 6-2 stunting defense, giving the Panther receivers one-on-one coverage – which was exactly what Pitt coach Johnny Majors wanted. Minutes after the opening kickoff, Matt Cavanaugh put the first points on the board.

Pitt, a two-and-a-half point favorite, zipped 80 yards on a 12-play drive on its second possession. Split end Gordon Jones caught a 13-yard pass to midfield, then fullback Elliot Walker beat linebacker Jim Griffith and took a pass over the middle that turned into a 36-yard gain. "On that first long pass," moaned linebacker Ben Zambiasi later, "the ball actually hit my finger. It was just broken coverage by one of our linebackers."

The play went to the Georgia 10, and two snaps later Cavanaugh scored on a keeper from the 6.

If there was any solace for Georgia, it was that Dorsett gained only 10 of the 80 yards.

The Bulldogs hung in from there until seven minutes were

gone in the second quarter when Cavanaugh, running along the line on an option, pulled up and threw to a slanting Jones who split two defenders and loped 59 yards to the end zone.

"They've got eight people up there to stop Tony," Cavanaugh explained, "and that means single coverage on our receivers. All you have to do is get them the ball."

Dorsett finally got loose, leaving defenders sprawled in his wake and scoring from the 11 before the half to make the score 21-0. That sealed Pittsburgh's national championship.

Repeating a question in the locker room, tight end Jim Corbett said, "When did I think we had it won? That's easy. At halftime. There's no way any team is going score 21 points on our defense in one half."

While statisticians were breaking down the figures of the first half, a reporter broke up the press box by glancing solemnly toward the Pitt locker room and saying, "Well, I guess they're drinking Bloody Marys."

The halftime stats read like a Georgia obit. The 'Junkyard Dogs' had done a reasonable job on Dorsett. Holding him to 65 yards on 17 carries. Cavanaugh, however, was 7-of-11 passing for 185 yards.

The Georgia offense was victimized in part by its own trends. On obvious running plays the Panthers went to a six-man line to which the Bulldogs never seemed to adjust. Georgia was unable to put together back-to-back first downs and, by game's end, one notation raised eyebrows: The Bulldogs gained only slightly more than a yard (a total of 17) on its first down opportunities.

In the second half, cracks in the Georgia line seemed to widen and Dorsett began swinging wide, left side or right, anywhere there was a sliver of daylight. He gained 137 yards on 15 carries in the final 30 minutes to set a Sugar Bowl record of 202 yards rushing.

Cavanaugh, who got Pitt over the hump, was the MVP, though.

Allan Leavitt kicked a 25-yard field goal for Georgia, but Panther kicker Carson Long countered with 42 and 31-yard field goals to end the scoring.

The Pitt defense was extraordinary, perhaps the finest unit of this exceptional collection of athletes. The three points Georgia tallied was not only 26 below its season average, but the Bulldogs' lowest output in 52 games. Georgia averaged 279.5 yards rushing during the regular season, but could manage just 135 against the Panthers. It wasn't until 22 playing minutes of the Sugar Bowl elapsed that Georgia crossed midfield. The Pitt defense caught more (4) of Georgia's passes than the Bulldogs did (3).

And three of Pitt's five scoring drives came after the defense forced a turnover.

"I think some people thought we might miss the 11:30 kickoff because we'd be hung over," middle guard Al Romano cracked, obviously relishing the early and practical end to the national championship question. "What they should do now is call off the Rose Bowl," Romano added puckishly.

"All year long," Majors said reflectively, "I haven't waved my finger in the air, and I haven't worn a No. 1 button." Now, waving a finger in the air and sporting a No.1 button, he added, "But after the game I told the team it was No. 1, and they all agree we are."

Vince Dooley covers skinhead after Pitt skinned Georgia.

	1	2	3	4	
Pittsburgh	7	14	3	3	27
Georgia	0	0	3	0	3

Pittsburgh: Cavanaugh, 6-yard run. PAT, Long kick.

Pittsburgh: Jones, 59-yard pass from Cavanaugh. PAT, Long kick.

Pittsburgh: Dorsett, 11-yard run. PAT, Long kick.

Georgia: Leavitt, 25-yard field goal.

Pittsburgh: Long, 42-yard field goal.

Pittsburgh: Long, 31-yard field goal.

Individual Leaders

Rushing
Pittsburgh: Dorsett 32-202, 1 TD.
Georgia: Goff 17-76.

Passing
Pittsburgh: Cavanaugh 10-18-0, 192 yards, 1 TD.
Georgia: Robinson 2-15-2, 33 yards.

Receiving
Pittsburgh: Walker 3-80; Taylor 4-72.
Georgia: Davis 1-19; Pyburn 1-14; McLee 1-13.

Pittsburgh		Georgia
24	First Downs	14
288	Rushing Yards	135
10-18-0	Passing	3-22-4
192	Passing Yards	46
480	Total Yards	181
5-36.8	Punts	8-42.1
2-1	Fumbles – Lost	4-2
6-66	Penalties – Yards	4-30

Attendance: 75,212.
Teams' remuneration: $1,801,600.
Miller-Digby Award recipient: Matt Cavanaugh, Pittsburgh quarterback.

Alabama 35 Ohio State 6

"You'd better get the grandfathers involved."

The look of the Sugar Bowl was changing in many ways. The football game was back on New Year's Day, with the Southeastern Conference champion automatically in one corner. Edna Engert, after 41 years of running the business office, decided to call it a career.

She had once said, "I was very involved with the piano as a young girl. My mother said I must make up my mind to either attend college and study music or take a job. I took a job and I've never regretted it. It led me to the Sugar Bowl." The feeling was obviously mutual. This woman, who started with 37 bosses, was entrusted with command of the Sugar Bowl's nerve center for most of her tenure with the Mid-Winter Sports Association. She served well. If Fred Digby was "Mr. Sugar Bowl," Edna Engert was the "Mrs."

At a testimonial given by her "bosses," Edna was presented with a gold charm and desk set. Until then, it was a gift reserved only for Sugar Bowl presidents.

Carl James, the 48-year-old athletic director of Duke University, was named executive director in July; but the position was again open the following year when James resigned to become Athletic Director at the University of Maryland.

Alabama and Notre Dame again seemed to be the champagne pairing for the holidays. After an early season loss to Nebraska, the Crimson Tide had developed into a potent football team. The Irish were in and out, and indeed a loss to a very weak Ole Miss seemed to knock the Notre Dame aspirations for No. 1 askew. But it was the only Irish loss.

What the pairing appeared to be riding on was a Texas defeat before November 19, the day the invitations would be issued. A loss by the No. 1 Longhorns should lift the Tide to No. 1, and Dan Devine's Fighting Irish would go wherever No. 1 went for the chance to swipe the crown.

A more likely occurrence would be Texas steaming into the Cotton Bowl with the Irish tagging behind, and Michigan edging Ohio State in the Big Ten's annual showdown. That would send Michigan to Pasadena and the co-champion Buckeyes looking for other vacancies on New Year's. Since the Big Ten and Pac-Eight had broken their Rose-only binds, their representatives had played in other bowls, though not in New Orleans.

Notre Dame was more desirable, but the novelty of a Big Ten team in the Sugar Bowl was intriguing—particularly if it were a game between Coach Bear

Bryant, with 270 victories, and Coach Woody Hayes, with 231 victories, the biggest winners on football's active roster. It was interesting also to ponder the insurance the Sugar had with the SEC tie-up. Without it, Bryant surely would have been angling for a No. 1 showdown.

In spite of being generally outplayed, Michigan somehow beat Ohio State. The fiery Hayes, gentleman and history scholar off the field and occasional firebrand on the field, slugged an ABC cameraman in the game's final moments. Hayes' temper had become part of football lore and New Orleans braced for it.

Alabama and Ohio State were 3rd and 8th in the polls at the time of the selections. The Tide's wishbone gained 416.7 yards a game, the 11th-best offense nationally. Ohio State was 14th with 413.8 yards a game and 2nd in rushing with 321.2 yards. On the opposite side of the ledger, the Buckeyes gave up only 230.8 yards a game (7th nationally) while 'Bama surrendered 252 yards. Sprinkled on the Buckeye roster were names like Pete Johnson (fullback), Chris Ward (tackle), Ron Springs (tailback), and Tom Cousineau (linebacker). Alabama had names like Ozzie Newsome (receiver), Jeff Rutledge (quarterback), and Tony Nathan (running back).

The only names the press seemed interested in were Bryant and Hayes. The growl vs. the scowl was the way the New Orleans press painted the game.

"I don't know why you people keep making such a big deal over Woody Hayes and Paul Bryant," rasped the Bear. "I can assure you that I'm not going to play ... and I hope Woody does." Hayes made a case for the vintage years. "When (Egyptian President Anwar) Sadat and (Israeli Prime Minister Menachem) Begin got together," said Hayes, "it's the same as when Bear and I get together. If you want a good contest or a good agreement, you'd better get the grandfathers involved."

Even the players got into the act. Springs said, "This is a game between Bear Bryant and Woody Hayes. They are the two best coaches of all time. We (Ohio State) wouldn't want to say we play for the second-best coach."

Gil LeBreton, who covered Ohio State for the *Times-Picayune*, however, believed the Buckeyes were priming themselves for a tumble. "They found a ready-made excuse and used it," said LeBreton, referring to an Ohio State feeling that the Buckeyes rightfully belonged in Pasadena as the undisputed Big Ten champion.

A victory and a Texas loss could put 'Bama on the top of the polls. Ohio State was trying to redeem itself for two losses and a conference co-championship instead of a national championship.

"Coach Hayes has been saying all along that there's one more great game left in this team," said Aaron Brown. "This has got to be the one." Springs added, "We really felt this was the best Ohio State team we've had here in a while. Those Oklahoma and Michigan losses were just so disappointing. They kinda all stay on your mind. "In a way I'm glad we're playing Alabama. It's like a second chance for us."

Woody Hayes and Bear Bryant prepare café brulot at Antoine's.

"We thought we had 'em then."

Lou Green, an Alabama guard, had Ohio State right where he wanted the Buckeyes – under his foot.

He had cut out pictures of Buckeye stalwarts like Aaron Brown, Tom Cousineau, Byron Cato and Dave Adkins and put them in his sock.

"I wanted to paste Brown's picture in my helmet," Green deadpanned, "but some of the guys talked me out of it. I just kept them down there where they couldn't raise any hell."

The Buckeyes never get out from underfoot – either Green's or the 'Bama team – despite 10 Crimson Tide fumbles, though only two were lost.

Even with that, from start to finish, Alabama was in command.

"The plan," center Dwight Stephenson said, "was to take it right to them." And 16 of Alabama's first 17 plays went right into the teeth of the Buckeye defense. The Crimson Tide held the ball for eight minutes, gaining 60 yards, while Ohio State appeared to be just hanging on, even at that early stage. David Sadler, Green, Bob Cryder and Jim Bunch, the 'Bama offensive line, thrashed their opposition as the Tide backs consistently gained yardage off tackle. The drive ended short of points when quarterback Jeff Rutledge was stopped on a two-yard pickup on fourth-and-goal from the 5.

"We had a little further to go than I thought," commented Alabama coach Paul Bryant. "We should have kicked the field goal. It was stupid call, and I made it."

The ease in which 'Bama handled Ohio State, points or not, on that drive carried a message: "We thought we had 'em then," Rutledge admitted.

With almost embarrassing efficiency, Rutledge guided the Tide 76 yards on its second possession. A 29-yard pass to Ozzie Newsome, with a 15-yard roughing the passer penalty tacked on, put the Buckeyes in serious trouble. Tony Nathan bounded into the end zone from the 1 after Bruce Bolton put the ball

there on a six-yard run that wasn't supposed to be.

"Ozzie came off when Bolton went in, and he (Newsome) was supposed to carry on the play," Bryant moaned with a smile. "The Good Lord called that one for us."

Bolton also figured in the next 'Bama touchdown, which came on a play Bryant hadn't used all season. Rutledge and the Crimson Tide line had Ohio State backpedaling on its next series, an 11-play, 76-yard touchdown drive. The points came when fullback Johnny Davis swung right on a fake at the Buckeye 27 while split end Bolton, who had lined up as a right halfback, rolled out of the backfield and shot down the sideline.

Anticipating the run, the Buckeye cornerback stepped forward – and Bolton was almost instantly clear. Rutledge dropped back and got the ball to Bolton, barely inbounds. The extra point was missed, but with 4:32 left until the half, Alabama led 13-0.

The Tide had scored on two of only three first half possessions.

Tony Nathan (22) holds ball high after Alabama touchdown as Ohio State linebacker Tom Cousineau (36) checks scoreboard.

Quarterback Rod Gerald had the Buckeyes in position to get back in the game, guiding Ohio State to the Alabama 3. Coach Woody Hayes, however, passed up a field goal attempt on fourth down. "I thought about it being bad football," he explained. "When you're down 13 points, field goals don't look so big ... if we had gotten the touchdown we may have played better ball."

But they didn't.

After 'Bama again held Ohio State at its 28, Rutledge took the Tide 72 yards where he hit Richard Neal with a three-yard TD pass. Another pass to Neal on a two-point conversion made the score an out-of-reach 21-0.

"There in the third quarter, when we had the ball on the short end of the 50 twice and didn't move," smoldered Hayes, "their defense rose to the occasion and our offense didn't. That definitely sealed the ball game right there."

Buckeye players continued to talk about their exhaustive beating to Michigan, and why they should've been in Pasadena as Big Ten champions. While embarrassed Sugar Bowlers cleared their throats and avoided eye contact after one of the game's worst matches, reporters wondered how one team could fumble 10 times and still win by 29 points.

Answers came from the Alabama locker room. Tackle Lloyd David Sadler felt it was because there simply was no better team. "Anyone who doesn't vote for us," he said with an eye toward the next day's final balloting after finding out that in the Cotton Bowl Notre Dame beat Texas, the only team ahead of the Tide in the poll, "isn't voting with a clear conscience."

'Bama fans tear down goalposts under the delusion that their Tide is No. 1.

	1	2	3	4	
Alabama	0	13	8	14	35
Ohio State	0	0	0	6	6

Alabama: Nathan, 1-yard run. PAT, Chapman kick.

Alabama: Bolton, 27-yard pass from Rutledge. Kick failed.

Alabama: Neal, 3-yard pass from Rutledge. PAT, Nathan pass from Rutledge.

Ohio State: Harrell, 38-yard pass from Gerald. Run failed.

Alabama: Ogilvie, 1-yard run. PAT, Chapman kick.

Alabama: Davis, 5-yard run. PAT, Chapman kick.

Individual Leaders

Rushing
Alabama: Davis 24-95, 1 TD; Crow 5-46.
Ohio State: Springs 10-74; Logan 13-57.

Passing
Alabama: Rutledge 8-11-0, 109 yards, 2 TDs.
Ohio State: Gerald 7-17-3, 103 yards, 1 TD.

Receiving
Alabama: Newsome 2-45; Ferguson 2-28.
Ohio State: Hunter 2-25; Springs 2-6.

Alabama		Ohio State
25	First Downs	13
280	Rushing Yards	160
8-11-0	Passing	7-17-3
109	Passing Yards	103
389	Total Yards	263
1-33.0	Punts	4-37.5
10-2	Fumbles – Lost	0-0
1-5	Penalties – Yards	4-40

Attendance: 76,811.
Teams' remuneration: $1,867,164.
Miller-Digby Award recipient: Jeff Rutledge, Alabama quarterback.

Alabama 14 Penn State 7

"It's not life or death."

"Everything coach told us turned out to be right – except the vote," said Alabama linebacker Barry Krauss of the 1978 bowl sequence. "He said we had to beat Ohio State convincingly. He said Oklahoma would lose, Michigan would lose, and Notre Dame would beat Texas. We just looked at him, feeling it couldn't all happen like he said. Damn if it didn't."

"Man, I was driving home, sure we'd be national champions. Then we go and get ripped off."

The victory Bear Bryant forecast for the fifth-ranked Irish over No. 1 Texas catapulted Notre Dame into the top spot in both polls while Alabama inched to No. 2, forcing a lot of fans to wonder if the pollsters voted for the name rather than the game. It was fair to speculate that had the positions been reversed – Notre Dame No. 3 and Alabama No. 5 before the bowls – and if the Tide beat No. 1 Texas 38-10, it would not have leapfrogged the Irish to the top.

It must have frustrated the man many considered the best collegiate coach of all time. Bryant had won three Associated Press national championships, four in United Press International. But Notre Dame was directly responsible for Bear not having an incredible seven AP No. 1s.

In 1966, Notre Dame had been voted No. 1 despite a 10-10 tie with Michigan State and despite Alabama's 11-0 record. Now the Irish had leapfrogged over Alabama to No. 1 despite the Tide's slaughter of Ohio State. The Irish beat him, 24-23, in the 1973 Sugar Bowl, and then upset him, 13-11, in the 1975 Orange Bowl.

There was a change in the masthead of the Mid-Winter Sports Association. The name was formally changed. No one bothered to call it anything but the Sugar Bowl, so after 44 years the membership gave up the ghost. The Sugar Bowl was now the Sugar Bowl.

An odd thing occurred in 1978 as the season opened and the time came to choose the participants for the Sugar Bowl: The weaknesses in the SEC-Sugar Bowl contract caught up with Alabama's Bear Bryant. After beating Nebraska and Missouri, the Crimson Tide lost 24-14 to Southern California in a game Bryant would say was "worse than the score." The loss was damaging to the Sugar because 'Bama was the SEC's best chance for a No. 1 team and, thus, the attraction for the highest-ranked opponent on January 1.

Georgia, which lost one early season non-conference game, was knocking on the Sugar's door most of the season. The Bulldogs were not a bad team but had little chance at No. 1. But they held the inside track for the Sugar Bowl. Bryant, it seemed, had written himself out of the Sugar Bowl. His Crimson Tide improved and continued to improve after the USC loss, rising to No. 3 in the polls. In some way, Bryant had to be able to play No. 1 Penn State in order

to have a shot at a national championship. With the Big Eight tie-up in the Orange Bowl and the SWC tie-up with the Cotton Bowl, the Sugar was the only major bowl in which such a pairing could occur.

When the original contract between the SEC and Sugar Bowl was drawn up, Bryant influenced the formula for selecting the conference representative. As the perennial champion, and because he wanted the freedom to go elsewhere on occasion, it was agreed in the event there was a tie for the conference title, the "most recent appearance rule" would prevail. That is, the team last appearing in the Sugar Bowl was free to go to another bowl. Alabama's better overall record would not come into play as the Sugar had less say in the representative than either the Orange or Cotton Bowls.

All Georgia had to do was beat Auburn to tie 'Bama for the conference championship, and the Bulldogs would host the Sugar Bowl, probably against Oklahoma. There was some talk of matching Penn State and Alabama in the Gator Bowl, but nothing came of it. Nothing had to.

Penn State Head Coach Joe Paterno had never won a national championship, nor had Penn State in 92 years of playing the game. He let the Sugar in on a secret. Penn State seemed ready to play in Miami, but Paterno allowed that should Missouri upset Nebraska and should Auburn beat Georgia, which would put Alabama in the Sugar, he wanted to play the Crimson Tide.

Sure enough, Missouri beat Nebraska, and Auburn and Georgia tied. After the Lions beat Pittsburgh and the Tide defeated Auburn, Alabama moved up a notch in the polls. The Sugar Bowl found itself with the No. 1 and No. 2 teams, only the fifth time this had happened in postseason football.

Why would Paterno look for the toughest foe? The answer was he had a team that could look anyone in the eye and not blink. The Penn State defense gave up an average of 54.5 yards rushing while quarterback Chuck Fusina, second in the Heisman Trophy balloting, directed an offense that averaged almost 31 points a game.

Paterno, unlike Bryant, did not believe winning a national championship was as important as the challenge of playing for a national championship. "This is my third 11-0 team," Paterno said in indirect reference to what seemed to be a prejudice by voters against Eastern football.

Paterno reiterated his fundamental belief in the chase for the title. "I think the important thing is that we have an opportu-

Penn State is stopped short of the goal line on fourth down preserving the national championship for Alabama.

nity to go for it," said Paterno. "Certainly it is important to have goals to attain." The talented quarterback Fusina echoed his coach. "We want to be No. 1," he offered, "and we're going to work as hard as possible. But it's not everything ... If we don't win a national championship, I won't feel the four years are a waste. There are a lot of things other than a national championship. It's not life or death."

Alabama's aspirations were clearly more single-minded. "Sure, I'd like to win another national championship," growled Bryant. "Every year I want that to be our goal and the objective of our team. Every day when they come in that's what we talk about. We write it down and we talk about how we're going to get there." "It is," said Barry Krauss, "the reason a lot of us came here."

Bryant and Paterno were, of course, more concerned with each other's teams. Bryant characterized his Alabama squad as "a bunch of average players who don't know they're not supposed to be able to play as well as they do." The figures backed Bear up. Uncharacteristically, this Crimson Tide team was not a reckoning force, particularly on defense where it surrendered 309.2 yards of total offense a game. "We used to not give up that much yardage in a season," moaned Bryant.

The thought came up that perhaps a replay of the 1978 bowl season could occur. If Alabama beat Penn State and 3rd-ranked USC (early season conquerors of Alabama) beat Michigan badly in the Rose Bowl, then the Trojans could rise to No. 1.

Tide defensive tackle Marty Lyons seemed self-assured. "If we beat the No. 1 team in the nation," he said, "... they're 11-0 and no one else could beat them. That has to say something for us ... We weren't brought here to play football for the fun of it. We were brought here for achievement."

"You better pass."

If there is a single image that paints the Sugar Bowl picture, it's this one: Alabama linebacker Barry Krauss, seemingly shot out of a missile silo, zeroing in on Penn State's Mike Guman at the goal line.

In one of the most fabled goal-line stands in college football history, in a game between the No. 1-and No. 2-ranked teams in the land, the Crimson Tide won – and Penn State lost – the 1979 national championship. It was the final of three touchdown-saving plays that preserved 'Bama's 14-7 lead in the fading minutes.

Even Krauss was surprised at his team's achievement. "They were down there at the 1-yard line, and I had to admit I was thinking they'd probably score, go for two and try to beat us.'' It was a fitting climax to a game that was a defensive classic before the fireworks two feet shy of the Superdome end zone.

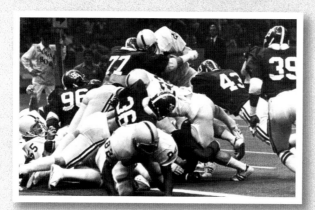

On fourth down, Mike Guman is denied a touchdown as Barry Krauss (77) and the Tide defense rise up.

Before then, Tide quarterback Jeff Rutledge threw a 30-yard touchdown pass to split end Bruce Bolton with eight seconds left in the first half for a 7-0 lead. The Nittany Lions tied it on a 17-yard pass from Chuck Fusina to Scott Fitzkee in the third quarter, but a 62-yard punt return by Alabama's Lon Ikner set up Major Ogilvie for an eight-yard touchdown that made it 14-7 in the third period.

What remained was a fourth quarter for all the marbles, and the Nittany Lions' one chance to claim it came when defensive

end Joe Lally recovered an Alabama fumble on the Tide 19 with 7:57 to play.

On the next play, fullback Matt Suhey ran 11 yards to the Bama 8 for a first down. Then Guman took a pitch and gained two yards to the 6.

On second down, Fusina dropped back and quickly delivered a pass to Fitzkee, who was flaring out near the right sideline. Fitzkee caught the pass at the 1, but before he could turn to find the end zone he was slammed out of bounds by cornerback Don McNeal two feet short of a touchdown.

It's a play that Fitzkee and Penn State fans have relived in their minds for years, but it always ends the same: coming up a little bit short.

"People still bring it up,'' Fitzkee said decades later. "I've heard a lot of criticism, and I'm sure those guys who didn't get in on third and fourth down have heard it too.''

That would be Suhey and Guman.

On third down, Suhey took the handoff up the middle, but he was wrapped up by linebacker Rich Wingo.

"Fusina came out to look at the ball,'' Bama tackle Marty Lyons recalled, "and I was standing in the way, in between him and the ball. He started smiling. 'How much is it?' he asked. I told him, ' 'Bout this much.' 'Ten inches?' 'Yeah,' I said. 'You better pass.' "

On fourth down, the Nittany Lions tried to muscle it in again, but Guman ran into Krauss.

"They had called timeout before the fourth down, and they were trying to figure out what they were going to do and what we were going to do,'' Krauss said. "We thought they'd go outside or throw because they had run it on third down (to no avail), so I had given myself a little more depth so I could flow to the outside. When he gave it back to Guman, and he came back inside, there was a hole. He saw it, and I did too.''

The Stand: Matt Suhey is stopped by Rich Wingo on third-and-goal from less than a foot away.

Bear Bryant, on the crest of No.1.

The collision was one that, as Krauss remembers it, made time stand still.

"He came over and I was able to hit him," Krauss said. "After that, I wasn't sure what happened."

Krauss, who had all but resigned himself to the likelihood that Penn State was going to score, never thought the hit would knock Guman short of the goal line. "It seemed like he was so close," Krauss said. "He was falling, and what was actually a couple of seconds seemed like five minutes."

But Guman did come down short, and so did Penn State, which never got close again.

The Alabama defense left the field jumping, whooping and hollering, not noticing that Krauss remained prone on the field. Eventually the dazed linebacker picked himself up and wobbily made his way to the sideline where Coach Bear Bryant embraced him. "A knock like that," the Bear growled with a grin, "is the nicest kind of feeling you can get."

	1	2	3	4	
Alabama	0	7	7	0	14
Penn State	0	0	7	0	7

Alabama: Bolton, 30-yard pass from Rutledge. PAT, McElroy kick.

Penn State: Fitzkee, 17-yard pass from Fusina. PAT, Bahr kick.

Alabama: Ogilvie, 8-yard run. PAT, McElroy kick.

Individual Leaders

Rushing
Alabama: Nathan 21-127; Whitman 11-51.
Penn State: Suhey 10-48; Guman 9-22.

Passing
Alabama: Rutledge 8-15-2, 91 yards, 1 TD.
Penn State: Fusina 15-30-4, 163 yards, 1 TD.

Receiving
Alabama: Bolton 2-46, 1 TD; Whitman 2-27.
Penn State: Guman 5-59; Fitzkee 3-38, 1 TD.

Alabama		Penn State
12	First Downs	12
208	Rushing Yards	19
8-15-2	Passing	15-30-4
91	Passing Yards	163
299	Total Yards	182
10-38.8	Punts	10-38.7
2-1	Fumbles – Lost	2-0
11-75	Penalties – Yards	8-51

Attendance: 76,824.
Teams' remuneration: $1,950,218.
Miller-Digby Award: Barry Krauss, Alabama linebacker.

Alabama 24   Arkansas 9

"I'll let y'all take care of the polls?"

New Sugar Bowl executive director Mickey Holmes' fear his initial brush at a bowl pairing would cause his red hair to change color. The University of Georgia was turning the hair of all the Sugar Bowlers white.

Vince Dooley's Bulldogs were unable to win outside the Southeastern Conference but were perfect within and knocking on New Orleans' door. It was possible, with Auburn wins over Georgia and Alabama coupled with a Bulldog loss to independent Georgia Tech, that a losing Georgia (5-6) team would hold down the host spot in the Sugar Bowl.

At the same time, Alabama, the nation's No. 4 offensive team, No. 1 defensive team, and No. 1-ranked team was cruising effortlessly to at least a share of the SEC championship with the Bulldogs. Alabama and Georgia didn't play, and the Bulldogs would earn the invitation in a tie because of the "most recent appearance rule." New Orleans could lose a possible national champion and gain a team with a losing season record. "We'd welcome them with open arms and go on with our bowl," Holmes said diplomatically of Georgia's chances.

Auburn, 15th-ranked but ineligible for bowls because of NCAA probation, put the Sugar on hold by unleashing James Brooks and Joe Cribbs on Georgia. Brooks gained 200 yards and Cribbs 166 in a 33-13 War Eagle whoop. But the Sugar Bowl could rejoice only momentarily. Alabama's last game was with these same War Eagles, a very good team. If Auburn beat the Crimson Tide, Georgia and Alabama would be tied in the final SEC standings and the Bulldogs would spend the holidays in New Orleans.

Coach Bear Bryant said of his state rivals and the bowl situation, "It's not up to me, but if we can't beat Auburn, I'd just as soon stay home and plow." The Auburn faction went up in arms over the

comment, which added more fuel to a rivalry that needed none.

Georgia officials removed the fear of having a losing team in the Sugar by requesting that the "most recent appearance" rule be waived should the Bulldogs lose to Georgia Tech. The request applied only in that instance, though. If Georgia won, and Auburn broke Alabama's longest-in-the-nation victory string at 19, the 'Dogs wanted their rightful berth.

The SEC Sugar Bowl opponent would be either Arkansas or Texas (tied with the University of Houston for the Southwest Conference lead). Texas appeared to be the odds-on choice; but the Longhorns were upset 13-7 by Texas A&M, and the Sugar had Arkansas, a 10-1 conference co-champion.

Bear Bryant, now hard on the heels of Amos Alonzo Stagg's all-time coaching record of 314 victories, showed up on the field more than an hour before the Auburn-'Bama kickoff. As he and Assistant Athletic Director Charlie Thornton strolled around Legion Field, Auburn students began chanting, "Plow, Bear, plow." Bryant had Thornton put his hands behind his back, whereupon the coach grabbed them, turning the bent-over assistant athletic director into a plow. The students roared approval.

With Vince Dooley in the press box along with some very nervous Sugar Bowlers, Bryant's team played an uncharacteristic Alabama game. The Tide had third-quarter fumbles on its 21, 23, 37, and on the Auburn 12-yard line. Alabama was letting a national championship slip away.

Auburn took an 18-17 lead with less than 12 minutes remaining; then the Tide composed itself and drove 88 yards for a touchdown and a 25-18 win. The Sugar Bowl had dodged a silver bullet.

Lou Holtz, the Arkansas coach who was knocked out of the Cotton and into the Sugar with Baylor's upset of Texas (because of the SWC's most recent appearance rule) said, "There were just four minutes left in the Alabama-Auburn game when we found out we'd be playing the Bear." He spoke of his first game against Bryant when he was an assistant on the South Carolina staff. "I was coaching the defensive secondary and, boy, it was going to be a great thrill. But it wasn't so because we got beat something like 42-0, or some ridiculous score like that. Heck, lots of teams get excited about playing Alabama before the game ... They're so good I don't vote for second and third place behind them. Nobody's is close to them."

Others thought differently. After the close call with Auburn, the Associated Press poll dropped Alabama to No. 2 behind Ohio State

by a point and a half, upsetting Tide fans who jammed the telephone circuits to AP headquarters in New York. The coaches who vote in the United Press International poll kept the Tide on top; but if 'Bama was to regain its AP ranking, it was going to have to be impressive in the Sugar Bowl and Ohio State would have to stumble in the Rose.

Holtz had done a masterful job with Arkansas. With five freshmen in his starting lineups and a defense ranked no higher than 6th in the SWC, he put together a team that played excellent field position football. "We use a rope-a-dope defense," said Holtz. "Everyone always seems to have us on the ropes." The "Cinderella Pigs" were sixth-ranked after giving up an astounding 320 yards but only 9.8 points a game. And if the bowls fell just right, Arkansas had as much claim to No. l as anyone.

"Polls, polls, polls," groused Bryant, "that's all I've heard about. I just want to beat Arkansas ... by one point or a half point, I don't care. Then I'll let y'all (the press) take care of the polls."

Which is what Crimson Tide defensive back Don McNeal, who unlike his coach had polls very much on his mind, was counting on. "This is it," said McNeal. "Everybody comes here (Alabama) to win the national championship. That was my goal when I came here. I've accomplished it once. I'm hoping for two."

"Steve just went pssst!"

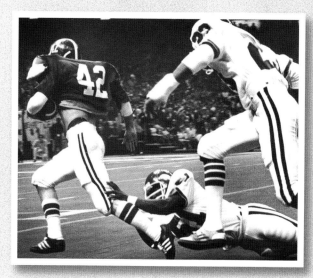

Major Ogilvie (42) rockets out of the arm of linebacker Ozzie Riley (51).

There was a new look to Alabama in the Sugar Bowl – a look Arkansas coach Lou Holtz didn't like. He liked it less after the game.

In the time since the end of the regular season, Bear Bryant installed a double wing with motion off the wishbone formation. The Crimson Tide could run its basic plays off the set – and give something else to concern Arkansas coaches.

After the Razorbacks got a 34-yard field goal, courtesy of a lost Alabama fumble on the opening kickoff, the Tide showed its new look.

Holtz watched a seven-play, 82-yard drive featuring a fullback in motion and a lot of counter-action to slow the Hogs' defensive charge. Major Ogilvie scored from 22-yards out after quarterback Steadman Shealy pitched out at precisely the last instant. It was the third straight year in which Ogilvie scored a Sugar Bowl touchdown.

"We weren't expecting as much double wing," Holtz admitted. "We weren't expecting an unbalanced line. We knew they'd run at least two wide-outs and two tight ends ... but with five freshmen (in his defensive alignment) we made some mistakes. We got in wrong calls, shifted the wrong way, and did a lot of wrong things."

There would be more.

Four plays after receiving the ensuing kickoff, another Razorback fumble was recovered by linebacker Thomas Boyd on the Hog 22. Ogilvie scored his second touchdown from the 1 to put the Tide ahead 14-3 with 3:46 left in the first period, forcing Arkansas into an accelerated passing game.

Alan McElroy kicked a 25-yard field goal, and with a 17-3 score at intermission, Alabama seemed content with the way the game was going.

Hogs quarterback Kevin Scanlon, hurried and hit on virtually every play in the first half by the relentless 'Bama defense, got hot, though, sweeping the Razorbacks downfield 80 yards after the second-half kickoff. Robert Ferrell made an over-the-shoulder three-yard catch for a touchdown, though the two-point conversion fell well short.

The score was now 17-9 and the game was taking on the look of a real dogfight.

When Mike Burchfield downed a punt on the Crimson Tide 2 in the fourth quarter, the nine-point underdog Hogs seemed to have

Major Ogilvie was a major problem for the Hog defense.

a real chance.

At that point Holtz got more of a look at Bryant's new wrinkle than he ever wanted to see. In three plays the Crimson were near midfield – 35 yards coming after Shealy timed a perfect pitchout by Billy Jackson. When the Crimson Tide reached the 12 – on a third-and-11, offensive coordinator Mal Moore suggested a play – "43 Read" – to Shealy. "I would not have called it," Shealy said. The quarterback glided down the line, "read" the right defensive end, and then stuck the ball into 230-pound frame of fullback Steve Whitman, who shot through the middle for the touchdown. He muscled his way over defensive back Kevin Evans at the goal. "I read the end on the play, and Steve just went psssst," Shealy recalled.

The 98-yard drive, Alabama's longest of the season, broke the back of the Razorbacks.

The two teams gained 696 yards between them. The double wing took the Hogs out of planned defensive schemes. Holtz addressed that change succinctly: "Alabama's defense is the fourth best in the nation, and it's their major weakness. How could we know the nation's best team would play a perfect game?"

Amidst all the clamor and reasons why Alabama should be ranked No. 1, Bear Bryant was saying injuries may have kept his team from being one of the greatest of all time. "We hit some peaks," Bryant said, "against Baylor, and later against Tennessee, when we came back from being down 17-0. No team has ever done that against Tennessee. It was a team that did what it had to do. When Auburn went ahead of us, we marched 82 yards (actually 88). When the Sugar Bowl was hanging in the balance, we went 98 yards. Things like that say something about a football team."

That football team said something about Bear, too, who had coached in nine Sugar Bowls, most of anyone, and where he showcased four of the six national championships Alabama claimed under him. The victory, in Bryant's last Sugar Bowl appearance, was not only his 296th, bringing him within 20 of Amos Alonzo Stagg's record 314, but this was the 17th of Bryant's 22 teams at Alabama to finish in the Top Ten, an unmatched feat since for a coach since the Associated Press began voting in 1936. Also, Southern Cal defeated Ohio State (17-16) that day, rectifying the AP voting and moving Bryant past Frank Leahy, who had won four AP national championships at Notre Dame in 1943-46-47-49.

	1	2	3	4	
Alabama	14	3	0	7	24
Arkansas	3	0	6	0	9

Arkansas: Ordonez, 34-yard field goal.

Alabama: Ogilvie, 22-yard run. PAT, McElroy kick.

Alabama: Ogilvie, 1-yard run. PAT, McElroy kick.

Alabama: McElroy, 25-yard field goal.

Arkansas: Farrell, 3-yard pass from Scanlon. Run failed.

Alabama: Whitman, 12-yard run. PAT, McElroy kick.

Individual Leaders

Rushing
Alabama: Jackson 13-120; Ogilvie 14-67, 2 TDs; Whitman 6-37, 1 TD.
Arkansas: Bowles 15-46; Anderson 6-28.

Passing
Alabama: Shealy 4-7-0, 70 yards.
Arkansas: Scanlon 22-39-1, 245 yards, 1 TD.

Receiving
Alabama: Jackson 3-62.
Arkansas: Anderson 7-53; Farrell 3-51, 1 TD.

Alabama		Arkansas
18	First Downs	21
284	Rushing Yards	97
4-7-2	Passing	22-40-2
70	Passing Yards	245
354	Total Yards	342
8-36.2	Punts	7-36.2
7-61	Penalties – Yards	1-15

Attendance: 77,484.
Teams' remuneration: $2,011,166.
Miller-Digby Award recipient: Major Ogilvie, Alabama running back.

Georgia 17 Notre Dame 10

"The road to the Sugar Bowl goes through I-85."

Auburn, in a very real sense, had been the key to the Sugar Bowl's national championship role. In consecutive years, the War Eagles had prevented Georgia, an SEC-challenging team with only average credentials, from playing in New Orleans. The complexion of the 47th Sugar Bowl would also be influenced by the Auburn-Georgia feud, but this time New Orleans had a strong hankering for the Bulldogs.

Vince Dooley had fashioned a textbook team in Athens, one that used limited resources to maximum efficiency. Georgia had a capable, big play defense (ranked only fourth in the SEC), excellent special teams and kicking units, and a battering ram offense based on the extraordinary talents of an 18-year-old freshman. Herschel Walker, a 220-pound tailback with sprinter's speed, became the ingredient that made Dooley's team the nation's best. Walker accounted for 40 percent of Georgia's 1980 offense.

Out first-downed, with less total plays and less possession time, Georgia outscored its opponents with a combination of Walker's running (which totaled 1,616 yards—30 yards better than Tony Dorsett's freshman record); Rex Robinson's place-kicking; and an opportunistic defense. It forced the opposition into a nation-leading difference in average turnovers (2.09 per game) and made the Bulldogs a fearful foe. Georgia also had a best-in-the-nation 16.6-yard average in punt returns while allowing only a half-yard. Georgia's 9-0 record and No.

2 ranking before the Auburn game made the Bulldogs the South's favorite.

The prospect that had the Sugar Bowl excited was a match between No. 1-ranked Notre Dame and the Bulldogs, though each had tough games at the end of the season.

After Georgia defeated Florida on a 93-yard pass play in the final minutes, a myriad of possibilities still existed for the Sugar Bowl's host berth. Alabama, LSU, and Mississippi State, right behind the 'Dogs in the conference standings, were waiting for Georgia to stumble. The complex SEC tie breaker had them all in the running should Georgia lose just once. If the Bulldogs could put Auburn away though, something they hadn't done since 1976, the shouting would be over.

Georgia vs. Notre Dame or Georgia vs. Alabama (SEC rivals that didn't play during the regular season) were the matches that intrigued the Sugar Bowl. The feeling in

Uniform of the day on the chain-gang.

New Orleans was that either the Irish or 'Bama, who had lost to Mississippi State, would be far more attractive against Georgia fans make a point for No. 1. than either Florida State or the winner of the Penn State-Pittsburgh game. Since Notre Dame and Alabama played late in the season, the Sugar wanted to tie up the victor. There were questions, however.

Rather than play Georgia, Notre Dame might well opt for the Cotton Bowl and its additional riches. An influential Irish alum told columnist Peter Finney, "Notre Dame would go anywhere if it meant $800,000." Finney disagreed, pointing to Baylor (with one loss) and Texas (with two) as the main contenders in the Cotton Bowl sweepstakes. "Could Notre Dame afford to pass up the challenge of playing No. 2 Georgia?" asked Finney. "I don't think so."

Another thought was whether Bear Bryant would enjoy the idea of an all-SEC bowl. For that to happen, Alabama would have to beat Notre Dame. Then Georgia, with a win over Auburn, could move to No. 1. Given those circumstances, Bryant's only chance at a third consecutive national championship would be to play Georgia. Bryant wouldn't commit himself for the record, but Crimson Tide running back Major Ogilvie summed up matters when he said, "If we beat Notre Dame and Georgia is the No. 1 team, I don't think there's any question we'd like to play Georgia. Our main objective all sea-

son has been the national championship. We'll do whatever it takes."

Would Vince Dooley like the idea of playing a fraternity brother? Probably not, but he didn't have to make the decision.

As it turned out, lowly Georgia Tech knocked the Irish out of No. 1 the week before the Alabama game with a 3-3 tie. That lifted Georgia to the top rung for the first time in 38 years and meant that the Irish would probably have to play the 'Dogs to have any opportunity to reclaim No. 1. Auburn couldn't wait for a chance to knock its conference next-door neighbor down a couple of pegs on the national ladder. The battle cry in the sleepy little Alabama hamlet that is home to the War Eagles was "The road to the Sugar Bowl goes through 1-85 (the highway that passes Jordan-Hare Stadium)."

Defensive back Greg Bell followed Georgia's season-long script by blocking a second-quarter punt that was picked up and returned for a touchdown. That put the Bulldogs ahead for the first time at 10-7 and was the catalyst in a 31-21 defeat of the gritty War Eagles. "We're shooting for No. 1," Buck Belue

Georgia fans make a point for No.1.

added as Vince Dooley accepted the Sugar Bowl invitation.

Two hours later, Notre Dame (which dropped to sixth after the Tech tie) awaited Coach Dan Devine in Legion Field's dressing room chanting, "Sugar Bowl, Sugar Bowl, Sugar Bowl!" Irish arms were held aloft as the bodies continually swayed, elated above a 7-0 victory over Alabama.

A 20-3 defeat by Southern California in the season finale put a practical end to Notre Dame's national championship aspirations, and the Irish opened a one-point favorite over the team no one could quite believe. Georgia was finally going to get its chance to play Notre Dame 34 years after Wally Butts had tried. The Bulldogs were an undefeated, No. 1-ranked underdog.

Scott Zettek felt it should have been more. "I hear we're favored," the Irish defensive end said. "My own personal (line), I give them 10 points. It's a chance to maybe be No. 1, and a chance to regain some of the respect we lost. We can prove

Herschel Walker begins his one-man destruction of the Nortre Dame defense.

ourselves again with a win. This game will get a lot of attention, not only because Georgia's No. 1 but because people want to see what Notre Dame does against them." Devine, who would be coaching his last game for the Irish, also figured in Zettek's handicapping. "We've been an emotional team all year, as all Notre Dame teams are, but the fact that it's Coach Devine's last game will be an additional factor."

The mammoth Notre Dame defense, outweighing Georgia's offense 15 pounds a man, had limited opponents to 109 yards a game rushing, a per-play average of 2.8 (in contrast to Georgia's offensive average of 4.5). The mobile Irish offensive line averaged 6-foot-6, 255 pounds against Georgia's front, which checked in at 6-foot-2, 236 pounds.

Notre Dame diehards spoke in smirks of Georgia's relatively easy schedule, and how South Bend troops were battle-hardened, conveniently forgetting some of the past paper-thin schedules the Irish had ridden to glory. Never, however, would Notre Dame have as much fraternity support as it would have against Georgia. There had not been a season quite like this, where so many schools remained alive for the national championship as New Year's Day approached. A Notre Dame victory and the right set of circumstances could vault Pittsburgh, Oklahoma, Florida State, Michigan, or even Baylor to No. 1. But any change hinged completely on one factor: Notre Dame had to defeat Georgia.

Former Bulldog idol Charley Trippi said it best, though, when he assessed, "Georgia can beat anyone because it's a very opportunistic team. And football often comes down to opportunism."

It was left to Rex Robinson, the second most prolific field goal kicker (59) in NCAA history, to capture just what this Georgia team was and what could be expected in its 12th game. "I know we've been a fortunate team in many respects," Robinson said on New Year's Eve. "What we've been, more than anything else, is a team of survivors. Somewhere, someone has been there to pick us up. The reason we're here is that we've survived."

"That was the only one we needed!"

It was an ugly stat: in a game when Georgia needed air-support to keep defenders off tailback Herschel Walker, quarterback Buck Belue was 0-for-11 passing.

Now, with 2:05 to play, and the Bulldogs trying to protect a precarious touchdown lead, Belue was looking at a third-and-seven at midfield.

He dropped back, looked, finally let loose, and completed his first – and only – pass, seven yards to Amp Arnold. That allowed Georgia to run out the clock, and secure its first consensus national title.

"That was the only one we needed," a relieved Bulldog coach Vince Dooley smiled.

This was a remarkable Georgia team, one that ran the table more because all its units meshed than on overwhelming talent, other than the redoubtable Walker.

Going into the Sugar Bowl against Notre Dame, conventional wisdom said to survive one more time in this memorable season, Georgia would need all its resourcefulness – and more. The Bulldogs had to have a passing threat to relieve pressure on its one-dimensional ground-game.

Although Belue didn't pass much on this infantry-oriented squad, he would have to pass, and pass well, in order to avoid having the Notre Dame Goliaths aim their defensive guns solely on Walker. Sprint-outs and play-action calls by Belue would be the only other offensive options in Georgia's limited offense.

The Bulldogs didn't get that needed air-support – even a halfback pass by Walker misfired - and still found a way to win.

Things didn't look good at the start: Notre Dame went ahead on a 50-yard field goal; a sack of Belue backed the Bulldogs up to their 6; Herschel Walker unknowingly separated a shoulder; and the Irish ended up at the Georgia 41, just nine yards from where Harry Oliver just kicked his field goal.

Reaching the 31, on a fourth-and-11, Oliver came back in for another kick. Everything appeared routine, until Bulldog Terry Hoage entered the game. Hoage was a reserve defensive back who had five minutes of game time during Georgia's season and who had made just two road trips. During Sugar Bowl practices the coaches had the backups attempt blocking kicks, simulating game conditions. Hoage had a knack for it and was placed on the Sugar Bowl travel squad.

As the ball was snapped the freshman sliced through the Notre Dame middle, leaped and caught Oliver's kick in the chest. "I saw kind of a little hole and just sailed through," Hoage explained.

That play, in essence, led to 10 of Georgia's 17 points.

From that blocked kick, Rex Robinson booted a 46-yard field goal to tie the score.

Robinson then kicked to Notre Dame's deep backs, Jim Stone and Ty Barber, each of whom drifted away from the ball before it hit near the end zone and began bouncing laterally. "I called for Ty to take the ball," Stone said, "but he didn't hear me. It was hard to hear with all that noise. Barber shrugged. "I guess he thought I had it, and I thought he had it. I think we were both too anxious to block (the on-coming Bulldogs)."

A brother act, Steve and Bob Kelly, closed in on the live ball.

Freshman phenom Herschel Walker goes up and over.

Steve dived at the offering, hit it, and, he said, "the ball popped into my brother's hand. At the 1. The play has come to be remembered in Athens as 'the world's longest on-sides kick.' "

Two plays afterward, Walker launched himself over the Notre Dame line to put Georgia in front 10-3.

After another Irish bobble, at the Notre Dame 22, Walker beat two defensive backs to the outside for a three-yard touchdown.

Taking advantage of three Irish miscues, Georgia was ahead at the half 17-3, but was behind in virtually every statistic – with the exception of three significant figures: Walker already had 95 yards rushing against a defense that hadn't surrendered a hundred yards to any runner all season; And Walker was getting his yards without benefit of a balanced offense; Belue had no completions in six attempts, and on five other plays he was unable to even get a pass off.

Irish coach Dan Devine decided to ignore Belue and shoot the works at stopping Walker. The Irish linebackers were moved up for a second-half salvo at Walker. Field position and size became Notre Dame's offensive components.

After weathering a Notre Dame touchdown drive in the third quarter, and another to the 20 – where DB Scott Woerner dropped Phil Carter for a yard loss on third down, forcing a missed field goal attempt, Georgia still had a task at hand.

That's when Belue completed on his only pass of the day.

Notre Dame outrushed (190-120), outpassed (138-7), and out first-downed (17-10) Georgia. Walker finished with 150 yards, 55 in the second half. His individual total may have been the most impressive rushing performance in Sugar Bowl history, considering his separated shoulder and the fact that his total was 30 yards more than his team's. Take away Walker's 36 carries and Georgia amassed a minus 30 yards of offense, partly due to four sacks of Belue. No winning team ever had such paltry figures in the Sugar Bowl.

Georgia did win two stats it had won all season: turnovers, 4-0 (not including Notre Dame's goal line gaffe), and the scoreboard, 17-10.

"I don't know how good we are," Vince Dooley said, "but I do know we're 12-0 and nobody else is."

In fact, Georgia was an undefeated, untied – and slightly unbelievable – national championship team.

Georgia players give Vince Dooley a ride following their Sugar Bowl triumph.

	1	2	3	4	
Georgia	10	7	0	0	17
Notre Dame	3	0	7	0	10

Notre Dame: Oliver, 50-yard field goal.

Georgia: Robinson, 46-yard field goal.

Georgia: Walker, 1-yard run. PAT, Robinson kick.

Georgia: Walker, 3-yard run. PAT, Robinson kick.

Notre Dame: Carter, 1-yard run. PAT, Oliver kick.

Individual Leaders

Rushing
Georgia: Walker 36-150, 2 TDs.
Notre Dame: Carter 27-109, 1 TD.

Passing
Georgia: Belue 1-12-0, 7 yards.
Notre Dame: Kiel 14-27-3, 138 yards.

Receiving
Georgia: Arnold 1-7.
Notre Dame: Holohan 4-44.

Georgia		Notre Dame
10	First Downs	17
120	Rushing Yards	190
1-13-0	Passing	12-28-3
7	Passing Yards	138
127	Total Yards	328
11-38.5	Punts	5-42.0
0	Fumbles – Lost	1-1
6-32	Penalties – Yards	8-69

Attendance: 77,896.
Teams' remuneration: $2,143,608.
Miller-Digby Award recipient: Herschel Walker, Georgia tailback.

Pittsburgh 24 Georgia 20

"Pitt was No.1 at the time."

The Georgia-Notre Dame game was a hit in every way. The pairing gave the Sugar Bowl one of its highest television ratings (23.3). But due to the nature of the Orange Bowl's prime-time telecast, and because the Sugar obviously lost a share of the afternoon audience to Dallas, Miami (24.1) was the ratings king. ABC, which had pressed the Sugar and the Southeastern Conference to switch to prime time, was pleased with the result, yet unhappy with the thought of what might have been.

ABC had a sweetheart deal with the Sugar Bowl because the Bowl gave the network all the high cards when the last contract had been signed in 1976. The Sugar, because of its contract with the network, could now pay competing football teams $1 million apiece. Meanwhile, CBS was paying the Cotton Bowl enough to allow its teams to get approximately $1.8 million. NBC's Orange Bowl contract was helping the Miami teams to pick up an estimated $1.3 million.

In four of the previous five years, the Sugar Bowl had showcased a No. 1 team in what was in effect, national championship games. ABC, the college football network, had the best of all worlds – the finest attractions for the lowest pay. And there were three more years remaining on the agreement.

In March at the conference basketball tournament in Birmingham, the SEC's Bowl Committee informed the Sugar that its tie-up would end after the January 1, 1982, game if more money was not forthcoming for the competing teams. The

Committee pointed out that under the existing contract, its champions had nothing to lose by being free to play in Dallas and Miami as well as New Orleans.

"We agreed to get back to the SEC people," said Mickey Holmes. "All we did here was to give our side and listen to their side. It's been a great relationship for both parties. As for raising the payoffs, the only way to do it is through TV money. You can't make any substantial increase in payoffs by increasing ticket prices."

The first thing the SEC-ABC-Sugar troika did was petition the NCAA Extra Events' Committee for the 7 p.m. kickoff that the network wanted. Mickey Holmes had to convince the Committee as well as suppress intense Orange Bowl lobbying. Miami, understandably, wanted to keep New Year's night to itself. For a prime-time kickoff, and a change in the SEC's most recent appearance rule in favor of letting the Sugar choose a representative in case of a championship tie, ABC was willing to come up with a $20 million, escalating, six-year

contract. Both were approved.

The Fiesta Bowl, a relative newcomer based in Phoenix, announced a move to New Year's Day opposite the Cotton Bowl. Nineteen eighty-two would be the first New Year's since 1961 that more than the traditional four bowl games would be played on January 1.

Finding quality teams to fill the bowl vacancies wasn't difficult. A record seven teams (Michigan, Notre Dame, Southern Cal, Texas, Penn State, Pitt, and Clemson) were ranked at the top of the polls at one time or another during the 1981 season. From the start, Pittsburgh and Penn State caught the Sugar's fancy. It was the SEC spot that caused the most headaches. Georgia lost its No. 1 ranking in the third week of the season when it lost nine turn overs and a game to Clemson, 13-3. Vince Dooley used the defeat as a springboard; his team constantly improved and headed toward the end of the season as a probable 10-1 entry. Alabama, which lost to Georgia Tech and was tied by Southern Mississippi, kept even with Georgia in the SEC standings.

Georgia recovered sufficiently from the Clemson defeat to climb back to No. 3 in the national polls. And, of course, Georgia had Herschel Walker as a calling card. Alabama, in the season that Bear Bryant eclipsed Amos Alonzo Stagg as college football's winningest coach, was ranked No. 6 when the Tide thrashed No. 5 Penn State 32-16. Alabama, seldom impressive during the 1981 season, was awesome. Penn State, a solid football team that probably played the most difficult schedule in the country, went down for its second loss.

Pittsburgh, ranked No. 1, was the obvious choice for the Sugar Bowl. But a local debate raged over the merits of the SEC co-champions. The argument for 'Bama, No. 4 after the Penn State game, was Bryant's record and the unpublicized fact that Bear was eager for a shot at Pitt and his protégé Jackie Sherrill. It was his most direct route for a chance at No. 1. There were those on the Sugar Bowl's Executive Committee acutely aware of what the organization owed Bryant.

The Sugar Bowl also had an obligation to itself, the SEC, and ABC to select what it felt was the best attraction. Georgia not only had the better record and the higher ranking, but the Bulldogs' only defeat was to Clemson, who would finish the season unbeaten. 'Bama's only loss was to Georgia Tech (1-

Herschel Walker breaks through the iron Pittsburgh defense.

9), a matter of striking significance. Also, the Sugar Bowl would have to choose between Bulldog running back Herschel Walker and Crimson Tide Coach Bear Bryant. The nod had to go to the combatant.

"We were in a 'can't win' situation with the SEC," said Holmes. "We had to choose between two excellent football teams. We made our choice. Now I feel we're in a 'can't miss' situation with No. 1 and No. 3."

Penn State made it a 'could miss' situation with a 48-14 comeback win over the Panthers, dropping Pitt to No. 8. Clemson, scheduled to play No. 4 Nebraska in the Orange Bowl, rose to the top spot in the polls. That, of course, put Miami in the position New Orleans had held before the kickoff: the game with the glitter.

No team may ever have lost as much talent at one time as did Jackie Sherrill when 21 members of his 11-1, 1980 Pitt Panthers decided to play professional football — 12 by way of the draft, nine as free agents. In what could only be expected to be a rebuilding year, Sherrill molded an extremely potent offense revolving around 6-foot-4 junior quarterback Dan Marino. With 2,615 yards and 34 touchdowns, Marino could already be throwing against pro defenses, observers believed.

The Pitt defense also glittered, leading the nation by allowing only 224.8 total yards a game. Seven turnovers and 13 penalties defused any chance Pitt may have had against Penn State, an extremely good team in its own right.

After the slow start, Vince Dooley was convinced his Bulldogs had evolved into a team better than the one that won the national championship the year before. Herschel Walker gained 1,891 yards, yet his longest run was 32 yards. As a sophomore he was more consistent, although less spectacular. Buck Belue, who led Georgia to 27 victories in his 29 starting assignments, completed 60 percent of his 188 passing attempts, taking pressure off Walker.

Both teams were downright miserly on defense. Pitt gave up 62.4 rushing yards a game, Georgia 72.5 yards. Both appeared vulnerable in the secondary. Pitt surrendered 162.5 passing yards, Georgia 164.5. That was only because opponents could-

n't run on either.

In 563 passing attempts over two seasons Marino had been sacked only 16 times, so Dooley suspected the course for his team was patience.

As much as Dooley respected Pittsburgh's capabilities, there was an intangible that kept gnawing at him. "Pitt being undefeated, and then jumping up with two relatively easy touchdowns (against Penn State) may have been the worst thing for Pitt, the best thing for Penn State. Pitt had not been in stress situations before and did not respond. Penn State (which had played a much more difficult schedule) had, and did. That loss was the worst possible thing for us. I would rather have had Pitt undefeated. Now they've been embarrassed and have an opportunity to make amends for that."

Sherrill studied the match-ups, went through the game plan at a chalk session two days before the Sugar, stopped and looked at the board again. With sudden insight he said, "They've got problems."

Dan Marino unleashes last minute pass.

"He'll burn you!"

Coach Vince Dooley can only taste defeat.

"There's one sure way to get in trouble against Pitt," Vince Dooley explained, "and that's to try to blitz Dan Marino. He'll burn you."

Jackie Sherrill agreed, saying, "Danny knows where the dots are going."

Seldom have two opposing coaches been so completely right on the same subject. They were almost prophetic. Marino knew exactly where the dots were going, and would torch Georgia with the same effectiveness as William Tecumseh Sherman, a field general of an earlier era.

It came down to this: down 24-20 with 42 seconds to go, Sherrill's Pittsburgh Panthers faced a do-or-die fourth and five at the Georgia 33.

Pitt was dominant all game, but Georgia, showing the same

incredible resiliency it displayed the year before against Notre Dame, spent most of the day in the lead. From the coaching booth at one point came the very loud voice of Panther assistant Joe Moore, bellowing, "I can't believe it. We're killing them, but we're losing!"

What would save the Panthers was "69-X," a play Pitt took out of mothballs on its last drive. And, of course, the right arm of Marino.

Georgia's lead was the result of two Herschel Walker touchdowns, and five turnovers against the Bulldogs' opportunistic and elastic bend-but-don't-break defense.

Seeming more aggressive after intermission when Georgia led 7-3, the Panthers took two leads, 10-7 and 17-13, but the Bulldogs found an answer each time and went ahead 20-17 on a leaping six-yard catch of a Buck Belue pass by tight end Clarence Kay with 8:13 to go.

After Pitt failed to convert on a fourth-down pass at midfield, with 5:29 remaining, all Georgia had to do was crank out two or three first downs for yet another hard-to-believe Sugar Bowl victory.

Instead, after three plays Georgia's Jim Broadway had to punt away.

Pitt took over at its 20 with 3:46 remaining. Marino and company picked up 10 yards, and then called "69-X." The Panther quarterback threw to Bryan Thomas, a tailback who Sherrill said he dreamed would outrush Walker. Thomas broke a tackle at the 35 and ran out of bounds at the Pitt 48. "It's a simple crossing pattern by our two backs," Marino explained. The backs become part of a five-receiver corps downfield, joining the tight end and two wide-outs. "The first time we ran it, they rushed only three men and Bryan was able to run away from a linebacker."

John Brown scores the winning touchdown after the catch.

By the time the Panthers reached the 33, they had almost run out of downs and time.

Timeout was called. Sherrill felt Pitt's best shot might be an attempt at a tying field goal. "But I asked Danny what he thought," the coach said, "and he wanted to go for the win. Since he thought he could do it, I went along with him."

Marino explained, "It comes down to this: It's a 50-yard field goal and, even if we don't make it, which is a longshot, it's still going to be a 20-20 score. If we go for it and make the first down, then we have a shot to win the game. And if we don't make the first down, then we don't deserve to win the game."

While Marino and Sherrill were deciding on 69-X as the best chance of picking up the first down, Georgia defensive coordinator Bill Lewis called for an all-out blitz – just the situation Dooley warned about the day before. "I wanted to minimize Marino's chances for a big play," Dooley explained. "It would have worked against most quarterbacks."

Marino took the snap. His backs picked up the on-coming linebackers. The other receivers adjusted and went deep against Georgia's single coverage. Instinctively, Marino took a deeper step than usual and singled out John Brown, a former wide receiver turned tight end, who was breaking down the center of the field. "He looked like he was bending to the outside on a short route," said a red-eyed safety Steve Kelly of Brown afterward, "to pick up the first down. I got my

To the victor, Coack Jackie Sherrill, goes the spoils.

shoulders turned around and he broke back behind me.''
Brown said, "When I looked up, there was the ball.''

There was the touchdown, and there was the Sugar Bowl. "It was a terrible thing to see," Kay said.

It turned out the Bulldogs couldn't control the ball against Pitt. Possession time (36:26-23:34) and virtually every other statistic was lopsidedly in the Panthers' favor. Even Georgia's awesome Walker was outrushed by Thomas (129 yards – 84 yards) – just as Sherrill had dreamed.

	1	2	3	4	
Pittsburgh	0	3	7	14	24
Georgia	0	7	6	7	20

Georgia: Walker, 8-yard run. PAT, Butler kick.

Pittsburgh: Everett, 41-yard field goal.

Pittsburgh: Dawkins, 30-yard pass from Marino. PAT, Everett kick.

Georgia: Walker, 10-yard run. Kick failed.

Pittsburgh: Brown, 6-yard pass from Marino. PAT, Everett kick.

Georgia: Kay, 6-yard pass from Belue. PAT, Butler kick.

Pittsburgh: Brown, 33-yard pass from Marino. PAT, Everett kick.

Individual Leaders

Rushing
Pittsburgh: Thomas 26-129; DiBartola 13-68.
Georgia: Walker 25-84, 2 TDs.

Passing
Pittsburgh: Marino 26-41-2, 261 yards, 3 TDs.
Georgia: Belue 8-15-2, 83 yards.

Receiving
Pittsburgh: Dawkins 6-77, 1 TD; DiBartola 8-64; Brown 6-62, 2 TDs.
Georgia: Walker 3-53.

Pittsburgh		Georgia
27	First Downs	11
208	Rushing Yards	141
26-41-2	Passing	8-15-2
261	Passing Yards	83
469	Total Yards	224
2-44.5	Punts	6-39.5
5-3	Fumbles – Lost	2-2
14-96	Penalties – Yards	5-35

Attendance: 77,224.
Total remuneration: $2,642,000.
Miller-Digby Award recipient: Dan Marino, Pittsburgh quarterback.

Penn State 27 Georgia 23

"If we win, I'll get a raise."

Pitt was a spectacular Sugar Bowl victor. In the Orange Bowl Clemson sealed the national championship with a victory over Nebraska. But CBS was the biggest New Year's Day winner. The Orange Bowl drowned the Sugar in the TV derby. The Sugar had 11.8 and 18 rating figures.

But even the rough spots couldn't detract from the absorbing drama of the 48th Sugar presentation.

Pittsburgh, with most of its high-octane offense and stunning defense returning, was the 1982 pre-season choice for No. 1. The biggest Panther loss was its coach, Jackie Sherrill, who went to Texas A&M; his replacement was assistant Foge Fazio.

The Panthers looked to be a hurdle and an influence for the entire 1983 bowl scene. Georgia and Alabama appeared to be the best SEC teams, and a Georgia-Pitt rematch had strong appeal. As the season progressed, several possibilities arose — Georgia-LSU or Georgia-Penn State.

Pitt won consistently throughout the 1982 season against a demanding schedule. LSU became a post-season favorite by turning a 3-7-1 record (1981) into a ranking 8-2-1 (1982). Penn State started weakly, lost to Alabama by a 42-21 misleading score, and then turned into a devastating machine.

Alabama led the Nittany Lions 27-21 in the fourth quarter, though Penn State seemed ready to take command. A Lion blocker backed into a Lion punt, though, to give the Tide an easy touchdown. An interception soon after accounted for the final margin. "In the locker room after the game," center Mark Battaglia later recalled, "Coach (Joe Paterno) was very calm. He said we had six games left and we should be thinking about winning them all, one at a time. Looking

back, I think that loss set the tone for the rest of the season."

Penn State didn't lose again, but even in their defeat to Alabama the Sugar Bowl scouts saw something in the Nittany Lions. "To be honest," said Penn State Athletic Director Jim Tarman, "Those of us around here thinking about bowls, started setting our sights at a different level after the Alabama game. But the Sugar Bowl people told us we were still in the picture. We have a little edge because we can deliver the TV markets in New York, Boston, Philadelphia, Washington, D.C., and Baltimore."

"We sent a representative to their game against Syracuse the week after Alabama," Mickey Holmes added. "We wanted to assure them they weren't out of it. I think it might have helped us when they saw we still were interested."

Paterno did a masterful job in throwing off the defeat to the Crimson Tide. Against one of the most difficult schedules in the country, including six bowl teams, the Lions pulled themselves together in an impressive forge down the stretch. After Mississippi State upset LSU, making Georgia the undisputed SEC king, the Sugar was faced with the same choice it had the previous year. They would invite a combatant in the Pitt-Penn State fracus, an intense rivalry that

The face of the 1983 Sugar Bowl.

would be played after the November 20 bowl signings.

Pitt was interested in the Cotton Bowl, but the Sugar had to decide whether to take Penn State. "There were three major factors in our decision to invite Penn State," said Holmes. "First, Penn State was finishing the season stronger. It beat Notre Dame while Pitt lost to Notre Dame. There was our gut reaction that Penn State was a better team. It was playing at home."

The Nittany Lions won, 19-10, and accepted the invitation to play the team that had risen to the top of the polls, 11-0-0 Georgia. Paterno, an advocate of a national championship tournament, always sought to have his teams play the highest-ranked opponent in a bowl. That philosophy cost him a national championship in the 1979 Sugar Bowl when his No. 1 team lost to No. 2 Alabama. Penn State got a chance to atone for that in 1982 when undefeated and second-ranked Southern Methodist was tied by Arkansas. Penn State rose to No. 2.

For the sixth time in bowl history, and for the second time in five Sugar Bowls, a No. 1 and No. 2 would tee-it-up. The national championship game was scheduled for New Orleans for the fifth time in seven years.

Penn State opened a four-point favorite, the third time in five years the No. 1-ranked team was a Sugar Bowl underdog.

The main attractions would be Herschel Walker, the Heisman Trophy winner and by now the third-leading ground gainer in NCAA annals with 5,097 yards, and Curt Warner and Todd Blackledge, the leg and

the arm of Penn State's success. The coaches, Paterno and Vince Dooley, were really the most compelling figures in the game.

Both were survivors in a demanding profession. Both enjoyed huge success and longevity, tributes to a pair of former journeymen quarterbacks, who were both articulate, fueled by competitive fire, long on insight, and long on discipline.

In 19 years at Georgia, Dooley had a 151-58-6 record (a winning percentage of .710), appeared in 14 bowl games, and won six conference championships. In 17 years with the Nittany Lions, Paterno's teams had made 15 bowl appearances and finished in the Top Ten 13 times while compiling a record of 161-34-1 (a winning percentage of .821).

The biggest professional difference between the men was the national title Dooley won on the Superdome carpet in the Sugar Bowl of 1981. Paterno, who coached three undefeated, untied teams, had lost his best chance at No. 1 in the same Superdome in 1979. "Our fans make more of that than I do," Paterno said of his lack of No. 1 rankings. "I think we were No. 1 in 1968, 1969, and 1973. We just weren't voted No. 1."

Dooley was struck by the offensive capabilities of Penn State, comparable, in his opinion, to the Pitt team he coached against in the 1977 Sugar Bowl. That team had the best opposing offense he had seen in almost 20 years at Georgia. Paterno had to brace for Herschel Walker and John Lastinger. Georgia quarterback Lastinger completed passes at only a 42 percent clip but had a 24-0-0 record as a starter in high school and college. The Bulldog secondary had intercepted 35 passes and led the nation.

Critics said Georgia was "one-dimensional" with Walker as its only real threat, but Paterno answered,

"Anytime Vince wants balance, he'll have balance. If you have a Herschel Walker, you run a Herschel Walker."

Paterno dismissed talk of what the national championship would mean to a school (with 95 years of excellent football tradition) that had never won it, or to a coach who won 82 percent of his games but never a No. 1. "If we win, maybe I'll get a raise," he chuckled lightly for the public.

But it had to mean more. Right after the Pitt victory, Paterno's thoughts returned to the 1979 Sugar when his Lions failed to score from the 1 and let the national championship pass to Alabama.

"This time we'll score," Paterno said to Jim Tarman as they walked off the field.

"I guess dreams are meant to be that way!"

Joe Paterno said he could "feel it beginning to slip away."

This was a nail-biter, too, just like the previous two Sugar Bowls, a very good team was in a Dawg-fight with Georgia. Except this time, if the game slipped away from Paterno's Penn State team, so would Paterno's first No. 1 pennant.

The Nittany Lions were clinging to a 20-17 lead in the third quarter — a period in which the Bulldogs climbed back into position for an unlikely victory; a period in which the long Penn State passing lanes were shut down; a period in which three of Georgia's five sacks occurred; and a period in which Paterno started getting queasy.

Georgia could only inch beyond its own 45 twice in the first half — though both times the drives resulted in points. The Bulldogs, though, closed the gap to 20-17 on the first series of the third quarter, going 69 yards in 11 plays with Herschel Walker scoring from the 1.

Suddenly, the Sugar Bowl was up for grabs — and Penn State's national championship could be down the drain.

The Nittany Lions seemed to have lost a bit of poise, and quarterback Todd Blackledge, who, by his own admission, said he had been playing "out of whack." Blackledge recalled later, "I told coach to give me a little while and I would be okay."

When Blackledge got the ball back, in the opening minutes of the fourth quarter, with a first down at the Bulldog 47, and Georgia in two-deep coverage and playing the run, Blackledge called "six-43," a routine play-action fake while four receivers streak downfield. Flanker Greg Garrity flew past freshman cornerback Tony Flack and made a diving, skidding catch in the end zone.

"Todd made a great throw, Garrity made a great catch," Joe Pa assessed. "It gave us some breathing room."

But the door was not completely shut on the Bulldogs. There would be more drama.

The only turnover Penn State would commit that night, a fumbled punt return by Kevin Baugh, made things close to the end. Bulldog quarterback John Lastinger pushed Georgia from the Nittany Lion 43 to the 9, where he scrambled and then threw back across the field to tight end Clarence Kay for a touchdown with 3:54 remaining.

A two-point conversion would put Georgia — with one of the nation's best kickers in Butler — in position to win with a field goal. But Walker was stopped short, leaving the score at 27-23.

Strategies from here on were simple: Georgia needed to get the ball back; Penn State had to hold on to it.

On third-and-one at the Nittany Lions' 23, Blackledge sneaked for two. On the next third down, three yards were needed at the 32. Instead of a plunge into the line by Warner, the call everyone expected, Blackledge said, "Let's go for it!" Paterno recalled later, "I just told him, 'Make sure you throw it far enough.' "

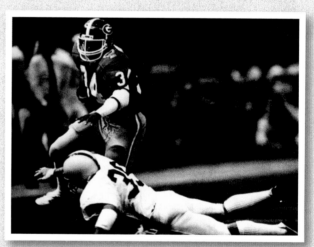

Dan Biondi cuts down Herschel Walker (34).

Chris McCarthy hits a wall of Nittany Lions.

Blackledge dropped back, and threw a darter to Garrity for a six-yard gain.

Walker said the Georgia offense was confident it could pull the game out ... "if we could just get our hands on the ball. But when they made that last first down, I turned to the guy who was standing next to me and said, 'We won't be going out there again.' "

Penn State had finally won its national championship by demonstrating clear superiority over a worthy opponent. Defenders like end Walker Lee Ashley and safety Mark Robinson, with nine tackles and two interceptions, performed above and beyond the call of duty. Walker was 'held' to 103 yards with his longest gain just 12 yards.

Curt Warner, on the other hand, out-rushed yet another Heisman Trophy recipient by gaining 117 yards. The previous year he ran for more yards than Southern Cal's Marcus Allen in the Fiesta Bowl.

The midseason 42-21 defeat to Alabama would be recorded as the largest defeat any national champion had then endured, showing just how far the Nittany Lions had come.

"We heard about the polls on the plane ride home," said Biondi. "We all cheered and basically went nuts." Receiver Kenny Jackson said, "Riding home tonight all this stuff was going on and I found myself thinking, 'Wait a minute. Is this for real?' ... I know it's the greatest feeling I've ever experienced, but, at the same time, it's unreal. I guess dreams are meant to be that way."

Joe Paterno, king, finally, of the hill.

	1	2	3	4	
Penn State	7	13	0	7	27
Georgia	3	7	7	6	23

Penn State: Warner, 2-yard run. PAT, Gancitano kick.
Georgia: Butler, 27-yard field goal.
Penn State: Gancitano, 38-yard field goal.
Penn State: Warner, 9-yard run. PAT, Gancitano kick.
Penn State: Gancitano, 45-yard field goal.
Georgia: Archie, 10-yard pass from Lastinger. PAT, Butler kick.
Georgia: Walker, 1-yard run. PAT, Butler kick.
Penn State: Garrity, 47-yard pass from Blackledge. Gancitano kick.
Georgia: Kay, 9-yard pass from Lastinger. Run failed.

Individual Leaders

Rushing
Penn State: Warner 18-177, 2 TDs.
Georgia: Walker 28-103, 1 TD.

Passing
Penn State: Blackledge 13-23-0, 228 yards, 1 TD.
Georgia: Lastinger 12-27-2, 166 yards, 2 TDs.

Receiving
Penn State: Garrity 4-116, 1 TD.
Georgia: Kay 5-61, 1 TD.

Penn State		Georgia
19	First Downs	19
160	Rushing Yards	139
13-23-0	Passing	12-28-2
228	Passing Yards	166
388	Total Yards	305
7-42.5	Punts	8-41.7
2-1	Fumbles – Lost	3-0
7-39	Penalties – Yards	7-42

Attendance: 78,124.
Teams' remuneration: $3,600,000.
Miller-Digby Award recipient: Todd Blackledge, Penn State quarterback.

Auburn 9 Michigan 7

"The situation sort of depends."

Auburn was a special team in a season when good teams abounded. The no-frills Tigers were the perfect SEC representative for the Golden Anniversary of the Sugar Bowl.

The trick this season was finding a suitable opponent, but one that would bring in television sets when the Sugar had no shot at the two top teams going into the bowls: No. 1-ranked Nebraska would be the host school in the Orange Bowl, and No. 2-ranked Texas would naturally be in the Cotton Bowl.

"I don't know whether we'll look at ranking or quality of schedule or whatever," said Mickey Holmes, executive director of the Sugar Bowl, on having to find a match that would excite the football public. "The situation (of picking a visiting opponent) really sort of depends ... Getting someone in the (visiting) spot will be a lot easier if the SEC representative is ranked third or fourth rather than ninth or 10th."

Exciting SMU was first choice, but when Mustangs Athletic Director Bob Hitch prematurely leaked to the press that his team was headed to New Orleans, the Sugar Bowl went with 9-2 Michigan, who rose to eighth after beating Ohio State to finish in second in the Big Ten. The Wolverines coming from an area with 25 percent of all the television sets in America didn't hurt the Wolverines chances.

"The highest-ranked teams don't necessarily make the best game possible," Holmes said.

There was never any doubt about Auburn, No. 3 by the time of the selection. Not flashy but fundamentally sound, the Tigers were a complete football team.

This was the intriguing match-up: Michigan's formidable defense, yielding an average of just 95 yards rushing, would try to contain the South's newest superstar – a multi-sport Superman in the mold of a Herschel Walker or Billy Cannon – an incredible specimen named Bo Jackson, a 6-foot-1, 228-pound sophomore who could high jump 6-feet-10 and hit a baseball 506 feet.

Jackson averaged 7.7 yards per carry while gaining 1,213 yards and scoring 13 touchdowns. Jackson, though, wasn't the only weapon in Auburn's arsenal.

Auburn – without overstating the case – was not simply a collection of gifted athletes. These young men had been steeled for anything life had in store. After young men, barely out of adolescence, see a teammate turn purple in death, Texas, Alabama, Georgia or Michigan football teams don't appear very imposing.

In August fullback Gregg Pratt collapsed and died after running a series of sprints. He was 20.

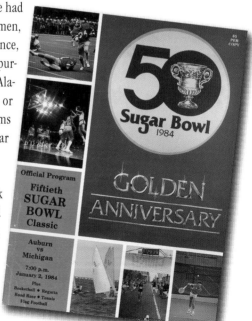

Coach Pat Dye had consistently told anyone who would listen that he was going to field a very good football team in 1983. He had recruited exceedingly well, and he wouldn't duck the truth. But there was also another reason: Auburn lived in the shadow of college football's greatest factory – Bear Bryant's Crimson Tide – so long that it had developed an inferiority complex as big as the state of Alabama.

Dye wasn't shy about telling folks just how good this squad could be. It was calculated strategy designed to pump confidence into the Auburn masses, and team.

Auburn, remember, won its only SEC championship in 1957 before Bryant, between 1961 and 1980, racked up six national championships. Auburn had flirted with excellence at several junctures, but could never really crawl out of the corner Bryant painted for it.

Dye, who spent three years assembling superior talent and trying to rid the program of negative vibes, finally had Tiger fandom believing in Auburn, and his athletes believing in themselves. Dye's strategy worked. He got Auburn's attention, and that brought high expectations.

The death of Gregg Pratt could have disrupted all that. But Auburn's players, suddenly older than their years, huddled in sorrow. They drew strength from their loss. They leaned on one another.

In the second week of the season, second-ranked Texas defeated Auburn 22-7. That was the only time the Tigers didn't play at maximum efficiency all season.

Auburn turned into a quiet, unemotional, efficient and excellent football team, slugging it out with the heavyweights of college football. Seven Auburn opponents were ranked in the Top 20 at the time of their game. Only twice in that entire awesome 11-game schedule did anyone see any emotion radi-

ate from this squad. The first was against Tennessee. Auburn led 10-7 at the half, but the Vols ran the second half kickoff back to the Tiger 30. Four downs later, Tennessee surrendered the ball without gaining an inch.

The defense ran off the field, uncharacteristically yelling and holding arms high.

The second display of emotion came immediately after the victory over Georgia, the win that represented the SEC championship. Players screamed and chanted, "SUGAR BOWL, SUGAR BOWL, SUGAR BOWL!"

Dye's third Auburn team lived up to every expectation. It was an unusual – and special – football team. It wasn't a team

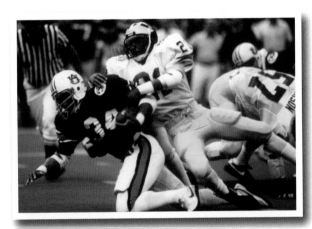

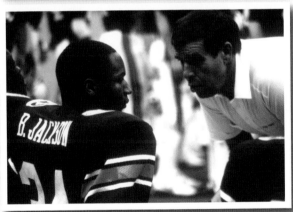

made of brick and mortar. It was a team made of heart and soul.

In the celebration after the Georgia victory, Terry Walker, Pratt's former roommate, looked into a television camera and said, "We've got one more to win for you, Gregg ... the Sugar Bowl."

"And I hit it good."

What goes through a kid's mind when playing games: Ninth-inning of the World Series, one run down and I'm at bat with two outs ... or 20-foot putt to win the Masters, and so on.

Auburn kicker Al Del Greco had been thinking along those lines for weeks. "Since the Alabama game," Del Greco said, "one of the coaches had me going to the 40-yard line. He'd say, 'Georgia beat (No. 2-ranked) Texas (in the Cotton Bowl), (and) Miami's leading (No. 1-ranked) Nebraska in the fourth quarter (of the Orange Bowl). Now, what you gonna do?'

"When the score was 7-6 in the fourth quarter and we got the ball, I said on the sideline, 'Well, that's just what's going to happen.' "

Michigan quarterback Steve Smith (16) takes a hard hit from the Auburn defense.

And it did. Del Greco had to make a kick for Auburn to beat Michigan in the Sugar Bowl and win the national championship – though the storybook finish turned into a horror tale for the Tigers.

Michigan, a three-and-a-half point underdog, scored on its second possession with quarterback Steve Smith rolling in from the 4 after the Wolverines got an interception at their 37. Then they used a combination of solid defense and timely turnovers in keeping the Tigers off-balance. The drive covered 63 yards in nine plays. At that juncture, halfway through the first quarter, Michigan had 83 yards in total offense, Auburn had "0."

The Wolverines had run 16 plays, the Tigers three, and, perhaps most importantly, Michigan had kept the ball away from the Auburn offense for all but two minutes and 30 seconds.

Two turnovers and the workmanlike Wolverine defense kept the Tigers at bay – and off the scoreboard – in the first half. This was only the second time all season Auburn had been held scoreless at intermission. Michigan's defensive plan was geared to stopping Auburn on first downs and limiting the number of carries by Jackson, who handled the ball only eight times for 67 yards at the half, was working to perfection.

Finally, though, after Auburn's second series of the second half, Del Greco put the Tigers on the scoreboard with a 31-yard field goal. It came, finally, after a typical Auburn offensive drive as the Tigers held the ball for 6:17.

Nursing a 7-3 lead early in the final quarter, Smith was caught trying to pitch at the Michigan 48.

Linebackers Jeff Jackson and Gregg Carr were coming in. Jackson hit Smith as the quarterback tried to bring his arm forward to launch the pass upfield. The ball flew weakly into the arms of Carr, who pulled the ball in at the Wolverine 41 and advanced it to the 39.

"It's going to sound like a fish story that gets better every time you tell it," Carr tried to explain afterward. "Basically, I had the good luck to be in the right place at the right time. I didn't have time to think about it."

The Auburn wishbone, which would spring Jackson for 131 yards, Tommy Agee for 93 and Lionel James for 84, was now operating at a high degree of efficiency, going to the 15 where Del Greco booted his second field goal, this one of 32 yards.

On the following Auburn series, at the end of a drive that consumed 7:21 while going 61 yards in 10 plays, Del Greco got to live his imaginary game: With 27 seconds to go, for what might be for the national championship, he booted a 19-yard field goal.

"If you hit it good," said the 5-foot-10 senior kicker from Miami after the 9-7 victory, "the angle doesn't matter. And I hit it good. I knew it was in the moment it left my foot."

Just as Al Del Greco's coach had imagined, Georgia beat Texas (20-9), and Miami upset Nebraska (31-30).

That only set up a major injustice to Auburn, however. The next day fifth-ranked Miami, which had been lobbying voters from the time the Hurricanes got its Orange Bowl invite, leaped from fifth place to No. 1, in what can only be construed as a political ballot. Third-place Auburn, after playing a schedule that included nine bowl teams, one that won a cumulative 70 percent of their games, remained at No. 3.

Though they both had the same 11-1 record, Miami's loss was to Florida, 28-3, the worst smudge on the resume' of any team to be named national champion. Auburn's was to Texas, by any measure a Top 5 opponent. Also, it should be noted, Auburn beat Florida 28-21.

The only poll that had Auburn on top at the end was the New York Times', in which, rare at the time, a computer was fed information and came up with its ranking.

"I kinda like that computer," Dye said wryly.

A mind picture was painted in Alabama when one group of Auburn students burned large replicas of the Associated Press and United Press International polls while another group of students had its head buried in the sports section of a Yankee newspaper.

The underlining caption read: "Auburn, Ala., where everyone reads the New York Times."

Sugar Bowl MVP, Bo Jackson (34), with teammate Lionel James (6).

	1	2	3	4	
Auburn	0	0	3	6	9
Michigan	7	0	0	0	7

Michigan: Smith, 4-yard run. PAT, Bergeron kick.

Auburn: Del Greco, 31-yard field goal.

Auburn: Del Greco, 32-yard field goal.

Auburn: Del Greco, 19-yard field goal.

Individual Leaders

Rushing
Auburn: Jackson 22-130; Agee 16-93.
Michigan: Rogers 17-86; Garrett 5-18.

Passing
Auburn: Campbell 2-6-1, 21 yards.
Michigan: Smith 9-25-1, 125 yards.

Receiving
Auburn: James 1-15.
Michigan: Markray 3-60; Bean 3-37.

Auburn		Michigan
21	First Downs	12
301	Rushing Yards	118
2-6-1	Passing	9-25-1
21	Passing Yards	125
322	Total Yards	243
4-42.0	Punts	8-38.3
4-3	Fumbles – Lost	2-1
3-15	Penalties – Yards	6-49

Attendance: 77,893.
Teams' remuneration: $3,600,000.
Miller-Digby Award recipient: Bo Jackson, Auburn tailback.

Nebraska 28 LSU 10

"I hugged the pilot."

The Jolly Roger was the pennant chased by the 10 Southeastern Conference schools during the 1984 season.

Florida and LSU opened the season with a memorable 21-21 tie that showed both teams in their best light.

But Florida was under the glare of a highly publicized NCAA investigation in which 107 recruiting allegations were finally compressed into 57. It was a situation which embarrassed the University of Florida and the SEC specifically, and college football in general. The only ones connected with the scandal who seemed to have no embarrassment were the Gators themselves.

After an opening defeat to Miami and the tie with LSU, the Gators, with a strong sense of "us against them," put on a powerful display of purpose and sheer ability. Charley Pell, the coach under whose command the violations were committed, was dismissed after Florida's third game. Offensive coordinator Galen Hall took over and directed Florida to a 9-1-1 season, its first at the top of the SEC standings.

Gator fans had an attitude of defiance. Banners with the inscription, "Hell, yes, we cheat," fluttered at Florida Field. Gator opponents seemed to have a collective attitude of awe. One coach after viewing film of Florida for a game the next week, uttered: "If they did, in fact, buy some of those players, all I can say is they spent their money wisely."

From the standpoint of sheer self-interest, the Sugar Bowl was panting for the opportunity to get Florida in its New Year's Day classic. If they had reached the Sugar, the Gators would not have been an underdog to anyone in the country on a neutral field.

One Sugar Bowler scowled at the headlines and said, "The NCAA can get anybody it really wants." Sugar Bowl president Elliott Laudeman said with proper decorum that his bowl would be happy with whatever decision the conference reached on the sticky situation. "We'll take the SEC champion with no questions asked," he said.

While the executive committee of the SEC was pondering how to deal with Florida, which put up no front of innocence, the Gators were thoroughly chewing up the league on the field. When Florida won its sixth consecutive game, against preseason favorite Auburn, the Gators were in position to win their very first conference title with another victory the following week against Georgia.

Nose guard Tim Newton philosophized that titles are won

on the field, not in boardrooms. "They can take the rings away, but they can't erase the scores," said the 280-pound Gator. "We'll be champions in our own minds. When my grandchildren ask me who was champion, I'm going to say, 'Well now, I got a story to tell.' "

Florida won the next week, and the SEC's decision was to ban the Gators from any postseason representation.

LSU had a strong shot to tie Florida for a co-championship, but a late-season upset at the hands of Mississippi State seemed to put Auburn in position to represent the SEC in the Sugar Bowl. But when Auburn missed a long field goal attempt in the fading seconds of a loss to Alabama, LSU was alone in second place of the SEC – and in the Sugar Bowl for the first time since 1968.

First-year LSU coach Bill Arnsparger was on a recruiting trip while Auburn was playing the Crimson Tide. "I was going to the airport in Monroe (La.) and couldn't hear the Auburn game until we were up in the air," Arnsparger said. "Then we got the game on the radio when Auburn had the ball and was trying that field goal. When I heard they missed it, I hugged the pilot. But he kept that little plane on course anyway."

Unquestionably the best team in the conference was not in the SEC corner of the Sugar Bowl. But, despite the predictable jeers at LSU getting in on a pass, given the circumstances the Sugar Bowl got the most deserving SEC team.

As it was, the most important games on the respective schedules of Auburn and LSU were Florida and Alabama. Auburn didn't beat either one, and LSU didn't lose to either one.

In the other corner of the Sugar was Big Eight co-champion Nebraska, an upset victim of Oklahoma but the only team the Vegas odds-makers felt was close to being the equal of Florida.

That was enough to make some Sugar Bowlers ill at the thought of what might have been – Florida-Nebraska, the two strongest teams in the country in terms of sheer talent.

The biggest news leading up to the Sugar Bowl between the fifth-ranked 9-2 Huskers and the 11th-ranked 8-2-1 Tigers wasn't the teams per se, but one coach.

Tom Osborne, who had never coached a team that won fewer than nine games in his nine-year career at Nebraska and who had an Eagle Scout reputation, was charged by Booker Brown, a former Southern Cal athlete who had been recruited by Osborne 14 years before, with irregularities in that process.

The continuing story from New Orleans had little to do with Nebraska's best-in-the-nation defense (averages of 203.3 yards and 9.5 points) or how that defense went from 73rd in 1983 to No. 1 in 1984.

Baby-faced coach Osborne was the story. Osborne subjected himself to a secret polygraph test that indicated he told the truth when he said he had no knowledge of Booker Brown's allegations. "I'll show you the wavy lines," a grim-looking and angry Osborne said of the test.

It was a milestone: A Sugar Bowl coach being strapped into a chair to defend his honor on a lie-detector machine.

"I knew I was heading to the end zone."

"It came down to the fourth quarter," exclaimed Harry Grimminger, a Nebraska offensive guard, "and nobody has been stronger in the fourth quarter than us."

That was the truth.

The 51st Sugar Bowl – a second guesser's delight – boiled down to the superior Huskers asserting themselves late, and a turn in the fortunes of the opposing quarterbacks.

By halftime, the white-shirted Cornhuskers, favored by a touchdown, resembled a groggy giant trying to catch its breath, having been stung by a squadron of swarming bees.

After 30 minutes of play under the Superdome gondola, the Tigers had eaten up 291 yards against the No. 1 defense in the land. And the Cornhuskers had to scrounge for a modest 141 yards of their own, 31 coming on one play.

LSU's problem was, at that point, it had only a three-point (10-7) lead that could have been 10 points or more.

The difference in the final outcome was Nebraska steaming for 184 yards and two touchdowns in the fourth quarter. That, and a switch in the Husker defense to one given to Tom Osborne by Bill Arnsparger years before. The switch limited

the Bayou Bengals to 113 yards in the second half. "We felt lucky to be behind by only three points at halftime," said quarterback Craig Sundberg, the MVP after passing for 143 yards. His counterpart, Jeff Wickersham, was called the goat after throwing for 212 yards (17-25-1) in the first half.

Sundberg, ill with the flu until hours before the game, though, passed for three touchdowns and Wickersham's second half totals were 3-of-12 for nine yards and three interceptions, stifling a charged up Tiger offense that had the vaunted Husker defense scratching its helmets for nearly three full quarters.

The real difference, though, was the inability of the Tigers to apply the vise once they had Nebraska in a headlock. Garry James caught a 26-yard touchdown that was nullified by a holding penalty. That series ended with a missed field goal. Later Coach Bill Arnsparger elected to take another field goal off the board after a roughing-the-kicker penalty, for a first down at the Nebraska 6 - and come away with no points.

Still, when the Tigers went 73 yards on 10 plays, and scatback Dalton Hilliard went from the 2, it was 10-0 with 13:11 to go in the second quarter. LSU fans had to be wondering what had happened to the feared Nebraska offense.

Doug DeBose (22) rushed for 102 yards for the Cornhuskers.

Cornerback Dave Burke (33) makes the tackle.

They soon found out.

The 'Huskers, methodically and quickly, went 70 yards on six plays, scoring when Sundberg hit tailback Doug Dubose with a 31-yard, against-the-grain, screen pass. "Craig faked a pass to the left and I snuck out there alone," Dubose said. "LSU's defense pursues real well, and as soon as I cut back across the grain, I knew I was heading for the end zone."

Just 2:40 after LSU took its surprising 10-0 lead, the score was cut to 10-7.

That's when Arnsparger took Lewis' field goal off – and then lost a shot at a touchdown and a possible 17-7 lead. Lewis then missed a 19-yard chip-shot.

It was an omen of things to come for LSU.

Osborne changed defenses from a four-man front to a three-man rush with eight back defenders. "We dropped (DB Chad Daffer) into the middle zone and that helped," the coach explained.

Daffer picked off two Tiger passes on LSU's first two second-half possessions, both leading to touchdowns, putting the Bengals behind for the first time.

Osborne said, "LSU had a tendency to run short crosses and then a deep cross, 15 to 17 yards downfield. We picked it up (the defensive scheme) from the Miami Dolphins a few years ago, and I think Bill (Arnsparger, who was then the Dolphins defensive coordinator) is responsible for that."

Momentum and fortune were shifting to Nebraska. And the Tigers were helpless to curtail the currents of the game.

DuBose, who gained 108 yards on 20 carries, accounted for 50 of the 80 total yards in the Huskers' clinching drive, which was sealed when Sundberg hit Todd Frain with a 24-yard touchdown pass with 10:54 left in the last quarter.

It was all Nebraska needed, though the Huskers would add one more score for good measure.

There were those, however, who wanted it recorded that Nebraska was not beating the SEC's best team.

An inscription on the Superdome scoreboard during the game read: "Congratulations Florida Gators, 1984 SEC champs."

	1	2	3	4	
Nebraska	0	7	7	14	28
LSU	3	7	0	0	10

LSU: Lewis, 31-yard field goal.

LSU: Hilliard, 2-yard run. PAT, Lewis kick.

Nebraska: Dubose, 31-yard pass from Sundberg, PAT, Klein kick.

Nebraska: Sundberg, 9-yard run. PAT, Klein kick.

Nebraska: Frain, 24-yard pass from Sundberg. PAT, Klein kick.

Nebraska: Frain, 17-yard pass from Sundberg. PAT, Klein kick.

Individual Leaders

Rushing
Nebraska: DuBose 108 yards.
LSU: Hilliard 16-86, 1 TD.

Passing
Nebraska: Sundberg 10-15-1, 143 yards, 1 TD.
LSU: Wickersham 20-37-5, 221 yards.

Receiving
Nebraska: Frain 4-53, 2 TDs.
LSU: James 4-25.

Nebraska		LSU
23	First Downs	19
280	Rushing Yards	183
10-18-3	Passing	20-38-5
143	Passing Yards	221
423	Total Yards	404
5-30.6	Punts	4-39.8
0-0	Fumbles – Lost	3-1
9-74	Penalties – Yards	5-36

Attendance: 75,608.
Teams' remuneration: $4,560,000.
Miller-Digby Award recipient: Craig Sundberg, Nebraska quarterback.

T U

Tennessee 35 Miami 7

"The pendulum always swings back."

Johnny Majors, witnesses said, lit up like Halley's Comet. Eyes big as saucers, the Tennessee coach raced from a Nashville banquet room to the nearest telephone.

Majors' breathless call took place shortly after the 1983 season, but it may have been the biggest single influence on the 1985 season: he hired Ken Donahue as the Vols' defensive coordinator.

Donahue shaped Bear Bryant's defenses for two glory-filled decades at Alabama. Defense was Bryant's trademark, but Bear was always smart enough to let genius take its course. There were times when the head coach would descend from his tower at practice and sit in his golf cart and watch Donahue's defenses go at it.

Bryant, the story goes, was entertaining a friend in Tuscaloosa. Toward the end of the evening, near midnight, they drove past the Alabama football offices. "Look," the friend said, "you forgot to turn out the light." "Naw," Bear said. "That's just that damn Donahue making me a legend."

Donahue was a B-team coach at Tennessee during Majors' All-American season of 1956, and later the two shared a desk as assistants at Mississippi State. "Ken Donahue," Majors said of the man whose greatest pleasure was going to work an hour early, "is one of a kind. His life, his soul, his recreation is football."

Now Tennessee had the sad-eyed, stoop-shouldered, single-minded defensive wizard, who was not retained at Alabama after Bryant stepped aside. Donahue was a recruiting coup for Majors.

A tie and a defeat blotched Tennessee's first four games of '85, but Majors' worst loss came when his spectacular quarterback Tony Robinson couldn't find a receiver in the third quarter against Alabama and ducked into the line. The crack was heard in the stands. Robinson's season (91 of 143 for 1,246 yards and eight touchdowns) was over – knee surgery followed.

Daryl Dickey, 24-year-old son of Tennessee athletic director Doug Dickey and a Vol backup for three-and-a-half years, excluding a redshirt season, raced in and got Tennessee home with a 16-14 victory.

After a 6-6 game with Georgia Tech a week later, Dickey responded with 10 touchdown passes

Tight end Jeff Smith (81) holds up the ball after catching a 6-yard touchdown pass.

Miami Head Coach Jimmy Johnson looks on as the Volunteers score 35 straight points.

and one interception in six regular-season starts – and five victories. A 64.9 (85 of 131) completion percentage and 106 consecutive passes without an interception were school records.

At the same time, Donahue's defense surged to the SEC fore, surrendering one meaningful touchdown in those last six regular-season games, allowing only a 13-point average in 11 games, forcing 37 turnovers and yielding a miniscule four-yards per completion.

Ray Perkins, who succeeded Bryant at Alabama, gave Majors another helping hand in late November, settling for a 14-14 tie against LSU with 1:23 remaining, putting both a half-game behind in the SEC standings while the Vols had only light-weights Ole Miss, Kentucky and Vanderbilt left to play.

"Air Italia" was blowing through the University of Miami schedule. Vinny Testaverde (216 of 352 for 3,238 yards), was the linchpin of an offense that averaged 461 yards and 36 points. The Hurricanes' defense was just as impressive, allowing 2.8 yards a rush, causing 30 turnovers (19 interceptions and 11 recovered fumbles) and scoring five defensive touchdowns.

Miami again lost its opener to Florida (35-23), then sailed through a treacherous schedule: Oklahoma (17-14) in Norman, Florida State (35-27) and Maryland (29-22). It was just that achievement that had Coach Jimmy Johnson fuming at the pollsters who voted Oklahoma third, a spot ahead of Miami, after the Sooners beat Nebraska in mid-November. "You always hear these people talking about playoffs," snorted the 44-year-old cherub-faced Texan. "I just wonder if those are the same people who voted Oklahoma over Miami," Johnson mimicked the apparent reasoning. "Well, they looked

so good (on TV) against Nebraska. Heck, Nebraska lost two games – and we beat both of those teams (Florida State and Oklahoma)."

Miami did move up to No. 2 in the AP poll after beating Notre Dame 58-7 at season's end, which meant that the Sugar Bowl had a national championship possibility, should the Hurricanes defeat No. 8 Tennessee and Oklahoma beat No. 1 Penn State in the Orange.

A new era was ushered in with the pairing. In the 51 previous Sugar Bowls, the University of Florida played in it twice, the only times teams from the Sunshine State had appeared in the game. Over the next 17 years there would be 14 combined appearances by Florida, Florida State and Miami – including three Sugar Bowls matching two of these in-state rivals against each other, with each of the three winning a national championship in New Orleans during that span.

This game was like a reunion. Majors had played and coached in the Classic, winning the national championship with Pitt in the '77 Sugar. Donahue had been to the Sugar with both Tennessee and Alabama. Johnson played for Arkansas in the 1963 game against Ole Miss, and was an assistant with Oklahoma in the early 1970s.

Furthermore, the man who signed Johnson to his grant-in-aid at Arkansas had coached in the 1974 Sugar Bowl, and was now the AD at Tennessee, Doug Dickey. And Johnson remembered when one of his old coaches had moved to Mississippi State and helped the eager young man get his first coaching assignment, at Picayune (Miss.) High. Later Johnson was his assistant at Iowa State.

It was, of course, Majors.

"Close, but no cigar."

It was the Sugar Bowl all right, in New Orleans, and in the Superdome – but anyone would have sworn that someone from the Orange Bowl was in charge of the color scheme.

Everywhere anyone looked, from the plaza level to the terrace, there were miles and miles of orange splashed across the visual sea of 77,432, and most of it was Tennessee orange.

In the decibel count, the Big Orange won, hands down. The din from Tennessee backers was almost a solid wall of Volunteer screams, chants, battle cries and roars. The crowd howled and sang the strains of "Rocky Top" from beginning to end. If the skimpy Miami gathering sang a fight song, no one heard it. The Volunteers' crowd dominated the Hurricanes' followers more than the Vols dominated the 'Canes on the field – and that's saying a lot, especially for the fans of an eight-and-a-half point underdog.

The Tennessee captains were ignored when they put out their hands for the traditional handshake at the coin toss. "They just looked the other way," UT safety Chris White said. Running back Jeff Powell snorted, "They were very cocky. I don't think they respected Tennessee. All this week, Coach (Jimmy) Johnson was talking about the Orange Bowl and who's going to win, and that they should be national champions because they beat Oklahoma. They should have paid attention to Tennessee."

That's for sure.

Testaverde, after having to call a timeout before his first snap because of crowd noise, threw an 18-yard touchdown to Michael Irvin on the game's first series. The looping, blitzing Vol defense appeared to have held, but the snap for an anticipated fourth-down punt from the 43 went to Marvin Bratton, who shot through the unsuspecting Vols for 25 yards to

Bryan Kimbro (55) and Darrin Miller (45) wrap up Miami quarterback Vinny Testaverde.

touchdown was scored by Jeff Smith from the 6 one play into the second quarter. Dickey cranked up another drive with just under five minutes to go until halftime. On first down at the Miami 9, Powell was stood up just short of the goal. The ball popped out and Tim McGee fell on it for a touchdown and a 14-7 Tennessee lead.

"I wasn't sure if they had blown the play dead or not," McGee said. "In fact, I didn't know it was a touchdown for a couple of minutes."

Miami quarterback Vinny Testaverde (14) struggled against the Tennessee defense throwing three interceptions.

the 18, setting up the Testaverde-to-Irvin connection.

"That kind of got us down," defensive tackle Mark Hovanic admitted. "But Coach Donahue knew what to do."

Donahue switched to a man-to-man defense in the secondary that allowed Tennessee to fire in as many as eight men on key passing downs. Pressure became the name of Tennessee's game against Miami.

"We looked at (Testaverde) on film and saw other teams had not blitzed him much, and they didn't have much success covering," Donahue said. "We changed up our blitzes and fired (alternately) our inside linebackers and safeties."

No one could have guessed, though, that at that juncture, with Miami up 7-0, the Hurricanes, averaging just under 40 offensive points, were through scoring for the night.

Daryl Dickey took the Vols on a 13-play drive, which resulted in no points but made a salient statement: Tennessee could move the ball.

On the next Vols possession, which began on the Miami 41 after a big sack of Testaverde by Richard Brown, the tying

Daryl Dickey (11) was named the game's MVP after leading Tennessee to a 35-7 upset.

Charles Wilson (32) leaps for the end zone.

By the time the score mounted to a jarring 34-7, with six minutes left and an extra point still to be kicked, the fans were treated to the sight of a player skipping off the field with his index finger raised to the Superdome ceiling. It was Dickey celebrating early the 6-0-1 record he had charted as a starter since Tony Robinson was injured.

Dickey was 15-of-25 for 131 yards and a touchdown in a "most outstanding" performance. The Tennessee defense squeezed Miami as it hadn't been squeezed in years. The Hur-

	1	2	3	4	
Tennessee	0	14	14	7	35
Miami	7	0	0	0	7

Miami: Irvin, 18-yard pass from Testaverde. PAT, Cox kick.

Tennessee: Smith, 6-yard pass from Dickey. PAT, Reveiz kick.

Tennessee: McGee, fumble recovery in end zone. PAT, Reveiz kick.

Tennessee: Henderson, 1-yard run. PAT, Reveiz kick.

Tennessee: Powell, 60-yard run. PAT, Reveiz kick.

Tennessee: Wilson, 6-yard run. PAT, Reveiz kick.

Individual Leaders

Rushing
Tennessee: Powell 11-104, 1 TD.
Miami: Williams 8-45.

Passing
Tennessee: Dickey 15-25-1, 131 yards, 1 TD.
Miami: Testaverde 20-36-3, 217 yards, 1 TD.

Receiving
Tennessee: McGee 7-94.
Miami: Irvin 5-91, 1 TD. Perriman 5-41.

Tennessee		Miami
16	First Downs	22
211	Rushing Yards	32
15-25-1	Passing	23-44-4
131	Passing Yards	237
342	Total Yards	269
6-39.1	Punts	6-37.6
2-1	Fumbles – Lost	5-2
11-125	Penalties – Yards	15-120

Attendance: 77,432
Teams' remuneration: $4,560,000.
Miller-Digby Award recipient: Daryl Dickey, Tennessee quarterback.

Tennessee Head Coach Johnny Majors receives a congratulatory hand shake after defeating Miami.

ricanes had a net of 269 yards, 92 in the fourth quarter. Testaverde was sacked seven times for losses of 84 yards, and was belted into losing the ball three times.

"It was fun while it lasted," Johnson said of Miami's long-shot reach for No. 1. "We came close, but no cigar."

As high as the Vols were flying, though, Sugar Bowl fears had come true. The game was a runaway – only the winner was a surprise – and Oklahoma beat Penn State for the national championship in the Orange Bowl. The rout translated into a 6.8 TV share, worst in Sugar Bowl history.

Yet, a mixture of chemistry, of an unheralded Daryl Dickey at quarterback and retread defensive coordinator Ken Donahue, gave Tennessee one of its most satisfying football moments. The Vols became the biggest underdog to win a Sugar Bowl.

Thursday, January 1, 1987

Nebraska 30 LSU 15

"Sounds of silence."

The furor was almost deafening.

The LSU Tigers, home-state heroes of hundreds of thousands of Louisianans, surprised Southern football observers with an eye-catching season, achieved against the nation's most demanding schedule, according to the NCAA computer.

It was a season that impressed many national football observers. But seemingly not, for the longest time, to the Sugar Bowl, located in the same state as the Tiger fan base.

Bill Arnsparger's Tigers stepped smartly into the late-season Top 10, despite an early 21-12 embarrassment to Miami of Ohio (the biggest upset in LSU history). By the time LSU defeated Alabama 14-10 in its eighth game, though, fans of the Bayou Bengals were making plans for their second Sugar Bowl appearance in the last three years.

A victory over Mississippi State would ensure no worse than a tie for the SEC championship. There were complications with the Sugar extending an early invitation, however. The Tigers, losers in the conference to Ole Miss, 21-19, could still be tied by the Crimson Tide if it won its season finale against Auburn.

Tiger fans reasoned that since their team had already secured no worse than a tie for the title, and it had beaten Alabama head-to-head, it was time to pick who'd be in the Sugar and to heck with the outcome of any future games that might play a role whether there was a tie or not. The Sugar, though, could not make that early commitment, angering many LSU fans.

The Sugar Bowl had to look at a broader picture: after Mississippi State, the Tigers still had to play Notre Dame and Tulane. There was the possibility that LSU and 'Bama could share the championship, but the Tide, if it won its remaining games, would finish 10-2 while LSU, if it lost one of its remaining games, would finish 8-3.

That's a huge differential in putting together the most attractive pairing possible. Still,

The LSU and Nebraska Bands perform at halftime.

Tiger fans thundered that their team had already earned its way in.

An Alabama victory over Auburn on Nov. 29 – the same night LSU was scheduled to play Tulane – would have forced the bowl's selection committee into the uncomfortable position of having to choose its SEC representative.

A last meeting of the selection committee was not necessary – Auburn beat Alabama and LSU was the undisputed SEC champion.

Nebraska, the team that defeated LSU 28-10 in the Sugar Bowl two years before, had already accepted an invitation six days earlier. The Cornhuskers took the offer right after playing, and losing in the last seconds, a magnificent 20-17 game against Oklahoma that determined the Big Eight championship. It was a pairing that gave LSU a chance to sooth its personal pride. The Cornhuskers had not only defeated the Tigers two years before, but held a 4-0-1 record against LSU, dating back to the 1971 Orange Bowl. In its storied history, of all the teams LSU had played at least three times, Nebraska is the only one it had never beaten.

The league tie-ups exacted a toll on postseason play in 1986, a year in which independents ruled the roost.

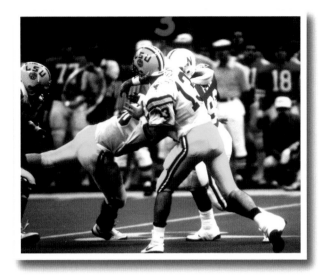

Miami was No. 1 for most of the season, with fellow independent Penn State No. 2 and aching for a chance to play the Hurricanes. After weeks of dealing with the Orange, Citrus, Gator and Fiesta bowls, the No. 1 and No. 2 teams in the land agreed to meet in the Fiesta, which, with no conference ties, could accommodate two independents. The Fiesta then moved its game back to Jan. 2, for maximum television effect.

LSU, meanwhile, was in the midst of an internal disruption. After the Mississippi State victory, Arnsparger tendered his resignation – it was later announced he'd become director of athletics at Florida – effective after the Sugar Bowl.

In the meantime, a deflated Nebraska team had to regroup for LSU.

Then LSU was hit with more adversity, when lineman Roland Barbay was barred from postseason football because of a positive drug test.

It was not a calm pre-Sugar Bowl interlude.

LSU receiver Wendell Davis (82) tries to run past Nebraska cornerback Brian Davis (32).

Tyreese Knox (34) scores on a 1-yard run to put the Cornhuskers up for good.

 53RD SUGAR BOWL CLASSIC

"They were going to crack."

After the game, Tom Osborne glanced at the Superdome scoreboard and put his team's effort in perspective: "We weren't playing for the national championship, the Big Eight championship was out the window. The only thing we had left was the Sugar Bowl."

The sixth-ranked Cornhuskers made the most of their season finale, running roughshod over the fifth-ranked Tigers, 30-15. If the Tigers ever had a real chance at victory, it dissipated with one late and lost opportunity, coupled with an amazing 100 yards of first-half penalties and Nebraska's brutal dominance of both lines.

On the game's first play from scrimmage, Wendell Davis, in full stride, caught a pass from Tommy Hodson for a 43-yard Tiger gain to the Nebraska 23. Six plays later, Harvey Williams scored from the 1 to give LSU a 7-0 lead.

That – with 2:54 gone in the first quarter – was the LSU high

point. Despite limiting Nebraska to 36 first period yards, the Tigers self-destructed in attempting to build on the lead.

One possession after the opening touchdown, LSU advanced into Cornhusker territory. Then the Tigers were beset with penalties. A personal foul and a holding call made it first-and-35, and punter Matt DeFrank eventually had to kick away.

The next time around, a sack of Hodson and an illegal receiver-downfield penalty killed another drive.

"We had the ball inside their 30 twice and didn't score," linebacker Ron Sancho said.

"It's hard for the defense to go out there and keep stopping them."

Tiger offensive coordinator Ed Zaunbrecher assessed, "If we stayed in a normal situation on first and second downs, we had

After intercepting an LSU pass Brian Davis (32) celebrates with Kevin Parsons (35) late in the 4th quarter.

a chance to do the things we wanted to do. Obviously, it's very hard to overcome the things that happened out there today."

From the second quarter, when Nebraska began to take control, until the final three-and-a-half minutes of the game, LSU made only two first downs and 32 plays that produced a total of 38 yards.

The mistakes frustrated the Tigers but didn't make a dent on the scoreboard until early in the second period. In punt formation, DeFrank, under a heavy rush from linebacker Dante Wiley, fumbled at the LSU 25. Nebraska got its first points minutes later on a 42-yard field goal.

LSU may have glimpsed at its fate on the next 'Husker series. Steve Taylor, who sat out the previous offensive possession, quarterbacked Nebraska 78 yards in nine plays. Taylor's score from the 1 gave the Cornhuskers a 10-7 halftime margin.

Nebraska began pulling away with a third-quarter touchdown, but one dramatic play made Tiger pulses race. Facing fourth-and-15 at the LSU 35, with a 10-point lead and a minute to go in the period, Osborne decided to go for a 52-yard field goal.

Noseguard Henry Thomas roared in, blocked the kick and put LSU in business at the Nebraska 17.

But Hodson was sacked twice for losses of 15 and nine yards. For the third time, the Bengals had penetrated the Huskers' 30 and were turned away pointless.

The Sugar Bowl essentially ended there.

"It's just like I said," Nebraska offensive tackle Tom Welter said. "We were going to pound 'em, and they were going to crack."

The defeat stung the Tigers because LSU was clearly and improved team and Nebraska not quite as good as it was two years before when the squads played a more competitive game in the Superdome.

"The thing I'll always wonder," Tiger center Nacho Albergamo reflected, "is that you don't know if they were really that good or if the penalties made us that bad."

On the following day, in the Fiesta Bowl, Penn State recorded the lowest offensive output (162 yards) and the highest defensive yield (445 yards) of any of the 10 teams that played on New Year's Day or Jan. 2.

To put it in perspective, LSU had 191 total yards and Nebraska had 352 total yards. But the little output Penn State generated against Miami was enough to win the national championship, 14-10.

In New Orleans, though, the day belonged to the Nebraska Cornhuskers.

Defensive end Broderick Thomas of the Cornhuskers broke into a wide grin when asked if the impressive Sugar Bowl showing was a stepping stone to a possible national championship in 1987.

"Tell the world," Thomas declared, "that Nebraska's 1987 hell-raising tour has begun."

Jake Moseley with USF&G presents the Sugar Bowl Trophy to John Custard.

	1	2	3	4	
Nebraska	0	10	7	13	30
LSU	7	0	0	8	15

LSU: Williams, 1-yard run. PAT, Browndyke kick.

Nebraska: Klein, 42-yard field goal.

Nebraska: Taylor, 2-yard run. PAT, Klein kick.

Nebraska: Knox, 1-yard run. PAT, Klein kick.

Nebraska: Millikan, 3-yard pass from Taylor. PAT, Klein kick.

Nebraska: Knox, 1-yard run. Kick failed.

LSU: Moss, 24-yard pass from Hodson. PAT, Lee pass from Hodson.

Individual Leaders

Rushing
Nebraska: Knox 16-84 yards, 2 TDs.
LSU: Williams 12-48, 1 TD.

Passing
Nebraska: Taylor 11-19-0, 110 yards, 1 TD.
LSU: Hodson 14-30-1, 159 yards, 1 TD.

Receiving
Nebraska: Banderas 4-42.
LSU: Davis 3-63.

Nebraska		LSU
22	First Downs	10
242	Rushing Yards	32
11-20-0	Passing	14-30-1
110	Passing Yards	159
352	Total Yards	191
4-30.5	Punts	6-42.0
5-2	Fumbles – Lost	6-1
5-78	Penalties – Yards	12-130

Attendance: 76,234.
Teams' remuneration: $5,100,000.
Miller-Digby Award recipient: Steve Taylor, Nebraska quarterback.

Syracuse 16 Auburn 16

"I just don't like that."

Had this game been played eight years later, a lot of football angst could have been avoided.

Tie games – which were always a big component of college football until overtime was installed in 1996 – and the way potential deadlocks were handled, colored the run-up to the 1988 Sugar Bowl.

Tennessee coach Johnny Majors took a lot of heat and second-guessing on Sept. 26th when he kicked an extra point with 1:20 remaining in the Vols' SEC game with Auburn, evening the score at 20-20, instead of going for the victory with a two-point conversion attempt.

That game haunted the Vols throughout the fall, as a three-way race developed between Auburn, which finished 5-0-1 in the SEC, LSU (5-1) and Tennessee (4-1-1). Had Tennessee gone for the win – and made it – the Vols would have been league champions.

A new power was flexing its muscles in the East where Syracuse, under Coach Dick MacPherson, with an exciting quarterback bearing a similar name, Don McPherson, was running rampant – until the last game of the Orangemen's so far unbeaten year.

It was a remarkable turnaround because Syracuse had gone 5-6 the previous season, but had won 10 straight going into the finale against West Virginia.

This was a heady experience for the Orangemen. It had been

23 years since Syracuse had last played in a major bowl game which was the historic Sugar Bowl of 1965 – and 28 years since its undefeated, untied national championship team of 1959. Now Syracuse was again among the elite, ranked fourth nationally.

The Mountaineers, though, gave the Orangemen almost more than they could handle on Nov. 21, in a game in which the opponents combined for 36 points in the fourth quarter. With seconds remaining, Syracuse scored the last touchdown to place the score at 31-30, West Virginia.

MacPherson had logical reason to settle for an extra point, and the tie: protecting what still would have been an unbeaten season. He opted take his chances for a one-point victory, chancing a one-point loss.

A successful end-around play on the PAT gave the Orangemen the win, still considered the single greatest football moment in Carrier Dome annals.

Just as thrilled was the Sugar Bowl. When it secured fourth-ranked Syracuse and sixth-ranked SEC champion Auburn, the

Auburn quarterback Jeff Burger (12) hands off to Reggie Ware (36).

Sugar Bowl had what it considered a natural match-up and an intriguing bowl game; a North vs. South pairing with an exciting offensive team, Syracuse, against an Auburn squad that played defense with cold efficiency.

A compelling match-up for aficionados, it came at a good time for the Sugar Bowl, which had partnered with USF&G Financial Services to become the corporate sponsor of the annual game. This was not an original concept. The first corporate sponsorship was the Florida Citrus Bowl in 1983. Florida Citrus Council is the name of the business that replaced the long-standing title of the Tangerine Bowl. Sponsorship, which eased the burgeoning expenses of putting on the games, was an idea that soon spilled across the postseason football landscape.

Syracuse in particular had the appearance of a godsend to the Sugar's selection committee. An Eastern team, especially an undefeated Eastern team, had the Sugar Bowl panting. After an extended run of No. 1 games that stretched from the early 1970s to the mid-1980s, the Sugar Bowl found itself having to fight the battle of holiday pairings with, figuratively, one arm strapped to the small of its back. Each year the bowl had to sit tight while the fiercely competitive Southeastern Conference, the Sugar's "anchor" league, where challengers would rou-

tinely cut each other up and eliminate each other from any No. 1 considerations.

Nov. 7 was a bloody Saturday for the Sugar Bowl because before that two SEC teams – Auburn and LSU – were legitimate national contenders, each undefeated but once tied. Florida State manhandled Auburn on that afternoon and Alabama upset LSU that night. The dual setbacks meant the Sugar Bowl would have to wait three weeks, until the Auburn-Alabama game, to find out which SEC team would play in New Orleans.

Auburn earned the right by beating 'Bama, 10-0.

Syracuse still had an outside shot at the national championship.

Don McPherson, runner-up to Notre Dame's Tim Brown in the Heisman Trophy balloting, was the ignition key to the Orange offense, having passed for 2,902 of his team's 4,843 total yards. Overshadowed somewhat in the Orangemen's 11-0-0 1987 was their defense. In the first six games of the season, before noseguard Ted Gregory was injured, Syracuse had the best statistical defense against the run (a 77.5 average) in the country. Gregory missed the last five games and Syracuse's average ballooned to 199 yards in that span.

Syracuse fullback Darrell Johnston (32) looks for more yardage on the Auburn defense.

The 285 yards of total offense averaged against Syracuse compared to the 280 yards averaged against Auburn, the SEC's best defensive unit, one that yielded just 10 points per opponent.

"Syracuse definitely has more to shoot for than we do," Auburn linebacker Aundray Bruce said. "We're here because we won our (conference) championship. What we have to do now is uphold the honor of the SEC."

The talk rankled the Orangemen. "We'd like for the people down South, and the nation, to know that we play good football in the East," said Syracuse free safety Markus Paul. "We haven't gotten any respect this season. As we built our winning streak this year, everybody kept waiting for us to get beat. We didn't. Now we're playing Auburn, a team with a loss and a tie, and we're still an underdog. I just don't like that."

He was fit to be tied.

Don McPherson (9) was named the MVP of the only Sugar Bowl to end in a tie.

"I was mad at myself."

Dick MacPherson would not let go of the trophy.

He went from interview to interview clutching the 35-pound, ornate, silver vessel, the symbol of Sugar Bowl supremacy.

"It's getting heavy," the Syracuse coach said an hour after the final whistle of a 16-16 New Year's Day deadlock with Auburn, "but they'll have to fight me to take it away."

The source of MacPherson's ire was the decision by Tiger coach Pat Dye to send place-kicker Win Lyle onto the field for a 30-yard field goal attempt with four seconds remaining. Dye, whose 9-1-1 team had no chance at a national championship or any other postgame laurels, was willing to settle for the tie.

Lyle's own frustrated teammates tried to wave him off the field before he made the tying kick, which produced boos from both sides, the only tie in the long annals of the Sugar Bowl (just the seventh in major bowl history, and the first since 1959), the only blot on Syracuse's record (11-0-1), and a fire in MacPherson's belly.

When Lyle's third field goal of the night sailed through the yellow uprights, MacPherson vented his anger by throwing his game plan – three sheets of rolled-up paper – to the Superdome turf. He had to walk onto the playing surface to retrieve it.

"I was mad at myself," MacPherson said.

Minutes before, when his team had to decide whether to go for it on fourth-and-inches at the Auburn 22, MacPherson's choice had been to kick for a 16-13 lead, feeling a team with no shot at No. 1 would have to go for the winning touchdown against an unbeaten, untied opponent in a bowl game.

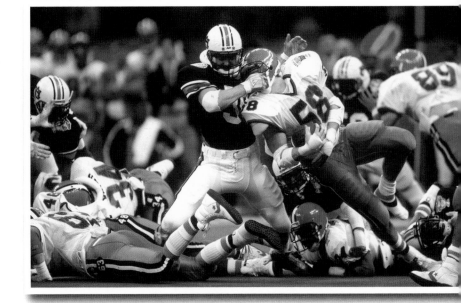

Roger Carges (58) opens the game with a 7-yard return.

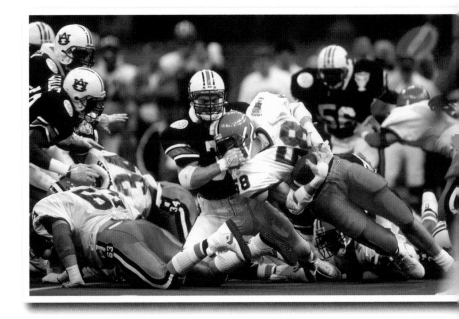

"I told my guys a field goal was like a touchdown," MacPherson said. "I told them if we made it, Auburn would have to go for the touchdown. If I had thought in my wildest imagination he'd go for a field goal, we would have gone for a first down."

At that point, all the Syracuse coach could do was smolder.

Dye said his Tigers – two and a half point favorites – simply played with "too much character and class" to risk going for

guard Stacy Searles reflected in the Sugar Bowl aftermath.

The disappointment, and the sniping and roaring between the Sugar Bowl foes on the first night of 1988, put a forlorn face on to the Sugar Bowl, a sharp contrast to the euphoria of a month earlier when the match was made.

This was the scenario: With just over two minutes remaining, with a fourth-and-inches at the Auburn 22, Tom Vesling

Win Lyle (6) kicks the game-tying field goal with one second left on the clock for Auburn.

a 13-yard touchdown in the fading seconds against the fourth-ranked Orangemen. "You win some, lose some and some end in ties," Dye said. "I made up my mind early on (in Auburn's last drive) what I was going to do. I wasn't going to let my team get beat. If they (Syracuse) wanted to win, they should have blocked the field goal."

The Tiger athletes, on the other hand, vividly remembered the Tennessee game. "I remember how happy Tennessee was with the tie and how disgusted I felt at the time," Auburn offensive

booted the go-ahead field goal.

MacPherson would second-guess himself later, but upon reflection said, "I think that was the right call." Dye agreed. "It put his team ahead (16-13)."

Auburn was 75 yards from their 10th victory of the season, and in that time span made up 62 of those yards.

At that point Dye sent in Lyle, to the accompaniment of boos

	1	2	3	4	
Syracuse	0	7	3	6	16
Auburn	7	3	0	6	16

Auburn: Tillman, 17-yard pass from Burger. PAT, Lyle kick.

Syracuse: Glover, 12-yard pass from McPherson. PAT, Vesling kick.

Auburn: Lyle, 40-yard FG.

Syracuse: Vesling, 27-yard FG.

Auburn: Lyle, 41-yard FG.

Syracuse: Vesling, 32-yard FG.

Syracuse: Vesling, 38-yard FG.

Auburn: Lyle, 30-yard FG.

Individual Leaders

Rushing
Syracuse: Drummond 17-82; Johnston 14-50.
Auburn: Danley 13-42.

Passing
Syracuse: McPherson 11-21-0, 140, 1 TD.
Auburn: Burger 24-33-1, 171 yards, 1 TD.

Receiving
Syracuse: Glover 6-91, 1 TD; Kane 2-30.
Auburn: Tillman 6-125, 1 TD. Danley, 7-34.

Syracuse		Auburn
23	First Downs	14
174	Rushing Yards	41
11-21-0	Passing	25-34-1
140	Passing Yards	229
314	Total Yards	270
5-35.6	Punts	6-44.8
2-0	Fumbles – Lost	1-0
2-20	Penalties – Yards	5-43

Attendance: 76,496.
Teams' remuneration: $5,400,000.
Miller-Digby Award recipient: Don McPherson, Syracuse quarterback.

from all ends of the Superdome. MacPherson made note of the fact that Auburn didn't throw into the end zone once on the last drive. "They were just fooling around with other things," he said, his anger showing through. "What the hell was (Dye) thinking? What the hell did they come here for in the first place?"

A Syracuse radio station, incensed by Dye's strategy, made a call for Orangemen fans to send Dye ties, the ugliest they could find. An estimated 2,000 ties flooded the Tiger athletic department in the days following the Sugar Bowl.

Dye, however, found a "moral victory" in the intended insult. He autographed each one, and included the score of the game, and had the athletic department sell them to fans for $100 apiece, with the proceeds donated to Auburn's general fund. Sales totaled $25,000.

A Montgomery radio station, WHHY, felt a response was in order, however. Disc jockey Blake Scott said sour grapes were exactly what Syracuse fans deserved. He asked Auburn fans to donate sour grapes to Dick MacPherson.

"We're looking for a warm warehouse to store them," Scott said, "then for the slowest transportation available."

Florida State 13 Auburn 7

"We got the most points."

Two games – each determined by a single point – colored the entire 1988 season, as well as the complexion of the bowl pairings and, eventually, the final polls.

Fourth-ranked Auburn was 4-0 and seemed to be a clear step above the rest of the SEC with a suffocating defense that would finish as the nation's best, when it visited unranked LSU (2-2) on Oct. 8.

Auburn's formidable defense pinned down the Bayou Bengals most of the night, so much so that LSU saw the far side of the field just once before the fourth quarter.

Still, the LSU defense was playing as well as Auburn's, keeping the home-standing Tigers behind just 6-0, within hailing distance. And LSU was able to pull itself together for one memorable late drive – and a very memorable 7-6 victory.

The Bayou Bengals lurched to life in the final minutes, made two unforgettable fourth-down plays – including the only touchdown of the evening with 1:41 to play – to stun an Auburn team that had legitimate national championship aspirations.

LSU gained but 28 yards rushing, and fullback Eddie Fuller, who caught the winning 10-yard touchdown pass from quarterback Tommy Hodson, was the Bengals' leading runner with 15 yards.

Assessed Hodson: "We didn't get a lot of first downs (13), a lot of completions (19-of-42) or a lot of yards rushing. But we got the most points."

A week later, resurgent Notre Dame, unbeaten under wisecracking third-year coach Lou Holtz, took on No. 1-ranked Miami.

In a game that wasn't determined until a two-point conversion attempt by Miami with 45 seconds remaining was knocked away, the Fightin' Irish nipped the Hurricanes 31-30.

Notre Dame ascended to No. 1, where the Irish remained the rest of the season.

The point is, had Auburn found a way to keep LSU out of the end zone in their game, Auburn and Notre Dame would have both been undefeated and would likely have met in the Sugar Bowl for the national championship.

As it was, Auburn was to face Florida State, which also finished with just one loss. But it was a whopper, 31-0 to Miami in the season opener.

"It was a storybook ending."

Florida State head coach Bobby Bowden leads
Florida State to its first Sugar Bowl.

Quarterback Chip Ferguson (5)
drops back to pass.

Auburn didn't impress Florida State. Not in the least.

This was expected to be a showcase game for Auburn's stifling defense – a much ballyhooed unit that came into the game surrendering 63.2 yards. No single back had cracked it for a hundred yards since 1986.

But on Florida State's first series, the Seminoles took straight aim at the Tigers, driving 84 yards for a touchdown, a two-yard run by fullback Dayne Williams. All but 23 yards of the drive were by rushing – just a hair under Auburn's per

game yield – and tailback Sammie Smith alone gained 34 of that yardage.

That is called making a statement.

Tiger tackle Tracy Rocker, winner of the 1988 Outland Trophy as the nation's top defensive lineman, said part of FSU's early success came from showing Auburn an offensive look it hadn't encountered all year.

"Teams usually come straight off the ball to block us," Rocker

Florida State quarterback Chip Ferguson can't avoid the sack by Ron Stallworth.

said. "This time they waited one count to see which way we were going. Then they would just go where we were and block us. Their backs would cut back."

After FSU's early touchdown, Auburn ran three plays and punted, and the Seminoles came right back with a 13-play drive that resulted in a 35-yard field goal by Bob Mason. Then Mason kicked another, giving the Seminoles a 13-0 lead.

Was the rout on?

Auburn finally got its offense untracked and climbed back

into the game when Reggie Slack hit Walter Reeves with a 20-yard touchdown pass after Deion Sanders bit on a fake pitch and left his zone uncovered.

"Auburn tricked us on that TD," Sanders said. "They lulled us to sleep during the drive, and that touchdown was my fault."

Then Bowden called a questionable play. Leading 13-7 early in the fourth period, the FSU coach sent in a pass play on third-and-goal from the 1. It was mishandled and wound up as a lateral pass/fumble that was recovered by the Tigers at the 18.

"We really needed to score there, at least a field goal," Bowden said. "... Three points there could have put the game away, because I don't think they could have scored twice on us. If I could do it again, I'd run."

Auburn coach Pat Dye wasn't dead yet, nor was he thinking of his controversial decision to go for a tie in the 1988 Sugar Bowl against Syracuse. Or so he said.

With 8:05 remaining, on fourth-and-nine from the FSU 15, Auburn went for it all. The Seminoles chased Slack out of the pocket and Slack was called for grounding the football.

"I didn't think there was enough (time) left for us to get down there again," Dye said. "If we had kicked the field goal then, we would have still needed a touchdown to win. I wasn't worried about what happened last year. We needed a touchdown to win and that's why we went to it."

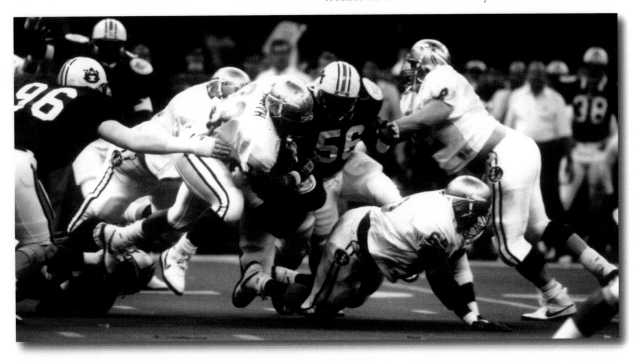

Sammy Smith (33) fights to gain yards on his way to winning the MVP award.

Fullback Dayne Williams (49) runs in for the 2-yard score in the first quarter.

Auburn did get the ball back and Slack mounted an impressive last-minute drive in a gallant attempt to beat the clock, and the Seminoles, converting three fourth-down situations to reach the FSU 22 with 12 seconds left.

He then lofted an end-zone shot to Lawyer Tillman. Sanders, though, timed his pursuit of the ball perfectly. Seemingly out of nowhere, Sanders stepped in front of Tillman and snatched the potential winning touchdown away from the receiver.

A split second later Sanders dropped to his knees in the end zone, securing the victory for the third-ranked Seminoles – and fulfilling his dream.

"When Deion Sanders doesn't make a big play," he said of himself in the third person afterward, "he has a bad game. It was a storybook ending, but I'm still not satisfied with my game. The ending made it OK, but I'm still not satisfied."

Deion Sanders (2) intercepts Reggie Slack's pass in the end zone to seal the win for FSU.

	1	2	3	4	
Florida State	10	3	0	0	13
Auburn	0	7	0	0	7

Florida State: Williams, 2-yard run. PAT, Andrews kick.

Florida State: Mason, 35-yard field goal.

Florida State: Mason, 31-yard field goal.

Auburn: Reeves, 20-yard pass from Slack. PAT, Lyle kick.

Individual Leaders

Rushing
Florida State: Smith 24-115; Carter 7-25.
Auburn: Danley 19-68; Joseph 8-47.

Passing
Florida State: Ferguson 14-26-1, 157 yards.
Auburn: Slack 19-33-3, 162 yards, 1 TD.

Receiving
Florida State: Anthony 3-47; O'Malley 2-31.
Auburn: Tillman 4-48; Taylor 5-35.

FSU head coach Bobby Bowden hoists the Sugar Bowl Trophy after defeating Auburn.

Florida State had every reason but one to be satisfied. The Seminoles gained 305 yards, most of any Auburn opponent in 1988, and Smith gained 115 of that total. Further, the Tigers managed only 270 total yards, 135 fewer than their season average.

"The only thing I didn't like was my play-calling on the goal line," Bowden said. "I let Auburn's defensive line intimidate me. I looked at 11 games on film, and nobody stuffed the ball on Auburn at the goal line. We could have scored a whole bunch of points."

A whole bunch of points would have been nice, but, as it was, 13 were enough. Just barely enough.

Florida State		Auburn
21	First Downs	18
148	Rushing Yards	108
14-27-1	Passing	19-33-3
157	Passing Yards	162
305	Total Yards	270
4-35.0	Punts	4-35.8
2-1	Fumbles – Lost	3-2
6-45	Penalties – Yards	5-65

Attendance: 75,098.
Teams' remuneration: $6,000,000.
Miller-Digby Award recipient: Sammie Smith, Florida State tailback.

Miami 33   Alabama 25

"It's an acceptance thing."

The hottest story in the off-season of 1989 was the continuing saga of the University of Miami, college football's program of the decade with two national championships and 88 victories.

Coach Jimmy Johnson abruptly left the Hurricanes in March to coach the Dallas Cowboys and a relative newcomer from Washington State, Dennis Erickson, replaced him.

Two weeks after Erickson's hiring, Steve Walsh, expected to be the premier college quarterback in '89, made himself available for the NFL supplemental draft, putting an apparent — and severe — crimp in the Hurricanes' offense. Junior Craig Erickson, no relation to the coach, was shoved up on the Miami depth chart.

The top games on an otherwise not-overly-demanding Hurricanes schedule were Florida State, a top-three finisher the last three seasons, and defending national champion Notre Dame. The Irish had benefited mightily from an erroneous fumble possession call at the goal line against Miami in 1988, thus aiding in securing a national title.

At the same time, at the University of Alabama, the 1989 season was a continuation of a fine and often unappreciated coaching job. Bill Curry had turned in an excellent 16-6 record with a modicum of talent in his first two years at Bama. But bricks were thrown through his office window

after one defeat, and Curry was constantly under attack from Crimson Tide fans with tunnel vision – and a nostalgic yearning to return Alabama football to its years under Bear Bryant. Curry, to some in Alabama, was a pariah because he had no previous Crimson Tide or Bryant ties, and because of his connection to Georgia Tech as a player and coach. The fact that he twice beat Bryant's Tide with short-handed Yellow Jacket teams always seemed overlooked. Or maybe too vividly remembered.

Miami, meanwhile, was operating just as efficiently as ever. Even in a new offense, the one-back, and with a new quarterback, the 'Canes scored 120 points in their first three games. Only when Erickson broke a finger and missed several games did Miami slow down. Four interceptions by Erickson's replacement, freshman Gino Torretta, and a failure to score on three possessions inside the Florida State 1, sealed a 24-10 defeat to the Seminoles.

But the Hurricanes, like all great teams,

University of Miami head coach Dennis Erickson.

So Miami, ranked seventh then, was invited and accepted.

Fourth-ranked Alabama was the likely opponent, making for a match of a pair of 10-1 squads.

The Sugar Bowl felt it was securely back in the national championship picture because if the right combination of wins and losses fell together, the No. 1 team would emerge from New Orleans for the first time since Penn State defeated Georgia in 1983.

All that had to happen was for Miami to beat Notre Dame, then for the Irish to defeat Colorado in the Orange Bowl, and for Southern Cal to whip third-ranked Michigan in the Rose.

"A victory tonight puts us back in the national championship picture," Hurricanes' athletic director Sam Janovich said a half-hour before the Miami-Notre Dame kickoff.

were not founded on offense. Miami led the nation in scoring defense (9.3 points per game) and total defense (216.5 yards per game) were No. 2 in rushing defense (69.1 ypg) and fourth in passing defense (147.4 ypg).

"Miami's defense arrives in the stadium in an angry mood," California coach Bruce Snyder said after losing to the 'Canes 31-3. "All coaches coach their defense to be that way. It's a physical game. It's a game for men. The more physical you can be, the more aggressive you can be, the better off you are.

"Not everybody accomplishes that. Miami does."

Try as it might, and it tried mightily, the Sugar Bowl couldn't lure the No. 1-ranked Irish to New Orleans.

Bowl bids were extended at 6 p.m., Nov. 25, approximately am hour before Notre Dame and the Hurricanes would kick off in Miami.

Alabama quarterback Gary Hollingsworth back to pass.

That night the 'Canes won a merciless 27-10 victory, moving the first block of the push to No. 1 into place.

"The Notre Dame game was a game that was really kind of fun," Dennis Erickson said, "regardless of the outcome, because of the intensity level of the game. I came here for a reason and the reason was that kind of game. To me, that game was what football is all about, even more than any game I've ever seen or experienced ... It's an acceptance thing. Winning that football game meant instant credibility, made the community realize we could coach."

The Hurricanes' victory propelled Colorado to No. 1, Miami to No. 2, while Notre Dame dropped to No. 3.

Alabama fell from the hunt for No. 1, sliding to No. 7, when Auburn, playing its archrival for the first time at home, beat the Tide 30-20, giving Auburn and Tennessee shares of the SEC title, the first tri-championship in the 57-year history of the league.

*The Alabama offense was lead by (top) senior quarterback Gary Hollingworth (14),
but (bottom) sophomore tailback Derrick Lassic (25) was just getting his first taste of the Sugar Bowl.*

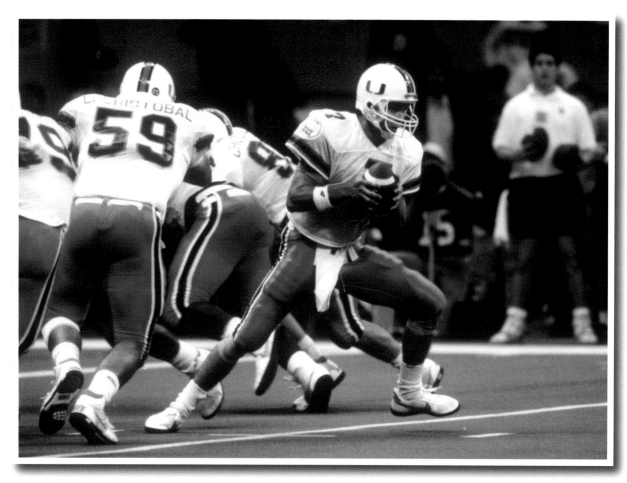

Miami quarterback Craig Erickson, Sugar Bowl MVP, finished the game with 250 yards and three touchdowns.

 56TH SUGAR BOWL CLASSIC

"Give them credit."

Whew! That was close.

Miami entered the Sugar Bowl as a nine-point favorite, the biggest spread of that New Year's Day, but, with 2:53 remaining, Alabama was suddenly within reach of tie – just as damaging as a loss for a team angling for the national championship.

With that much time to go, the Crimson Tide pulled to within 33-23 on Gary Hollingsworth's nine-yard pass to Prince Wimbly, then Hollingsworth completed a 2-point conversion to Lamonde Russell.

It was a long shot, but with an onside kick, another touchdown and another two-point conversion, 'Bama could foil the dreams of the Hurricanes. In one game anything can happen.

But it was the 'Canes who got the kick and who were then able to run out the clock.

In the end everything fell precisely into place for Miami's third No. 1 trophy in eight years, but Craig Erickson had to throw two of his three touchdown passes in the fourth quarter for that to happen. The question was, was that enough?

The cadre of Miami fans in the Superdome were ecstatic and celebrating when they started hearing scores of other games of major interest that day – Notre Dame defeated Colorado 21-6, and Southern Cal beat Michigan 17-10. But Miami's close shave dampened the revelry. It could have repercussions with voters.

"To have the opportunity to possibly win the national championship is a credit to our players and coaches," said Dennis Erickson, but he cautioned, "people still have to vote."

Alabama looked like it might do the voting in the first half, after which the Hurricanes led only 20-17. Those opening 30

Fullback Kevin Turner looks for yardage on a tough Miami defense.

minutes produced more yards – 412, the Crimson Tide garnering 163 – than either of the coaches expected. 'Bama's 17 points were the most allowed in a half by Miami all season, although there was a general feeling in the Superdome that the Crimson Tide was an outmanned team that just kept dodging the knockout blow.

Looming large at game's end were four extra points for Miami, coming on an offside penalty against 'Bama, which took the 'Canes' field-goal unit off the field and kept their drive alive at the Tide 3. Stephen McGuire scored on the next play, going over left guard with 4:55 to go in the opening period.

Two possessions later, the Crimson Tide returned fire, taking full advantage of field position created by its punt team.

Alabama quarterback Gary Hollingworth (14) is overwhelmed by the Miami defense.

After pinning Miami back at its 7, Gene Jelks returned a kick to the Alabama 36. In nine plays, Hollingsworth speared flanker Marco Battle with a four-yard TD pass at 14:07 of the second.

"I saw the pressure coming," Hollingsworth said. "It was to pick up the blitz. What they did all day was to put man-on-man single coverage on our receivers and try to get pressure on me. I didn't see Marco catch the ball, but I was happy that he did."

Erickson established Miami's passing game for good on the 'Canes' first series of the second quarter when he hit Wesley Carroll with three passes for 60 of the necessary 78 yards for a go-ahead touchdown. Carroll caught a 19-yard scoring pass. "After that we had to watch for everything," cornerback John Mangum said. "I mean, they just beat us. That's all there is to it."

Later, a Hurricanes fumble led to a 47-yard 'Bama field goal by Phillip Doyle, which made the score 13-10 with 8:28 left until halftime.

Miami safety Charles Pharms (2) intercepts an Alabama pass late in the 3rd quarter.

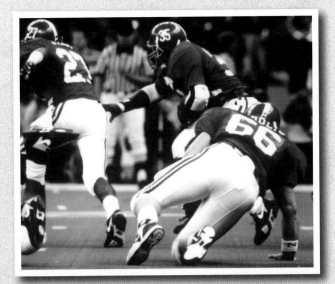

Fullback Martin Houston (35) looks for blocking.

The score jumped to 20-10 as Miami drove 62 yards on nine running plays. At the 3, Alex Johnson juked none other than Keith McCants, considered the best linebacker in the college game, on the outside and hit the end zone.

Alabama responded, coming right back and driving 80 yards on 11 plays as Hollingsworth found Russell with a seven-yard touchdown pass. Russell beat free safety Charles Pharms on a slant pattern.

The Hurricanes got downright stingy in the second half, limiting the Crimson Tide to 89 yards. The game was relatively close, but Miami was clearly the superior squad.

Miami, primarily a passing team, once untracked, rushed for 227 yards on 50 attempts. Erickson finished with 17 completions on 27 attempts for 250 yards and the three touchdowns.

"Give them credit," Ozmint said. "They're the best team we've played and Erickson is the best quarterback we've faced." But there was at least a little consolation for the Tide in the fact that the Tide had played hard and well – against the national champions.

The next day the Hurricanes were voted No. 1, making history on more than one front. Erickson became the first man to win a national title in his first season as head coach at a school since Bennie Oosterban at Michigan in 1948.

	1	2	3	4	
Miami	7	13	6	7	33
Alabama	0	17	0	8	25

Miami: McGuire, 3-yard run. PAT, Huerta kick.
Alabama: Battle, 4-yard pass from Hollingsworth. PAT, Doyle kick.
Miami: Carroll, 19-yard pass from Erickson. Kick blocked.
Alabama: Doyle, 45-yard field goal.
Miami: Johnson, 3-yard run. PAT, Huerta kick.
Alabama: Russell, 7-yard pass from Hollingsworth. PAT, Doyle kick.
Miami: Chudzinski, 11-yard pass from Erickson. Pass failed.
Miami: Bethel, 12-yard pass from Erickson. PAT, Huerta kick.
Alabama: Wembley, 9-yard pass from Hollingsworth. PAT, Russell, pass from Hollingsworth.

Individual Leaders

Rushing
Miami: McGuire 17-80, 1 TD; Johnson 9-58, 1 TD.
Alabama: Stacy 9-21; Lassic 4-13.

Passing
Miami: Erickson 17-27-1, 250, 3 TDs.
Alabama: Hollingsworth 27-43-1, 214, 3 TDs.

Receiving
Miami: Carroll 5-88, 1; Chudzinski 2-21, 1 TD.
Alabama: Battle 4-42, 1 TD; Russell 3-25, 1 TD; Wimbley 3-48, 1 TD.

Miami		Alabama
24	First Downs	17
227	Rushing Yards	38
17-27-1	Passing	27-43-1
250	Passing Yards	214
477	Total Yards	252
5-31.4	Punts	8-38.3
2-2	Fumbles – Lost	0-0
11-77	Penalties – Yards	3-24

Attendance: 77,452.
Total remuneration: $6,500,000.
Miller-Digby Award recipient: Craig Erickson, Miami quarterback.

Tennessee 23   Virginia 22

"Mirror, Mirror on the wall..."

It may have been a rare occurrence, but looking at the mystical football mirror in 1990, if the image of Thomas Jefferson was reflected, then his university's football team seemed to be among the fairest of them all.

Seemed to be.

If Davy Crockett popped up, then it was known his state university's school was looking good.

As usual.

Virginia and Tennessee were mirror images of orange offensive nitro. One of the stories of the 1990 season, the Cavaliers and the SEC champ Volunteers were football Siamese twins – too similar to separate.

"Johnny Majors has been a good friend of mine for 15 years," George Welsh, the Cavs' coach, said of Tennessee's head man. "We've exchanged information the last few years, and we're doing some of the things they do. Tennessee is an awfully good offensive football team with a very fine quarterback and great receivers – a little like us – and an underrated defensive team."

A big-play offense that scored on 71 of its 146 possessions

(48.6 percent) over the course of the season, Virginia's volatile offense, directed with uncommon precision by Shawn Moore, averaged 500 yards and 40 points.

"We really get upset when we don't score on every drive," receiver Derek Dooley said. "I guess it's a matter of greed."

Tennessee, with Andy Kelly as the offensive trigger, scored exactly the same amount of points (442) as Virginia and gained just 53 yards a game fewer.

Those quarterbacks each had arsenals of receivers to work with: The Cavs' Herman Moore, who tied the NCAA record of 10 consecutive games with touchdown catches. His 1,190 yards was an ACC record, and his 54 receptions, 13 touchdown catches, and 2,504 career-receiving yards were all Virginia records.

Nikki Fisher (33) lead the Cavaliers running game with 90 yards on the day.

"He's the best in the country," Georgia Tech coach Bobby Ross said unequivocally of Moore. "If there is anyone better in the country, you'll have to show him to me."

Vols wide receiver Carl Pickens, one of college football's most versatile performers and who set a school record with 13 receptions against Notre Dame on Nov. 10, led the SEC with 53 catches, one less than Herman Moore, for 971 yards.

Alvin Harper, another Vol pass-catcher, had another 37 receptions from Kelly for 567 yards. Harper was second on Tennessee's all-time pass-catching chart in career touchdowns (15), fifth in career receiving yardage (1,520) and sixth in career receptions.

Pickens was a throwback to an earlier football age, a man able to play on both sides of the ball. The year before Pickens made the All-SEC freshman team as a receiver and *Sporting News'* All-SEC freshman team as a defensive back.

Now a 6-foot-2, 188-pound redshirt sophomore, Pickens was a backup on offense and started the last five games in the secondary. As a wide receiver, Pickens caught seven passes for 81 yards, an 11.6 yards per-reception average. As a DB he intercepted five passes in the five games he played.

"And every one was a play of consequence," Majors emphasized.

Tennessee's Kelly strongly believed he, not Florida's All-SEC quarterback Shane Matthews, was the conference's best at that position.

And he had a case.

Kelly also compared favorably with Shawn Moore, acknowledged as one of the best, if not the best, in the nation.

* Kelly completed 58.9 percent (179-of-304) of his passes for 2, 241 yards.
* Shawn Moore completed 59.8 percent (144-of-241) of his passes for 2,262 yards.

This was going to be a fun game, a fans' game. What it was not going to be was a game that impacted on the national championship. Virginia, which rose to No. 1 for the first time in school history, finished 8-3. Tennessee, considered a pre-season national title contender, ended up 8-2-2 and far from any serious thoughts of No. 1.

This would be a historically significant moment, though, a first step in the postseason we know today.

What happened in the 1991 pairing greatly bothered Mickey Holmes, the Sugar Bowl's executive director. Holmes was mesmerized when he visited Virginia, at the time a scintillating 7-0 and on top the polls, and made no secret that the Cavaliers were also on top of the Sugar's wish-list.

The school and the bowl agreed – that the Cavs would spend New Years in New Orleans. Virginia then lost three of its last four games, but the Sugar was still on the hook.

Still, this would be an interesting Sugar Bowl. For one thing, Majors was going to have to defend two Heisman-class Cavs.

Shawn Moore finished fourth in the '90 vote, and battery mate Herman Moore finished sixth. That vote represented the first time since 1964 that a quarterback and receiver from the same school ended up in the top 10 of the balloting. Notre Dame quarterback John Huarte, who won the trophy, and Jack Snow (fifth) were the last pitch-and-catch tandem to finish among the Heisman elite.

Before that, the last combo from the same school was Navy end Ron Beagle, who was seventh, while finishing third was his quarterback George Welsh – the current Virginia coach.

"He was masterful."

Gary Steele (44) looks to run up the middle on a tough Tennessee defense.

Andy Kelly handed off to Tony Thomson, who banged into the end zone.

There were 31 seconds left in the Sugar Bowl and this was the last of 20 fourth-quarter points Kelly staked his team to – every one obviously consequential in what turned out to be a one-point victory.

"He was masterful," Tennessee coach Johnny Majors said, wiping sweat from his forehead after Kelly had moved his team 79 yards in the game's last 2:31 to stake the Vols to a 23-22 victory.

On that drive, Kelly accounted for 64 yards of the total by himself, connecting on 7-of-9 passes before Thompson, who gained 151 yards on the night, crashed in from the 1.

"A great feeling swept over my body when I saw Tony going in for the winning touchdown," a relieved Kelly exalted.

This is how close the difference between victory or defeat was: Perhaps the game's most important play came seconds earlier, on fourth-and-one at the Virginia 23, with 50 seconds to play, Kelly sent Greg Amsler into the line. Amsler gained six yards. If he had been stopped, Tennessee would have been beaten.

And the difference between Tennessee and Virginia, a team bent on redeeming itself, was Kelly, who finished the night with 24 completions in 35 attempts for 273 yards, plus the engineering of three last quarter drives.

The halves of the Sugar Bowl were complete contrasts.

Tennessee was its own worst enemy early. The Vols had to overcome three first-half turnovers, including two critical Kelly interceptions near the Cavs' goal line, for the victory. The first half also marked the first time in 13 games that Tennessee had failed to score in the opening 30 minutes.

Tennessee had been surprised by a new Virginia blocking scheme, and to which the Vols did not adjust until the second half. Quarterback Shawn Moore dislocated the thumb on his throwing hand early, but still the Cavs moved almost at will, holding the ball for nearly 22 minutes in the first two quarters.

So dominant were the Cavaliers in the first half that they outgained the SEC champions 210-125, converted on 9-of-11 third downs, and rolled to a 16-0 lead that could have been bigger had the lingering effects of Moore's injury not been so evident, with his passes fluttering. On the game's first series, the Cavs' quarterback completed three short passes, two to his receiver-deluxe Herman Moore. All were third-down conversions to keep the drive going.

Carl Pickens (15) of Tennessee and Len Izzo (16) of Virginia both juggle for the ball.

But for the most part, the Cavs relied on the running of Terry Kirby and Gary Steele. It was Steele who scored from 10 yards out 5:41 into the game. Tennessee linebacker Darryl Hardy blocked Jake McInerney's PAT (only his second miss of the season) to keep the score at 6-0.

Considering what happened later, Hardy may have saved the Sugar for the Vols.

The next time Virginia got the ball, it took a 9-0 lead on McInerney's 22-yard field goal with 35 seconds left in the opening period. A tipped-pass interception in the end zone, gathered in by Tyrone Lewis, started the Cavaliers on a grueling 80-yard push that took 6:59 off the clock and gave them a 16-0 lead. The touchdown came on Terry Kirby's one-yard run out of the wishbone.

While Virginia's best defense in the first half was its offense, the defensive unit was very opportunistic. The Cavaliers forced three turnovers on the Volunteers' first five possessions, a fumble at the Virginia 36, an interception at the Virginia 1, and another at the Virginia 19.

Tennessee quarterback Andy Kelly (8) celebrates as Tony Thompson (24) dives into the end zone.

The Cavs built their imposing halftime lead, sending many of the Tennessee (un)faithful to the French Quarter.

Though Tennessee was able to pick up only three points during the third quarter – Greg Burke toed a 27-yard field goal at the end of the Vols' first possession – a change in the game's tenor began to show. Tennessee had the ball for 8:07 of the period, compared to 8:06 of the entire first half.

A Cavalier drive deep into Tennessee territory was cut short when an under-thrown pass by Moore was picked off by Floyd Miley. Tennessee then drove 94 yards – in the process picking up its first third-down conversion of the game – to slice the margin to 16-10.

The foes traded shots – but field goals for Virginia, touchdowns for Tennessee – until quarterback Moore ignited a drive that led to a 44-yard McInerney kick that made the score 22-17 with 2:31 left to play.

From then on it was Kelly against the clock.

Amsler said accurately, "He was a cool customer in the fourth quarter."

 ## 57TH SUGAR BOWL CLASSIC

Epilogue

It was February and in Chicago. It was after a meeting of the Big Ten athletic directors. Mickey Holmes, executive director of the Sugar Bowl, and Jim Brock, his counterpart at the Cotton Bowl, had just heard the conference plead for guaranteed inclusion for its runner-up team in another of the postseason classics, other than the Rose Bowl, where the Big Ten champion annually played.

Both knew that such a move was not the answer to a lot of questions swirling around the bowl system. Ever since Virginia lost three of its last four regular-season games, Holmes had been wrestling with finding a new way to make pairings. "There has to be a better way," Holmes said of being forced to take chances on teams long before the season was concluded.

He thought he may have found it.

Heading to the airport, Holmes told Brock he had an idea he wanted to try on him: if the concept was sound it could, Holmes thought, improve immeasurably the postseason pairings and the timing when the matches were made.

That meeting with the Big Ten, a league which had just been fortified by the inclusion of long-time independent power Penn State, had followed hard on the heels of Big East Football Conference discussions in which the new league, made up entirely of previously independent schools, was aggressively pursuing a tie-up with a bowl.

At the same time the Atlantic Coast Conference was putting pressure on the Citrus Bowl to come up with more money and looking around for other football harbors in case it didn't – the move fortified by the imminent joining of Florida State, heretofore also an independent.

The great pool of independents from which the bowls had drawn for years to fill berths against their associated league champions was evaporating.

Thus the Sugar, like the Cotton and the Orange, was looking squarely at a potentially negative reality. If the ACC and the Big East each tied up with a bowl, leaving Notre Dame virtually the only independent in the college sport, and therefore the only open possibility, the bowls would be matching conference champions against second-place opponents in almost all cases.

At the same time, Holmes knew that if the Sugar Bowl were to jump ahead and effect a tie-up with either the ACC or Big East to play the SEC champ each New Year's it would be forfeiting an opportunity each year to have Notre Dame or the champion of other conferences.

Then, too, there was the ongoing problem of early selections which sometimes occurred as much as four weeks before the season ended.

During that session with the Big Ten, Holmes had begun putting together a scenario, which could keep the champions of the ACC and Big East, plus Notre Dame, in the mix available to all three bowls each year.

Then, he figured, if a fourth bowl, which would be open for both berths, were added, two more "at-large" teams, the best available to college football, could be added.

Born, though Holmes didn't know it for sure then, was the "Pool of 5."

Later, with Brock at the Chicago airport on their ways back to their respective bases, Holmes sprung the idea on his longtime colleague. Brock liked it.

Approached next, at a meeting later that week in Dallas, were Steve Hatchell (executive director) and Harper Davidson (president) of the Orange Bowl and John Stuart (president) of the Cotton Bowl.

"Cut holes in it, tear it apart and put it back together again, and then rip it apart again," Holmes urged the others.

They did and the hybridization was started. Next came a meeting with the ACC, the Big East and Notre Dame. The "Pool of 5" was unveiled by the three bowls, with reference to the fourth designated as "Bowl X."

"Though we didn't know it, the ACC and the Big East (as rep-

resented by then-commissioners Gene Corrigan and Mike Tranghese) had been discussing a plan as well," Holmes recalled. "We had very mixed reactions to their proposal (primarily a three-bowl approach), though Notre Dame quickly picked up on the four-bowl concept. The two commissioners had problems with our idea and I was worried."

What came about was a "relative" of the original outline, having benefited at every turn from the input of all, including "Bowl X," which was the Fiesta, as selected by all.

The system sounded complicated, though it was actually very simple.

Just remember the Sugar, with its host berth allocated to the champion of the Southeastern Conference, the Orange, its host team being the champion of the Big Eight, and the Cotton, with its anchor team being champion of the Southwest Conference, each need one "visiting" team to fill their games for a total of three. The Fiesta had no conference affiliation and therefore would have two openings for a total of five open berths within the four bowls.

The "Pool of 5," the teams to fill those berths, would be composed of the champions of the ACC, the Big East, Notre Dame, and two "at-large" schools, from which the four bowls would select.

Once the components of that "Pool of 5" were established, AND THE SEASON IS OVER (meaning after the conference championships were decided), then the pairings for the four New Year's Day bowls would be put together.

The bowls with postseason affiliations would pick from the "Pool of 5" in the order of their league champions' national rankings, with the bowl with the highest-ranked "host" team having first pick, and so forth.

The only exception to this formula would be in a year when the No. 1 and No. 2-ranked teams in the country are within the "Pool of 5" (champions of the ACC, Big East, Notre Dame and the two at-large squads). Those teams would then automatically play in the Fiesta, and the other three pairings would be made with selections made on national rankings of the bowls' host teams, as above.

Contrary to what some writers penned when the plan was revealed, the Bowl Coalition, as it was called, was never conceived to be a playoff plan and was never discussed as such among the bowls, among the conferences involved or Notre Dame, as a playoff plan.

Yet by establishing that "Pool of 5," which would keep teams generally worthy of top-draw consideration in a mix available to all four bowls, with no pairings set in stone most years, there was a real possibility of the best games for each of the four bowls most seasons.

"I think the real advantage is that it slows down the selection process to allow for all the major New Year's Day bowl games to put together some healthy match-ups," SEC commissioner Roy Kramer said.

When all aspects had been hammered out, the next logical step was taken – the three "host" conferences were brought in, as represented by their commissioners, Fred Jacoby of the Southwest, Carl James of the Big Eight, and Kramer.

It was the belief of all involved that the intent to create at least four exceptional postseason games for the benefit of fans and college football had been met.

"We believe it will do that and do that for a number of years," said Holmes. "And the best part is, the pairing of for these marquee games won't be put up until the season is over."

	1	2	3	4	
Tennessee	0	0	3	20	23
Virginia	9	7	0	6	22

Virginia: Steele, 10-yard run. Kick blocked.
Virginia: McInerney, 22-yard field goal.
Virginia: Kirby, 1-yard run. PAT, McInerney kick.
Tennessee: Burke, 27-yard field goal.
Tennessee: Thompson, 7-yard run. PAT, Burke kick.
Virginia: McInerney, 43-yard field goal.
Tennessee: Pickens, 15-yard pass from Kelly. PAT, Burke kick.
Virginia: McInerney, 44-yard field goal.
Tennessee: Thompson, 1-yard run, Run failed.

Individual Leaders

Rushing
Tennessee: Thompson 25-154, 2 TDs.
Virginia: Fisher 15-90; Moore 11-76; Kirby 21-75, 1 TD.

Passing
Tennessee: Kelly 24-35-2, 273 yards, 1 TD.
Virginia: Moore 9-22-2, 62 yards.

Receiving
Tennessee: Moore 7-97; Pickens 6-87, 1 TD.
Virginia: Kirby 4-27.

Tennessee		Virginia
28	First Downs	25
191	Rushing Yards	287
24-35-2	Passing	9-24-3
273	Passing Yards	62
464	Total Yards	349
2-20.0	Punts	1-48.0
1-1	Fumbles – Lost	1-0
5-65	Penalties – Yards	5-30

Attendance: 75,132.
Teams' remuneration: $7,100,000.
Miller-Digby Award recipient: Andy Kelly, Tennessee quarterback.

Notre Dame 39 Florida 28

"Wake up the echoes."

One little fact escaped college football pundits before the Sugar Bowl, and that was Florida and Notre Dame were football teams going in opposite health directions. The Irish had a rash of serious injuries, particularly defensively, in their seventh game against Air Force.

Players such as Demetrius DuBose, Notre Dame's leading tackler, and the rest of the linebacking corps – Pete Bercich, Anthony Peterson, Greg Davis – and tackle Bryant Young were, at various times, unavailable during Notre Dame's crucial last three games, two of which it lost, creating cries the Irish didn't deserve a spot in a major bowl game. The 18th-ranked Irish somehow blew a 31-7 second-quarter lead in what became a 35-34 defeat to Tennessee, lost 35-13 to Penn State, and then squeezed out a 48-42 win at Hawaii to give Notre a 9-3 record.

So not everybody thought Notre Dame deserved a match against the third-ranked, 10-1 Gators.

But, the Irish would all be healed and ready for the game in New Orleans. That would have to make a difference.

Conversely, Florida was largely injury-free until its last game, against Florida State. After that backyard battle, quarterback Shane Matthews needed arthroscopic surgery on a knee, and All-SEC linebacker Tim Paulk was lost because of a severe hamstring pull. Later, starting defensive end Harvey Thomas was hurt in a moped accident and lost for the Sugar Bowl.

This was a significant matchup for both Florida and the Sugar Bowl. It marked the first time Gators coach Steve Spurrier took a Florida team to the Sugar. Spurrier would eventually bring five Gator

Notre Dame players do the Gator chomp after Jerome Bettis (6) scored late in the 4th quarter.

squads to New Orleans in just nine seasons. Other coaches would have that many or more, but none would have as many Sugar Bowl teams in so short a period of time.

Notre Dame coach Lou Holtz, after defensive coordinator Gary Darnell resigned to take a similar job at the University of Texas, took direct command of the unit. He put in a four-man rush and seven-man cover scheme (called the "rope-a-dope" defense) to keep Matthews from connecting on the big play

and tried to stir his team's emotions, stoking the fire of the Irish by reminding them no one thought they belonged on this stage, against a big-time opponent like Florida. And, the night before the game, he showed them the film *Wake Up the Echoes*, which chronicles the unsurpassed tradition of Notre Dame football.

If the Irish weren't ready after that emotional bloodletting, they never would be.

"Lou Holtz doesn't give tips."

Seldom have a football coach's orders been carried out so perfectly.

After the Sugar Bowl, Notre Dame fullback Jerome Bettis reiterated his frustrated coach's halftime speech: "Coach (Lou) Holtz told us we could move the ball on the ground – and that we *WOULD* move the ball on the ground in the second half."

At that point, the Irish were behind 16-7, and had a grand total of 34 yards rushing.

But Holtz did wake up the echoes – or something.

And Bettis took Holtz's orders to heart. In the dying minutes of the game – in an imagination-stretching span of 2:44 – he broke loose for three touchdown runs of 3, 49 and 39 yards, rushed for an even 100 yards, and brought Notre Dame back to a deceiving 39-28 victory.

It was an uphill grind all night for the Irish.

Florida quarterback Shane Matthews guided the Gators 85

Shane Matthews (9) takes a hit from a relentless Notre Dame defense.

yards on their first series, topped by 15-yard touchdown pass to Willie Jackson. Arden Czyzewski then kicked a field goal to put Florida ahead 10-0 at the end of the first quarter, then another to make the score 13-0 with just under five minutes gone in the second.

The only echoes Notre Dame was waking up at this point were those of its ragged regular-season finish.

Still, despite everything, the Irish were winning small battles. Florida's first two field goals came after a combined 29 plays that covered 146 yards. The Gators were ahead, but a disturbing pattern was building – big drives, no touchdowns. Florida was moving from 20 to 20, but was leaving points on the goal line.

The Gator injuries continued to mount as well. Inside linebacker Carlton Miles suffered a back injury in the second quarter and couldn't return. Third-stringers Kevin Freeman and Gregg Diamond filled in. Until this game Diamond had played strictly on special teams.

The thin Gator defense was beginning to tear. Linebacker Ed Robinson lamented later, "I was trying to do too much."

Notre Dame finally got on the board on a 40-yard pass from Rick Mirer to Lake Dawson.

Then, however, the Florida bug-a-boo again turned up, as Czyzewski kicked a 36-yard field to make the halftime score 16-7. That drive covered 51 yards in 10 plays. Florida was absolutely dominant in the first half, but Notre Dame, with just its 34 rushing yards, so far was very much in the game.

Jerome Bettis celebrates after scoring one of his three touchdowns.

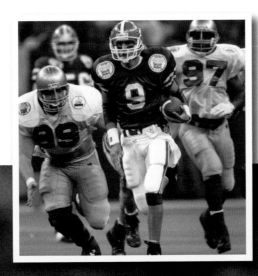

The Florida offense struggled to get accross the goal line having to settle for field goals.

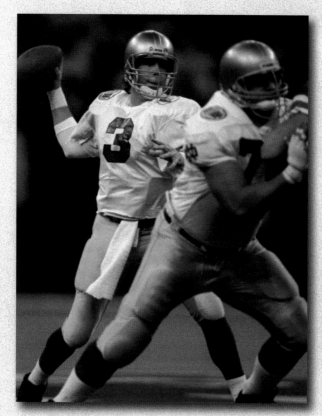

Notre Dame was led by quarterback Rick Mirer (3).

That's when Holtz gave his halftime ultimatum.

Notre Dame, whose offensive line outweighed the Gator defensive front 35 pounds a man, showed brute strength on its first second-half possession. The Irish drove 64 yards on 11 plays – without throwing one pass. Kevin Pendergast kicked a 23-yard field goal to draw Notre Dame to within six at 16-10. The Irish went ahead for the first time when Mirer rolled out and passed four yards to tight end Irv Smith. Pendergast's PAT made it 17-16, Notre Dame.

Twice more Florida swept down the field. Twice more Czyzewski kicked field goals – 37 and 24 yards (the first after a 10-play, 50-yard sortie, the second after a fumble recovery at the Notre Dame 12) – to give Florida a 22-17 lead with 11:21 remaining.

Twice more that Holtz-drawn defense had bent but hadn't broken.

Then Bettis and the Irish front line truly came to the fore.

Notre Dame finished with 279 yards for the night, of which 141 came in the fourth quarter. The Gators gained an eye-popping 511 total yards. Still, the major Florida shortcoming was obviously the inability to punch in touchdowns when the Gators got close to the end zone. In the highest scoring Sugar Bowl up to that time, the Gators had the ball inside the Notre Dame 20-yard line seven times and could come away with only two touchdowns and a record five field goals by Czyzewski.

"We had plenty of time to throw," said center Cal Dixon. "We held them out for five or six seconds – they were only rushing four guys. It's frustrating. Not getting touchdowns when you have as many chances as we did will usually come back to haunt you."

Bettis, who led all runners with 150 yards, a 9.4-yards per carry average, had one main comment for everyone within earshot in the locker room: "I never did like Cheerios."

All week long a "Cheerios" riddle, attributed to a waiter, had been in vogue – "What's the difference between Notre Dame's

Tailback Rodney Culver (5) tries to break outside on the Florida defense.

Jerome Bettis rushed for 150 yards on his way to being named MVP.

football team and Cheerios?" Answer: "Cheerios belong in a bowl."

It was Notre Dame, Holtz, and the Sugar Bowl who got the last laughs.

The game's overnight television ratings reached 11.4, a 19-percent share in the nation's 25 largest cities, a share two points higher than the Orange Bowl game between Penn State and Texas and the Sugar's best TV showing in six years. Yes, the Notre Dame selection had paid off handsomely.

It was only the Cheerios jokester who didn't see a payoff. Holtz admitted his team was not just the butt of the puzzle, but that he slipped in a verbal counter-jab for the waiter who made the crack. The coach said he responded by with a question of his own: "Do you know the difference between a golf pro and Lou Holtz?"

Answer: "Lou Holtz doesn't give tips.

	1	2	3	4	
Notre Dame	0	7	10	22	39
Florida	10	6	0	12	28

Florida: Jackson, 15-yard pass from Matthews. PAT, Czyzewski kick.
Florida: Czyzewski, 26-yard field goal.
Florida: Czyzewski, 24-yard field goal.
Notre Dame: Dawson, 40-yard pass from Mirer. PAT, Hentrich kick.
Florida: Czyzewski, 36-yard field goal.
Notre Dame: Pendergast, 23-yard field goal.
Notre Dame: Smith, 4-yard pass from Mirer. PAT, Hentrich kick.
Florida: Czyzewski, 37-yard field goal.
Florida: Czyzewski, 24-yard field goal.
Notre Dame: Bettis, 3-yard run. PAT, Brooks, pass from Mirer.
Notre Dame: Bettis, 49-yard run. PAT, Pendergast kick.
Florida: Houston, 36-yard pass from Matthews. Pass failed.
Notre Dame: Bettis, 39-yard run. PAT, Pendergast kick.

Individual Leaders

Rushing
Notre Dame: Bettis 16-150, 3 TDs; Culver 13-93; Brooks 13-68.
Florida: Rhett 15-63; McClendon 7-34.

Passing
Notre Dame: Mirer 14-19-1, 154 yards, 2 TDs.
Florida: Matthews 28-58-2, 370 yards, 2 TDs.

Receiving
Notre Dame: Smith 7-75; Dawson 2-49, 1 TD.
Florida: Jackson 8-148, 1 TD; Houston 3-52, 1 TD; Sullivan 4-47.

Notre Dame		Florida
23	First Downs	29
279	Rushing Yards	141
14-19-1	Passing	28-58-2
154	Passing Yards	370
433	Total Yards	511
2-34.0	Punts	2-52.5
4-3	Fumbles – Lost	0-0
3-15	Penalties – Yards	4-40

Attendance: 76,447.
Teams' remuneration: $7,400,000.
Miller-Digby Award recipient: Jerome Bettis, Notre Dame fullback.

Alabama 34 Miami 13

"They laughed at us."

Nobody saw this coming.

On the other hand, maybe we should have.

It was eerie to think Alabama was back in the hunt for a No. 1 pennant, 10 years after the passing of Bear Bryant, a period in which the fortunes of the Crimson Tide ebbed and flowed, just like any other program.

But, it seemed fitting, especially since this was Alabama's football centennial season. After going through a couple of other coaches, who did fair jobs by most measurements, at the 'Bama helm was Gene "Bebe" Stallings, who played for Bryant at Texas A&M, in fact was one of the famed "Junction Boys," and coached under Bear. When he went on his own, Stallings became the first of Bryant's disciples to become a head coach and beat the Master when the Aggies whipped the Tide in the 1968 Cotton Bowl. He also had a deep, resonant voice like Bryant.

Stallings had a losing record as coach at A&M and in the NFL, but once he returned to Tuscaloosa to replace Bill Curry, he seemed to have found a magic touch. In fact, Stallings took some of Curry's outstanding recruits, infused the Tide with some of his own, and within three years was fielding a team that strongly resembled some of Bryant's. The Tide featured a solid running game and a suffocating defense.

And, because of that ball-control offense, was underrated. Seriously so.

This was also a juncture in the evolution of the national championship system, the first year of the Bowl Coalition, and the agreement between most conferences and the major bowls to try to pair the best two teams for the title despite the league tieups of their champions to play in specific postseason games.

It wasn't perfect, but it was a step in clearly deciding college football's No. 1 football team.

Things, however, were going to be tougher for any SEC team to make the title game. The league divided into two divisions that year with the top team from each meeting in a championship game – a high hurdle none of Bryant's squads ever had to overcome.

And, that season, waiting after the SEC championship game

State, Penn State and Syracuse), had the look of a Team of Destiny, one which featured a sophisticated passing attack with quarterback Gino Torretta, the Heisman Trophy recipient.

An exclamation point to the Hurricanes' ranking was a 29-game victory streak, longest in the nation.

The Miami offense faces off against a formidable Alabama defense.

would be No. 1-ranked and defending national champion Miami, who spanked the Crimson Tide for the national championship in the Sugar Bowl 33-25 just three years before.

Miami, after coming through in the late going in four impressive victories against quality opponents (Arizona, Florida

Conversely, Bama was almost an afterthought in the polls. The Tide was not picked as a national contender before the season, and deep into its schedule was not receiving any first-place votes. Bama, while winning and leading the nation in four defensive categories, was unimpressive to voters until things started jelling in November.

Miami quarterback Gino Torretta (13) takes a hard hit from Alabama strong safety Eric Turner (39).

Miami quarterback Gino Torretta (13) scrambles for the loose ball.

In it's 10th game, Alabama blew a 17-point lead to fall behind Mississippi State 21-20 in the fourth quarter. Quarterback Jay Barker guided the Crimson Tide to 10 late points and a 30-21 victory; In the regular-season finale, it took the 61-yard return of a third quarter interception for a touchdown by cornerback Antonio Langham to break open a scoreless defensive struggle against Auburn, 17-0; Against Florida in the inaugural SEC Championship Game, Langham again picked off a fourth-quarter pass and returned it 27 yards for the deciding points in a 28-21 victory.

This Alabama team may not have been all that impressive to the uneducated eye, but the Tide was coming together. Now they were No. 2, and headed to New Orleans with a 22-game victory streak – which failed to impress the Hurricanes, who made it a point to taunt and laugh at Bama with the message that Miami was too good to lose to "a one-dimensional team."

Yet it was the dimensions of the Hurricanes that gave heart to the Tide coaching staff, which put in a new scheme for the Sugar Bowl. Convinced that Miami could not run on his team, Bama coach Gene Stallings decided to gamble, installing a scheme that sometimes used as many as seven defensive backs and, at other times, put all 11 defenders on the line.

Miami's confidence – or overconfidence – became a real weapon for the Crimson Tide.

"In all my years, I've never heard such stuff," Alabama defensive coordinator Bill Oliver said of the 'Cane's notorious 'trash talk.' Oliver said with a post-game snort, "They laughed at us when we were warming up. Imagine that!"

"I expected it to be a whole lot tougher."

The Hurricanes never knew what hit them.

"The whole second half is a blur," Gino Torretta, who entered the game with a 26-1 record as a starter, said afterward.

The plan was simple. Alabama suspected it could run on Miami, while believing the 'Canes could not against the Tide. The key was foiling the Miami passing game.

The handwriting was on the wall in the opening 30 minutes, a span in which the Tide outrushed the Hurricanes 152-6. Bama, an eight-and-a-half point underdog, took a 13-6 lead before turning the lights out on Miami.

Then the Tide hit the Hurricanes with a roundhouse blow by scoring two more touchdowns in the span of 16 seconds.

The first of two consecutive interceptions of Torretta, by cornerback Tommy Johnson at the Miami 44, was returned to the 20, leading to Derrick Lassic's 1-yard touchdown run.

The second pickoff of Torretta, on the first play of Miami's next possession, was a quick pass pilfered by George Teague, who stepped in front of receiver Jonathan Harris at the 31, took off down the right sideline and high-stepped into the end zone.

That play, for all practical purposes, ended matters.

George Teague returns an interception for a touchdown as Alabama scores twice in less than thirty seconds.

Gene Stallings gets a victory ride after winning the National Championship and 1993 Sugar Bowl.

The resultant 27-6 lead was the biggest Miami deficit since the Hurricanes lost to Tennessee 35-7 in the 1986 Sugar Bowl.

Stallings' conviction that the Tide could run on the 'Canes was vindicated. Bama rolled up 267 yards on the ground. The flip side also showed the acumen of the Alabama staff. Miami runners gained a paltry 48 rushing yards – 42 coming on an inconsequential drive after Alabama had already started its celebration.

Kevin Williams provided Miami's most potent weapon, returning a punt 78 yards with 12:08 to play. But Miami never really threatened to get back in the game.

Miami did garner 278 passing yards, as Torretta was 24-of-56, but most of that yardage came after the Crimson Tide had the victory salted away. Besides, the three interceptions thrown by Torretta more than offset that statistic. He had thrown just seven in the entire regular season.

"I think we confused him a lot," Tide defensive back Sam Shade said. "There were times he thought we were in man (defense) and we were really in zone. I don't think they expected us to use seven defensive backs. But they don't have a very good running game, and we were able to do that."

This is how dominating the Alabama defense was: it almost

*Miami wide receiver Lamar Thomas (36) covers his face
as the Tide rolled over the Hurricanes.*

	1	2	3	4	
Alabama	3	10	14	7	34
Miami	3	3	0	7	13

Alabama: Proctor, 19-yard field goal.
Miami: Prewitt, 49-yard field goal.
Alabama: Proctor, 23-yard field goal.
Alabama: Williams, 2-yard run. PAT, Proctor kick.
Miami: Prewitt, 42-yard field goal.
Alabama: Lassic, 1-yard run. PAT, Proctor kick.
Alabama: Teague, 31-yard interception return. PAT, Proctor kick.
Miami: Williams, 78-yard punt return. PAT, Prewitt kick.
Alabama: Lassic, 4-yard run. PAT, Proctor kick.

Individual Leaders

Rushing
Alabama: Lassic 28-135, 2 TDs; Lynch 5-39; Williams 7-23, 1 TD.
Miami: Jones 5-28; Bennett 3-26.

Passing
Alabama: Barker 4-13-2, 18 yards.
Miami: Torretta 24-56-3, 278 yards.

Receiving
Alabama: Wimbley 2-11.
Miami: Jones 3-64; Thomas 6-52; Williams 3-49.

Alabama		Miami
15	First Downs	16
267	Rushing Yards	48
4-13-2	Passing	24-56-3
18	Passing Yards	278
285	Total Yards	326
6-44.5	Punts	5-41.6
0-0	Fumbles – Lost	4-1
7-46	Penalties – Yards	6-37

Attendance: 76,789.
Teams' remuneration: $8,300,000.
Miller-Digby Award recipient: Derrick Lassic, Alabama halfback.

didn't need anything more than a straightaway running offense. Consider that Jay Barker, who quarterbacked Bama to its 18th victory in his 18 starts, completed only four passes in 13 attempts – for a total of 18 yards.

Though the score would never reflect an upset, Miami was the biggest favorite ever to lose a Sugar Bowl game – a dubious distinction previous held by the 1985 Hurricanes, eight-point favorites when they lost 35-7 to Tennessee.

Cornerback Antonio Langham put Alabama's national championship victory into perspective: "I was shocked," Langham said. "I expected it to be a whole lot tougher. But we rattled them before they could think clearly.

Florida 41 West Virginia 7

"We've got some firsts."

Surprising, and luckily for a new hierarchy, the Sugar Bowl found itself in a no-lose situation as pairings began to take shape for the postseason.

There was a change in leadership as Mickey Holmes stepped down as executive director of the Sugar Bowl, and his recommendation for the job was his protégé, 29-year-old Troy Mathieu. Perhaps as an indication of how much times had changed, not much was made of the fact that Mathieu was African-American. Still, it was noteworthy that after all the trials and tribulations of the segregation years of the late '50s and early '60s, the Sugar Bowl was now operated by a black man.

Though on the surface things did not look promising for Mathieu's first game at the helm, given that the Sugar Bowl was slated to pick after both the Orange Bowl and Cotton Bowl. Yet the Sugar wound up with attractive options.

All the sporting world knew the Orange would chose to pair Nebraska against Florida State, the No. 1 and No. 2-ranked teams in the final Bowl Coalition poll. After that, though,

things got interesting. Available to face the Cotton Bowl's host team, SWC champion Texas A&M, were No. 3 West Virginia, the undefeated champion of the Big East, and No. 4 Notre Dame, owner of a 10-1 record that included a regular-season victory over Florida State. Whichever team the Cotton by-passed would then end up in the Sugar Bowl.

And that's exactly what happened ... almost. The Cotton Bowl tabbed West Virginia, but the Mountaineers elected to exercise an option in the Bowl Coalition contract allowing a school to pass on a bowl invitation for "financial reasons." Subsequently, Notre Dame found itself with an invite to Dallas.

There were several reasons for West Virginia's "Thanks, but no thanks" response to the Cotton. At least a million of those were the Sugar's higher payout, more than $4 million, but the Mountaineers insisted there were other important issues to consider.

WVU coach Don Nehlen explained he considered the Sugar Bowl one of the premier football classics and that he and his 11-0-0 team would be honored to participate in it.

He didn't say this, but even though Florida State and Nebraska would be playing for the national championship in the Orange Bowl, Nehlen also must have thought he could plant a seed of doubt with a West Virginia victory over Florida (10-2) rather than one over out-of-the-running Texas A&M in Dallas.

"We feel strongly (that) playing a team the caliber of Florida, if ... *if* we won that game, we'd be a 12-0 football team and we'd deserve a part of that national championship," Nehlen said.

"We all know that Florida State is a great, great football team. But, on the other hand, they stubbed their toe (31-24 at Notre Dame), and Nebraska didn't stub their toe. And neither did we."

Jay Kearney gives the Mountaineers a lift with his touchdown grab from Jake Kelchner.

West Virginia had, of course, an outstanding record, but its real strength was questionable – just, ironically, as the Mountaineers of 40 years before who also played in the Sugar Bowl. *New Orleans Item* sports editor Hap Glaudi dubbed the '54 match with Georgia Tech the "Lemon Bowl" and ridiculed the selection. On that day, Georgia Tech drubbed West Virginia 42-19 in a game that was never close.

Gators coach Steve Spurrier's New Year's night goals were less ambitious than Nehlen's. There was no possible national championship awaiting Florida. "We've got the opportunity to win 11 games for the first time in the history of our school, and we've never won in the Sugar Bowl (0-3), so we've got some firsts out there that we can try to accomplish without worrying about what's happening in the Orange Bowl."

"It felt real sweet."

Florida running back Errict Rhett (33) strecbes for one of his two 3rd quarter touchdowns.

Gator defensive back Lawrence Wright, before the end of the first half, ran himself into every highlight film the Sugar Bowl will ever again produce – straight into the West Virginia end zone and into Florida football lore.

Wright tip-toed his way through the Mountaineers, not once but twice, in perhaps the most exciting dash in the six-decades-old annals of the Sugar Bowl, slipping and sliding maybe 120 yards from sideline to sideline on his way to the

end zone with an interception – and the touchdown that put Florida ahead for the first time, 14-7.

The play was born with West Virginia playing a first-and-10 at its 30-yard line and quarterback Darren Studstill scrambling out of the pocket. Rover Monty Grow fired in on a blitz, zeroed in on Studstill and caught him chest-high just as the ball was being released. Studstill's head shot backward as his mouthpiece flew off to the side.

Mountaineer quaterback Jake Kelchner scrambles as Florida's Mark Campbell gives chance.

"The shot was definitely one of my best this season," Grow, a 6-foot-3, 222-pound senior, said in explaining how it lifted Florida from early lethargy. "It was a good solid shot, and it felt real sweet. After that hit everybody was smacking each other around before the next play, saying, 'C'mon, let's play ball!' "

Wright said simply, "Monty's hit got Studstill rattled. Once you take a big hit like that, you don't focus in on the game the same way you normally would."

The route Wright took to Sugar Bowl fame is a story unto itself. Out of high school he had signed not with the Gators

Grow's shot turned Studstill's pass into a wounded duck that fluttered into the open arms of Wright, who made the Mountaineers dizzy with his broken-field virtuosity that was right out of a game of "touch" and which officially ended 52 yards from the point of the interception.

"That was a key play," Gator coach Steve Spurrier understated.

Indeed. The game was never really close again.

but with the Miami Hurricanes, which was no surprise seeing as how he was a blue-chipper out of North Miami High School. But as fate would have it, he didn't have the necessary grades and wound up at a prep school, Valley Forge Military Academy in Fort Wayne, Pa.

Jerome Evans (34) rushes for 7 yards late in the 4th quarter.

When Wright lifted his grades and was ready to re-enter college, his young life took a sudden twist. Because his high school dream was to build a recreation facility in his depressed neighborhood, he decided on the University of Florida, not Miami, when he discovered Florida's School of Building Construction ranked No. 1 in the U.S.

Wright went quickly from being academically suspect to a spot on the SEC's All-Academic Team, thanks to a 3.2 GPA.

As Paul Harvey would say, now you know the rest of the story of how Lawrence Wright galloped into the Florida Hall of Fame.

It was the second time West Virginia was victimized by the blitz in the first half – one by the Mountaineers themselves – after motoring for an easy first-quarter touchdown. Florida countered with a tying scoring drive in the second period before the pyrotechnics began.

Behind by the margin of Wright's touchdown with less than a minute to play in the half, Mountaineer linebacker Wes

Robinson came in on a blitz as Gator quarterback Terry Dean got off a sideline pass to wide receiver Willie Jackson. Jackson had to slow down for the under-thrown ball, and as he jumped for it, West Virginia cornerback Mike Logan slipped. Jackson made the catch near the 20-yard line, then casually trotted into the end zone to complete a 39-yard scoring play with 51 seconds to go until intermission. Florida led 21-7 at the break.

If West Virginia had any serious notions of coming back, they were dispelled in the third quarter when Florida scored twice in the first six minutes to push the lead to 35-7, including a 1-yard run by Errict Rhett, his third touchdown of the game, with 8:58 to go in the third quarter.

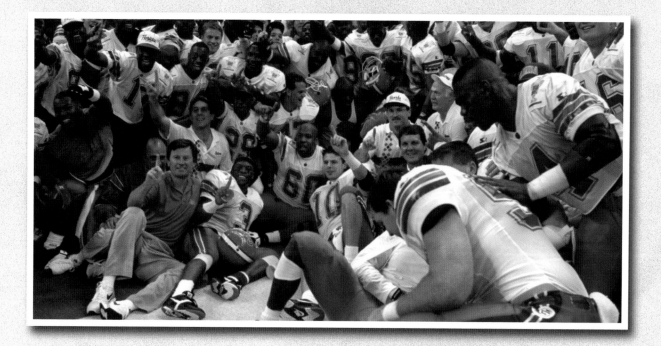

	1	2	3	4	
Florida	7	14	14	6	41
West Virginia	7	0	0	0	7

West Virginia: Kearney, 32-yard pass from Kelchner. PAT, Mazzone kick.
Florida: Rhett, 3-yard run. PAT, Davis kick.
Florida: Wright, 52-yard interception return. PAT, Davis kick.
Florida: Jackson, 39-yard pass from Dean. PAT, Davis kick.
Florida: Rhett, 2-yard run. PAT, Davis kick.
Florida: Rhett, 1-yard run. PAT, Davis kick.
Florida: Davis, 43-yard field goal.
Florida: Davis, 26-yard field goal.

Individual Leaders

Rushing
Florida: Rhett 25-105, 3 TDs; Foy 10-53.
West Virginia: Walker 13-59; Woodard 2-18.

Passing
Florida: Dean 22-37-1, 244 yards, 1 TD.
West Virginia: Kelchner 13-27-0, 123 yards, 1 TD.

Receiving
Florida: W. Jackson 9-131; J. Jackson 3-32.
West Virginia: Kearney 4-59, 1 TD; Baker 4-46.

"We felt like we were still in it at the half," said West Virginia wide receiver Jay Kearney. "When they scored those two quick touchdowns, that was it. There really wasn't any way we were coming back from that." Spurrier agreed. "After we scored on those first two (second-half) possessions," he analyzed, "we were pretty much in control."

There is one very important coda to this game: Wright eventually became one of the University of Florida's most renowned building construction graduates. And he did build the recreational facility for the kids in his old neighborhood.

Florida		West Virginia
30	First Downs	16
201	Rushing Yards	122
24-39-1	Passing	16-40-1
280	Passing Yards	143
481	Total Yards	265
3-52.7	Punts	8-42.0
2-1	Fumbles – Lost	2-1
5-43	Penalties – Yards	8-71

Attendance: 75,437.
Teams' remuneration: $8,387,000.
Miller-Digby Award recipient: Errict Rhett, Florida tailback.

West Virginia players look on in disgust as Florida scored 34 unanswered points.

Florida State 23 Florida 17

"And we got it."

The famed Al Michaels query – "Do you believe in miracles? ... YES!" – echoed across time, space and sports.

If there was ever any doubt that miracles do indeed happen, even in sports, it was dispelled in the collective mind of the Sugar Bowl of 1995, a decade and a half after the noted sportscaster made it famous at an Olympic hockey match.

The Sugar Bowl was in a vise. It was no joke, and there was no minimizing it. The way College Football '95 shook out, the Sugar was in a quandary. Florida and Alabama were Top 10 SEC teams, but there were very few viable opponents to pair either up with in the postseason. Nebraska and Penn State, the nation's top two teams, were ticketed by conference affiliation to the Orange and Rose bowls, respectively; Miami, as usual, wanted to stay home to play the Huskers; the Sugar couldn't take Colorado, the second place Big Eight team, and then have to go against the Orange and Big Eight champion Cornhuskers at the same time on TV.

Florida State was there, but the Seminoles had a date with their archrival Gators on Nov. 26. An FSU pairing with undefeated Alabama would be dynamite, but if Florida beat 'Bama for the SEC championship, the Sugar Bowl would then have to talk reluctant participants into a second "Braggin' Rights" game. All parties have to agree on any bowl pairing of teams that have met during the regular season, and that wasn't likely with such fierce football antagonists.

Still, the Sugar Bowl took measure of the remote possibility – and both the Gators and Seminoles discouraged the notion. Executive Director Troy Mathieu, however, recalled later, "Both said they would consider it (but) only under a few sets of circumstances."

A tie in their regular-season game was one of those circumstances. Other than that unlikely scenario it strongly appeared the winner of the Southern Cal-Notre Dame game would be the choice of ABC, which televised the Sugar Bowl. Each of those teams would give the Sugar a visitor with more than three defeats. Notre Dame finished 6-4-1 and USC was 7-3-1 after the regular season.

1970 Sugar Bowl MVP, Archie Manning, shakes hands with FSU team captains before the coin toss.

The Sugar Bowl was praying. Hard.

Miracles do happen.

When they played in Tallahassee, the fourth-ranked Gators ran roughshod over the seventh-ranked Seminoles for almost 49 minutes, holding a gargantuan 31-3 lead. Then, with 11 minutes to play, FSU quarterback Danny Kanell dropped into a shotgun, not even trying to fool anyone about his intent to pass, and marshaled his forces. Kanell rocketed the Seminoles to blurring drives 84, 60, 73 and 60 yards. With 1:45 remaining, after Rock Preston scored from the 4-yard line, the

Seminoles were in a flabbergasting 31-31 deadlock.

Florida State actually had a chance to win it, but Coach Bobby Bowden changed his mind and sent in kicker Dan Mowrey rather than go for two and chance losing the most stunning comeback in FSU annals.

"I didn't want to lose the game," Bowden mused. "I simply didn't want to lose it. From 31-3 with what was it? Eleven minutes left. Uh-uh, didn't want to lose that one."

Had Bowden gone for the two-point conversion and made it,

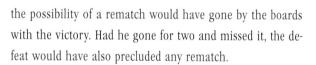

Danny Wuerffel (7) set the record for most passing yards with 394 in a losing effort to the Seminoles.

the possibility of a rematch would have gone by the boards with the victory. Had he gone for two and missed it, the defeat would have also precluded any rematch.

To make the events of the day even more miraculous, that night Notre Dame and USC also played to a tie, eliminating both from Sugar consideration.

"We knew we needed a miracle – and we got it," Sugar Bowl president Chuck Zatarain gushed after announcing the Seminoles (9-1-1) had agreed to play the SEC champion – even the Gators again, should they defeat unbeaten Alabama in

the SEC title game, which Florida (10-1-1) did, 24-23.

It was an important game because the 1995 classic was the last to be played with the old automatic tie-up between the SEC and the Sugar Bowl because of a new bowl configuration, one in which the Sugar, Fiesta and Orange would rotate national championship games.

But the tie-up would go out with a bang, in no small measure because of events with all the earmarks of divine intervention.

"You've got to trade punches with them."

The trouble with highly anticipated rematches, it was pointed out – and this one was billed as Overtime II – is that you never really know what you're getting.

Would it sizzle like the first game, or fizzle like so many sequels?

Until an hour before kickoff, the Superdome scoreboards read: Florida 31, Florida State 31 going into the fifth period. The Sunshine State foes immediately picked up where they left off.

This game would sizzle.

The 'Noles and Gators engaged in a high-powered, volatile blood-match that erased seven Sugar Bowl records that had weathered the test of time for upwards of 40 years – though two of the new records lasted less than nine minutes before they were broken again.

Warrick Dunn, the Louisiana product who was FSU's work-horse, threw a halfback pass that became the longest com-

Florida State kicker Dan Mowrey (9) converts one of three field goals.

pletion and longest scoring pass – 73 yards to O'mar Ellison – in Sugar Bowl annals. Eight minutes of the second quarter later, Gator quarterback Danny Wuerffel hooked up with another native Louisianian, Ike Hilliard, for an 82-yard strike.

There was razzle-dazzle on both sides because the head coaches, Bobby Bowden and Steve Spurrier, each believed victory was attainable only by pulling out all the stops.

"We're just going to get there and let that thing rip," Bowden said just before kickoff regarding an opponent he was well aware had averaged 43.4 points. "I don't think anybody can beat them in a ball-control game. You've got to trade punches with them."

The teams traded haymakers all night long.

Spurrier threw everything he had at FSU, including the kitchen sink – in the form of the Emory & Henry formation, which involves three-player triangles at both ends of the line. One player is a tackle, separated from his interior brethren, and is named for a college in Virginia that used it in the 1950s. A lateral, then a forward pass is the upshot.

But after the Gators lost 10 yards on their second play of the game in that exotic alignment, Spurrier junked it for a four-receiver set. Florida threw on four of its first five plays, and Florida State opened in the shotgun that was so successful during the fourth quarter of the earlier meeting.

With the score 3-3, the Seminoles forced a Fred Taylor fumble, which proved pivotal.

After the recovery at the FSU 36, Dunn – whose last visit to the Superdome had been two years before when his Catholic High of

Danny Kanell led the Seminole offense to victory over the Gators.

The Florida State players pour onto the field after defeating the Gators.

Baton Rouge team was humiliated by Ruston High, 52-10, in the Louisiana Class 5A state championship game – brought practically every one of the 76,224 fannies in the building out of their seats by taking a lateral from Danny Kanell. Dunn, a prep quarterback, had never thrown a collegiate pass. But he pulled up and lofted the ball to Ellison, who made a spectacular reception in double coverage – making the catch off the helmet of Gator safety Michael Gilmore – and sprinted into the end zone.

"You're one-for-one now," Bowden said to his game-breaking

back. "That's good enough," said Dunn, who added he was perfectly content with his regular duties. "Believe me," Dunn, who finished with 182 all-purpose yards, said. "I'm happy with just playing running back right now. That stuff (passing) was in high school."

Next possession, the Seminoles came right back for another touchdown, and a 17-3 lead, on a 16-yard scoring pass from Kanell to Kez McCorvey. It was the greatest deficit Florida had faced all season.

But the Gators pulled themselves back into contention in the third quarter when Wuerffel connected on the 82-yard TD pass to Hilliard, who bounced off Sean Hamlet, shook off Brooks, then outran the rest of the Seminoles to the goal line.

FSU, though, would have to weather a late storm by the Gators. Wuerffel took Florida on a 17-play, 80-yard drive that ate up four minutes and 50 seconds of the fourth quarter that Florida could hardly afford – and closed the scoring oddly. Wuerffel, on a third-and-goal from inches away, stuck his arm out and appeared to break the plane of the goal line with the ball. As he held the ball out, it was knocked loose. Corey Fuller recovered for the 'Noles and sprinted to midfield. He then spiked the ball in frustration when officials ruled Wuerffel's maneuver a touchdown. Florida State was penalized 15 yards on the kickoff, but recovered an on-sides kick to preserve the satisfying victory.

"I do not want to play them twice ever again unless I'm coaching at Mississippi State or someplace," Bowden said of the rematch (though he would play Florida again two years later in a rematch, and also Miami in the 2004 Orange Bowl). "It's no fun to coach against your in-state rivals ... well, it hasn't been for six days here. It's pretty good now."

	1	2	3	4	
Florida State	3	17	3	0	23
Florida	3	7	0	7	17

Florida State: Mowrey, 21-yard field goal.
Florida: Davis, 22-yard field goal.
Florida State: Ellison, 73-yard pass from Dunn. PAT, Mowrey kick.
Florida State: McCorvey, 16-yard pass from Kanell. PAT, Mowrey kick.
Florida: Hilliard, 82-yard pass from Wuerrfel. PAT, Davis kick.
Florida State: Mowrey, 24-yard field goal.
Florida State: Mowrey, 45-yard field goal.
Florida: Wuerrfel, 1-yard run. PAT, Davis kick.

Individual Leaders

Rushing
Florida State: Dunn 14-58; Crockett 5-19.
Florida: Williams 10-27; Taylor 8-18.

Passing
Florida State: Kenell 23-40-0, 252 yards, 1 TD.
Florida: Wuerffel 28-39-1, 394 yards, 1 TD.

Receiving
Florida State: Ellison 4-102, 1 TD; McCorvey 4-84, 1 TD.
Florida: Jackson 6-128; Hilliard 3-119, 1 TD.

Florida State		Florida
21	First Downs	23
76	Rushing Yards	5
24-41-0	Passing	30-43-1
325	Passing Yards	449
401	Total Yards	454
4-39.0	Punts	3-45.7
0-0	Fumbles – Lost	2-2
7-62	Penalties – Yards	8-57

Attendance: 76,224.
Teams' remuneration: $8,900,000.
Miller-Digby Award recipient: Warrick Dunn, Florida State tailback.

Virginia Tech 28 Texas 10

"Who was that man?"

Joel Ron McKelvey was one of the three biggest stories leading up to the 62nd Sugar Bowl.

If you can't place him, don't worry. Nobody else could either.

But first, there was an another interesting change in the leadership of the Sugar Bowl. Dr. Leonard Burns became the first African-American to serve as the Sugar Bowl's president, putting persons of color in both the executive directorship with Troy Mathieu and the presidency. Coincidently, this landmark moment came the same year women were also brought into the organization.

There was a change in Sugar Bowl sponsorship, too. The game was now affiliated with Nokia Communications.

There was a change in the configurations for the postseason, as well, as the second step in the formula to pair the best two teams was implemented. The Bowl Alliance went into effect, encompassing the SEC, Big 12, ACC and Big East along with provisions for Notre Dame. For the first time the "host" teams in the Sugar, Fiesta, and Orange bowls would leave their traditional homes to play in a No. 1 game.

That's what happened to the Sugar as SEC champion Florida, ranked No. 2, went to the Fiesta to meet No. 1 Nebraska.

The system still wasn't perfect because the Big Ten and Pac-10 still weren't part of it, making a true title somewhat iffy. Things worked out this particular season, however, with Nebraska blitzing the Gators, 62-24.

Meanwhile, back in New Orleans, chuckles were produced as Texas and Virginia Tech were pitted in the first Sugar Bowl without an SEC presence in 24 years.

It was a worthwhile pairing of conference champions, and Texas was ranked ninth and Virginia Tech 11th.

But it was also a match in which no one could tell the players even with a roster. Really.

Leading up to the Sugar Bowl, McKelvey was listed as a Texas defensive back. Two days before the game, a California newspaper identified McKelvey as Ron Weaver, a 30-year-old man who assumed the name of a person seven years younger to play football for the Longhorns. He had already played six years of college football, ending in 1989. McKelvey/Weaver was a reserve cornerback who played in all 11 Texas games in '95 but was a real factor in none.

An investigation ensued when Texas officials learned of a story in *The Californian*, a newspaper in Salinas, Calif., which McKelvey listed as his hometown. The paper had been doing stories on local athletes playing in college bowl games when it was discovered no one knew of an athlete named Ron McKelvey from Salinas.

According to the paper's account, several people in Salinas identified a photograph of McKelvey as Weaver, including his mother, Sung Weaver.

The Californian reported Weaver played for two seasons at Monterrey Peninsula and two years at Sacramento State. In 1992 Weaver told his parents he was enrolling in graduate school.

Jim Druckenmiller looks for an open receiver.

Instead, he assumed an alias and went to L.A. Pierce Junior College. After two standout seasons, Weaver was signed by Texas.

Upon learning of McKelvey's ruse, the Longhorns were left to explain how they had been fooled. Coach John Mackovic said the school doesn't normally check players' birth certificates for identification, but rather relies on the transcripts from the high schools or junior colleges.

The Salinas newspaper reported Weaver had revealed in an interview that he took on the identity of Joel Ron McKelvey so he could sell his story. "I'm here for no other purpose than what you think," McKelvey was quoted as saying in the paper. "I'm working on a book. In L.A., I have a publisher. It's on the scandals of college football."

But he never explained himself to his Texas teammates, coaches or administration. When they went looking for him, Weaver had already skipped town.

James Brown (5) was sacked five times by the Hokies defense.

Taje Allen (2) and the rest of the Texas defense couldn't stop the Virginia Tech offense.

"We only had two fingers."

Ron Weaver/Joel Ron Weaver was long gone when Texas and Virginia Tech kicked off – and the Longhorns could have used him. Texas needed every available hand, and even a largely inconsequential defensive back just might have slowed the Hokies' Bryan Still.

Still was the fuse to Virginia Tech's greatest football moment up 'till then, with 179 all-purpose yards and two touchdowns.

In comparison, gathering momentum as the game progressed, the Tech defense intercepted Texas quarterback James Brown three times, sacked him five times and limited the 'Horns to a mere 78 yards rushing.

"When you write about Virginia Tech, write about how well they played," Texas offensive tackle John Elmore said in a daze afterward. "We never could plug all the holes against

Dwayne Thomas (42) looks to slip by Chris Carter (16) and the Longhorns.

them. There were three holes and we only had two fingers.''

The Longhorns jumped out to an early 7-0 lead and had an opportunity to give themselves a comfortable cushion, intercepting Tech quarterback Jim Druckenmiller at the Hokies' 31 in the opening moments of the second quarter. But the Tech defense pushed Texas back two yards and the Longhorns settled for a 52-yard field goal by Phil Dawson to make it 10-0 with 13:19 to go to the half.

That, as it turned out, was the high point of Texas' night.

The beginning of the Longhorns' end came a few moments later when they kicked from their 15. Still, who led the Big East in punt returns the season before but whose return duties in '95 were curtailed by his value to the offensive unit, took the kick at his 40, sprinted through a crease in the middle and broke to the right sideline, running untouched into the end zone.

"The punt return in the first half was a big play that gave them a shot of confidence," Texas coach John Mackovic said. "We had control of the game at 10-0. That gave them a lift."

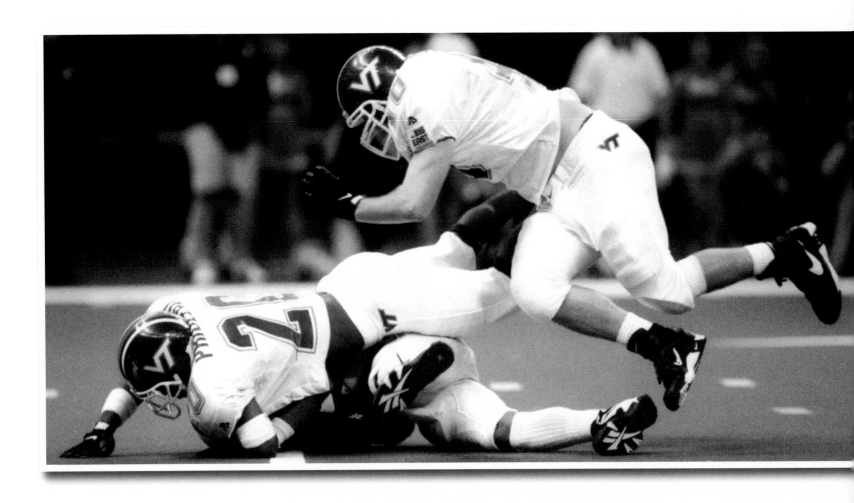

Bryan Still returns a punt to get the Hokies on the board.

Actually, history seemed to still favor the Longhorns when the teams broke at intermission with Texas ahead 10-7. Texas was 21-0-1 when leading at the half since Mackovic's arrival in 1992.

But Still, on offense, and the Tech defense took complete control from that point. First, Still made a 27-yard catch to reach the Texas 2, from which point fullback Marcus Parker scored to put the Hokies ahead 14-10 in the third quarter. Then he raced beyond the Longhorn secondary and hooked up on a 54-yard scoring rainbow to make it 21-10 in the fourth period.

"Bryan ran right by all the defensive backs, and I just lofted it right up there for him," Druckenmiller said.

That was more than enough for the Hokies' dominating defense. Gradually, and with emphasis, Tech's defense began turning the screws. With well-timed blitzes and with speed up and down the line, the Hokies penned up the reeling Longhorns. On three straight possessions they picked off errant throws by Brown. Finally, with issue settled, Brown was sacked, the ball squirted out, and the Hokies administered the knockout blow with a 20-yard fumble return by tackle Jim Baron to close the scoring with 5:06 to go.

Chris Malone (51) holds the Sugar Bowl Trophy after the Hokies' victory over the Longhorns.

Almost unbelievably, that was the seventh touchdown scored by the Hokies' defense in their last six games.

"All the talk was that we didn't belong here," Still said with satisfaction afterward. "We showed we do belong with the great teams of college football."

Yes, indeed. Not only did Virginia Tech tatter the Texas defense for 371 yards, but ruled supreme defensively. The Longhorns, who averaged 433 yards per game during the regular season, had the ball seven times in the second half. On those possessions, Texas punted three times, threw three interceptions and lost a fumble.

	1	2	3	4	
Virginia Tech	0	7	7	14	28
Texas	7	3	0	0	10

Texas: Fitzgerald, 4-yard pass from Brown. PAT, Dawson kick.

Texas: Dawson, 52-yard field goal.

Virginia Tech: Still, 60-yard punt return. PAT, Larson kick.

Virginia Tech: Parker, 2-yard run. PAT, Larson kick.

Virginia Tech: Still, 54-yard pass from Druckenmiller. PAT, Larson kick.

Virginia Tech: Baron, 20-yard fumble return, PAT, Larson kick.

Individual Leaders

Rushing
Virginia Tech: Thomas 15-62; Oxendine 8-31.
Texas: Williams 12-62; Mitchell 15-59.

Passing
Virginia Tech: Druckenmiller 18-34-1, 266 yards, 1 TD.
Texas: Brown 14-36-3, 148 yards, 1 TD.

Receiving
Virginia Tech: Still 6-119, 1 TD; Jennings 6-77.
Texas: Adams 6-92; Fitzgerald 3-21, 1 TD.

Virginia Tech		Texas
20	First Downs	15
105	Rushing Yards	78
18-24-1	Passing	14-37-4
266	Passing Yards	148
371	Total Yards	226
8-37.0	Punts	9-40.0
5-2	Fumbles – Lost	2-1
11-99	Penalties – Yards	9-91

Attendance: 70,283.
Teams' remuneration: $15,650,000.
Miller-Digby Award recipient: Bryan Still, Virginia Tech flanker.

Florida 52 Florida State 20

"It was an exhilarating moment."

A startling whoop went up behind the party dining at Commander's Palace. In the middle of the world-famous restaurant, Paul Hoolahan and Jon Litner yelled and gave each other high-fives.

The last piece of a four-month-long puzzle had just fallen into place.

Hoolahan, executive director of the Sugar Bowl, and Litner, vice president of ABC programming, headed a group into Commander's on New Year's evening, and caught sight of a diner with a miniature television viewing the last seconds of the Rose Bowl. Peeking over the man's shoulder, the pair saw Ohio State's Joe Germaine throw a five-yard touchdown pass to David Boston to give the Buckeyes a 20-17 lead over undefeated and second-ranked Arizona State – a lead that would stand up for the remaining 19 seconds of play.

"It was an exhilarating moment," Hoolahan, overseeing his first Sugar Bowl, said. "That play put us back in the driver's seat."

It set up a match for all the football marbles – a head-to-head game for the right to plant the No. 1 pennant on the 1996

season – the next night at the Superdome. Florida State, perched atop the polls, and third-ranked Florida were scheduled for a rematch of their regular-season blood-letting – and a rematch of their 1995 rematch in the same setting.

Somebody up there must have been looking out for the Sugar Bowl this time. Divine Providence is the only way to explain the rejuvenation of what could have been a Sugar Bowl disaster.

The Sugar was one of three postseason games in the Bowl Alliance, designed to bring together the best teams, and hopefully a No. 1 vs. No. 2 national title game. In the '96 game there was very little interest in Virginia Tech and Texas. But in '97 the Sugar had the first two picks.

Coach Steve Spurrier's Gators, at their best, clearly were the nation's finest overall team and were ranked

No. 1 most of the season. Ohio State seemed to be a worthy contender to the throne, and was ranked No. 2 most of the season – a regular season finish that would hurt the Sugar Bowl since the Big Ten and Pac-10 were not part of the Alliance and, as Big Ten champions, the Buckeyes were tied to the Rose Bowl, precluding a No. 1 vs. No. 2 game in New Orleans.

On top of that, upstart Arizona State shocked defending national champion Nebraska early in '96, then rolled merrily undefeated through its regular season. Nebraska righted itself after the loss to the Sun Devils and at the end of the season was an impressive football team, as good as the Cornhuskers who manhandled Florida 62-24 the year before in the national championship game at the Fiesta Bowl.

Florida State was unbeaten and untied as the season wound down, so there were plenty of challengers when the banged-up Gators started gimping in the home stretch. The Seminoles drove what seemed to be a stake in Florida's No. 1 aspirations when, on Nov. 30, Warrick Dunn – the Baton Rouge native who was MVP in the 1995 Sugar Bowl – was unleashed for

185 yards, and the FSU defensive front either sacked or threw quarterback Danny Wuerffel for losses 27 times, literally beating the eventual Heisman Trophy recipient to a pulp in a 24-21 Seminole victory.

FSU assumed the top spot, but, if things fell right, it was the Rose Bowl, with undefeated Ohio State and unbeaten Arizona State, that could have college football's showcase game. Nebraska, with that one defeat, appeared a likely opponent for the 'Noles in New Orleans, but the Huskers were a very long shot for No. 1 consideration.

Someone must have heard the Sugar Bowl's prayers. Michigan upset Ohio State 13-9 in the regular-season finale, and Texas

stunned Nebraska 37-27 in the Big 12 championship game.

That scenario eliminated Nebraska from Sugar consideration and put Florida back in the national title picture at No. 3. Despite Seminole coach Bobby Bowden's reluctance, the Sugar exercised its right for the best game possible and invited FSU and the Gators – hoping against hope Ohio State could prevail in the Rose over the No. 2 Sun Devils, which would, in essence, make the Sugar a showdown for the championship.

That's exactly what happened, though the Gators feigned disinterest in what was happening in California. Playing the Seminoles was motivation enough, they tried to make everyone believe. After a workout on New Year's Day, as the Buckeyes

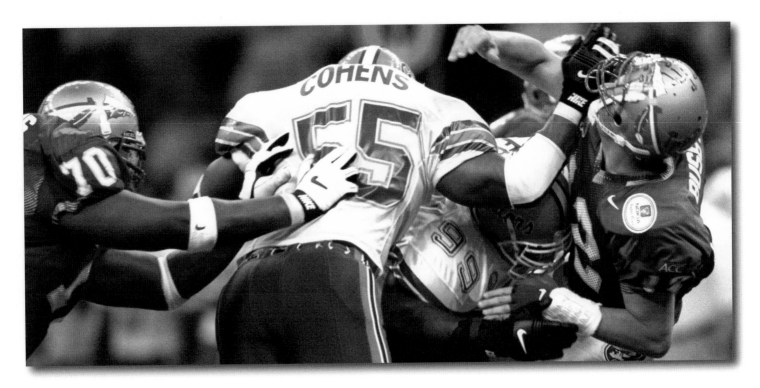

and Sun Devils prepared to kickoff in Pasadena, the Gators boarded buses in New Orleans and traveled to Gonzales, La., 50 miles west, to rest up and get away from the distraction.

But at the end of the Rose Bowl, screaming players and laughing coaches streamed out of their rooms, whooping it up and high-fiving each other in the motel courtyard.

Technically, it wasn't the No. 1 vs. No. 2 game the Bowl Alliance had tried to achieve; but, in effect, it was. The Rose Bowl outcome put Florida and Florida State in a head-to-head battle for the national championship.

At the same instant the Gators were euphorically hugging each other in Gonzales, Hoolahan and Litner, whose network was the Sugar's broadcast partner, were in the midst of their own boisterous moment – though they did their howling in the middle of a staid, normally quiet and reserved Old World restaurant.

"Without them we don't have a chance."

Looking back, you'd have to say Bobby Bowden put the gun to his own head. In a deep irony, it was Florida State which forced Steve Spurrier to do something he said he'd never do: go to a shotgun offense. In the process, Bowden gave Florida a potent weapon for the Sugar Bowl.

It went back to Nov. 30, the day the Seminoles beat the

Gators 24-21 and savaged quarterback Danny Wuerffel, leaving him bruised and battered. Wuerffel was sacked six times and hit behind the line 21 times.

A week later, facing Alabama for the SEC championship, Spurrier made the shotgun a part of his offense, placing his quarterback five yards behind the center to give him an extra

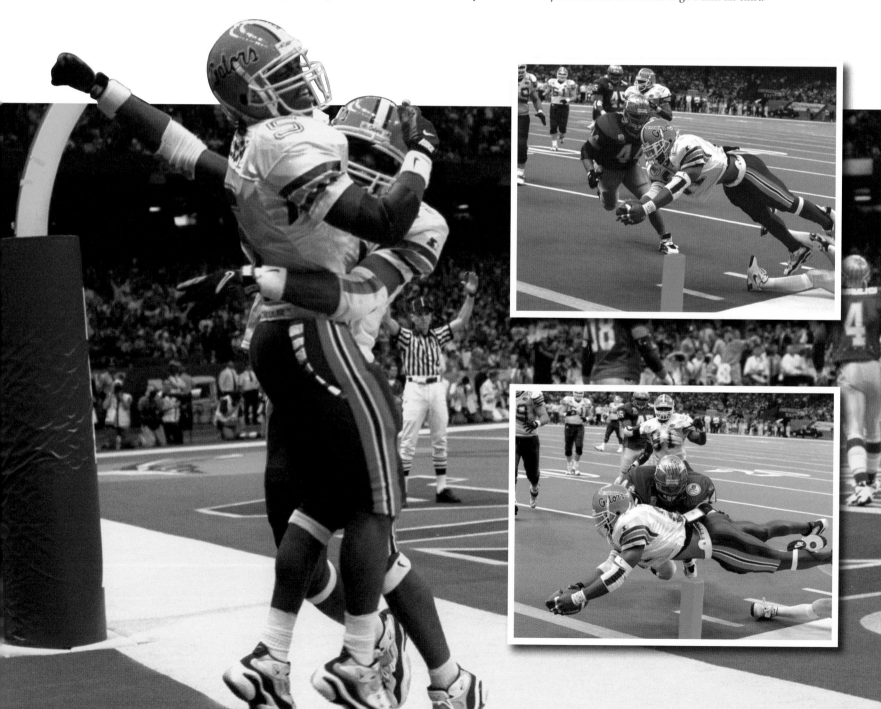

After rushing up the middle against the tough Florida Gator defense, Warrick Dunn (28) lays on the turf after being shaken up during the 52-20 pounding.

split-second to get off his passes to Florida's usually gifted receiving corps – and to try to keep Wuerffel out of the emergency room.

The result: Wuerffel passed for six touchdowns against the Crimson Tide, four of them from the shotgun formation. The stage was set for the Sunshine State rematch – just like the 1995 game - pairing the nation's best offensive team, Florida, against the nation's third-best defense, FSU.

As it turned out, the Seminoles were sliced, diced and left for dead.

The Sugar Bowl began with FSU quarterback Thad Busby completing a 33-yard rainbow to Andre Cooper, and the Seminoles going down to a fourth-and-one at the Gators' 23. Declining the field goal attempt, FSU went for the yard but Reggie Mc-Grew and Mike Peterson stopped Pooh Bear Williams cold.

Wuerffel went to work. Riding shotgun, Wuerffel, keeping his distance from an FSU front that represented a thousand pounds of beef on the hoof, completed five passes for 73 yards, including a nine-yard touchdown to Ike Hilliard, another Louisiana native playing for a Sunshine State program.

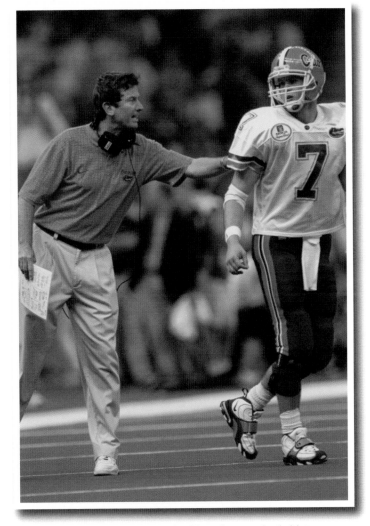

Florida coach Steve Spurrier (1966) and quarterback (7) Danny Wuerffel (1996) both won the Heisman trophy and were named Sugar Bowl MVPs as quarterbacks for the Gators.

That was the start of a volatile first half in which 41 points were scored in a football game that resembled a tennis match for 30 minutes.

When Wuerffel marched the Gators 73 yards in 26 seconds in the second quarter to put Florida in front 17-3, it marked the first time the 'Noles were behind by more than seven points the entire season. FSU closed to 17-10, only to watch the Gators' shotgun go off once more, this time for 65 yards in four plays. Wuerffel and the Gators' wide-receiver wrecking crew had the FSU secondary baffled as they operated in near-perfect sync, running slants and stop-and-go routes.

Still, Busby was having a good night, too, and, with the Gators in front 24-10, FSU answered with a fast-break of its own, traveling 66 yards in 77 seconds, the last 12 yards coming on a gallop by Warrick Dunn, who had been silent in a half dominated by the pass and by his own leg cramps.

Intermission came with Florida ahead 24-17, a score largely based on Wuerffel's 246 yards passing and Busby's 216.

FSU's Scott Bentley kicked a 45-yard field goal for the first points of the second half, but that would be all the Seminoles wrote. Florida took complete command en route to its ultimate 32-point victory – piling up the most points ever scored by a single team in Sugar Bowl history – and the first national championship in Gators history.

Florida's 12-1 record merited it, although there were four other teams in America with just one loss (Ohio State, 11-1; Brigham Young, 14-1; Arizona State, 11-1; and, of course, Florida State, 11-1). But put Florida's accomplishments in perspective: there were four other 1996 SEC teams (Tennessee, Alabama, LSU, and Auburn) that won bowl games, and Florida beat them all by an average of 26 points.

The victory made amends for the blowout defeat to Nebraska the year before in the Fiesta Bowl, after which 'Husker defensive coordinator Charlie McBride gave symposiums on stopping the vaunted Gator offense. Spurrier said wryly: "I don't think anyone's going to give clinics on how to stop Florida this offseason."

For sure, no one was up to stopping Wuerffel all season long, and certainly not in the Sugar Bowl. He was the game's MVP after passing for 306 yards and three touchdowns – all to Hilliard – and running for a fourth.

"Now do you see why we didn't want to play them again," asked a glum Bobby Bowden afterward.

Bobby Bowden exchanges a few words with Steve Spurrier
after the game.

"If Texas hadn't beaten Nebraska, if Ohio State hadn't beaten Arizona State, we wouldn't be here – we ought to send (Ohio State coach John) Cooper and (Texas coach John) Mackovic a ring or something," Spurrier said, "because without them we don't have a chance."

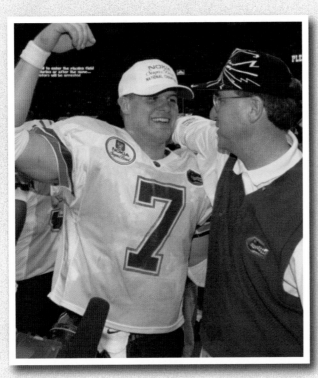

Danny Wuerffel (7) Heisman and Sugar Bowl MVP celebrates
after upsetting the #1 ranked Seminoles 52-20.

	1	2	3	4	
Florida	10	14	14	14	52
Florida State	3	14	3	0	20

Florida: Hilliard, 5-yard pass from Wuerffel. PAT, Edmiston kick.
Florida State: Bentley, 43-yard field goal.
Florida: Edmiston, 32-yard field goal.
Florida: Taylor, 2-yard run. PAT, Edmiston kick.
Florida State: Green, 29-yard pass from Busby. PAT, Bentley kick.
Florida: Hilliard, 31-yard pass from Wuerffel. PAT, Edmiston kick.
Florida State: Dunn, 12-yard run. PAT, Bentley kick.
Florida State: Bentley, 45-yard field goal.
Florida: Hilliard, 8-yard pass from Wuerffel. PAT, Edmiston kick.
Florida: Jackson, 42-yard run. PAT, Edmiston kick.
Florida: Jackson, 1-yard run. PAT, Edmiston kick.

Individual Leaders

Rushing
Florida: Jackson 12-118, 2 TDs; Taylor 18-60, 1 TD.
Florida State: Dunn 9-29, 1 TD.

Passing
Florida: Wuerffel 18-34-1, 306 yards, 3 TDs.
Florida State: Busby 17-41-1, 271 yards, 1 TD.

Receiving
Florida: Hilliard 7-150, 3 TDs; Green 5-79; Anthony 4-50.
Florida State: Green 3-86, 1 TD; Cooper 4-82.

Florida		Florida State
26	First Downs	13
203	Rushing Yards	70
18-34-1	Passing	17-42-2
306	Passing Yards	271
509	Total Yards	341
7-48.1	Punts	8-46.4
1-0	Fumbles – Lost	0-0
15-102	Penalties – Yards	14-115

Attendance: 78,347.
Teams' remuneration: $16,850,000.
Miller-Digby Award recipient: Danny Wuerffel, Florida quarterback.

Florida State 31 Ohio State 14

"They've been good forever."

Peyton Manning, a hometown product, entered the 1997 season as the most renowned quarterback in college football.

His team, the Tennessee Volunteers, was formidable, but was not seen as the SEC champion. Defending champion Florida held that distinction.

That changed as the season went along. The Gators did defeat the Vols, but lost later games to LSU and Georgia. Tennessee overcame its only loss to win the SEC East, then nipped Auburn 30-29 in the SEC championship game.

The problem for the Sugar Bowl was that the Vols inched to No. 3 in the polls. No. 1 Michigan was ticketed for the Rose Bowl, but the Orange Bowl, with its pick in the Alliance, grabbed Tennessee to play No. 2-ranked Nebraska.

The Sugar Bowl also was hoping to land a Big Ten team, three of which were hovering in the Top 10 most of the sea-

son, with Penn State a prime candidate. A 49-14 defeat to Michigan State removed the Nittany Lions from the picture. So on selection day the Sugar, using the third and fifth picks, took fourth-ranked Florida State (10-1) – the third time in four years the Seminoles would ring in the New Year in New Orleans – and ninth-ranked Ohio State (9-2).

There were some mild criticisms of the Sugar Bowl for not taking No. 6 UCLA, higher than Ohio State but with a reputation of not bringing many fans. "We looked at what we call the Five Rs," said Paul Hoolahan, the game's executive director, "record, rankings, (TV) ratings, reward (for the ath-

Sebastian Janikowski (38) attempts a field goal with Marcus Outzen (14) as the holder.

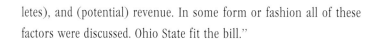

letes), and (potential) revenue. In some form or fashion all of these factors were discussed. Ohio State fit the bill."

It really was a very good matchup. Florida State was felt by many to be the best team in college football, done in only by a narrow, last minute defeat to Florida. The Ohio State team, anchored by sophomore All-American linebacker Andy Katzenmoyer, was solid but very, very young with only four seniors in the Buckeyes' starting 22. A case could be have been made that this could have been a preview of the national championship game of 1999. The Seminoles averaged 452 yards and 39 points a game; the Buckeyes averaged 412 yards and 31.7 points.

"This could be a heck of a game," said FSU coach Bobby Bowden. "You know, Ohio State has the name. We've been pretty good lately, but they've been good forever."

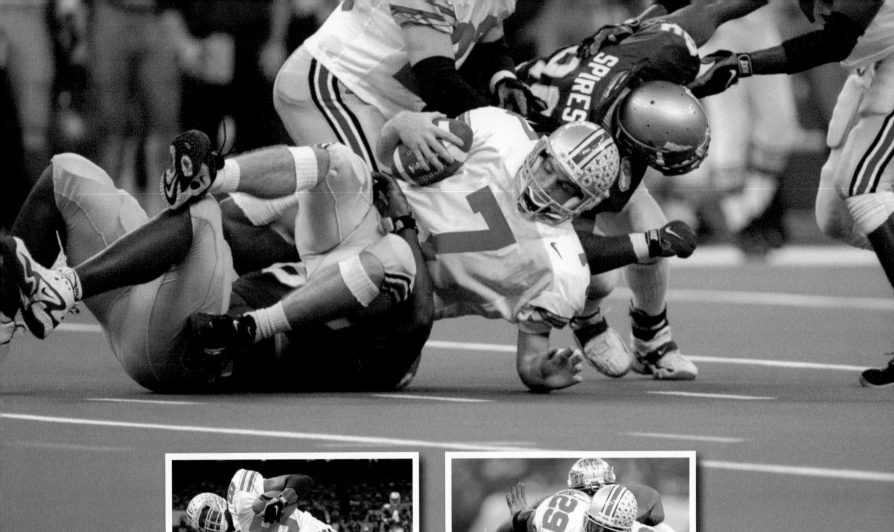

E.G. Green (19) strolls into the end zone with Peter Warrick (9) on a 27-yard touchdown pass from Thad Busby at the end of the first qurater.

"We did not have time."

Football, of course, is a 60 minute game.

But the 64th Sugar Bowl was really a 30-minute game. It was over by the half.

Despite an early 3-0 Ohio State lead on a 40-yard field goal by Dan Stultz, Florida State dominated the trenches and the passing lanes while the game was on the line.

In the first half, the Seminoles had a stretch of eight plays in which they did not allow Ohio State to gain a yard. The Buckeyes' offensive line simply couldn't stop the charges of FSU defensive end Andre Wadsworth.

Split end E.G. Green caught six passes for 134 yards and a touchdown in the first 30 minutes. "It's kind of like you hear Michael Jordan say, 'if you can get in the zone, the basket gets so big you can't miss,' " said Green, who was the game's MVP. "The coaches kept feeding me."

FSU quarterback Thad Busby completed 18-of-25 passes for 242 yards and a touchdown in the first half, but he also threw two interceptions – one in the end zone with 6:08 left in the first quarter – that prevented the Seminoles from taking command even sooner.

Complete command came just before halftime when, with Florida State ahead 14-3, Seminole defensive back Shevin Smith picked off a Joe Germaine pass and returned it 51

Dan Stultz (47) kicks one of two field goals for the Buckeyes with Brent Bartholomew (41) as the holder.

yards to the OSU 23. That set up a two-play drive that lasted 17 seconds, ending when fullback William McCray scored from the 1 with 10 seconds remaining.

The way the Seminoles were manhandling the Buckeye offensive line, no one in the disappointing crowd of 67,289 could have logically believed Ohio State would be able to come back and score three touchdowns.

Florida State allowed Ohio State to move up and down the field in the second half, getting a touchdown before firing back with a touchdown and field goal. "Quick, relentless pres-

sure throughout the ballgame," marveled OSU coach John Cooper. "Their pass rush was the best I've seen in a long time. We did not have time to throw the football."

Cooper's assessment was backed up by his team's quarterback statistics: field generals Stanley Jackson and Germaine combined for six interceptions and were sacked six times.

The big story, as it turned out, from the Sugar Bowl was the continuing saga of Bobby Bowden's magic carpet ride at Florida State.

Florida State's E.G. Green (19) tries to run by Gary Berry (1) and Antoine Winfield (11) of Ohio State.

FSU coach Bobby Bowden congratulates Kevin Long (51) after the Seminoles beat the Buckeyes 31-14 in the 64th Sugar Bowl.

Twelve months after losing 52-20 to the Florida Gators in the Superdome, Bowden's Seminoles returned for a notable bowl victory: his 16th in the postseason, one more than Alabama's Bear Bryant, two shy of the record held by Penn State's 71-year-old Joe Paterno.

And the superlatives didn't end there.

The victory pushed Florida State to a final No. 3 ranking. Since 1987, the Seminoles had finished No. 2, 3, 3, 4, 4, 2, 1, 4, 4, 3 and 3.

Coaches and programs have won more mythical titles, but none comes close to matching such a 10-year claim to excellence.

	1	2	3	4	
Florida State	7	14	0	10	31
Ohio State	3	0	5	6	14

Ohio State: Stultz, 40-yard field goal.
Florida State: Green, 27-yard pass from Busby. PAT, Janikowski kick.
Florida State: Busby, 9-yard run. PAT, Janikowski kick.
Florida State: McCray, 1-yard run. PAT, Janikowski kick.
Ohio State: Stultz, 34-yard field goal.
Ohio State: Safety.
Florida State: Janikowski, 35-yard field goal.
Ohio State: Lumpkin, 50-yard pass from Germaine. Pass failed.
Florida State: McCray, 1-yard run. PAT, Janikowski kick.

Individual Leaders

Rushing
Florida State: Minor 12-53; Feaster 2-10.
Ohio State: Pearson 22-60; Keller 6-20.

Passing
Florida State: Busby 22-33-2, 334 yards, 1 TD.
Ohio State: Germaine 10-26-2, 173 yards, 1 TD.

Receiving
Florida State: Green 7-176, 1 TD; Warrick 3-82.
Ohio State: Miller 6-79; Lumpkin 2-61, 1 TD.

Florida State		Ohio State
18	First Downs	21
60	Rushing Yards	118
22-33-2	Passing	16-36-3
334	Passing Yards	207
394	Total Yards	325
6-42.7	Punts	7-45.4
0-0	Fumbles – Lost	1-0
9-74	Penalties – Yards	10-70

Attendance: 67,289.
Teams' remuneration: $15,650,000.
Miller-Digby Award recipient: E.G. Green, Florida State flanker.

Ohio State 24 Texas A&M 14

"Why not us?"

The buzzer ending the Florida State-Ohio State game, the final Sugar Bowl of the three-year Bowl Alliance, also sounded the start of a new postseason system.

The Conference Commissioners Association began putting together a more intricate – and complete – ranking to determine a true national championship just a year into the Bowl Alliance setup. This wasn't possible until the Rose Bowl agreed in 1997 to join forces with the participants of the Bowl Alliance, meaning the other major bowls, in a format to be called the Bowl Championship Series.

Because of the high marks received by the bowls (Sugar, Fiesta and Orange) sanctioned originally by the Alliance, and after each underwent another interview process, all were again entered into a rotation. They were joined by the Rose, which freed up the best teams in the Pac-10 and Big Ten, making as close as possible, without a playoff system, a true national championship pairing.

One of the major changes was the concession by the Commissioners that each bowl would again tie-up with the champion of its natural conference, as they did before the Alliance, placing, say, the winner of the SEC back in the Sugar, unless

that team was involved in the No. 1 vs. No. 2 game. That change would ease the possibility of weak match-ups with little national or local interest.

Under the new format, polls, computer rankings, strength of schedule and, obviously, the won-loss records were components in determining the top two teams.

The ranking system consisted of the Associated Press, and USA Today/ESPN polls, a combination of the computer rankings compiled by Jeff Sagarin and published in USA Today, the Seattle Times and the New York Times.

It was a formula that kept fans guessing who would play for No. 1 in the Fiesta Bowl (the first title site in the rotation) throughout the '98 season. The Sugar drew the BCS' second spot, which meant New Orleans would host the first – or the last, depending on how you

looked at it – title game of the millennium, that football showcase scheduled for January 4, 2000.

The preseason and near-universal favorite for the championship was Ohio State, a team manned by such standouts as linebacker Andy Katzenmoyer, guard Rob Murphy, receivers David Boston and Dee Miller, and cornerback Antoine Winfield.

The Buckeyes were ranked No. 1 for most of the season – until losing a 17-point lead and absorbing a 28-24 defeat to four-touchdown underdog Michigan State on Nov. 7.

Texas A&M clawed and scratched its way into the national limelight, defeating No. 2-ranked Nebraska (28-21) during the regular season, then upsetting No.

1-ranked Kansas State (36-33) in double-overtime in the Big 12 championship game.

Undefeated Tennessee, the SEC champion, made it to the Fiesta against 11-1 Florida State, and the third-ranked Buckeyes (10-1) and eighth-ranked Aggies (11-2) were ticketed to New Orleans – with visions of a possible share of the national championship still dancing in Ohio State's head. (It's notable that the Sugar Bowl selection committee never seriously considered hometown team Tulane, unbeaten for the first time since 1925, because of the Green Wave's weak strength of schedule.)

John Cooper, the Buckeye coach, made the argument that should his team, a 12-point favorite, win convincingly, and should second-ranked FSU defeat the Vols

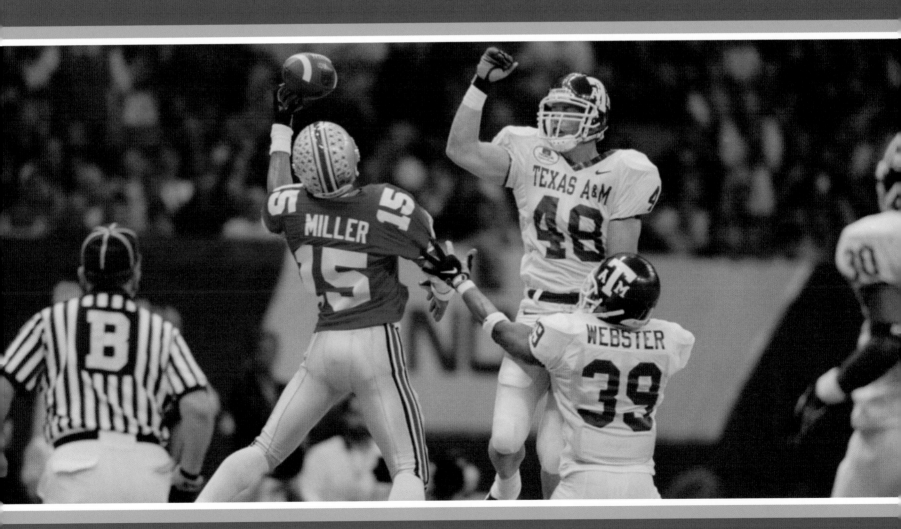

Dee Miller (15) attempts to make the catch as Rich Coady (48) and Jason Webster (39) defend for the Aggies.

in an unimpressive game, the nation's three highest-rated teams (Tennessee, Florida State, and Ohio State) would all have one loss and the Buckeyes had a case that they were as good or better than anyone. The BCS championship would, of course, automatically go to the winner of the Tennessee-FSU game, as the system was designed, but Cooper seemed to be trying to impress the AP voters.

"If Tennessee lost and there would be three teams with a loss, I'm not one to take handouts, but why not us as champions?"

Cooper mused. "Until that door is completely shut, anything's possible."

A&M, naturally, didn't take well to Ohio State's looking past the Aggies and to the polls.

"We've been the underdog all season long," Kyle Lednicky, A&M's long snapper, retorted. "We were almost a three-touchdown underdog against Kansas State. We proved everybody wrong, and we plan to do it again."

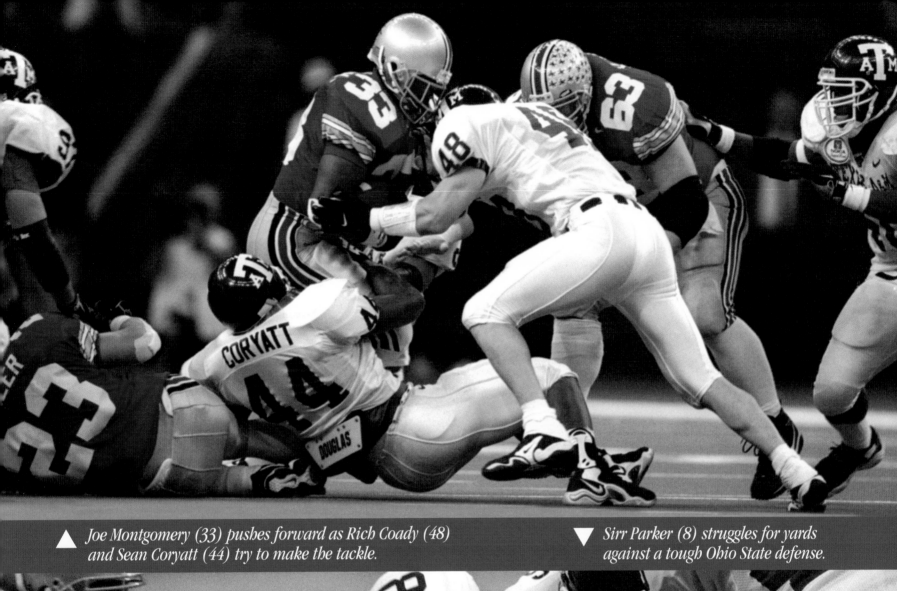

▲ *Joe Montgomery (33) pushes forward as Rich Coady (48) and Sean Coryatt (44) try to make the tackle.*

▼ *Sirr Parker (8) struggles for yards against a tough Ohio State defense.*

"We'll play head-to-head with anybody."

The Buckeye contingent loudly let its unhappy feelings be known when the Superdome's video screens showed a piece on the Bowl Championship Series that called the game at the Fiesta Bowl "the first true national championship."

But the Aggies quickly quieted the Buckeyes.

In a game bracketed by big plays in the kicking area, Texas A&M put the first points on the board, driving 59 yards, gain-

ing ground on each of its six plays against the country's No. 2-ranked defense, and getting a touchdown on a nine-yard run by Dante Hall.

Then, though, Ohio State flew to a near-insurmountable lead with three touchdowns in a span of six minutes, 35 seconds. That, in a nutshell, was the story of the 65th Sugar Bowl.

Ohio State's spurt included an 18-yard scoring pass from

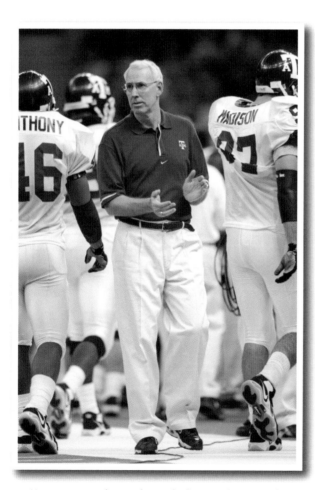

Texas A&M coach R.C. Slocum looks on as his Aggies fall to the Ohio State Buckeyes.

Texas A&M wide receiver Chris Taylor (42) battles Ahmed Plummer (19) of Ohio State for the ball.

Ohio State kicker Dan Stultz (47) hits a 31-yard field goal.

quarterback Joe Germaine to Reggie Germany after overcoming a third-and-15 situation. Germaine hit Dee Miller for 28 yards, and five plays later the Buckeyes tied the game. Then Ohio State went ahead on a 10-yard run by Joe Montgomery.

Even though the game was still in the first quarter, the outcome may have been put out of reach for the Aggies when A&M's Shane Lechler suffered the first blocked punt of his career. Rich Coady missed a block on Derek Ross, and Ohio State's outside rusher came firing through, smothering the ball as Lechler dropped it toward his foot. Kevin Griffin picked up the loose ball and returned it 16 yards for the touchdown that gave the Buckeyes a 21-7 first period margin.

It was the first blocked punt allowed by A&M since its 1993 Oklahoma game, and was the first blocked punt returned for a touchdown in the Sugar Bowl since 1965, when Syracuse's Brad Clarke brought one back 28 yards against LSU.

Ohio State, which stretched its advantage to 24-7 by the half, should have had this one tucked away, but really couldn't breathe easily. The Buckeyes converted only one of six third-down situations in the first half, and kicker Don Stultz missed two field-goal attempts of 49 and 47 yards in the second half, the latter ricocheting off the right upright.

The Aggies, with the help of three Ohio State penalties that accounted for 40 of the necessary 68 yards, scored a third-quarter touchdown on an seven-yard pass to LeRoy Hodge to cut the Buckeye lead to 10.

A&M was in position to again pull off one of its late-game heroics.

But just when it was needed most by Ohio State, senior linebacker Jerry Rudzinski stood tall. In a series of clutch plays, Rudzinski helped brake A&M's late momentum.

With 10:30 to play in the fourth period, with a first down at the Buckeye 43, quarterback Branndon Stewart flung a swing pass – actually a lateral – out to Hall. Rudzinski tipped the pass, then beat Hall to the ball, recovering at the Aggies' 48.

He later broke up a pass, and Winfield deflected yet another, forcing a punt with 6:40 remaining.

Rudzinski's final tackle, an open-field stop of fullback Ja'Mar Toombs after a short reception, helped stymie what turned out to be A&M's last possession.

Other than the game's opening drive and the penalty-aided touchdown drive in the third period, the Aggies never advanced beyond their 47, and even that was on a meaningless 19-yard completion on the final play of the first half.

"We played a great football team in Ohio State, and we came up a little short," Aggie coach R.C. Slocum said. "When you're playing a team as talented as Ohio State, you can't fall behind like we did."

Yet Ohio State never did quite shake the Aggies, who outgained the Buckeyes 152-140 in the second half. The Buckeyes, who scored no points after intermission, hardly had a powerful case for the dominance they needed to impress voters.

No matter. Tennessee beat Florida State 23-16 in Tempe to settle matters in the AP poll. Ohio State finished second.

"We'll play head-to-head with anybody," a frustrated Boston said, knowing full well Ohio State would never get that chance.

But the stage was set for football's next big coming attraction: the showcase Sugar Bowl of 2000.

	1	2	3	4	
Ohio State	21	3	0	0	24
Texas A&M	7	0	7	0	14

Texas A&M: Hall, 9-yard run. PAT, Bynum kick.

Ohio State: Germany, 18-yard pass from Germaine. PAT, Stultz kick.

Ohio State: Montgomery, 10-yard run. PAT, Stultz kick.

Ohio State: Griffin, 16-yard blocked kick return. PAT, Stultz kick.

Ohio State: Stultz, 31-yard field goal.

Texas A&M: Hodge, 7-yard pass from Stewart. PAT, Bynum kick.

Individual Leaders

Rushing
Ohio State: Montgomery 9-96 1 TD; Wiley 16-88.
Texas A&M: Toombs 10-68; Hall 11-53, 1 TD.

Passing
Ohio State: Germaine 21-38-0, 222 yards, 1 TD.
Texas A&M: Stewart 22-39-0, 187 yards, 1 TD.

Receiving
Ohio State: Boston 11-105; Wiley 5-40.
Texas A&M: Taylor 5-52; Spiller 5-43.

Ohio State		Texas A&M
25	First Downs	17
210	Rushing Yards	96
21-38-0	Passing	22-39-0
222	Passing Yards	187
432	Total Yards	283
6-38.3	Punts	10-39.8
3-0	Fumbles – Lost	1-1
6-61	Penalties – Yards	6-43

Attendance: 76,503.
Teams' remuneration: $25,000,000.
Miller-Digby Award recipient: David Boston, Ohio State receiver.

Tuesday, January 4, 2000

Florida State 46 Virginia Tech 29

"They've got to worry about these computer rankings."

This was a watershed moment for the Sugar Bowl. In the ever-evolving road to the national title, the Bowl Championship Series system, which put the major bowls in an annual line and rotated the site of the match between teams deemed No. 1 and No. 2, making this New Orleans' turn.

This time the football battles across the country throughout the fall were of only passing interest to Paul Hoolahan. The executive director of the Nokia Sugar Bowl was sitting in the catbird's seat, knowing no matter who or what did the rankings, that when all was said and done, the best two teams were going to be paired in his venue. And Hoolahan wouldn't have to strain himself analyzing every possible angle in the determinations.

He could sit back and wait to see what would present itself.

"Taking the decision-making out of our hands is nice when you know you're going to have the championship game," Hoolahan said with a chuckle.

In the trenches, Coach Bobby Bowden had most of his Florida State Seminoles back from the team that came within a game of taking the national championship the year before, including wide receiver Peter Warrick. He was seen as very possibly the best senior player in the land. Bowden also had a superb quarterback in Chris Weinke, who had played several seasons of professional baseball and at 27 was very likely the oldest junior in college football.

Though ranked No. 1 from the preseason polls and on through

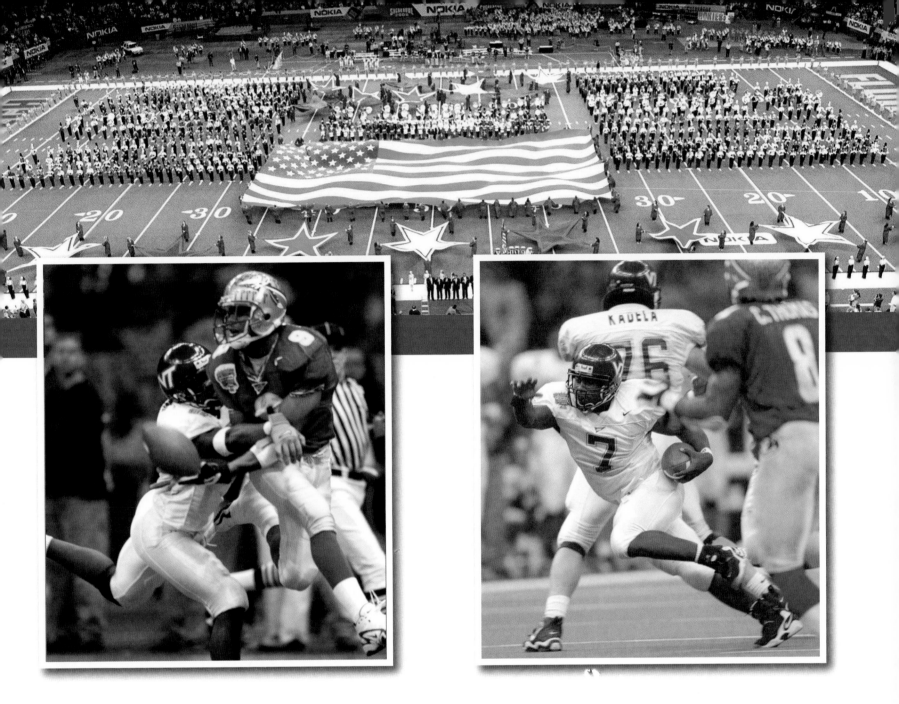

the regular season, FSU wasn't always impressive in the early season. Sometimes, as in a 17-14 victory over Clemson, coached by Tommy Bowden, son of the 'Noles headmaster, Florida State seemed to be getting by strictly on talent, not effort. Still, the Seminoles were getting by.

The 'Noles weren't always in sync because a major part of their offense wasn't always there. Warrick was the missing – then occasionally unsure – component.

He and teammate Laveranues Coles ran into legal problems which resulted in a two-game suspension for Warrick while Coles was dismissed from the squad. Bowden's team over-

came that embarrassing adversity, continued to win – and continued to stay perched atop the computer rankings.

The battle for the No. 2 spot was spirited with unbeaten Virginia Tech, of the perceived not-so-powerful Big East – powered by a will-o'-the-wisp freshman quarterback named Michael Vick – and once-beaten Nebraska of the highly respected Big 12 Conference jockeying for position near season's end.

The computer rankings seemed to color what transpired on the field. When Tech piled up a 62-7 win over Temple near

Virginia Tech quarterback Michael Vick (7)
with Jerry Johnson (92) right behind.

the last three touchdowns, that the Hokies ran it up to impress the computers.

"I know exactly the position (Tech) is in, so I had no problem at all with what happened," Coach Bobby Wallace of the Owls said. "They've got to worry about these computer rankings."

Indeed, they did. As they reached the last week of the regular season, just 0.63 points separated Tech and Nebraska. The 10-0 Hokies prepared to play 8-2 Boston College and the 9-1 Cornhuskers had to beat 6-4 Colorado to get a spot in their league's title game against Texas.

Virginia Tech did what it had to do, rapping the Eagles 38-14, while Nebraska struggled to nip the Buffaloes 33-30 in overtime. The difference in those games allowed the Hokies to stretch their lead in the computer tabulations – and clear a path to the Sugar Bowl and a shot at No. 1.

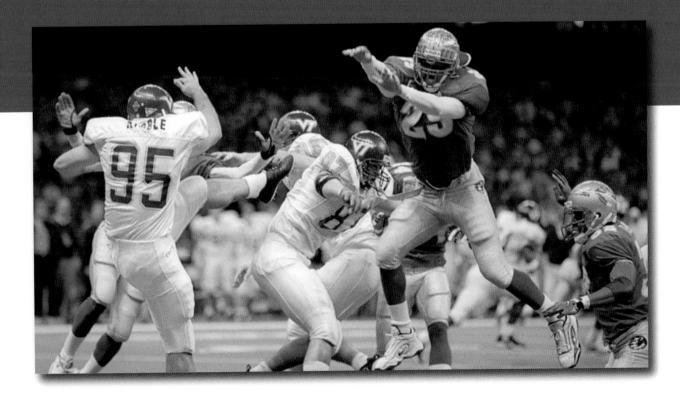

"No one can ever take this away from me."

The first Sugar Bowl of the new millennium was a kaleidoscope of mesmerizing football.

With a backdrop of a Superdome filled to the rafters with a festive and raucous crowd, FSU's Peter Warrick caught six passes for 163 yards and set a Sugar Bowl record by scoring 20 points. Michael Vick, Virginia Tech's redshirt freshman quarterback, guided his team to 503 yards, most ever in a losing Sugar Bowl effort.

There was seldom a moment for anyone to catch their breath.

Warrick helped stake the Seminoles to a 28-7 lead in the first half; Vick galvanized the Hokies to a stupefying comeback that actually put Virginia Tech ahead 29-28 at the end of the third quarter. Then Warrick and Florida State took over again.

In a game that spent the energies of fan and athlete alike, Vick began lighting the fuse to blow up Florida State's No. 1 dream from the opening kickoff, driving the Hokies to within hailing distance of the Seminole end zone three times, only to come up empty. Most costly was a lost Tech fumble at the FSU 1 in the Hokies' first drive.

Warrick, who was held to one catch for seven yards in the '97 title game, erased that memory quickly. After a Tech threat was quelled, he opened the scoring by grabbing a 64-yard touchdown from Chris Weinke.

Until that moment, Virginia Tech had outgained the Seminoles 123-8.

"I've never been so focused before a game in my life," the 5-foot-11 Warrick mused afterward. "I was just going to go into this game to do what I've done all season – go out and make plays.'

Then Tech yielded another quick touchdown to FSU when the 'Noles blocked a Hokie punt, and Jeff Chaney grabbed the bouncing ball and ran into the end zone from the 6-yard line. All of a sudden, the Sugar had the appearance of a rout-in-the-making until Andre' Davis latched onto a 49-yard pass

Peter Warrick (9) returns a Virginia Tech punt 59-yards for a touchdown.

Florida State celebrates its wire-to-wire National Championship after defeating Virginia Tech 46-29.

from Vick with 30 seconds left in the first quarter.

Weinke threw another scoring strike of 63 yards to Ron Dugans in sort of a landmark for Tech. The 21 points the Hokies gave up in the first sixteen and a half minutes were more than they had in any game all season.

And Warrick still had some magic to weave.

Still early in the second quarter, standing on the FSU 40, Warrick raised his arms in the air – then raised the roof. Fielding a punt on the bounce, Warrick dodged one defender, blew past two more, then sprinted down the sideline for a 59-yard touchdown that ratcheted the Seminoles' lead to a very comfortable 28-7.

The fireworks, though, were just beginning. Vick closed the margin with a three-yard TD run just before the half, setting the stage for a spectacular quarter.

The 19-year-old virtuoso sidestepped Seminoles all across the Superdome floor, disappearing like smoke as they zeroed in on him. Dashing right, then left, Vick gained 43 yards to set up the Hokies' second touchdown.

Scrambling so much as to make the FSU defense dizzy, Vick kept breathing life into his bunch of underdogs, accounting personally for 81 of Tech's 140 yards in the period and whipping the Hokies to two touchdowns and a field goal for a stunning one-point lead with two minutes left in the third quarter. Vick had energized his Hokies enough to drive them to four touchdowns in five possessions.

This was the moment of truth for the Seminoles. "All the hard work in the offseason," FSU nose guard Corey Simon reflected, "It all came down to this. We couldn't quit when they got ahead."

And FSU didn't, reclaiming control and blowing open the game with 18 unanswered points in the fourth quarter – with the senior Warrick giving Florida State fans something to remember him by, a juggling catch in the end zone for a 43-yard touchdown, despite obvious interference by a defensive back.

The two teams combined for 10 touchdowns, a Sugar Bowl record 75 points, 862 yards, and Virginia Tech scored the most points ever by a losing team in the Sugar. Something to think about was Vick's 322 total yards of offense – despite being sacked seven times.

FSU coach Bobby Bowden holding the National Championship Trophy.

Bobby Bowden finally joined his sons Terry and Tommy by completing his first perfect season in his 40 years as a head coach.

The Seminoles found a little notch in history, too. They became the first team to go wire-to-wire as the top team since the preseason rankings began in 1950. In the half-century since then, eight teams were ranked No. 1 in the AP preseason poll, fell out of the top spot at some point, but went on to win the national title: Tennessee (1951); Michigan State (1952); Oklahoma (1956, 1974, 1975, 1985); Alabama (1978); and Florida State (1993).

Before 1950 there were two regular season wire-to-wire champions, Notre Dame in 1943 and Army in 1945.

Now there were three, in no small measure because of the determination of Warrick, who knew he had something to atone for.

"When I leave Florida State," he said thinking of his slow start in the early season, "I want people to think of me as a good person, on and off the field. I went out as a champion. This is the national championship. No one can ever take this away from me.

	1	2	3	4	
Virginia Tech	7	7	15	0	29
Florida State	14	14	0	18	46

Florida State: Warrick, 64-yard pass from Weinke. PAT, Janikowski kick.
Florida State: Chaney, 6-yard blocked punt return. PAT, Janikowski kick.
Virginia Tech: Davis, 49-yard pass from Vick. PAT, Graham kick.
Florida State: Dugans, 63-yard pass from Weinke. PAT, Janikowski kick.
Florida State: Warrick, 59-yard punt return. PAT, Janikowski kick.
Virginia Tech: Vick, 3-yard run. PAT, Graham kick.
Virginia Tech: Graham, 23-yard field goal.
Virginia Tech: Kendrick, 29-yard run. Pass failed.
Virginia Tech: Kendrick, 6-yard run. Pass failed.
Florida State: Dugans, 14-yard pass from Weinke. PAT, Warrick pass from Weinke.
Florida State: Janikowski, 32-yard field goal.
Florida State: Warrick, 43-yard pass from Weinke. PAT, Janikowski kick.

Individual Leaders

Rushing
Virginia Tech: Vick 23-97, 1 TD; Kendrick 12-69, 2 TDs; Stith 11-68.
Florida State: Chaney 4-43; Minor 9-35.

Passing
Virginia Tech: Vick 15-20-0, 225 yards, 1 TD.
Florida State: Weinke 20-34-1, 329 yards, 4 TDs.

Receiving
Virginia Tech: Davis 7-108, 1 TD; Hawkins 2-49.
Florida State: Warrick 6-163, 2 TDs; Dugans 5-99, 1 TD.

Virginia Tech		Florida State
24	First Downs	18
278	Rushing Yards	60
15-29-0	Passing	22-33-3
225	Passing Yards	334
503	Total Yards	394
6-29.3	Punts	7-44.3
3-3	Fumbles – Lost	0-0
6-65	Penalties – Yards	9-74

Attendance: 79,280.
Teams' remuneration: $26,000,000.
Miller-Digby Award recipient: Peter Warrick, Florida State receiver.

343

Miami 37 Florida 20

"I'm not concerned."

Paul Hoolahan and fans of Florida's major schools were in a state of football euphoria.

In a year when the executive director of the Sugar Bowl could logically be expected to be scrambling, he was in uncommonly good position to fill his postseason extravaganza, which had played host to the national championship game in 2000. The Bowl Championship Series rotation indicated the Sugar should be fourth in the four BCS games this time. But the Sugar was in unexpectedly high clover, and the potency of the Sunshine State troika was the primary reason why.

Florida State was having its usual superlative year, this one with 10 regular-season victories; the University of Florida, sputtering at times compared to recent years, still beat 10 opponents, winning the SEC; and the University of Miami returned to the elite of the college game, with FSU counted among its victims in a 10-1 regular season.

Hoolahan almost couldn't miss, listening attentively to the sales pitches of such programs as Nebraska and Notre Dame. But Hoolahan and the BCS couldn't resist the lure of the outside possibility of a second straight national championship game.

This is how that potential could be factored in: FSU (second-ranked in the BCS but third-ranked in the polls) was taken to challenge No. 1-ranked Oklahoma in the BCS game of the year at the Orange Bowl. The winner of that game would automatically be No. 1 in the final USA Today/ESPN rankings, determined by coaches.

But Miami (10-1), which beat FSU 27-24 and rose to No. 2 in the Associated Press poll, could conceivably jump to No. 1 in that tabulation, which is determined through voting by sportswriters and sportscasters, with a Sugar Bowl victory over SEC champion Florida (10-2 and seventh-ranked) coupled with a Seminole win – and FSU was favored over the 12-0 Sooners.

And don't think the Hurricanes didn't play that angle for all it was worth, making the case for weeks that

Miami running back Clinton Portis (28) runs past the out streched hands of a Gator defender.

their 27-24 victory over Florida State should have put them in the title game in their own hometown. Conveniently ignored in Miami's case, however, was a 34-29 defeat at the University of Washington in the second week of the season. The Huskies had the same 10-1 record and were ranked fourth at the end of the regular season.

"Hey, there's 116 other teams or however many Division I schools there are out there that would love to be in our position," said Miami sophomore tight end Jeremy Shockey, a native of Oklahoma who didn't believe his home-state team had a shot against Florida State. "This is a great opportunity for us," Shockey said. "You can't let good opportunities like this slip past you."

Both Miami and Florida, in-state rivals who had not played in 13 years, featured a numbers of game-breakers. For the 'Canes they included receiver/kick returner Santana Moss, receiver Reggie Wayne, running back James Jackson, middle linebacker Dan Morgan and quarterback Ken Dorsey, a sophomore who threw for 25 touchdowns and just five interceptions during the regular season.

This is how resourceful the 2000 Hurricanes were: they turned eight turnovers (six interceptions, two fumbles) and five punt returns (four by Moss) into touchdowns.

Countering the Hurricanes was a potent Gator force that included quarterback Rex Grossman, receivers Jabar Gaffney and Earnest Graham, running back Robert Gillespie, cornerback/return specialist Lito Sheppard, defensive end Alex Brown and defensive tackle Gerard Warren.

The opponents couldn't and didn't wait to get it on. On their first night in the Big Easy, a week before the Sugar Bowl, a near-brawl occurred between 15 to 20 players from both sides on the downtown corner of Bourbon and Canal streets. Apparently the Hurricanes started taunting and threatening the Gators, who responded. New Orleans police broke up the altercation, though no arrests were

Florida receiver Reche Caldwell is pushed out of bounds.

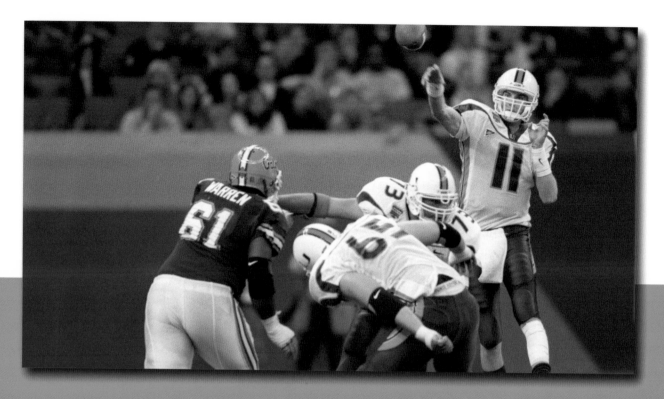

made and neither Miami coach Butch Davis nor Florida coach Steve Spurrier felt any disciplinary action was necessary.

What was necessary was getting the players' minds on the task at hand, though Davis insisted attaining a No. 1 pennant was not as important as playing well in the last game of a memorable season.

"I'm not concerned in the least about the Florida State-Oklahoma game," Davis said. "It has some implications, potentially. But the only thing I'm really concerned with is us playing as well as we can, giving ourselves a chance to beat Florida. We'll be happy with a one-point win. I can't control the other teams; I can't control the other games; I can't control voters; I can't control the computers. All we can do is play the very best we can on Tuesday night, and whatever happens is going to happen.

"Regardless what happens, nothing will diminish or take away from this season. This is going to be remembered as a great season."

Florida running back Earnest Graham is gang tackled by Miami's Quincy Hipps (90), Dan Morgan (44), Leonard Myers (22) and James Lewis (23).

"We got what we deserved."

In a super-heated Sugar Bowl, Miami's Ken Dorsey cooled the Florida Gators.

The sophomore from Orinda, Calif., was the main difference in a clear-cut victory that kept the Hurricanes' hopes for at least a share of the national title alive for one more day.

After misfiring on his first three passes, Dorsey finished with 22 completions in 40 attempts for 270 yards and three touchdowns. His last two scoring passes came in the decisive third quarter, holding his team together after throwing an interception that led to a 36-yard touchdown run that put Florida ahead, 17-13.

At that point, Dorsey marched his mates 80 yards to a lead the Hurricanes would not surrender.

"He's a winner," exuded Miami coach Butch Davis. "He's always making the right decisions. And tonight our guys helped by making some big-time catches."

After Florida went ahead 17-13 − courtesy of the Dorsey interception − with 13:10 to go in the third quarter, he threw two touchdowns, 17-yards to D.J. Williams with 8:23 to go in the period, and, five playing minutes later, two-yards to Najeh Davenport.

When Miami put the game out of reach on a three-yard run with 4:21 left in the game, the Hurricane faithful in the stands began chanting "We're No. 1!"

Not quite, as it turned out, circumstances being as frustrating to Miami as both defenses were early in the Sugar Bowl.

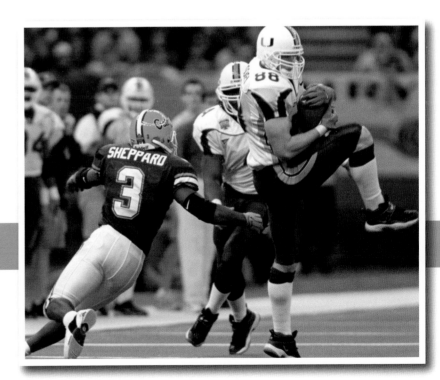

Miami players dump water on head coach Butch Davis.

Miami's mascot proclaims the Hurricanes as "State Champs" after defeating the Gators 37-20.

The two defenses, playing on their respective heels, spent most of the opening 30 minutes thwarting the offenses near the end zones. For teams that averaged 42 points (Miami) and 37 points (Florida) over the regular season, the first half had a decided defensive accent, this despite the fact the teams combined for 497 yards and 52 passes. The Hurricanes ran and passed for 231 yards, the Gators for 266. At intermission Miami was holding a 13-10 lead.

After slow starts, each of the quarterbacks warmed up on their second possession, with Rex Grossman finishing a seven-play, 70-yard drive with a 25-yard touchdown pass to tight end Kirk Wells for a 7-0 Florida lead.

Dorsey responded by taking the Hurricanes on consecutive scoring drives for a 10-7 advantage after one quarter. Todd

Sievers kicked a 44-yard field goal. Then Dorsey collaborated with tight end Jeremy Shockey on an eight-yard touchdown pass.

Sievers increased the 'Canes' lead to 13-7 with a 29-yard field goal with 10:44 left in the half. Jeff Chandler trimmed the margin with a 51-yard kick of his own.

With 13 seconds left in the half, Spurrier passed up a 43-yard field goal attempt from the Miami 26 to take a shot at the red zone. The decision backfired. Grossman's pass, intended for receiver Taylor Jacobs, was badly under thrown, and Miami cornerback Leonard Myers picked it off.

Then came the swing period, the third quarter. Just three plays into the second half, Gator cornerback Keiwan Ratliff pilfered

Miami coach Butch Davis celebrates the Hurricanes victory over the Florida Gators in the 2001 Sugar Bowl.

a Dorsey pass and returned it nine yards to the 'Canes' 36.

On first down running back Earnest Graham bounced outside and broke arm tackles by Miami defensive backs Edward Reed and Al Blades – one of the principals in the near-fight six days earlier – and ran 36 yards for the 17-13 Florida lead.

Then Dorsey turned on Miami's afterburners.

A downcast Gator coach Steve Spurrier said bluntly afterward, "We got what we deserved. You've got to give Miami credit, because they were better than us. It was sort of embarrassing the way we played."

Twenty-four hours later, though, Miami's long-shot dream ended when Oklahoma beat Florida State and swept the polls.

	1	2	3	4	
Miami	10	3	14	10	37
Florida	7	3	7	3	20

Florida: Wells, 23-yard pass from Grossman. PAT, Chandler kick.
Miami: Sievers, 44-yard field goal.
Miami: Shockey, 8-yard pass from Dorsey. PAT, Sievers kick.
Miami: Sievers, 29-yard field goal.
Florida: Chandler, 51-yard field goal.
Florida: Graham, 36-yard run. PAT, Chandler kick.
Miami: Williams, 19-yard pass from Dorsey. PAT, Sievers kick.
Miami: Davenport, 2-yard pass from Dorsey. PAT, Sievers kick.
Florida: Chandler, 26-yard field goal.
Miami: Sievers, 29-yard field goal.
Miami: Davenport, 3-yard run. PAT, Sievers kick.

Individual Leaders

Rushing
Miami: Portis 18-97; Jackson 12-62.
Florida: Graham 15-136, 1 TD.

Passing
Miami: Dorsey 22-40-2, 270 yards, 3 TDs
Florida: Grossman 18-41-3, 312 yards, 1 TD.

Receiving
Miami: Moss 6-89; Shockey 4-47, 1 TD.
Florida: Caldwell 6-100; Gaffney 7-75.

Miami		Florida
28	First Downs	25
184	Rushing Yards	140
22-40-2	Passing	24-51-3
270	Passing Yards	312
454	Total Yards	452
2-44.0	Punts	5-46.8
0-0	Fumbles – Lost	0-0
11-109	Penalties – Yards	9-79

Attendance: 64,407.
Teams' remuneration: $26,000,000.
Miller-Digby Award recipient: Ken Dorsey, Miami quarterback.

LSU 47 Illinois 34

"Talk about a windfall!"

America's "second Day of Infamy," 9-11-2001, colored everything that happened afterward – including the sports world.

The terrorists who crashed hijacked passenger planes into New York's World Trade Center towers, the Pentagon complex in Washington, D.C., and into a Pennsylvania field, instantly changed one aspect of the U.S. lifestyle: travel.

In no time, though briefly, air-travel was reduced to less than half of what it was on that fateful morning. The perceived threat of more air-piracy understandably caused more Americans to stick closer to home – particularly for such comparatively unimportant happenings as long-distance sports events.

With that mind-set as a backdrop, one of the season's most interesting stories began unfolding in Baton Rouge, 80 miles away from the Superdome. After a bumbling start in which underachieving LSU started 4-3, Coach Nick Saban righted the Tigers in eye-catching fashion.

With such weapons as receiver Josh Reed, college football's most productive pass-catcher, Rohan Davey, one of the SEC's premier quarterbacks and LSU's all-time passer, and tailback LeBrandon Toefield, who tallied an SEC-record-tying 19 touchdowns, the Tigers were dangerous offensively. LSU's Achilles'

heel was its secondary, which gave up so many big pass plays that in pass defense the Tigers were ranked 108th of the NCAA's 117 football-playing schools. That stat, perplexing for a conference championship team, however, was more of a reflection of the first half of LSU's season than the second half.

After a 35-24 loss to Ole Miss in which LSU did as much to beat itself as did the Rebels, the defense against the pass improved markedly, dramatically slicing almost 50 yards off opponents' passing averages. At the same time, and this was crucial in the turnaround, the Tiger offense became more efficient and time-consuming, keeping the defense – and opposing offensive units – on the sidelines for longer periods of time.

Five victories later, LSU claimed its unlikeliest SEC championship, not only upsetting second-ranked Tennessee 31-20 (by outscoring the Volunteers 24-3 in the second half), in the

Illinois fans cheer as the Illini take on the Tigers of LSU.

league's championship game but also doing it with backups at key positions. Davey went out after taking a second jarring shot in the first quarter, and Toefield soon followed with a torn anterior cruciate ligament. But reserve Matt Mauck filled in capably at QB, finishing off one drive for Davey and guiding the Tigers to all their points. Domanick Davis – who split his previous playing time in the secondary – performed superbly in Toefield's stead by rushing for 78 yards. Davis especially shone in the fourth period on LSU's last touchdown drive, when he carried six times for 32 yards, not only eventually scoring the put-away TD, but helping the Tigers run 6:04 very valuable minutes off the clock.

That victory, against a team that had beaten the Tigers 26-18 in September, put LSU in its home-state's major postseason game for the first time in 15 years. After all the animosity through the years between the bowl and the school, both were elated to have each other.

As it turned out, the Tigers' opponent would be once-beaten and seventh-ranked Big Ten champion Illinois, making for an alluring game of contrasts: Illinois' heralded quarterback Kurt Kittner threw for a school-record 26 touchdowns and 2,994 yards, putting the Tiger defense again under the gun. At the same time Illinois brought a more-than-capable secondary, which allowed an average of 214 yards for the season, to challenge LSU's aerial prowess.

In another year Illinois would have been unavailable to New Orleans. For the first time the Rose Bowl, for a half-century the postseason home for Big Ten and Pac-10 champions, was to host the BCS national championship game. This season Miami and Nebraska would be in Pasadena.

Illinois fell into the Sugar's lap.

It also reunited two old friends, Saban and Illini coach Ron Turner, who used to enjoy beers together when both were NFL assistants, Saban in Cleveland and Turner in Chicago. Also, although the schools had never played before, they had a major bond. Mike Chambers, LSU's trainer in the 1930s, played for Illinois in the Red Grange era. He became such a beloved figure in Tigertown that LSU's mascot, Mike the Tiger, whom Chambers helped secure, was named for him.

Warm feelings aside, more than anything the pairing

was a boon to the Sugar Bowl, Executive Director Paul Hoolahan said ticket demands ranked as high as the bowl's recent record national title games.

"Talk about a windfall!" Hoolahan said two days before the Sugar Bowl. "This is as good a situation as we could have possibly hoped for. We were obviously concerned, as were the other bowls, that plane travel would be an issue for some people. So if we had our druthers, we were hoping to secure a local team.

"Sure enough, the way the stars were lined up, it all fell into place."

Domanick Davis (31) is congratulated by fellow teammates after scoring one of four touchdowns.

"It was pitch and catch."

This Sugar Bowl was one for the books – the record books.

In a game being played more for poll position and the old-time bowl goal of pure fun than anything else, LSU was rollicking in the first 30 minutes, and by halftime sending press box statisticians flipping furiously through the records.

By then the one faint doubt of the outcome was whether Kurt Kittner would once again manage to bring his team a come-from-behind victory, which he had done five times during the regular-season.

In that opening half the Illini simply could not slow down the Tigers. After a couple of self-inflicted miscues (both by tight

Illinois quarterback Kurt Kittner (15) tries to escape the reach of Jeremy Lawrence (56).

Josh Reed (25) led the LSU receivers with 239 yards and two touchdowns.

ends – a flag on Robert Royal that killed one drive and a drop by Joe Domingeaux that could have gone the distance), LSU scored touchdowns on five of its next six possessions. That span included the biggest scoring spurt in Sugar Bowl history, with 27 Tiger points in the second quarter.

It came down to this: Tiger receivers were running helter-skelter across the Superdome rug almost unimpeded, through an Illini secondary that featured three All-Big Ten athletes.

"There came a point in the second quarter when Coach had to tell me to settle down," Davey said. "I was trying to hit a home run on every play. It was just pitch-and-catch."

Davis, on his way to an unprecedented four Sugar Bowl

touchdowns, scrambled in from the 2 in the opening period; in the second quarter he reached the end zone on a quick-hitter from 25 yards out; then did the same thing from the 16. Both times Illinois was trying to shoot the gaps with its cornerbacks and both times Davis ran into the vacant spaces untouched.

In the air, even when Davey was missing his mark, Illinois was unable to cover the Tiger wideouts, which showed in the stat sheets: 33 Davey passes and 19 completions, covering 246 yards. As it turned out, Davey's two touchdowns came when LSU was at point-blank range, and both came on third down with Illinois playing zone defense. First, from the 5-yard line after Josh Reed found his way to the back of the end zone where Davey speared him. Then, from the 7, Royal did the

Nick Saban is dowsed after the Tigers defeated the Illini 47-34.

same thing for the final points of the half.

The LSU defense was no less spectacular. Illinois simply couldn't hold out the Tiger rush, coming at Kittner with hands high to disrupt his low passing trajectory. It was a successful strategy, making a basket case of Kittner, who was trying to throw over a picket fence of outstretched limbs and digits. He had more first-half passes batted down at the line of scrimmage (6) than completed ones. At one point he was 1-for-13 for a grand total of one yard.

One play told the story of Illinois' frustration: Illini go-to receiver Brandon Lloyd's only catch of the first half resulted in an LSU touchdown, when corner Randall Gay stripped him after a four-yard gain, picked up the fumble and returned it 19 yards to the Illini 5. Moments later the score was jacked to 27-0 when Davey hit the embarrassingly open Reed.

Kittner finished the first half 5-of-17 passing for 80 yards and a touchdown. But 75 of those yards came on a three-play scoring drive, leaving Illinois' best quarterback in history 2-for-14 for five yards the rest of the half.

"The best way I can describe their defense is ferocious," said Lloyd, who eventually finished with two touchdown receptions and passed for another score. "They kept coming 100 miles per hour and never relented."

At intermission the Tigers had a commanding edge in total offense, 344-134, and led 34-7.

The Sugar Bowl was over, but Illinois showed its mettle by making it respectable in the second half. Kittner completed 7-of-10 passes for 142 yards and three touchdowns in the third quarter, and he ended the night 14-of-35 for 262 yards

LSU (top) celebrates as an Illinois player (bottom) looks on in disgust.

for four touchdowns and one interception.

"We found some offense in the second half, but it was too little, too late by then," Lloyd said. LSU linebacker Trev Faulk said, "We did everything we could to stop them in the first half. It would only be a matter of time before Kittner got going in the game."

When the smoke cleared, no fewer than a dozen records were set in the highest-scoring Sugar Bowl in history, including 595 yards of total offense, 444 passing yards by Davey, and 239 receiving yards by Reed on yet another record 14 receptions.

"I was in a zone," Davey gushed later. "There was no pressure on me. I was going to make the most of my opportunity. I was going to go out there and have fun."

	1	2	3	4	
LSU	7	27	7	6	47
Illinois	0	7	14	13	34

LSU: Davis, 4-yard run. PAT, Corbello kick.
LSU: Davis, 25-yard run. PAT, Kick failed.
LSU: Davis, 16-yard run. PAT, Corbello kick.
LSU: Reed, 5-yard pass from Davey. PAT, Corbello kick.
Illinois: Hodges, 2-yard pass from Kittner. PAT, Christofilakos kick.
LSU: Royal, 7-yard pass from Davey. PAT, Corbello kick.
Illinois: Lloyd, 17-yard pass from Kittner. PAT, Christofilakos kick.
Illinois: Young, 17-yard pass from Kittner. PAT, Christofilakos kick.
LSU: Reed, 32-yard pass from Davey. PAT, Corbello kick.
Illinois: Lloyd, 10-yard pass from Kittner. PAT, Christofilakos kick.
Illinois: Young, 17-yard pass from Kittner. PAT, Christofilakos kick.
LSU: Davis, 4-yard run. Pass failed.
Illinois: Young, 40-yard pass from Lloyd. Pass failed.

Individual Leaders

Rushing
LSU: Davis 29-129, 4 TDs; Henderson 13-55.
Illinois: Harvey 9-42.

Passing
LSU: Davey 31-53-0, 444 yards, 3 TDs.
Illinois: Kittner 14-35-1, 262 yards, 4 TDs.

Receiving
LSU: Reed 14-239, 2 TDs; Clayton 8-120.
Illinois: Young 6-178, 2 TDs; Lloyd 5-56, 2 TDs.

LSU		Illinois
32	First Downs	14
151	Rushing Yards	61
31-53-0	Passing	15-36-1
444	Passing Yards	302
595	Total Yards	363
6-39.4	Punts	9-40.4
2-1	Fumbles – Lost	1-1
13-113	Penalties – Yards	4-39

Attendance: 77,688.
Teams' remuneration: $26,000,000.
Miller-Digby Award recipient: Rohan Davey, LSU quarterback.

Georgia 26   Florida State 13

"There's a direct line connecting the good things."

Mark Richt was speaking of Bobby Bowden: "He taught me all I know about football," the Georgia coach said of the Florida State coach – and lovingly isn't too strong a description for his tone and obvious emotions.

This was an intriguing storyline: the old master going against his most devoted student.

Through a series of twists and turns, and in a year in which the Sugar Bowl would not be the site of the game for No. 1, the Superdome became the playing field for the matching of wits between Bowden and his former long-time assistant, Richt.

Georgia was the hot team in the Southeastern Conference, revitalized under the hand of Richt, who was persuaded to leave FSU two years before after 14 seasons of serving as Bowden's quarterbacks coach/offensive coordinator. The fourth-ranked Bulldogs went 12-1 in 2002, won the SEC for the first time since 1982, and earned a Sugar Bowl berth for the first time in two decades.

For a while it appeared the Sugar would have a glamour game with its first Pac-10 school, Southern California, against the Bulldogs. The Orange Bowl, however, used a one-time option to snatch the Trojans from New Orleans, one granted because at the birth of the Bowl Championship Series the Miami game put up more money (approximately $200,000) than the Sugar.

That put the familiar face of Bowden and 16th-ranked Florida State, which played in five Sugar Bowls in the previous 14 years, back in New Orleans – but this time against Richt, who was like a son to Bowden. "I sort of feel like I raised Mark," Bowden said in just thinking of being on opposite sides of the field.

As Bowden's chief offensive assistant, in 14 years Richt developed

Florida State head coach Bobby Bowden and Georgia head coach Mark Richt, with broadcaster Lynn Swann (middle).

two Heisman Trophy recipients, one runner-up, and five quarterbacks who went on to the NFL. In that same span, Florida State had a 169-26-2 record, won nine Atlantic Coast Conference titles and two national championships.

"There's a direct line connecting the good things that have happened at Georgia to Florida State," Richt said. "Bobby Bowden was my mentor. Just about everything I learned about coaching, learned about handling people, and about people in general, I learned from him and from being at Florida State.

"I was blessed just to be around him."

This was not one of Bowden's most memorable teams, having lost four games and his top two quarterbacks. Starter Chris Rix overslept for a final exam, rendering him ineligible. Backup Adrian McPherson was dismissed from school after running afoul of the law.

That put third-stringer Fabian Walker, a sophomore who was in on only 13 plays all season, behind center for the Sugar Bowl.

Walker may have been the least experienced quarterback to start in a major bowl since Steve Sloan replaced the suspended Joe Namath for the 1964 Sugar.

"I don't think I've ever heard of a quarterback in this situation before," Bowden reflected while prepping receiver Anquan Boldin, who would be Walkers backup and who last played quarterback in high school. "It's certainly going to be an adventure for him."

Still, outwardly at least, Georgia was preparing for a battle royal. "First of all," Richt said, "Florida State is a quality team. They beat an opponent we couldn't (Florida, 31-14) and they made (No. 1-ranked) Miami (in a 28-21 Hurricane victory) look like just another team.

"And I always thought Coach Bowden is at his best when his back is against the wall, after something has jolted him or the team. I've always admired how he handles these situations, and how he is able to get everyone focused at the task at hand. I remember well when we lost (Heisman Trophy-winning quarterback) Chris Weinke before the 1998 Florida game. Everybody wrote us off, but Florida State followed Coach Bowden's game plan to

near-perfection and we beat the Gators (23-12).
"Bobby Bowden is a coach who can find a way to get his team to rise to the occasion. I know that from experience."

Richt also knew, though, that a football team with an inex-

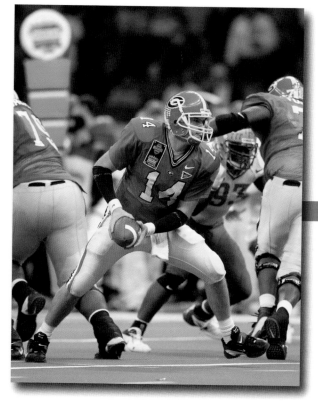

Anquan Boldin (4) fills in at quarterback for Florida State.

▲ *Georgia's Tony Milton (9) is stopped by Florida State's B.J. Ward (24) and A.J. Nickolson (54).*

▼ *Noles wide receiver P.K. Sam (81) is tackled by Sean Jones (6).*

"That doesn't overcome my sadness for me."

It's rare for an untested quarterback not to make game-turning mistakes.

This was not one of those times.

Florida State took the early fight straight to Georgia, but Bruce Thornton's second-quarter interception of a Fabian Walker pass and 71-yard return for a touchdown was just the miscue for which the Bulldogs had been waiting, and they used it as the springboard to victory.

"I wanted to make a big momentum swing," said Thornton, whose touchdown came with Georgia trailing 7-3. "We needed something to happen because they had all the momentum."

The victory put a fitting cap on Georgia's first SEC championship in 20 years. The 13-1 final record placed the Bulldogs third nationally, their highest ranking since 1983.

Florida State (9-5) ended with its most defeats since 1981.

"I'm happy for Mark," FSU coach Bobby Bowden said of his former aide. "But that doesn't overcome my sadness for me."

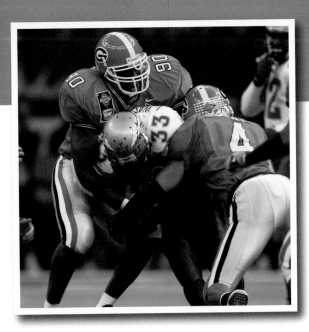

Bulldog wide receiver Michael Johnson (25) makes the grab over the Seminole's Rufus Brown (7).

It might have been different had Rix or McPherson been quarterbacking for the Seminoles. Walker played well early on, throwing a touchdown pass to Anquan Boldin in the second quarter. But he did little after the game-turning pick, and was replaced by Boldin.

"We had to do what we had to do, and things weren't very structured," Bowden said. "The split-second timing wasn't there, and we were just kind of hoping someone would make some plays. We made a couple, but it seemed like we had to work hard for everything we did, and they got it a little easier."

Boldin threw a 40-yard touchdown pass to Craphonso Thorpe on the last play of the third quarter to make the score 23-13, but that was as close as the Seminoles got.

Georgia's Billy Bennett kicked the last of his four field goals with 10:39 left, and Florida State's last real chance to at least make it interesting ended when Tim Jennings stopped Boldin on the Georgia 32, three yards short of a first down on a fourth down carry with 6:50 to go.

Georgia, outgained 131-118 in the first half and in control of the ball for only 8:17 with just four first downs, did a better job in the second half, chiefly on the running of Musa Smith.

Smith carried 23 times for 145 yards, 108 after intermission, and earned the Miller-Digby Award as the game's MVP.

"When a defense like ours is playing as good as it did tonight, you have a great kicking game and a running back like Musa Smith, you're going to win a lot of games if you don't mess up," Richt said. "It might have been a little boring. But in a game like this, you'll take boring if that's what wins for you."

Things certainly weren't boring before Thornton's interception.

Florida State, as an eight-point underdog, was leading more than midway into the second quarter and had the ball in Georgia territory with a third-and-six at the Bulldog 34. Walker lofted the ball and Thornton, a junior with only one previous career interception, picked it off and had little trouble negotiating the left sideline for the score.

"I think he (Walker) got pressure on him," Thornton said.

Georgia wide receiver DeMario Minter (2) joins the crowd after Georgia defeated Florida State 26-13.

"Maybe he was trying to throw it away. I just happened to come up and catch the ball."

Four plays later, after a 26-yard punt return by Damien Gary, Georgia had the ball at the FSU 37. The Bulldogs' backup quarterback, D.J. Shockley, came in and wasted no time passing to Terrence Edwards, who had beaten Seminole cornerback Stanford Samuels at the goal line for the touchdown to make the score 17-7.

That was Georgia's only offensive touchdown of the night, but with a defense that ranked fourth nationally in points allowed, it proved to be enough.

"Coach Richt taught us how to win," Edwards said. "That's what this whole season's been about."

Richt gave credit to Bowden for teaching him how to coach a winning team. "Coach Bowden is just one of the best men I've ever known," Richt said. "We just had to play against him, and no matter who you play you want to win.

"They made it a great game until the very end."

	1	2	3	4	
Georgia	3	14	6	3	26
Florida State	0	7	6	0	13

Georgia: Bennett, 23-yard field goal.
Florida State: Boldin, 5-yard pass from Walker. PAT, Bennett kick.
Georgia: Thornton, 71-yard interception return. PAT, Bennett kick.
Georgia: Edwards, 37-yard pass from Shockley. PAT, Bennett kick.
Georgia: Bennett, 42-yard field goal.
Georgia: Bennett, 25-yard field goal.
Florida State: Thorpe, 40-yard pass from Boldin. Run failed.
Georgia: Bennett, 35-yard field goal.

Individual Leaders

Rushing
Georgia: Smith, 23-145; Milton 5-13.
Florida State: Washington 10-48; Boldin 13-34.

Passing
Georgia: Greene 9-14-0, 88 yards.
Florida State: Boldin 6-14-0, 78 yards, 1 TD.

Receiving
Georgia: Edwards 3-60, 1 TD; Johnson 1-34.
Florida State: Thorpe 1-40, 1 TD; Boldin 3-34, 1 TD.

Georgia		Florida State
11	First Downs	18
151	Rushing Yards	115
10-15-0	Passing	13-26-2
125	Passing Yards	147
276	Total Yards	262
4-48.2	Punts	5-40.4
1-1	Fumbles – Lost	2-1
6-59	Penalties – Yards	5-37

Attendance: 74,269.
Teams' remuneration: $27,000,000.
Miller-Digby Award recipient: Musa Smith, Georgia running back.

LSU 21 Oklahoma 14

"This is the spotlight game."

How short memories can be.

For years, decades, really, fans had complained – almost always when their favorite team was not in the top spot – about the biases of sportswriters voting in the polls. The coaches' poll (now under the auspices of USA Today/ESPN) was also questioned, but to a lesser degree because coaches, by their own admissions, often don't vote; they let underlings do it for them, at least until the end of the regular season.

In a way, that's what brought on the advent of the Bowl Championship Series, with its series of factors – knowledgeable observations and the data from various polls fed into computers – to come up with the most deserving two teams to meet for the national championship.

The idea was to have as close to a true No. 1 game as possible, while preserving the bowl system, and not, as was the case for most of the 20th century, a championship based on opinion. Educated opinions for the most part, but opinions nevertheless.

Yet that's exactly what was at the heart of the great college football debate of 2003 – not to mention the national championship.

Here's the crux of the matter: Oklahoma spent the entire regular season at the top of the two polls, then, when it was released in October, the BCS standings. OU obliterated the other contenders, and was talked about and written about as perhaps the greatest team of all-time – until the Sooners stunningly lost 35-7 to Kansas State in the Big 12 championship game. Southern Cal had a remarkably fine season, losing once

to a so-so California squad, but finishing atop the sportswriters and coaches polls. Not flashy but efficient LSU came out of nowhere after losing to Florida at midseason then stampeding the rest of its way to the SEC championship game.

The trio were obviously the nation's best college football teams, all with one defeat.

The BCS formula was then a combination of computer rankings, schedule comparisons, quality-win bonuses and a composite of the AP writers and USA Today/ESPN coaches polls.

The human opinion polls had USC ranked No. 1 at the end of the regular season, but the cold, calculating, dispassionate seven computers that figured the BCS standings had Oklahoma and LSU ranked 1 and 2, based largely on strength of schedule, a factor that was not determined until the last weekend of the season with Syracuse defeating Notre Dame and Boise State beating Hawaii. Both of the losing teams had been USC opponents and deflated the Trojans' accomplishments.

Those games turned out to mean everything because, coupled with LSU beating Georgia in the SEC title match, the Trojans suddenly

trailed both OU and LSU in six of the seven computer rankings and in overall schedule strength. In the final BCS rankings, Oklahoma, 12-1, was first with 5.11 points based on its No. 1 position in five of the seven computers. LSU, 12-1, was second at 5.99, edging USC (11-1) by 0.16 in the second- closest finish in the BCS's six-year history.

Nebraska nipped Colorado by 0.05 in 2001.

The howl that went up in Los Angeles (home base of the Trojans) and by voting sportswriters made the weeks leading up to bowls a media-spitting match. Southern Cal, No. 1 in the AP poll, was set to play fourth-ranked Michigan in the Rose Bowl. A victory would give the Trojans first place in at least one poll.

But Oklahoma and LSU were ticketed to play for the BCS national championship in the Sugar Bowl, a title, site and formula designated years before and agreed to by every school in the NCAA's Division 1-A, including Southern California.

An irony is that the system was tweaked the previous year to take margins of victory out of the computers' computations because of thinking that the equation shouldn't be a factor, that a victory was just a victory and a defeat was just a defeat. So Oklahoma's lopsided loss to Kansas State had no more weight than USC's or LSU's. Also, as opposed to years gone by, a late-season defeat was no worse than an early setback. USC lost in September, LSU in October, and Oklahoma in December.

Had those computations remained in the equation (and apparently they did in the minds of the sportswriters), it's very likely LSU would have been playing Southern Cal in the Sugar Bowl.

But all the computers could factor was one defeat for each of the contenders, and one fewer victory for USC than Oklahoma or LSU. If the argument was difficulty of schedule, the Trojans came up short there, too. USC and LSU had two common opponents, Auburn and Arizona. The Trojans beat Auburn 23-0 in the opening game of the season; LSU defeated Auburn 31-7 eight weeks later. LSU beat Arizona 59-13 in its second game. USC whipped Arizona 45-0. Diplomatic Auburn coach Tommy Tuberville said he wouldn't want to be playing LSU right now (at the end of the regular season when the LSU defense was performing with the cold precision of an execution squad). Arizona senior Clay Hart was asked to make a comparison and said, "I thought they were really good," he said of the Trojans, "but I personally think LSU was the best team we've faced since I've been a Wildcat."

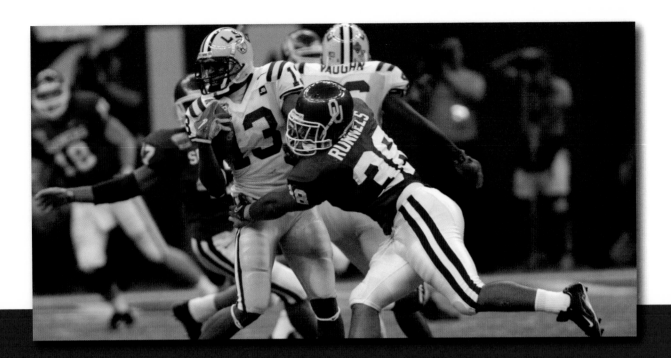

"Everybody wants to sit here and say they got screwed," Oklahoma defensive tackle Dusty Dvoracek said of Southern Cal, "but they actually got the easier row to hoe. They got to stay at home (in the Rose Bowl), play the lesser team (Michigan).

BCS coordinator Mike Tranghese put things in a smiley-face scenario: "If you're a USC fan, you're very, very disappointed," he said. "On the other hand, if you're an Oklahoma or LSU fan, you're happy because you're being given an opportunity to play. In the old (pre-BCS) system, these teams would have gone to separate bowl games. USC would have gone to the Rose Bowl, and LSU would have gone to the Sugar and Oklahoma in the Fiesta Bowl. And none of them would have played (each other). So I think our system is better than we had."

Tiger defensive tackle Kyle Williams would've liked to put the title on the line between the winners of the Rose and Sugar bowls. "Would I like to play them? Sure, we'd love to play them and decide it (who's No. 1)," he said of the Trojans. "I'm sure USC is looking at it the same way we are. To them, their game is the one that matters. But to us, this is the spotlight game. It's us against Oklahoma for all the marbles ... Well, most of them."

"Rub it like a genie?"

The Sugar Bowl really had the look of a monumental collision comin' on.

Oklahoma was the highest-scoring team in college football, averaging an eye-popping 45.2 points. And the Sooners were also the nation's third-best overall defensive team, giving up an average of 255.7 yards a game.

Consider this heady statistic: In its first 12 games, Oklahoma was behind for fewer than six of the 720 minutes played.

Not only did the Sooners have seven first-team All-Americans, but they practically swept the major individual awards that go to the sport's crème de la crème. They were: the Heisman Trophy, to quarterback Jason White, as the nation's top player; the Fred Biletnikoff Award, to Mark Clayton, as the nation's top receiver; the Chuck Bednarik Award, to Tommie Harris, the top defensive player; the Dick Butkus Award, to Teddy Lehman, the top linebacker; the Lombardi, to Harris, the top interior player; the Bronco Nagurski, the Jim Thorpe, to Derrick Strait, the top defensive back; the Davey O'Brien, to White, the top quarterback; and AP Player of the Year to White.

No wonder they were being compared with the best teams of all time.

Next to the Sooners, the Tigers just had two All-Americans, defensive tackle Chad Lavalais and cornerback Corey Webster.

Conversely, despite its relative anonymity, LSU was a complete team, scoring an average of 35 points behind Matt Mauck, a 24-year-old former minor-league catcher who had the SEC's highest quarterback rating, along with a dangerous combination of running backs and receivers and a big, fast offensive line that combined for 156 starts.

It was on defense, though, where LSU separated itself from the rest of college football. The Tigers led the nation in rushing defense, yielding a miniscule 68.2 yards, and were atop the statistical list in scoring defense, allowing a paltry 10.5 points a game.

This is how lethal LSU could be: In the SEC championship game, against a Georgia squad that was still in the Top 10 despite its earlier defeat to the Tigers, at one point LSU led the Bulldogs 17-0 and outgained them 196 to minus 8.

It was obvious that in the Sugar Bowl something would have to give – but not the self-discipline of the Tigers, very much aware LSU hadn't won a national title in 45 years.

LSU offensive lineman Stephen Peterman eyed the crystal trophy that goes to the BCS champion as it was displayed on the 25-yard line of the Superdome two days before the Sugar Bowl. "I ain't touching it," he said. "Rub it like a genie? Has anyone ever touched it and lost? Not me. It's a jinx.

"You can't touch it – it's not ours yet."

Oklahoma running back Kejuan Jones (20) is stuffed by Cameron Vaughn (46) and Lionel Turner (29).

Tiger defensive back Jonathan Zenon (33) was just late in getting to Oklahoma quarterback Jason White (18).

LSU running back Justin Vincent (25) rushed for 117 yards, one touchdown and averaged 7.3 yards a carry. Vincent proved to be too much for the Oklahoma defense, as the Tigers went on to defeat the Sooners 21-14.

 70TH SUGAR BOWL CLASSIC

"It's like winning the lottery."

LSU made a convincing case: Start to finish, with Tiger freshman Justin Vincent juking linebacker Gayron Allen and shooting 64 yards in the open field on the game's first play to set the tone, LSU was in command.

"Any time you make (big) plays, they have a lot to do with momentum," LSU coach Nick Saban said of Vincent's opening streak. "That play did."

On the last meaningful play, with Jason White searching for someone – anyone – open enough to get fingers on the ball and tie things up, Tiger linebacker Lionel Turner fired through the middle on a delayed blitz and flattened the quarterback and any OU hopes.

In between this may have been the biggest seven-point rout in football history. Put this in focus: LSU held Oklahoma, which averaged 461 offensive yards coming into the Sugar Bowl, to 152 total yards – 52 of that rushing on 70 plays, an average of 0.74 yards a try; LSU held OU, which averaged those 45 points coming into the Sugar Bowl, to a couple of touchdowns, arrived at on a combined 33 yards.

And the Tigers spent the night, as they did all season, responding positively to adversity.

What had all the earmarks of an 80-yard touchdown run by Vincent turned into mere field position when Sooner defensive back Derrick Strait ran him down at the Oklahoma 16. Four

TIGERS 21 · 1 BALL 19 2:25
HIBERNIA National Bank SOONERS 14 0 T.O.L DOWN 4 TO GO 4 QTR 4

▲ *LSU Head Coach Nick Saban holds up the National Championship Trophy as the team looks on.*

plays later, playing a first-and-goal at the 1, quarterback Matt Mauck fumbled the snap and the Sooners recovered.

In just two plays, though, Corey Webster intercepted White's first pass at midfield and returned it to the 32. LSU was on the boards in short order as speedster Skyler Green turned right end and tiptoed along the sidelines 24 yards to the end zone.

In the second quarter, Oklahoma showed its first signs of life when it blocked a Tiger punt two yards from the LSU goal. It took an OU offense that scored on its first possession 11 times during the season, and on its second possession the other two times, four plays (after a penalty) to punch it in and tie the score. The Sooners had been outgained 204-50 at that point, yet the teams were even on the scoreboard.

LSU put together a big-time response, driving 80 yards before Vincent ran the final 18 on the same play with which he opened the game. The Tigers again had the lead with 4:21 remaining until the half – a half in which Oklahoma managed a total of 44 yards.

"That was the turning point of the game," Saban said of the go-

ahead drive. "They blocked a punt and scored (an easy touchdown), and our offense came right back."

What proved to be the final nail in Oklahoma's coffin came with 47 seconds gone in the third quarter when White unleashed his first pass of the second half – and hit Tiger defensive end Marcus Spears in the flat. "I dropped back and it was like a gift," Spears, a former tight end, said. "When I saw it coming, I said, 'Man, put your hands up and try to get the thing to the end zone.' "

Twenty yards later, that's exactly where Spears found himself.

After a Tiger field goal, which would have given LSU a 24-7 lead, was wiped away by a penalty, Oklahoma got new life, and after LSU's only major mistake of the game, a third-down interception of Mauck that Brodney Pool returned 49 yards to the Tiger 31, somehow Oklahoma was seriously back in the fray. Kejuan Jones went in from the 1 with 11:01 – plenty of time – to play.

The Sooners had Tiger fans gripping their seats from that point to the end, as White, taking over at the 5:45 mark, moved Okla-

With their win over the Sooners the Tigers celebrated ▲ their first National Championship since 1958

	1	2	3	4	
LSU	7	7	7	0	21
Oklahoma	0	7	0	7	14

LSU: Green, 24-yard run. PAT, Gaudet kick.

Oklahoma: Jones, 1-yard run. PAT, DiCarlo kick.

LSU: Vincent, 18-yard run. PAT, Gaudet kick.

LSU: Spears, 20-yard interception return. PAT, Gaudet kick.

Oklahoma: Jones, 1-yard run. PAT, DiCarlo kick.

Individual Leaders

Rushing
LSU: Vincent 16-117, 1 TD; Mauck 14-27.
Oklahoma: Jones 20-58, 2 TDs; Clayton 4-38.

Passing
LSU: Mauck 13-22-2, 124 yards.
Oklahoma: White 13-37-2, 102 yards.

Receiving
LSU: Jones 3-54; Clayton 4-38.
Oklahoma: Clayton 4-32; Wilson 3-31.

LSU		Oklahoma
13	First Downs	12
159	Rushing Yards	52
14-24-2	Passing	13-37-2
153	Passing Yards	102
312	Total Yards	154
8-34.0	Punts	8-45.9
1-1	Fumbles – Lost	2-0
8-65	Penalties – Yards	11-70

Attendance: 79,342.
Teams' remuneration: $28,000,000.
Miller-Digby Award recipient: Justin Vincent, LSU tailback.

homa from its 39 to the LSU 12 in eight plays. From there, however, the Tigers threw up their prickly defense, giving OU no openings in the passing lanes. Only on fourth down did the Sooners come close.

The tying touchdown pass was tipped by safety Jack Hunt and trickled off the fingers of Mark Clayton in the end zone. "I just tried to give somebody a chance to catch it," White said. "He almost caught it."

LSU, despite the controversy, finished with its first national championship in four decades, even if Southern Cal also claimed a piece of it. "It doesn't bother me," tackle Chad Lavalais said. "It's like winning the lottery but you have to share the Powerball with someone else. It's still a good deal."

Mauck had no doubt who was No. 1. "All I know is the powers that be selected us to be in this game; (and) we just received the (championship) trophy."

There was something else that should convince any disbelievers who made preseason bets on the eventual No. 1 team: Las Vegas paid off on Sugar Bowl champion LSU.

That was as official as any poll.

Auburn 16 Virginia Tech 13

"Things are as they are."

After the flap that left Southern Cal out of the Bowl Championship Series loop in the 2004 Sugar Bowl, the BCS decided to tweak its computer compilations without perhaps the most important ingredient, and the one that put LSU into that season's title game: strength of schedule, feeling it was already built into the equation.

That change would come back to haunt Auburn University.

The Tigers from the Alabama plains were an unlikely national challenger. Coach Tommy Tuberville was so unpopular with school administrators that the president, board members and athletic director took a flight to interview another potential coach during the 2003 season.

Somehow, Tuberville survived. Auburn's president and AD did not.

Tuberville put together a superb team in 2004, one that would win 12 games in the regular season, win the SEC Championship Game, beat four nine-victory opponents and four Top 10 teams, and trail at halftime only twice.

For all that, there was one obstacle Auburn could not overcome: Tigers were ranked 17th in the preseason polls. Southern Cal and Oklahoma entered the season ranked No. 1 and No. 2 and neither ever lost. Auburn never really had a chance at the national championship.

With exceptional quarterbacking from Jason Campbell and two outstanding tailbacks in Carnell Williams and Ronnie Brown, Auburn rose to No. 3, but could never crack the top two to play in the national title game in the Orange Bowl, becoming the first SEC team since Alabama in 1966 to go undefeated and untied and not have a shot at finishing No. 1.

The consolation prize, and not a bad one, Tuberville was quick to

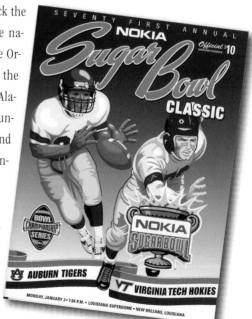

Halftime activities in the Superdome with over 2,000 perfomers.

acknowledge, was the SEC's Sugar Bowl berth. Perhaps a pairing between the Tigers and the equally unde-feated Utah would have been an eye-catcher, but Atlantic Coast Conference cham-pion Virginia Tech, 10-2, was picked.

It was abundantly clear that for all Auburn's credentials, nobody was giving any-thing to the Tigers, the fifth-best defense (269.5)

in the land, and the best (11.2) in scoring defense. In those same categories, Tech was fourth (265.3) and third (12.6), so the Tigers didn't draw any gimme.

The pairing, though, was especially interesting since one of the Hokies' defeats came in the season-opener to Southern Cal (24-13).

Tech coach Frank Beamer said he thought Auburn should be in Miami playing for more than pride, and had so indicated in his ballot in the coaches' poll. "I certainly believe, and the way I voted, is that (Auburn) should be playing in the na-tional championship game," Beamer said. "I think anytime you go through the SEC and the title game in that league, you deserve to play for the national championship.

"But things are as they are."

Auburn coach Tommy Tuberville.

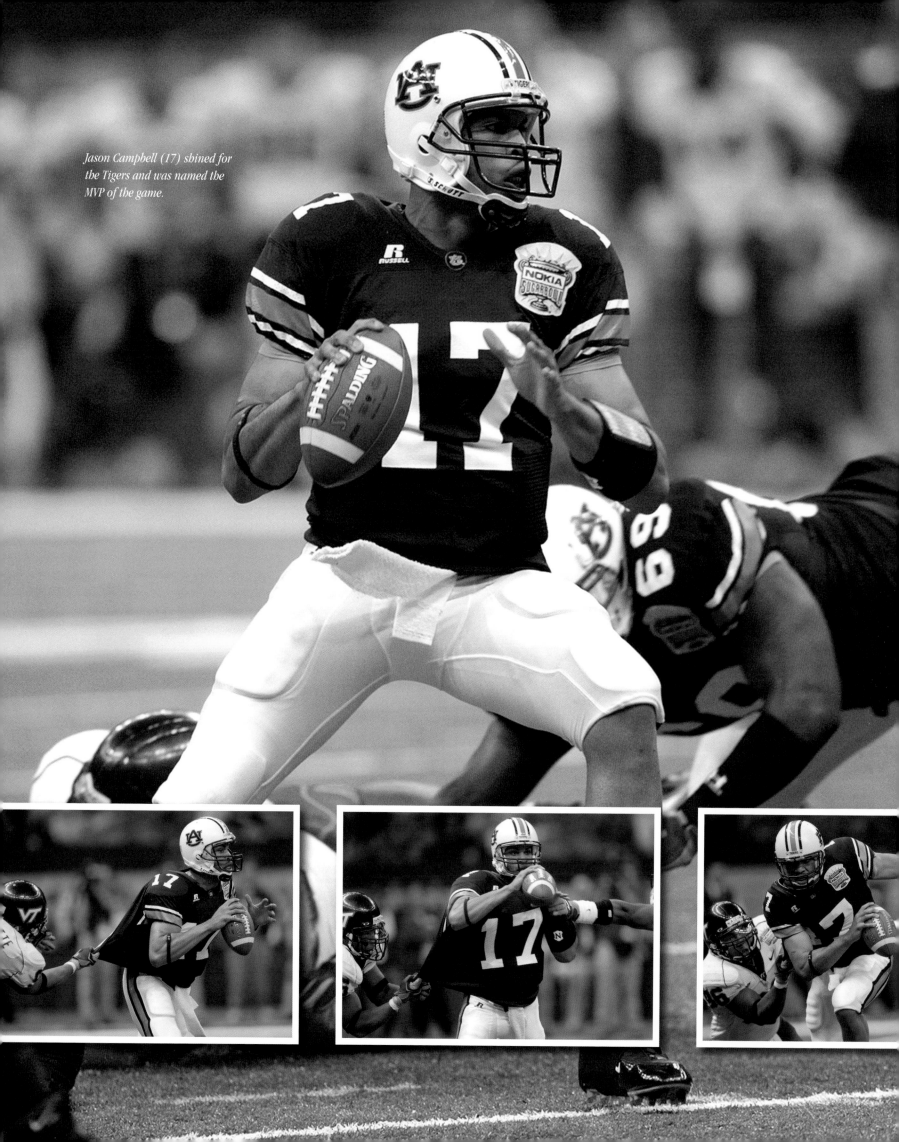

Jason Campbell (17) shined for the Tigers and was named the MVP of the game.

"We have them backed up."

The Auburn Tigers wanted to make a statement.

What they made was sort of more of a stammer.

Starting out like it was going to show the college football world what an injustice its omission from the national championship game had perpetuated, the Tigers could never put Virginia Tech away – and, in fact, could well have lost the game along with their argument in the end.

Early though, the Tigers were making a strong case. On the night's first series, quarterback Jason Campbell drove Auburn to the Hokies' 8. But the Tigers couldn't put the ball in the end zone. John Vaughn kicked a 21-yard field goal.

An interception of Tech quarterback Bryan Randall by Junior Rosengreen eventually put the Tigers at the 1 – where the Hokies forced a second Vaughn field goal.

Auburn was in front and in charge – but not convincingly, even though Virginia Tech was unable to seriously dent the formidable Tiger defense.

By the end of the quarter, Tech had two first downs and just 30 yards of offense, nine of which came on scrambles by Randall.

The first real signs of offensive life for Virginia Tech came in the second period when Randall drove the Hokies to the Tiger 2 and the opportunity to seize the lead against an Auburn team that was settling for field goals instead of touchdowns.

After two futile plays, on third down Randall ran a quarterback draw and, for an instant, had a clear path to the end zone.

But free safety Will Henning shot up the middle and stopped Randall a yard short. Then, on fourth down, passing up a field goal

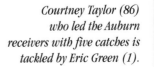

Courtney Taylor (86)
who led the Auburn
receivers with five catches is
tackled by Eric Green (1).

and with everyone expecting another power run, Randall rolled out and flung a pass between two defenders to sophomore fullback Jesse Allen – who had it for an instant, then dropped it. The ball may have been brushed by a defender's finger, but no one was certain.

"I wasn't sure if it was tipped or not," Allen said. "Randall usually puts the ball in there where you can get it. It was my job to catch it."

Coach Frank Beamer explained his rationale in going for seven points instead of the almost sure three at that point thusly: "We had a chance to go up 7-6, and I felt we were lucky to be down (just) 6-0 at that time," Beamer said. "I felt even if we don't make it, we'd have them backed up."

Instead, not only did Virginia Tech fail to take the lead but Auburn took over at the 1, and then proceeded to march 92 yards to the Hokies' 7, where John Vaughn kicked another field goal, this one of 24 yards.

The 9-0 halftime lead gave Auburn breathing room, and, then, on the opening drive of the third quarter, the Tigers extended the lead with their lone touchdown of the night. Campbell hit Anthony Mix with a 53-yard completion to the Tech 13, then threw five yards to Devin Aronashodu for the TD that put Auburn up 16-0.

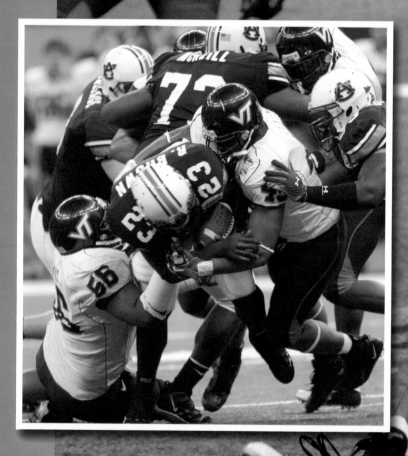

*Josh Morgan (17) scores one
of his two touchdowns.*

Ronnie Brown (23) breaks free from the tough Virginia Tech defense.

John Vaughn (37) kicks one of his three field goals to help lead the Tigers to victory over the Hokies.

An indication of Auburn's control of the game at this point would be that at the end of three quarters, the Hokie running backs had a total net of 26 yards.

Virginia Tech, though, was about to throw a major scare into the Tigers. A recovered fumble led to Tech's first points with a 29-yard scoring pass from Randall to Josh Morgan.

Time was running out, but Tech made the ending a heart-stopper when Randall-to-Morgan struck again, this time on a stunning 80-yard pass – the longest against the Tigers all season – with 2:01 remaining.

Suddenly Tech, dominated almost all evening long, had a chance to steal the Sugar Bowl – and the thunder from Auburn's argument that it may well have been the nation's best college football team. Cooper Wallace's recovery of Tech's on-sides kick, though, ended matters for all practical purposes.

In a way, Tech deserved a better fate. The Hokies, whose running backs had only 34 yards but lived on a controlled passing offense, outgained the Tigers 375-299, and the Tech defense turned in a sterling performance, holding Auburn in check for all but five plays.

Those five plays, though, were the difference. The Tigers gained 179 yards on their five plays of 20 yards or longer. Auburn had 120 on its other 54 plays. "We held them to field goals, but the big plays hurt us," Hokies cornerback Eric Green said.

"We wanted to make the quarterback (Campbell, who was the game's MVP) beat us, and he made a couple of huge plays tonight," defensive end Nolan Burchette said. "I think we did very well against their two tailbacks. Up front we did very well containing them – better than any other team did this year."

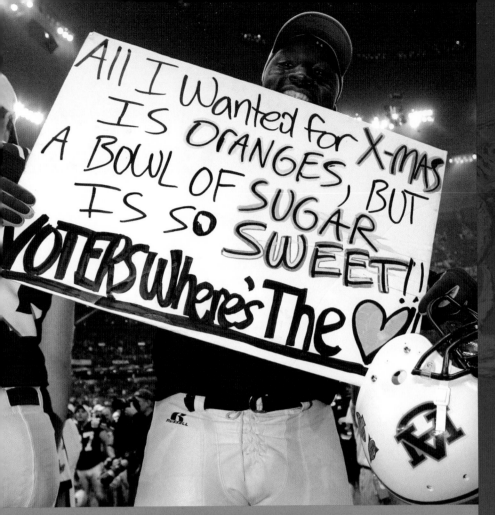

Jay Ratliff sends a message after defeating Virginia Tech.

	1	2	3	4	
Auburn	6	3	7	0	16
Virginia Tech	0	0	0	13	13

Auburn: Vaughn, 23-yard field goal.

Auburn: Vaughn, 19-yard field goal.

Auburn: Vaughn, 24-yard field goal.

Auburn: Aronashodu, 5-yard pass from Campbell. PAT, Vaughn kick.

Virginia Tech: Morgan, 29-yard pass from Randall. Run failed.

Virginia Tech: Morgan, 80-yard pass from Randall. PAT, Pace kick.

Individual Leaders

Rushing
Auburn: Brown 15-68; Williams 19-61.
Virginia Tech: Randall 9-45; Imoh 6-16.

Passing
Auburn: Campbell 11-16-1, 189 yards, 1 TD.
Virginia Tech: Randall 21-38-2, 299 yards, 2 TDs.

Receiving
Auburn: Taylor 5-89; Mix 2-68.
Virginia Tech: Morgan 3-126, 2 TDs; Hyman 5-71.

Williams and Brown combined for 129 yards, 60 less than their season average. Still, Auburn became just the 10th school in NCAA history to finish a season 13-0 or better.

It didn't do the Tigers any good, however. They still were left in the cold as far as national recognition went.

Coach Tommy Tuberville got something out of the memorable season, however. He cracked after the Sugar Bowl that maybe if the more recognized national media polls didn't pick Auburn No. 1, perhaps someone else would, like maybe *Golf Digest.*

The tongue-in-cheek comment brought a quick response. A representative of the magazine contacted the Tiger coach and informed him that he would be receiving a lifetime subscription.

Auburn		Virginia Tech
14	First Downs	19
110	Rushing Yards	76
11-16-1	Passing	21-38-2
189	Passing Yards	299
299	Total Yards	375
4-42.0	Punts	5-35.2
1-1	Fumbles – Lost	0-0
4-35	Penalties – Yards	7-57

Attendance: 77,349
Teams' remuneration: $28,000,000.
Miller-Digby Award recipient: Jason Campbell, Auburn quarterback.

West Virginia 38   Georgia 35

"This has been our ultimate challenge."

Kickoff of the 72nd Sugar Bowl was like watching the flag raising on Mount Suribachi: powerful and inspiring.

In its almost three-quarters of a century history, through the most frightful events of the last eight decades: global economic depression, the world's bloodiest war, terrorist attack on America, the Sugar Bowl not only endured but flowered.

Hard times – and an ability to deal with them – helped the Sugar Bowl flourish.

But nothing could have prepared the Sugar, or any other sports, civic or government entity, for anything like Katrina.

Hurricane Katrina, one of the strongest storms in recorded history, made landfall on Aug. 29, 2005, damaging large tracks of three states, flattening huge portions of the Gulf Coasts, and lower areas of New Orleans, which for a while recast the Big Easy into a brackish bog. Breaches in the levee system surrounding the city, much of which sits below sea level, caused extensive flooding, ruining many neighborhoods.

Tens of thousands of homes were destroyed, and hundreds of people killed.

Life in New Orleans would never be the same.

Even that mighty structure that had become the modern symbol of the old town, the Superdome, the home of the Sugar Bowl, was a casualty. Its roof was partly stripped by the winds, and later, after it was used as a shelter of last resort for thousands who could not, or would not, evacuate, it became a huge but hellish hovel. Utilities went out, as they did all over New Orleans, meaning air-conditioning and plumbing were also gone. The Dome floor was inundated, and some of the defenseless crowded into the Dome were bullied by thugs, who also looted some of the offices in the building, including the Sugar Bowl's.

All of a sudden, in this football-mad region, sports was the last thing on the minds of the people. The stadium was unusable, hotels were too damaged for a multitude of visitors, and the city was essentially on its knees.

The status of the Sugar Bowl was really in the balance. The game could be played in Baton Rouge, or in At-

lanta, or perhaps elsewhere. But did such a New Orleans sporting institution – one worth an estimated $200 million annually to the regional economy – be played anywhere outside the area?

Executive Director Paul Hoolahan noted it was imperative that the Superdome be reopened by the 2008 game because that is the year in which New Orleans is scheduled to host both the national championship game and the "regular" Sugar Bowl under the BCS' new double-hosting format.

That aspect of New Orleans' recovery was taken care of in time for the 2007 game.

For the 2006 Sugar Bowl, though, the game would be played 500 miles away. In the end, lack of the approximate 32,000 necessary hotel rooms in Baton Rouge needed was an obstacle that could not be overcome if the game was played at LSU.

"We couldn't have fans scattered from Mobile to Lafayette to Jackson, Miss. driving in to Baton Rouge on the day of the game," one bowl official said. "That's not what the Sugar Bowl experience is supposed to be."
Hotel rooms were not a problem in Atlanta.

"I think Paul was surprised to learn he had a choice of four different headquarters hotels," said Bob Schuler, vice president of the Atlanta Convention and Tourist Bureau. "The period around the Sugar Bowl is one of low occupancy for our hotels, so we can easily accommodate the fans.

"We're going to do everything to create a quality bowl experience. It won't be New Orleans, but the teams and fans will have plenty to do."

The Sugar Bowl would be played Jan. 2, following Atlanta's Peach Bowl on Dec. 30 and a Falcons-Carolina NFL game on Jan. 1.

With the help of the Atlanta Convention and Tourist Bureau, Hoolahan, who lost two homes in the storm,

West Virginia quarterback Pat White (5) scrambles against the Bulldog defense.

▲ *Martrez Milner (87) attempts to catch a pass from D.J. Shockley.*

▼ *Pat White (5) tries to break free from a Georgia defender.*

gathered his bedraggled staff, and set up hearth and home at the Omni Hotel adjacent to CNN, a short walk from the Inforum building where their offices were located as well as the Georgia Dome, site of the first Sugar Bowl to be played outside New Orleans.

"If we had to do this, we're in the perfect city," Hoolahan reflected. "The infrastructure of hotel rooms, entertainment venues and the like was already here. People pointed us in the right direction, and from then on it was a matter of plugging to the resources instead of having to spend a lot of time trying to find our own way."

Along with more than 50 members of the Sugar Bowl committee, on hand to lend their assistance, the staff did yeomen-like work. And they all needed to after losing about six weeks of work after Katrina and having to adjust to their new city.

The staff consisted of associate executive director Jeff Hundley, business manager Kathy Gaspard, ticket manager Sandy King, receptionist Kelli Bourgeois, interns Deidra Church and Megan Mathis – who just started work a week before Katrina – and director of communications Greg Blackwell, one of the Sugar's major heroes.

When personnel was first allowed into the Superdome about a month after the storm to briefly check the condition of their offices, Hoolahan and Blackwell found the Sugar Bowl office broken into, trashed and looted. The thieves got into petty cash boxes and took the insignificant sum, but overlooked an irreplaceable historical treasure.

An elegant and classic silver cup was still standing in its place. It was handmade in England in 1830 during the reign of King George IV by the silversmiths Rebecca Emes and Edward Barnard. Samuel Waldhorn, a renowned New Orleans antique dealer obtained the rare piece on one of his yearly European business trips. When the Sugar Bowl was getting off the ground in 1935 it was donated to the effort – and became its symbol.

Blackwell secured the trophy and took it with him and his wife – across the country to California, where his family lives, until it could be returned to a safe place. Then he – and the Sugar Bowl – buckled down for its 72nd game.

"This has been our ultimate challenge," Hoolahan said.

"We've taken a major event, transferred it to another city, kept it to the high standards we've always set for ourselves, and when it's over, we'll pack up, go back home and start anew.

"There is a great amount of satisfaction of knowing that we've still got all the moving parts in place. There is no doubt I'm awfully proud of this group."

Ironically, the University of Georgia earned the SEC berth by beating LSU 34-14 – at the same Georgia Dome where the Sugar would be played and in the same city where the Bulldogs beat arch-rival Georgia Tech weeks before. The No. 7 Bulldogs, with a 10-2 record and the nation's fourth-best defense, yielding just 14 points a game, was essentially playing a home game. With all its perceived advantages, Georgia was a touchdown favorite over West Virginia, 10-1 but champions of the lowly regarded Big East Conference, a league which was already 0-3 in the season's bowl games. The No. 11 Mountaineers, coached by former Tulane offensive coordinator Rich Rodriguez, were ranked behind six teams that lost more games, including Georgia.

"Nobody gives us much respect," Craig Wilson, a Mountaineer defensive end from New Orleans, said. "Everybody claims the Big East is a weak league, and that makes us a weak team. We know that's not true, but the only way to prove it is by beating Georgia."

That would be a tall order. At the controls of the Bulldogs offense was D.J. Shockley, a superb quarterback who completed 153 of 277 passes for 2,311 yards with 21 touchdowns and just five interceptions. He also ran for 251 yards and four TDs.

It was thought the 'Dogs going against the Mountaineers would be like men going against boys. And with reason. Eleven redshirt and eight true freshmen, including Steve Slaton, dotted the West Virginia starting units. Slaton came in with 924 yards rushing and 16 touchdowns. WVU QB Pat White, a redshirt freshman, entered the game with 708 passing yards and seven touchdowns, and ran for 875 yards and seven more touchdowns, a prime reason why the Mountaineers and their spread offense averaged 262.5 yards rushing, ranking fifth nationally.

"Practice makes perfect," Georgia roverback Tra Battle said. "They've almost perfected their running game. They have the talent and the athletes to do it.

"That was weighing on my heart."

Disasters seemed to be the order of the day. Just as the Sugar Bowl was determined to put on a good show as a demonstration that it and New Orleans were still standing, the Mountaineers entered the game with extra resolve. Yet another catastrophe occurred that morning in their home state when an explosion in the Sole Sago coal mine in Tallmansville trapped 13 men in a shaft two miles deep in the earth.

At game-time no one knew how many, if any, survived. Eventually one man was rescued.

"It's only football," Rich Rodriguez, a native West Virginian, said, "but we wanted to do something to lift our people's spirits. We always want to play well, but tonight especially."

What he got from his Mountaineers was so startling that it caused TV viewers from Maine to Oregon to blink in disbelief. West Virginia's spread offense had the Bulldogs' defense as befuddled as the viewers.

It took West Virginia fewer than three minutes to gash the vaunted Bulldog defense. Steve Slaton, the freshman tailback, took a handoff on a draw play and shot through three attempted tackles for a 52-yard touchdown at 12:12 of the opening quarter.

On its second possession, West Virginia scored again, this time on a 3-yard reception by Darius Reynaud, another Louisianan, from Pat White. The touchdown followed a 30-yard catch by Brandon Myles and a 17-yarder by Reynaud.

Pat White (5) rushed for 97 yards on the Bulldog defense.

In quick order, Slaton scored again on an 18-yard burst, and Reynaud ran in from 18-yards out on an end-around.

In four possessions, West Virginia had Georgia – and the college football world – stupefied with a 28-0 lead by the opening minute of the second quarter, running only 21 plays and having to convert just three first downs.

There would be more surprises, but not before the Bulldogs, stung by the turn of events, roared back into the hunt.

The Georgia defense, finally asserting itself, found a way to stop the Mountaineers. In its next six possessions, WVU got only a lone field goal. Meanwhile, Shockley jump-started the UGA offense. The Bulldogs, who at that point had not yet crossed midfield, went on lightning-quick drives of 80 and 90 yards, climaxed by a 34-yard run by Kregg Lumpkin and a 52-yard dash by Thomas Brown. Shockley hit tight end Leonard Pope with a four-yard touchdown pass to close to 31-21 with 58 seconds remaining until the half – a far more manageable score than Georgia was looking at just minutes before.

Now the Sugar Bowl had a game again.

It got even closer in the third quarter when Shockley hit A.J.

Bryant for a 34-yard touchdown in the opening minutes.

But the Mountaineers weren't about to roll over. Backed up to their 5 with 10 minutes left, they ground their way to the 48. Slaton, with 8:32 remaining, then burst up the middle for a 52-yard touchdown, his third of the night.

▲ *The West Virginia offense out ran the Bulldogs in Atlanta.*

The touchdown was just enough to survive another Georgia score, a 43-yard pass from Shockley to Bryan McClendon that brought the score to its final figures with 3:12 to play.

But the drama wasn't over. Not by a long shot.

With less than two minutes to go, WVU found itself at its 45 with a fourth-and-six. Phil Brady faked a punt and ran for 10 yards, sealing the victory.

It was a Sugar Bowl to remember for a variety of reasons. Slaton finished with 204 yards rushing to break the 30-year old Sugar Bowl record of 202 set by Pittsburgh's Tony Dorsett; West Virginia racked up 502 yards and five touchdowns against the nation's fourth-ranked defense. That was one more yard than Georgia in a game that saw the Sugar Bowl record for total yardage eclipsed.

West Virginia proved it belonged among the big boys of college football. It also gave a lift to dispirited folks at home.

"That was weighing on my heart," Rodriguez, a native of Grant Town, said of the efforts at the coal mine. "It was a tough day for the state and hopefully the victory, because we have so

▲ WVU coach Rich Rodriguez receives the
Sugar Bowl Trophy.

▲ Sugar Bowl President Mark Romig presents
the Miller-Digby Trophy to Steve Slaton.

much pride, will help people feel good about themselves."

It was the same for the Sugar Bowl, still functioning at a high level despite the desperate conditions in New Orleans.

"This game had to come off smoothly for us to continue to show we are one of the premier bowl experiences," Sugar Bowl president Mark Romig said. "That has been our driving inspiration through all of this. Katrina knocked us down but did not knock us out, and we have done what we had to do to put on this game in its grand tradition."

	1	2	3	4	
West Virginia	21	10	0	7	38
Georgia	0	21	7	7	35

West Virginia: Slaton, 52-yard run. PAT, McAfee kick.
West Virginia: Reynaud, 3-yard pass from White. PAT, McAfee kick.
West Virginia: Reynaud, 13-yard run. PAT, McAfee kick.
West Virginia: Slaton, 18-yard run. PAT, McAfee kick.
Georgia: Lumpkin, 34-yard pass from Shockley. PAT, Coutu kick.
Georgia: Brown, 52-yard run. PAT, Coutu kick.
West Virginia: McAfee, 27-yard field goal.
Georgia: Pope, 4-yard pass from Shockley. PAT, Coutu kick.
Georgia: Bryant, 34-yard pass from Shockley. PAT, Coutu kick.
West Virginia: Slaton, 52-yard run. PAT, McAfee kick.
Georgia: McClendon, 43-yard pass from Shockley. PAT, Coutu kick.

Individual Leaders

Rushing
West Virginia: Slaton 26-204, 3 TDs; White 24-77.
Georgia: T. Brown 9-78, 1 TD; Shockley 8-71; Lumpkin 9-67, 1 TD.

Passing
West Virginia: White 11-14-0, 120 yards, 1 TD.
Georgia: Shockley 23-33-0, 277 yards, 2 TDs.

Receiving
West Virginia: Reynaud 6-48, 1 TD.
Georgia: Pope 6-50, 1 TD; McClendon 3-72, 1 TD.

West Virginia		Georgia
27	First Downs	27
382	Rushing Yards	224
11-14-0	Passing	20-33-0
120	Passing Yards	227
502	Total Yards	501
4-36.0	Punts	3-45.7
0-0	Fumbles – Lost	3-3
9-74	Penalties – Yards	4-50

Attendance: 77,458.
Teams' remuneration: $36,000,000.
Miller-Digby Award recipient: Steve Slaton, West Virginia tailback.

LSU 41 Notre Dame 14

"I couldn't have scripted it any better."

The statement was made softly, but it crackled with emotion. "The fact that we're here, I think it's right," Les Miles said. "I can't imagine it any other way, to be honest."

The LSU coach was reflecting on the presence of his team in the first Sugar Bowl in New Orleans after the destruction and horror of the worst natural disaster in American history, Hurricane Katrina, which submerged large portions of the Crescent City for weeks.

After a year away from the disheveled, scaled-down and still traumatized city and the storm-wrecked Superdome for a sojourn to Atlanta, the Sugar Bowl was, more or less, back in its natural surroundings, and with an ideal pairing that even some members of the media characterized as divinely inspired: America's Team (Notre Dame, 10-2, not quite a member of the football elite at No. 11 in the BCS rankings, though certain to hold the country's interest – and television sets) vs. Louisiana's Team (LSU, 10-2, ranked No. 5 and once again, like after 9/11, a godsend to the Sugar Bowl).

If Florida and Ohio State, the top two teams in the country, played the national title game in the ravaged Big Easy instead of in Arizona where they did, that pairing wouldn't have provided more of an emotional lift.

Paul Hoolahan, the Sugar Bowl's chief executive officer, reiterated the general feeling, saying, "I'd be less than honest if I didn't say I was tremendously excited. I just felt, to myself, we're back and we're up and running. It's a great feeling, exhilarating ... This will give everybody in the country full confidence that we are back and able and capable of doing the job we have in the past. I think it's very important to get that message out. This game is a testament to that."

The Sugar Bowl itself was a bit ginger: it hadn't been played in New Orleans in two years; its day-by-day operations were now housed in new, temporary headquarters in suburban Metairie; as part of the BCS arrangement it was now working with a new television network, Fox; and with a new corporate sponsor, Allstate Insurance.

So the Sugar was truly traveling through some uncharted waterways.

CHARLIE WEIS

LES MILES

LSU head coach Les Miles, and Notre Dame head coach Charlie Weis, answer questions before the 2007 Sugar Bowl.

But the game itself was pure serendipity, and Miles conveyed genuine feelings in tying in the circuitous route LSU took to its home-state BCS bowl game with the stunning and surprising success of New Orleans' NFL team Saints in the same season. He said, "I couldn't have scripted it any better ... LSU plays in the first Sugar Bowl (in New Orleans) after the storm (and) the Saints have a great year. Maybe there's an overall plan for this."

There really was a near-sense that something unreal had occurred in matching these teams. Remember, Ohio State was No. 1 and Michigan No. 2 following the Buckeyes' 42-39 victory against the Wolverines in their final game on Nov. 18, making a rematch in the first stand-alone BCS championship game a possibility. Southern Cal was third and Florida fourth. Then, after the Nov. 25th games, the Trojans jumped to second place after an impressive victory against Notre Dame, and the Gators climbed to third after beating archrival Florida State.

LSU was out of the SEC-title picture, but after the USC-Notre Dame game, the Rose Bowl expressed interest in the Tigers to play either the Trojans or Michigan, depending on which team

got left out of the national championship game, and LSU fans responded by pledging money for more than 40,000 tickets.

But things went haywire.

First, USC lost to UCLA, 13-9 on Dec. 2, taking the Trojans out of title contention, although they did still go to the Rose Bowl as Pac-10 champion.

Then, Florida beat Arkansas, 38-28 in an exciting SEC title game, and suddenly the USA Today and Harris Interactive poll voters were looking on the Gators in a new light.

The next day, Florida passed Michigan in both polls and split with the Wolverines in the computer rankings, sending the No. 2 Gators to Glendale, Ariz., for a national championship meeting with Ohio State.

Not surprisingly, the Rose Bowl chose Michigan to replace Ohio State in its game, leaving the Sugar Bowl with the next two selections.

In a blink, Hoolahan & Co. jumped on LSU and Notre Dame,

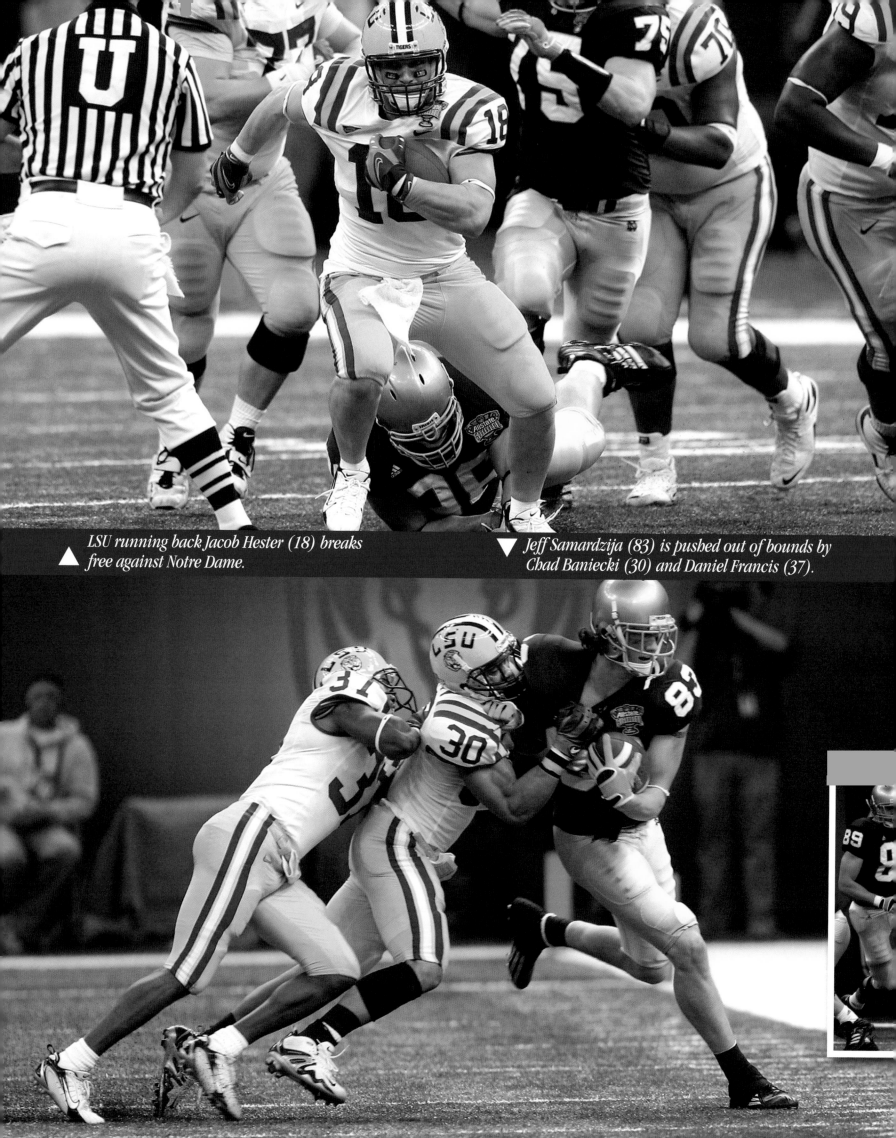

LSU running back Jacob Hester (18) breaks free against Notre Dame.

Jeff Samardzija (83) is pushed out of bounds by Chad Baniecki (30) and Daniel Francis (37).

choosing the Irish over No. 6 Louisville, No. 8 Boise State and No. 13 West Virginia.

It was an intriguing selection on several levels, perhaps the biggest being an on-the-field comparison between two of the better quarterbacks in college football, Notre Dame's Brady Quinn, a finalist for the Heisman Trophy, and LSU's JaMarcus Russell, one of the sport's most accurate passers.

LSU fans got over the disappointment of not making a first-ever appearance in the Rose Bowl about two minutes after the announcement. For one thing the Tigers were still in a high-quality bowl being played close to home; for another thing, there was the anticipation of playing against college football's most renowned program.

There was another fortuitous benefit in the pairing: New Orleans hotels had not fully recovered. There were 8,000 fewer rooms than two years before. Also the number of flights into and out of New Orleans had not returned to pre-Katrina levels, but because many LSU fans live in the surrounding area, the crush wouldn't be as bad as usual.

The empathy of both schools for the battered region, though, was what caught the attention of many observers. Notre Dame and LSU coaches and players all visited devastated areas, visited with the affected, uplifted some spirits and helped in some of the rebuilding efforts.

The Tiger contingent spoke often, and movingly, of their sense of obligation.

"I'm just happy to be here in my hometown again, playing in front of my fans," said LaRon Landry, a Tiger safety from nearby Hahnville. "It's my last game, we're playing in my hometown. After the disaster of last year, playing in the city of New Orleans, it would be great if we come out with a win in the first Sugar Bowl back here.

"My goal is just to give it all back to the city and state."

His chances, and LSU's, were pretty good. The Tigers opened as a nine-point favorite, the widest spread of the major bowls. But Notre Dame is Notre Dame, the most storied football program in the land, and there was a feeling the Irish, for one night, could put everything together, particularly since few in the national media were giving them much of a chance. Plus, under the tutorage of Coach Charlie Weis, the offensive coordinator on three Super Bowl champion teams, if he could get the Irish offense untracked, some felt this could be a trap for LSU.

Everyone was aware of Weis' gilded background of finding soft spots in stout defenses, a trait for which he had already left his fingerprints in New Orleans.

When Notre Dame practiced inside the Superdome, Weis told his squad of being part of the New England coaching staff when the Patriots won Super Bowl XXXVI there when Adam Vinatieri's last-second field goal defeated favored St. Louis. "He pointed to the spot where Vinatieri made the kick," Irish receiver Jeff Samardzija said of Weis. "It was pretty cool to think of all the history that's taken place in there."

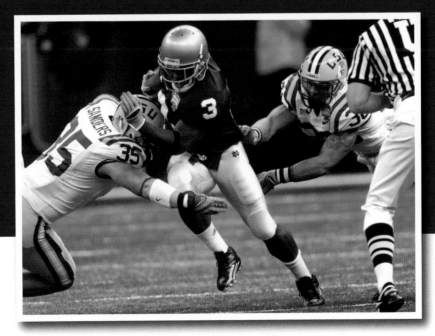

Running back Darius Walker (3) was the lone standout for the Irish, rushing for 128 yards.

"They really laid the wood to us."

If this was to be a head-to-head comparison between two of the better quarterbacks in college football, LSU's JaMarcus Russell and Notre Dame's Brady Quinn, it was Russell who made the most of it.

The strong-armed Tiger threw for 332 yards and two touchdowns, ran for 16 more yards and another touchdown. Quinn wasn't bad, somehow keeping his team in it for a half. But there was no real comparison between the two quarterbacks.

Or the two teams.

Tiger dominance was illustrated in the second half when Notre Dame was outgained by the astonishing margin of 333-30. For the night, the Bayou Bengals gained an eye-rolling 577 yards and scored 41 points – the most ever surrendered by Notre Dame in a bowl game.

"They came to play," Irish safety Chinedum Ndukwe said simply, "and we didn't."

LSU certainly did come to play – right from the start.

Trindon Holiday (8) gains 11 yards down the sideline.

Mike Richardson (30) intercepts a JaMarcus Russell pass in the end zone.

Early Doucet (9) leaps to make the one of his eight catches on the night.

The Irish opened the gates wide for LSU when they went for it on fourth down at their own 34 on their first possession. The fake punt failed, and the Tigers turned that into an easy touchdown that gave LSU early momentum. Russell immediately lofted a ball to a leaping Early Doucet, who made the catch 31 yards downfield, at the 3. The next play freshman Keiland Williams went in for the first points of the night. Then the Tigers went 80 yards on eight plays – with Russell rumbling for 21 yards to the Irish 15 on a quarterback draw. The drive ended with Dwayne Bowe latching onto an 11-yard Russell throw.

Twice the Tigers had the ball and twice they scored. Just nine minutes into the game LSU had a 14-0 lead.

To their credit, though, the Irish fought their way back. On two 80-yard drives, with 2:25 remaining until halftime, Notre Dame surprisingly tied the score with two short Quinn touchdown passes, to David Grimes and to Jeff Samardzija. The last came against a tiring LSU defense, which, because of the Tigers' quick scores, had spent most of the first half on the field.

The Tigers welcome the Sugar Bowl back to New Orleans with an impressive win over Notre Dame.

The upshot, though, was that Notre Dame had actually pulled even against a clearly superior opponent. But that didn't last long, 70 seconds to be exact.

As if someone flipped a light switch, LSU cruised easily 82 yards downfield with Russell hitting Doucet with a 58-yard on-the-money bomb that carried to the 5. On the fifth play of the drive, Russell took it in himself on a quarterback draw. It was his first rushing TD of the season.

"That one right before the half got our morale down," cornerback Mike Richardson sighed.

Notre Dame had been hanging in by keeping the ball away from the Tigers. At halftime the Irish had run 50 plays to LSU's 26; controlled the ball for 19:31 of 30 minutes; had rushed for 137 yards to LSU's 74; and had 15 first downs to LSU's 12. Furthermore, Darius Walker had 125 yards rushing

against the vaunted Bayou Bengal defense, and the Irish caused the only turnover of the half.

Yet, LSU was ahead 21-14.

"We gave up that big play before the half, which is never good," Weis agreed. "And then they really laid the wood to us in the second half."

Yes. The worst for Notre Dame, on its way to losing an NCAA-record ninth straight bowl game, was still to come.

Distancing themselves from the Irish in every conceivable way, the Tigers scored on their first four drives of the second half to end early any suspense about the outcome. In the third quarter, in which LSU scored on two Colt David field goals and another 58-yard pass from Russell to freshman Brandon LaFell, the Tigers out-gained the Irish 205 yards to

	1	2	3	4	
LSU	14	7	13	7	41
Notre Dame	7	7	0	0	14

LSU: Williams, 3-yard run. PAT, David kick.
LSU: Bowe, 11-yard pass from Russell. PAT, David kick.
Notre Dame: Grimes, 24-yard pass from Quinn. PAT, Gioia kick.
Notre Dame: Samardzija, 10-yard pass from Quinn. PAT, Gioia kick.
LSU: Russell, 5-yard run. PAT, David kick.
LSU: David, 25-yard field goal.
LSU: David, 37-yard field goal.
LSU: LaFell, 58-yard pass from Russell. PAT, David kick.
LSU: Williams, 20-yard run. PAT, Gaudet kick.

Individual Leaders

Rushing
LSU: Williams, 14-108 yards, 2 TDs; Vincent, 12-71 yards.
Notre Dame: Walker, 22-128 yards; Aldridge, 3-7 yards.

Passing
LSU: Russell, 21-34-1, 332 yards, 2 touchdowns.
Notre Dame: Quinn, 15-35-2, 148 yards, 2 touchdowns.

Receiving
LSU: Doucet, 8-115 yards; Bowe, 5-78 yards, 1 touchdown.
Notre Dame: Samardzija, 8-59 yards, 1 touchdown; McKnight 3-22 yards.

26; rolled up 11 first downs to 1; 25 to 7 in offensive plays; and had the advantage in time of possession, 12:13 to 2:47.

A couple of unit tweaks by defensive coordinator Bo Pelini had allowed the Tigers to overwhelm the Irish offense, yielding one first down and a total of 30 yards in the entire second half. Walker didn't gain a single yard in the final 30 minutes, and Quinn completed just 15 of his 35 passes for the game, good for a season-low 148 yards and two touchdowns along with two interceptions.

"Our defense was stingy all day," LSU coach Les Miles said afterward. "It was dominant in the second half."

So was Russell, who was not only the game's MVP, but his eye-catching performance played a role in his selection as the No. 1 player in the NFL draft. Quinn went 22nd.

Miles couldn't have scripted things any better.

LSU		Notre Dame
31	First Downs	17
245	Rushing Yards	143
21-34-1	Passing	15-35-2
332	Passing Yards	148
577	Total Yards	291
2-42.0	Punts	5-47.4
2-1	Fumbles – Lost	0-0
9-95	Penalties – Yards	4-40

Attendance: 77,781.
Teams' remuneration: $36,000,000.
Miller-Digby Award recipient: JaMarcus Russell, LSU quarterback.

Georgia 41 Hawaii 10

"Dixie vs. the Ha'a Dance."

The Georgia Bulldogs felt they earned a postseason trip to New Orleans. They just thought they should have been in the Big Easy a few days later.

A young team that started slow but finished fast, Georgia was considered a "hot" team at the end of the regular season, playing at a high level of efficiency and winning its last six games impressively.

The problem for Coach Mark Richt's Bulldogs was the fact that the body of work for any team is the season as a whole, and Georgia lost two of its first six games, ultimately keeping the fourth-ranked Bulldogs out of the SEC Championship Game – and out of the BCS national championship, to be played in the Superdome six days after the Sugar Bowl.

When the top two teams lost on the last day of the regular season, Richt lobbied the media hard that his team should be in the No. 1 mix. It was not to be.

"We've still got that little ache in our stomach about not being able to go for the national championship," UGA senior defensive end Marcus Howard said. "We thought we should have moved up to No. 2, but it didn't happen."

The Sugar Bowl was ecstatic to get the Bulldogs in what appeared to be an intriguing match-up with BCS party-crasher Hawaii, which had to be taken for the BCS' final berth because it finished in the top 12.

The bowl picture following the 2007 season opened like the parting of the Red Sea on December 1 in a series of games: LSU defeated Tennessee in the SEC Championship Game; No. 1-ranked Missouri lost to Oklahoma in the Big 12 Championship Game; No. 2-ranked West Virginia was upset by four-touchdown

underdog Pittsburgh; and Hawaii preserved its standing as the nation's only undefeated team by coming back from a three-touchdown deficit to beat the University of Washington.

The upshot was that Ohio State, ranked third in the standings of the Bowl Championship Series, rose to No. 1, and LSU, ranked seventh, ascended to No. 2. Two of the headline teams of the season would play in the BCS national championship game.

In the end, Georgia, which dropped from fourth to fifth, was done in by the fact that LSU won the SEC while the Bulldogs failed to qualify for the league's title game; that the Tigers defeated South Carolina and Tennessee, both conquerors of Georgia; and LSU's body of work, 6-1 against ranked opponents at season's end.

Georgia's reward was its trip to New Orleans – even if it was a week earlier than hoped – against Hawaii, with its eye-catching offense run by a breath-taking quarterback, Colt Brennan.

This would be not only a clash of the nation's highest-scoring team (Hawaii) at 46.2 points a game and one of the nation's best defenses (Georgia), yielding 21 points a game, but a striking contrast in cultures. As Baton Rouge sportswriter Scott Rabal-

Georgia and Hawaii show their team spirit before the 74th Sugar Bowl.

ais succinctly put it: "This was as much a distinction as you could get in the postseason, Dixie vs. the Ha'a dance; Grits vs. mahi-mahi; Mint juleps vs. something frothy with an umbrella sticking out of it."

And Hawaii had a bit of a chip on its shoulder, too.

The 10th-ranked Warriors (12-0) had to fight for any respect because they play in the Western Athletic Conference, one of the lower-tier leagues that get little consideration for the prestigious BCS bowls – never mind that in the previous three seasons two schools in similar conferences had upset "the big boys" in the postseason: Boise State of the WAC embarrassed

Oklahoma of the Big 12 in the 2007 Fiesta Bowl, and Utah of the Mountain West Conference beat the Big East's Pittsburgh in the 2005 Fiesta Bowl.

Hawaii coach June Jones, playing the underdog role to the hilt, put his team's task of playing a representative of the perceived best conference in college football thusly: "It's sort of like the Bad News Bears coming east to play the SEC."

Ray Jeandron, the Sugar Bowl president, was in Atlanta on December 1, taking in the SEC Championship Game, but he was keeping an eye on the other games on television while trying to keep awake to watch Hawaii-Washington, which came on at midnight Eastern Time. "By the time I put my head on my pillow, it was 20 hours from the time I had gotten up. To say I was bushed would be putting it mildly, but I went to sleep with a smile on my face."

And visions of sugar plums – with a genuine SEC powerhouse in one berth and an exciting and undefeated opponent in the other, overlooking the comparative small-bore caliber schedule the Rainbow Warriors' schedule was built on – danced in Jeandron's head. "It was more than we dared hope for," Jeandron said.

Georgia, playing in its third Sugar Bowl in six years, had a team that harkened back to the high-point of the Vince Dooley era with a stout defense (one which allowed an average of just 119 yards passing), and an outstanding freshman running back named Knowshon Moreno, who ran for 1,335 yards and 12 touchdowns during the season, and who reminded some of another Bulldog of years past, Herschel Walker.

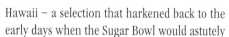

*Hawaii quarterback
Colt Brennan*

Hawaii – a selection that harkened back to the early days when the Sugar Bowl would astutely take teams with more game than name, like Santa Clara, Carnegie Tech, and St. Mary's – would be playing in its first major bowl.

Part of the Warriors' attraction was the presence of a kid who took a wrong path on the way to football paradise on the volcanic and coral islands 2,400 miles west of San Francisco. As a walk-on at Colorado, Colt Brennan spent a night doing what young people sometimes do: something stupid. He got drunk and entered a female student's dorm room uninvited. He eventually served one week in jail on ancillary charges.

Only a couple of schools were willing to give a second chance to Brennan. One was Hawaii, where he fit perfectly into Jones' run-and-shoot, accumulating 29 NCAA records, including 58 touchdown passes in 2006. As a senior Brennan completed 71 percent of his passes for 4,174 yards and threw for 38 touchdowns on an offense that rolled up 529.2 yards a game.

The combination of Jones' offensive genius on the blackboard and Brennan's ability to execute the coach's Xs and Os on the field transformed Hawaii's sporting culture: football became the "in" sport. For the latter part of the 2007 season, Aloha Stadium was packed with 50,000 fans, with football-crazed fans setting off fireworks every time – and that was a frequent occurrence – the Warriors scored a touchdown.

The night that Hawaii earned its Sugar Bowl bid – the one Jeandron sleepily watched from Atlanta – the Warriors played at the University of Washington. At the same time a symphony was in progress in downtown Honolulu.

During a timeout between numbers, the maestro tapped his baton and made an announcement to the audience: "21-0, Washington," he intoned solemnly.

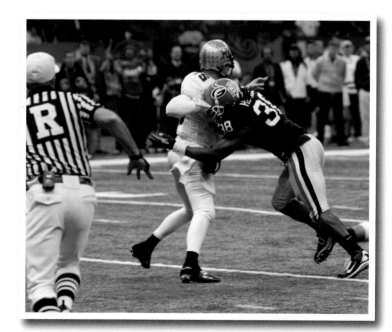 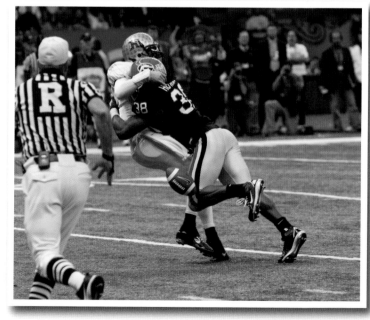

Georgia defensive tackle Marcus Howard (38) knocks the ball loose from Colt Brennan and recovers for the touchdown.

Thomas Brown leaps into the end zone.

Georgia quarterback Matthew Stafford.

Ryan Grice-Mullen scored Hawaii's lone touchdown.

A groan went up, causing the conductor to reassure the audience, "Do not worry, there's plenty of time left.

There was, but just enough, with the Warriors scoring the last points of a 35-28 victory with 44 seconds to play.

With 15 minutes remaining, Hawaii was behind 28-21. With three minutes to go, and the score tied at 28, Brennan took the Warriors the length of the field on six consecutive completions, the last a five-yard touchdown pass.

Another miracle finish produced Hawaii's 12th victory in 12 regular season games.

Still, Hawaii was going to need Brennan & Co. at their very best – and much more – against Georgia.

At the Heisman Trophy ceremonies, where Brennan finished third, winner Tim Tebow, the quarterback at Florida, warned him about the Bulldogs. "Get rid of the ball quickly," the Gator said, "because they (the Georgia defense) will be coming at you hard, in a hurry, and all night long."

"That was the fastest team I've probably ever seen."

"Aloha," most people on the U.S. mainland know, means both "hello" and "goodbye" in Polynesian.

College football learned a new word from the islands on New Year's night: "Ho'ohilahilo," which translates roughly to "butt-kicking."

That's what Georgia administered to the out-manned Warriors in the Sugar Bowl, a game characterized by one play: Marcus Howard sped through the shredded Hawaii line, took aim at his target, and crashed into a back-peddling Colt Brennan at the Warriors' 5. The ball popped free and rolled into the end zone, where Howard recovered.

That was the signature moment of the 74th Sugar Bowl.

▲ *Georgia fans express their support for the Bulldogs.*

Hawaii dancer's show off their unique style. ▼

Georgia players strike a victory pose with fans after cruising past Hawaii.

The touchdown for Georgia's defensive end gave him as many as the vaunted Warrior run-and-shoot offense would get for the night. It lifted the third-quarter score to 31-3 as the Bulldogs barely broke a sweat in dispatching the upstarts from the islands.

There would be no Boise State-like shocker this night.

Brennan – and Hawaii – got a stiff dose of reality in going against the SEC's Bulldogs. The Warriors quarterback was sacked eight times for minus 53 yards, and was hurried or hit on at least that many when he did get a pass off; He threw three interceptions and lost two fumbles.

Brennan went 22-of-38 for 164 yards, less than half of his 348-yard average, and Hawaii as a team was held to 306 yards, 228 fewer than its average – and 151 of that total came in the fourth quarter.

"It just shows it's not always about offense," said Howard, the game's MVP after recording three sacks, forcing two fumbles, and tipping a ball that turned into a Bulldog interception. "Defense wins ball games, and that's what happened tonight."

Bulldogs coach Mark Richt, a little surprised himself, said, "Our guys just kept coming. We wanted to force Colt to throw faster than he wanted to. We really didn't think we'd get that many sacks, and we knew when they did complete passes we had to give up no yards after the catch. Our guys tackled extremely well today."

The only time the game was close was at the last notes of the national anthem. Georgia scored the first four times it had the ball, on runs of 17 and 11 yards by Knowshon Moreno, a 52-yard field goal by Brandon Coutu, and an 11-yard touchdown pass from Matt Stafford to Sean Bailey. That made the score 24-3 midway through the second quarter, and school was out for Hawaii.

"That was the fastest team I've probably ever seen," a dazed

Georgia Coach Mark Richt hoists the Sugar Bowl Trophy.

	1	2	3	4	
Hawaii	3	0	0	7	10
Georgia	14	10	14	3	41

Georgia: Moreno, 17-yard run. PAT, Coutu kick.
Hawaii: Kelly, 41-yard field goal.
Georgia: Moreno, 11-yard run. PAT, Coutu kick.
Georgia: Coutu, 52-yard field goal.
Georgia: Bailey, 11-yard pass from Stafford. PAT, Coutu kick.
Georgia: Howard, fumble recovery in end zone. PAT, Coutu kick.
Georgia: Brown, 1-yard run. PAT, Coutu kick.
Georgia: Coutu, 45-yard field goal.
Hawaii: Grice-Mullen, 16-yard pass from Graunke.
PAT, Kelly kick.

Individual Leaders

Rushing
Hawaii: Pilares, 7-26.
Georgia: Brown, 19-73, 1 TD; Moreno, 9-61, 2 TDs.

Passing
Hawaii: Brennan, 22-38-3, 169 yards; Graunke, 13-19-1, 142 yards, 1 TD.
Georgia: Stafford, 14-23-1, 175 yards, 1 TD.

Receiving
Hawaii: Rivers, 10-105; Bess, 7-53; Grice-Mullen, 6-37, 1 TD.
Georgia: Massaquoi, 5-54; Durham, 3-48.

Brennan said afterward. "We just couldn't get into our groove and do what we wanted."

After their total victory, the Bulldogs couldn't resist chiding the BCS for what they perceived as an injustice. "We're No. 1," Georgia safety Kelin Johnson proclaimed. "We're supposed to be in the national championship game. The nation knows it, everyone knows it."

Howard said reflectively, "It just doesn't sit well with us. We were No. 4 in the BCS and thought we should have been No. 2. We felt we got snubbed. But it doesn't matter now. We came out and won the ballgame and let everyone know we should be No. 1.

"It's great to be here in New Orleans and win this game. I just wish we would have been here one week later."

Hawaii		Georgia
20	First Downs	19
-5	Rushing Yards	159
35-57-4	Passing	14-27-1
311	Passing Yards	175
306	Total Yards	334
3-34.0	Punts	3-48.3
2-2	Fumbles – Lost	1-0
11-90	Penalties – Yards	11-100

Attendance: 74,383.
Teams' remuneration: $36,000,000.
Miller-Digby Award recipient: Marcus Howard, Georgia defensive end.

"They were the pathfinders."

The Sugar Bowl was the concept – a mission, really – of one man in the 1920s, and since then has grown and developed into a major event on America's sportsworld, a destination either physically or mentally for millions of college football fans.

It has moved from a barely adequate stadium to one almost four times its original size – built on the appeal, and crowds, that one football game of the year. Then moved to the magnificent structure, the Superdome, that the New York Times termed "the Eighth Wonder of the World" when it opened.

Conceived in the ridicule of some, the Sugar Bowl now lives in the acclaim of the sportsworld. Its roots stretch from legendary coaches Glenn "Pop" Warner and Frank Thomas to Bear Bryant and Vince Dooley, and then onto Joe Paterno and Bobby Bowden, and from stellar, unforgettable players like Monk Simons and Slingin' Sammy Baugh to Tony Dorsett, Herschel Walker and JaMarcus Russell.

Not every step the Sugar Bowl took was the right one. It is an association of men, and men are fallible.

An "open" bowl concept was clung to in the early and adolescent years, and often New Orleans was treated to pairings of the very best of college football. Times changed. Getting the cream of the game became harder. The Sugar Bowl considered a conference tie-up very carefully. Finally, the Southeastern Conference and the Sugar Bowl joined forces.

Times may change again, but for now it can be safely argued that this is truly a marriage made in football heaven.

The Sugar Bowl was struggling at the start of the 1970s; it could not quite shake the effects of the segregation years, which handcuffed the classic. A decade later the Sugar Bowl was in the forefront of postseason college football, having hosted three straight national championship games. The string

grew, before the advent of the BCS title game, to a total of eight No. 1 Sugar Bowl games since the tie-up with the SEC. Three more were played under the aegis of the BCS. Payouts to participating teams has grown to more than $30 million – a figure that would stagger the 37 men who founded the Sugar Bowl during the Great Depression, when the $55,000 divided between Tulane and Temple in 1935 seemed a king's ransom.

"We knew things would probably be easier with a tie-up," said Cliff Kern, a past president of the Sugar Bowl. "We just didn't know how much easier. It's really been incredible."

Just as incredible is the fact that the Sugar Bowl is still functioning at its usual high level even after the crucible of killer Hurricane Katrina, which put New Orleans under water, forcing the game out of its racked and ruined environs and temporarily into another city. The efforts of Chief Executive Officer Paul Hoolahan and the Sugar Bowl membership were nothing short of remarkable in keeping the operation going.

Considering the circumstances, Hoolahan & Co. didn't skip a beat with – somehow – successful attractions in 2006 in Atlanta and 2007, when the Sugar returned to the Crescent City. The Sugar Bowl pulled off what seemed impossible in grand fashion. "We're back," Hoolahan said to himself at kickoff time of the 73rd Sugar Bowl. "We're back and able and capable of doing the job we have in the past."

Fred Digby had a vision. Thirty-seven men forged that vision into reality. Considering the times in which it was born – and considering the times in which it survived America's most apocalyptic natural calamity – the Sugar Bowl is a near-miracle. The founders, and their successors, have not only built a sports monument, they've kept a pledge. Over the long course of three-quarters of a century, more often than not, the Sugar Bowl has presented the best game possible.